W9-CTJ-550

THE FUNDAMENTALS OF FUNDAMENTAL ANALYSIS

JOHN C. RITCHIE

PROBUS PUBLISHING COMPANY
Chicago, Illinois
Cambridge, England

ISBN 1-55738-473-8

First paperback edition 1993

Printed in the United States of America

3   4   5   6   7   8   9   0

Contents

Preface

This book is for the individual investor, professional analyst, or portfolio manager who desires to select common stocks in an intelligent manner. It offers a thorough and rigorous approach to the selection of common stocks and the management of a common stock portfolio.

Many people are achieving the financial affluence that requires a sophisticated approach to investment decisions. Common stocks have long been an important component of the investment portfolios of successful individuals recognizing their growth potential and the possibility they offer of offsetting the adverse effects of inflation.

Ibbotson and Sinquefield have carefully studied historical rates of return for six major classes of financial assets in the United States: (1) common stocks, (2) small capitalization stocks (3) long-term U.S. government bonds, (4) long-term corporate bonds, and (5) U.S. Treasury bills. Common stocks, on average, more than doubled the returns recorded by the other financial instruments over the period 1926–1986, offering further support to the attractiveness of including well-selected common stocks in a portfolio.

Success in investments in common stocks depends on a knowledge and application of sound principles of investment analysis in a consistent manner. The emphasis should be on long-run growth of capital committed. We do not advocate rapid in-and-out trading, which has not typically produced good results. This book will help you learn to avoid investment pitfalls and mistakes that have plagued an army of unsuccessful investors.

Successful investors need reasonable intelligence, a knowledge of market history, a value oriented and fundamentally sound analytic approach, patience, the courage of their convictions, and the ability to ignore crowd psychology. The background information and analytic techniques presented in the book supply the reader with the tools and approach needed for successful investment. Selectivity, based on long-run fundamental considerations and consistency, is the key to success.

Part I of the book carefully develops useful background information and a value oriented fundamental analysis approach used by many successful investors. The book recommends coupling the fundamental analysis approach with a low price–earnings ratio approach which is supported by several studies, including one recently completed by the author, with financial support from Provident Capital Management, a Philadelphia fund manager. Mr. Paul Lesutis, a senior vice-president of that organization has been generous with his time and help in developing my appreciation of this approach.

I also wish to express gratitude to Bernice Harris, Hugh Treloar, Ernestine Hopson, and Mary Blount, members of the secretarial staff at Temple University, for typing of this manuscript. Mr. Treloar also provided useful editing comments.

Most importantly, I thank my wife for her help, encouragement, editing of material, and total support throughout the process of writing this book.

PART I

Investment: Analytical Foundations and Background

CHAPTER 1

Investments: An Introduction

This book provides an investor with the background information and an analytical framework needed for wise investment decision making. Fundamental security analysis provides the sophisticated analytical framework designed to assess important economic, political, and social dynamics as well as company data and suggest their potential impact on the capital markets and security values. We will concentrate on analyzing common stocks, though the framework developed also can be used to analyze bonds and other investments.

Serious application of the approach suggested will enable an investor to structure an investment program with security and capital appreciation over a lifetime. The book does not provide guidelines for traders—those who expect to build capital by attempting to forecast the short-term (less than one year) action of the market. The record of short-term, in-and-out traders generally has been poor, though it is difficult to gain objective information on the performance of such individuals. Sidney Weinberg, a highly respected member of the investment community and successful investor, emphasized that he did not believe that one builds capital by short-term trading. Bernard Baruch agreed with this conclusion. Moreover, the longer-term approach advocated in this book has been well tested by investors such as Graham and Dodd, Douglass Bellemore, Warren Buffett, Walter Schloos, Charles Munger and William Ruane.[1]

Short-run speculation can be profitable and carried out in an intelligent manner. An intelligent speculation differs, however, from the long-term investment viewpoint advocated in this book. Speculators who stress short-term, as opposed to long-term capital appreciation, operate on more limited information and assume a higher degree of risk than the average investor is willing or able to assume. Moreover, a speculator tends to trade on the basis of information that he or she believes is not yet known or fully understood, while an investor makes no such assumption.

---

1 See "Can You Beat The Stock Market?," *Fortune*, December 26, 1983, p. 83.

For a great many speculative situations, careful appraisal almost is impossible for there are insufficient facts and the information that is available is of questionable reliability. The purchase of stocks on "market tips," a glamorous name, or other rather casual approaches is more akin to gambling than investment. It is interesting to note that many individuals believe that while their chosen vocation requires a long period of training, experience or ability, successful investing can be accomplished with little training, experience, ability, or hard work. Successful investment or intelligent speculation requires a relatively high degree of technical knowledge, good judgment, and diligence in seeking facts and information.

Risk and Return

Investment decisions are based on the expectations of receiving a positive return in the future. One sacrifices the opportunity for current consumption when making an investment, and requires reward for making this sacrifice. Investors need large expected returns to compensate for deferring consumption and for undertaking the risks associated with holding financial assets.

Investors logically aim at maximizing the expected return for the degree of risk accepted. Webster's dictionary defines risk as "the chance of injury, damage or loss." Risk is a significant constraint for all investors. A key determinant is the degree of risk an investor is willing to accept for a given rate of return or the probability of realizing a given rate of return.

Financial Investment Risk

Risk is a part of any financial investment decision and must be analyzed along with other facets of a potential investment. Various types of risk can affect an investment decision. Thus, a comprehensive analysis of risk for investment decisions is one that attacks the problem simultaneously from various points of view.

Expectations: Concept of Risk.   Decisions made under conditions of certainty will turn out to be correct. When these conditions apply, there is no variation of outcomes relative to one's expectations and there is no risk. In a reasonably efficient capital market, the reward for investing in a riskless asset should approach a limit that we refer to as the *riskless rate of return*. For example, the purchaser of a short-term treasury bill is certain of realizing the calculated rate of return on the purchase price. The purchase of treasury bills, however, is not truly a riskless investment when one considers opportunity costs, changing yield patterns over time, and inflation.

Because the outcome of an investment decision is determined by chance events, the environment of investment decision is deemed *uncertain*. A financial asset purchased on the basis of imperfect knowledge about future events is called a *risky asset*. The degree of risk differs for different financial assets, but all financial assets are risky assets, in the opportunity sense. For example, uncertainty exists over whether the issuer of a bond will make all promised payments, what the price will be at various times prior to maturity if liquidity is desired, and what the impact of inflation will be over a relatively long investment horizon. Predicting the future cash flows to be generated through investment in a common stock and the impact of inflation on the returns from such an investment could be considered even more uncertain, since no contractual promises have been made.

Traditional Risk Concepts.   Traditional analysis discusses specific types of risk that could lead to an investor not realizing an anticipated return that led to a specific investment decision.

Purchasing Power Risk.   Table 1–1 shows the Consumer Price Index (CPI) for the years 1967 through 1985. The value of a dollar relative to the base year 1967 also is shown. The effect of inflation on the purchasing power of payments received under a fixed-income contract, such as a bond or a nonparticipating, nonconvertible preferred stock, is obvious. If the market correctly anticipates inflation it will be built into required returns that are an important determinant of security valuation, as we will see in Chapter 3. It is unanticipated inflation, therefore, that brings the purchasing power risk.

To illustrate the impact that purchasing power risk can have, assume that a savings account was opened on January 1, 1967, with a deposit of $1,000 and that a five percent interest rate, compounded annually, was paid from then until the end of 1985. By December 31, 1985, the dollar value of the account would have grown to $1,000 (1.05 ^{19}) = $2,526.95. By year-end 1985, however, the value of a dollar would have shrunk to just $.31 in terms of 1967 purchasing power. Therefore, $2,526.95 spent at year-end 1985 would not purchase as much as $1,000 spent in 1967:

$$\text{1967 Purchasing Power} = \$2,526.95\,(.31)$$

$$= \$783.35$$

Table 1-1   Consumer Price Index (CPI), 1967-1985

Year	CPI	Price Relative	Year	CPI	Price Relative
1967	100.0	1.00	1977	181.5	.55
1968	104.2	.96	1978	195.4	.51
1969	109.8	.91	1979	217.4	.46
1970	116.3	.86	1980	246.8	.41
1971	121.3	.82	1981	272.4	.37
1972	125.3	.80	1982	289.1	.35
1973	133.1	.75	1983	298.4	.34
1974	147.7	.68	1984	311.1	.22
1975	161.2	.62	1985	322.2	.31
1976	170.5	.59			

The holder of the savings account lost $216.65 in terms of 1967 purchasing power because of inflation. The compound interest payments on commercial bank passbook savings accounts (typically paying a five percent interest rate) were not sufficient to maintain the purchasing power of the funds originally deposited over the period 1967-1985.

Interest Rate Risk.   Interest rate risk comes about as a result of unanticipated changes in interest rates. To the extent that future changes in the *interest rate are anticipated*, such changes will be reflected in the current period prices of fixed-income securities. The double-digit inflation of 1973 and 1974 was not anticipated by the market, and thus its impact was not reflected properly in the prices of fixed-income securities before the fact. For example, investors who purchased investment quality corporate bonds late in 1973 would (in horror) have seen market prices drop by as much as 20 percent from 1973 highs to 1974 lows, reflecting rising interest rates.[2] With the tapering off of the rate of inflation in 1975 and an easing of monetary policy by the Federal Reserve, the average price of investment quality corporate bonds came back up to a point approaching their 1973 highs. Many bondholders were forced to take substantial losses during the period. Interest rates reached historic highs in August 1981, again causing serious losses for many earlier purchasers of bonds. Such outcomes are evidence that substantial interest

---

2 The inverse relationship between change in interest rates and security prices is carefully developed in Chapter 3.

substantial interest rate risk is taken by participants in the securities market and that efficient markets are able to predict the future only imperfectly.

Further evidence of the high degree of interest rate risk present in bond markets is offered in Table 1–2. Interest rates over the period rose strongly through 1981, and as a result, bond prices generally were falling until 1981. Bond prices then recovered sharply by 1986 as interest rates fell to early 1970s levels.

Business Risk and Financial Risk. When purchasing a fixed income security, an investor enters into a contract that provides for a promised and legally obligatory periodic cash flow over the life of the contract and the return of the principal amount at maturity of the instrument. A common or preferred stock offers no certain future cash flows but is bought on the expectation of realizing some minimum in terms of future cash flow. In the event of default or temporary disruptions in the cash flows received by a business, the promised or expected future cash flows may not be received (or only received in part) by an investor.

Table 1–2   Bond Yields and Prices

	Yield			Related Bond Price Index		
Year	U.S Government Long-Term (%)	Corporate AAA (%)	Municipal High Grade (%)	U.S. Government Long-Term (%)	Corporate AAA (%)	Municipal High Grade (%)
1946	2.19	2.44	1.64	110.40	123.40	140.10
1960	3.99	4.26	3.73	88.94	94.64	103.90
1967	4.90	5.47	3.98	80.04	81.75	102.50
1970	6.75	7.76	6.51	65.00	61.55	72.34
1975	8.21	8.43	6.89	55.52	56.23	68.94
1980	11.22	11.56	8.51	41.17	41.38	57.43
1981	13.20	13.72	11.23	34.18	33.74	43.25
1982	12.51	13.03	11.57	36.68	35.79	41.92
1983	11.09	11.50	9.47	41.56	41.15	51.36
1984	12.34	12.43	10.15	36.97	*	47.96
1985	10.74	10.94	9.18	43.06	*	53.02
1986	7.68	8.53	6.93	58.70	*	68.58

* No longer reported by Standard & Poor's.

Source: Standard & Poor's Statistical Service, Security Price Index Record, 1986 Edition.

Business risk is intrinsic in the firm's operations. This type of risk is defined in terms of the ratio of fixed to variable costs and the resultant implications for the variability of the firm's net cash flows under changing business conditions and sales levels. *Financial risk* stems from the firm's capital structure decisions. The higher the proportion of capital raised through the issuance of fixed-income contracts (debts and preferred stocks), the greater the variability of the firm's net cash flows under changing business conditions and sales levels.

Calculations of the degree of operating and the degree of financial leverage are discussed as leverage measures in most business finance texts,[3] and is further developed in this book in a later chapter. Much controversy surrounds the use of various accounting data in making such calculations, and these approaches make assumptions that can limit their usefulness. But the concepts have been found to be useful by investment analysts and practicing financial analysts, in spite of the limitations.

Risk and Return—An Historical Overview

History may not repeat itself, but it is reasonable to utilize past performance as a basis for forming realistic investment goals.

Figure 1–1 shows the growth of an investment, assuming a buy and hold approach, in a common stock portfolio represented by the stocks included in the Standard & Poor's Index: small capitalization stocks, long-term government bonds and Treasury bills, as calculated by Ibbotson Associates over a 59-year period from 1926 through 1984. Each of the series is initiated at $1.00 at year-end 1925. Compound growth is highlighted by presenting the vertical scale as a logarithmic scale.

Stocks clearly were the best performers over the study period by a substantial margin, though risk (in terms of variability) also was higher for stocks. The substantially higher returns earned by the stock series, based on casual observation, seems to compensate well for the added risk associated with stock investment. The key is to maintain broad diversification and adequate liquid funds (invested in Treasury bills or money market funds) to meet emergencies and avoid forced sales of stock. One could also become much more liquid when fundamental analysis suggested sales of many stocks, accumulating cash for a more favorable buying opportunity. In general, however, it is better to invest consistently and gain the

---

3 For example, see Lawrence D. Schall and Charles W. Haley, *Introduction to Financial Management*, 4th Ed. (New York: McGraw-Hill Book Company, 1986), Chapter 13, especially pages 439–445.

Figure 1–1   Wealth Indices of Investments in the U.S. Capital Markets

Year–End 1925 = 1.00

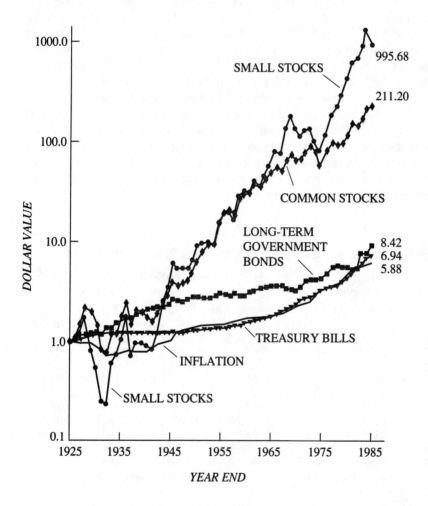

Source: *Stocks, Bonds, Bills and Inflation: 1985 Yearbook,*
Chicago: Ibbotson Associates, 1985, p. 8.

the advantages of dollar averaging. Figure 1–1 does assume continuous investment in the given instrument.

Table 1–3 shows the yearly results over the 10-year period 1975–1984 for each type of investment in terms of annual total returns (dividends or interest plus or minus capital gains or losses). Returns for common stocks have been calculated over the years 1926–1984. They have ranged from an exciting 53.99 percent in 1933 to a dismal loss of 43.34 percent in 1931. Data was not available for 1987 at the time of writing this book. Though losses in October 12, 1987 were at historically high levels, investors actually gained from January 1, 1987 through December 31, 1987 based on data for the Standard & Poor 500 Index.

Sharpe has noted that Table 1–3 leads one to the conclusion that the "past pattern of stock returns provides little help in predicting next year's return."[4] He suggests that one uncover the value for 1941 and preceding years and try to guess the return for 1942. If one continues to proceed in this manner year-by-year, we are confident one will agree with the above conclusion. One cannot accurately estimate short-term market movements.

Table 1–3   Basic Services: Year-By-Year Total Returns, 1975–1984

Year	Common Stocks	Small Stocks	Long-Term Corporate Bonds	Long-Term Government Bonds	U.S. Treasury Bills	Consumer Price Index
1975	0.3720	0.5282	0.1464	0.0919	0.0580	0.0701
1976	0.2384	0.5738	0.1865	0.1675	0.0508	0.0481
1977	–0.0718	0.2538	0.0171	–0.0067	0.0512	0.0677
1978	0.0656	0.2346	–0.0007	–0.0116	0.0718	0.0903
1979	0.1844	0.4346	–0.0418	–0.0122	0.1038	0.1331
1980	0.3242	0.3988	–0.0262	–0.0395	0.1124	0.1240
1981	–0.0491	0.1388	–0.0096	0.0185	0.1471	0.0894
1982	0.2141	0.2801	0.4379	0.4035	0.1054	0.0387
1983	0.2251	0,3967	0.0470	0.0068	0.0880	0.0380
1984	0.0627	–0.0670	0.1639	0.1543	0.0985	0.0395

Source: *Stocks, Bonds, Bills and Inflation: 1985 Yearbook*, Chicago: Ibbotson Associates, 1985, p. 26.

---

4 William F. Sharpe, *Investments*, 3rd Ed. (Englewood Cliffs, New Jersey, Prentice-Hall, Inc., 1985), p. 11.

Fortunately, if a long-term view is taken, precise measurements are not necessary for establishing sound investment policy.

Finally, the results for the entire period (1926–1984) are summarized in Table 1–4. While the standard deviations are large, this table would suggest that it is reasonable to anticipate a nine percent compound annual return for an investment in a well diversified portfolio of stocks over a long period of time. The nine percent return is before taxes and is not adjusted for inflation. Several studies have estimated the real national income of the U.S. economy has grown at about a three percent compound rate over long periods of time.[5] If we allow for inflation at a rate of five percent (based on experience since 1970), again it seems reasonable to expect investment returns of about eight to nine percent. Compound returns do assume that all interim cash flows (such as dividends) are reinvested over the time period of the calculation. We advise adhering to this assumption, paying taxes on the dividends from regular income. A consistent and systematic savings and investment program incorporates the advantages of dollar averaging. To illustrate the potential of compounding when a systematic program is put in place, consider a 30-year-old individual who saves $500 a month until retirement at age 70. This individual would accumulate a total of $2,358,214.60 by the end of the 40-year period if a return of nine percent compounded annually were realized and all interim cash flows were reinvested. Compounding is a powerful force, and recognition of this allows setting reasonable goals. At a nine percent rate compounded annually, an initial investment will double about every eight years. We would aim at doubling an investment in six to seven years, which experience also suggests is a reasonable goal when selecting securities.

A Realistic Approach

Successful investing for the average investor should:

1. Aim at realistic rather than spectacular results;
2. Remain immune to changing moods and emotions of the market place while concentrating on long-run value and fundamental considerations;
3. Purchase only securities that represent reasonable values based on rigorous analysis as developed in this book;

---

5 For example, see E.F. Denison, *The Sources of Economic Growth in the United States*, Supplemental Paper No. 13 (New York: Committee for Economic Development, 1960) and Table 6–1 in this book.

Table 1–4   Basic Series: Total Annual Returns, 1926–1984

SERIES	GEOMETRIC MEAN	ARITHMETIC MEAN	STANDARD DEVIATION	DISTRIBUTION
COMMON STOCKS	9.5%	11.7%	21.2%	
SMALL STOCKS	12.4	18.2	36.3	
LONG TERM CORPORATE BONDS	4.4	4.6	7.6	
LONG TERM GOVERNMENT BONDS	3.7	3.9	7.5	
U.S. TREASURY BILLS	3.3	3.4	3.3	
INFLATION	3.0	3.2	4.9	

-90x   0x   +90x

Source: Stocks, Bonds, Bills and Inflation: 1985 Yearbook, Chicago: Ibbotson Associates, 1985, p. 23.

4. Sell securities purchased only when targets set for these securities have been realized and/or more attractive alternative investment opportunities exist; and

5. Keep an efficiently diversified portfolio.

The culmination of fundamental security analysis for a common stock is an estimate of "intrinsic" value based upon the expected cash flows that an investment will generate, the return required by the investor, and the relative risk associated with that stock. These estimated values offer a consistent framework for purposes of comparing alternative investment opportunities, and providing a mechanism for testing the reasonableness of the assumptions that seem to make a particular stock an attractive purchase candidate. Professor Graham (a successful investor) once said,

> To establish the right price for a stock, the market must have adequate information, but it by no means follows that if the market has this information it will thereupon establish the right price. The market's evaluation of the same data can vary over a wide range, dependent upon bullish enthusiasm, concentrated speculative interest and similar influences, or bearish disillusionment. Knowledge is only one ingredient on arriving at a stock's proper price. The other ingredient, fully as important as information, is sound judgment.[6]

This book provides the background material and analytic approaches needed to render sound judgment.

Organization of the Book

As noted, the objective of this book is to present a sound comprehensive framework for analyzing investment in stocks and bonds. The book is divided into three parts. Part I develops the investment environment that underlies an investor's perspectives. A perspective for analysis is offered in Chapter 2.

In Part II of the book the logic and analytical structure of fundamental security analysis begins with an in-depth study for the economy and its implications for industries and companies to a valuation of a security based on its future earning power and dividend paying expectations utilizing valuation approaches developed in Chapter 3. Both qualitative and quantitative information and analy-

---

6 Benjamin Graham, "The Decade 1965–74: Its Significance for Financial Analysts," *The Renaissance of Value*. The Financial Analysts Research Foundation, Charlottesville, Virginia, 1974, p. 10.

ses are used in developing valuation estimates. The stock's intrinsic (present) value is then compared with market value for purposes of determining whether or not a desirable investment candidate has been found.

Statistical evidence supporting the *efficient market* hypothesis questions the ability of analysts to produce superior returns through fundamental analysis. Proponents of the efficient market hypothesis argue that the impact of all information publicly available concerning a company's future prospects already is reflected in the price of that company's common stock. Moreover, new information enters the market on a random basis. Therefore, stocks are appropriately valued by market price and an investor using fundamental analysis cannot "beat the market."

Impressive evidence does exist supporting the idea that the market is efficient. The evidence of market inefficiencies has been accumulating rapidly; however, especially, when longer time horizons underlie the investment decision. One can, at a minimum, avoid bad situations by careful analysis. Sound analysis can estimate return expectations, the riskiness of investment in different securities, and the impact of changing market conditions. We believe that fundamental analysis can help recognize temporarily undervalued situations and develop strategies for improving returns by investing in such situations, especially when longer run considerations are present.

Part III of the book develops a framework for analyzing special classes of securities. There are differences between industrial securities and those of companies in regulated industries that should be recognized.

CHAPTER 2

Security Analysis: Approach and Basic Issues

The objective of security analysis is to screen and classify financial assets in terms of investment quality and expected return. A security analyst utilizes expectations for the economy and for industry groupings (product line analysis) to forecast earnings, dividends, and intrinsic values for particular companies. Estimates of expected return and relative risk rankings serve as a basis for appraising relative attractiveness of the particular securities under consideration. This approach to security selection is called *fundamental analysis*.

Fundamental analysis is concerned with the historical performance of the economy, industry, and firms for the insight into future firm performance that these data may offer. Financial analysis explores not only the financial relationships that exist for a given firm at a moment in time, but more importantly trends in those relationships over time. The composition and liquidity of corporate resources, the company's capital structure and leverage, the competitive position of the company, and company earnings are all studied for the clues they provide as to future firm performance. Share prices reflect expected future profitability, risk (as reflected in the financial condition of the firm, the competitiveness of its markets, and leverage considerations), dividend policy, and supply and demand conditions for the given financial asset.

Published Ratings and Quality Grading

Several reporting services compile and publish financial data useful for evaluating companies and also rate bonds and some common stocks.

Bond Ratings

The major emphasis when grading bonds is on the ability of the firm to meet all obligations in years of poor as well as good economic conditions. The highest bond ratings suggest coverage for obligations by earnings and cash flow such that the probability a firm will not be able to meet its obligations, even in a recession, is close to nonexistent. Bonds are rated in terms of probability of default. Moreover, such quality ratings are based on analysis of one type of risk—the financial risk—and ignore other aspects of risk. The ratings of the two most widely used agencies and a brief summary of their meanings are shown in Table 2–1. An old study concluded that "The record of the agencies over the period studied (1900–1943) was remarkably good insofar as their ratings pertain to default."[7] Defaults and losses were larger during the period studied for issues rated low-grade (below BBB) than for higher rated issues as indicated below:

Rating Category	Default Rate (% of Par Value)
I (AAA)	5.9
II (AA)	6.0
III (A)	13.4
IV (BBB)	19.1
V-IX (BB and below)	42.4

Hickman concluded that the high default risk associated with bonds rated below BBB make them unsuited for individual long-term investors who are not in a position to diversify away default risk.

The information above is not meant to imply that agency ratings are an infallible guide. For example, the agencies failed to predict (i.e., by lowering ratings) the difficulties experienced by holders of New York City obligations during the early 1970s. Moreover, there are hundreds of issues that attain an investment quality rating. An independent analysis still is necessary to help spot the most desirable bonds within a given rating category and to possibly reveal fundamental changes that have not yet been reflected in the ratings.

---

7 W. Braddock Hickman, *Corporate Bond Quality and Investor Experience*, National Bureau of Economic Research (Princeton, N.J., Princeton University Press, 1958).

Table 2-1   Description of Agency Ratings

Moody's	Standard & Poor's	Quality Indication
Aaa	AAA	Highest quality
Aaa	AA	High quality
A	A	Upper medium grade
Baa	BBB	Medium grade
Ba	BB	Contains speculative elements
B	B	Outright speculative
Caa	CCC & CC	Default definitely possible
Ca	C	Default, only partial recovery likely
C	DDD-D	Default, little recovery likely

Stock Ratings

Quality ratings for common stocks also emphasize the risk that a series of expected cash receipts for a given security will not be realized. The less the uncertainty foreseen in realizing expected dividends and earnings growth, and the stronger the underlying financial condition of the company, the higher the rating. Standard and Poor's, for example, explains that their common stock ratings are designed to indicate…the relative stability and growth of earnings and dividends of the most recent years while also making adjustments for corporate size and "special considerations such as natural disasters, massive strikes and nonrecurring accounting adjustments."[8] Standard and Poor's point out that "a ranking is not a forecast of future market performance, but is basically an appraisal of past performance of earnings and dividends…"[9]

Published quality ratings for common stocks are less widely used and quoted than those for bonds, possibly because bonds typically have been purchased as a defensive investment, emphasizing the yield to maturity and relative certainty of receiving that yield rather than growth.

8 *Stock Guide* (New York: Standard and Poor's Corporation, November 1981) p. 7.

9 Ibid.

Valuation: A Cornerstone of Fundamental Analysis

Valuation of common stocks rests on the ability of the analyst to anticipate future performance of the firm and the market in which the financial asset trades. Valuation would be easy in a world of certainty, but once uncertainty about future earnings, dividends, and stock prices is recognized, one realizes that fundamental analysis can offer only a range of values based on assumed conditions.

Such an analysis does provide a basis for varying assumptions concerning the factors underlying valuation—the analyst can ask "what if" questions. Moreover, one could assign probabilities to key assumptions and develop estimates with given probabilities.

Portfolio Selection and Fundamental Analysis

The fundamental approach suggests selecting that stock whose intrinsic value, as determined in the valuation process, is highest relative to current market price. Risk is taken into account by varying the discount rate or capitalization factors used in calculating intrinsic value. This does not imply a one stock portfolio, as suggested by Markowitz.[10] If all investors calculated the same highest intrinsic value relative to market price for a given security, the resultant demand for that security quickly would push up its price until the margin of intrinsic value over current market price would be greater for other securities. A given security would be most attractive only at a given moment in time. Since investors commit funds over time, have different expectations, and change their expectations over time, they would acquire more than one security.

It is correct to say that valuation analysis incorporates a different and less complete concept of risk than that developed in the literature of modern portfolio theory. By concentrating on individual securities, it overlooks the importance of covariation of returns and the logically related idea that risk for an individual security and risk for that security as part of a portfolio of securities are two different things. Risk reduction through diversification can be attained only when the covariance relationships are taken into account. Modern portfolio theory has added a new and important dimension to the problem of security selection that is not considered in the fundamental analysis approach to selecting securities. An integration of the two approaches is needed, though not really available in the current literature.

---

10 Harry Markowitz, "Portfolio Selection," *Journal of Finance*, Vol. 7, No. 1 (March 1952), pp. 77–78.

Basic changes occur in a firm's characteristics over time, such as changes in product mix, technological change, the introduction of new products, variations of capital structure, and merger. It is important to assess the implications of these changes for the cash flow of a firm and the value of its stock. Fundamental analysis provides a framework for analyzing such changes.

Capital Market Theory and Fundamental Analysis

In an efficient capital market, stock prices always reflect all publicly and privately available information concerning the securities traded. Security prices would adjust instantaneously and in an unbiased manner to new information as it enters the market. Furthermore, price changes in such efficient markets would perform a random walk—that is, behave in a patternless manner reflecting the random introduction of new information.

It is true that in a perfectly efficient market no technique or analytical tool can be expected to yield systematically above-average returns. However, security analysis is essential to market efficiency—only if investors make conscientious and competent efforts to learn about and apply relevant information promptly and perceptively can efficient markets exist. In a real world, users of available information do not necessarily agree on the implications that information has for future corporate performance and stock prices. Furthermore, information is not costless to market participants. Finally, transactions costs do exist. Existing capital markets probably are efficient, but disequilibrium situations are likely to exist in the short run. Such disequilibrium situations come about because of varying and changing interpretations by the various participants in the market and are likely to be short-lived.

The analyst must recognize that acceptance of the idea that capital markets are efficient and that stock prices perform a random walk does not imply that security analysis is useless. Fundamental analysis, unlike technical approaches and charting, is not based on historical price data. The analyst is attempting to uncover information that is not known generally. It is consistent with the concept of relatively efficient capital markets to recognize that proper use of such information could result in above-average gains.

The major contribution of security analysis in relatively efficient markets will be the understanding it brings about of effects of firm and economy-wide events on security prices and alertness in directing attention to new developments. Opportunities for gains that may result from effective analysis may well be short-lived in our capital markets, and originality in analysis and alertness in applying the results are necessary conditions for successful security analysis.

The Ingredients of Security Analysis

In making an analysis of securities, both qualitative and quantitative factors are considered. *Qualitative factors* refer to subjective information (such as the quality of management or research and development effort) and to projections of quantitative data such as earnings and dividends. *Quantitative factors* are historical numerical data as reported in financial statements or concerning the economy and financial markets. Quantitative data appear to be objective, but the determination of the figures reported often depends on numerous subjective judgments. Expressing qualitative factors in quantitative terms does not change the fact that such data are subjective in nature. The data that analysts utilize in their decision-making process often are thought of as probability distributions rather than point estimates as typically presented. The job of the analyst is to develop the probability distributions. The fact that projections and other data are qualitative and subjective in nature does not mean that such data are not useful or even essential—the data merely emphasize the uncertainties and the need for an analysis capable of dealing with uncertain situations.

Ratio Analysis: A Basic Tool of Security Analysis

Investors have long used ratio analysis as a major tool for evaluating and interpreting the financial statements of companies. The object of ratio analysis is to reduce the large number of items contained in the statements to a relatively small number of meaningful relationships. Mere examination of the absolute figures included in financial statements cannot be expected to lead to definite conclusions in regard to the financial status of a business. Assume, for example, that Company A reports earnings after taxes of $100,000 while Company B reports earnings after taxes of $1,000,000. To assume that Company B is ten times as profitable as Company A, and therefore worth ten times as much, would be incorrect. Suppose the balance sheet of Company A showed total investment capital of $200,000, while that of Company B showed total investment capital of $10,000,000. Company A is earning 50 percent on invested capital while Company B is earning only 10 percent. The overall objective of a business is to earn a satisfactory return on the funds invested in it, consistent with maintaining a sound financial position. An acceptable return on invested capital ratio is a logical test of the success experienced in achieving this objective.

Interpretation requires comparison of meaningful components. Appropriate relationships (ratios) will depend on the purpose of the ratios selected and should relate components in which a logical decision-making relationship exists between the two variables, as for profits and invested capital; the numerator and denominator chosen should be based on commonly calculated values. For example, cost of sales (not net sales) should be used as the numerator in an inventory turnover ratio since the denominator (inventory) is valued at cost and the purpose is to access the adequacy of the physical turnover of that inventory.

Screening Procedures

Screening processes are used by analysts to select from the thousands of stocks and bonds offered in the market a limited number worthy of extensive analysis. The screening process should be based on the objectives and risk tolerance of the investor. Provident Capital Management, for example, follows a low price-earnings (P/E) ratio philosophy in selecting stocks, based on historical studies indicating that low P/E stocks have consistently outperformed high P/E stocks over most time periods considered. They, therefore, concentrate their analytical efforts on those stocks whose P/E ratios fall among the lowest 40 percent of those applicable to all firms at a given moment in time.

Computers are a valuable aid for purposes of screening stocks. Obviously, the computer can screen only on the basis of data already gathered and stored in the system. The Compustat tapes, prepared by Standard & Poor's Investors Management Sciences, Inc., provide detailed financial data on thousands of firms that could be helpful in a screening effort.

Stock screens could be set up to reflect any of the following criteria:

A. Growth Criteria

1. A minimum compound annual growth rate for a specified time period for sales and/or earnings could be required.
2. Risk could be limited by specifying a minimum standard deviation of sales or earnings data around the above-mentioned growth rate. Steady growth usually is preferred to growth that comes in fits and starts.
3. A minimum growth rate, and possibly standard deviation, could be required for dividend payments, the dividend payout ratio and/or dividend yield by an investor to whom current cash flow is highly important.

B. Profitability Screens

1. A minimum return on total assets and/or owners' equity could be required. The efficiency with which the firm utilizes assets or owners' capital is a

significant indicator of performance. A study by Faulkner, Dawkins, and Sullivan, Inc., indicated that high rates of return on owners' equity were well related to investment performance.[11]

C. Price Related Screens

1. A screen could be based on the P/E ratio, either in relation to past history, to other firms in the industry or to all firms. Provident Capital Management ranks P/E ratios relative to all firms.
2. One could build a market price to book value component into a screen.
3. The P/E ratio could be related to earnings or other characteristics in a screen.

D. Risk Characteristics

1. Beta, as calculated in modern portfolio theory, could be entered as a risk constraint in a screen. Beta could also, of course, be related interactively with other characteristics of the firm in preparing a screen.
2. A liquidity standard could be entered as a requirement. Liquidity might be defined in terms of the current ratio, the acid-test, turnover ratios or the interest coverage or fixed charges coverage ratios. A cash flow variable could also be built into a screen.
3. A minimum debt to equity;as screening criteria requirement could also be part of a screen. Again, firm differences in terms of revenue stability would make it unlikely that a single standard would be useful.

E. Marketability Tests

1. An investor could be interested in assuring reasonable marketability for a commitment. A minimum number of shares outstanding and/or a minimum daily or weekly trading volume requirement for the stock of a firm could be included in the screen.

The computer also could be used to test the efficiency of screens that have been developed and improve them. Returns performance of securities selected by the screen could be checked over time and other characteristics could be tested to see if inclusion could improve the screen. Such tests only can be based on historical performance, and the future may not mirror the past. The tests are not conclusive; on-going evaluation is useful.

---

11 Robert P. Colin and Howard E. Willie, *Interrelationship of Stockholder and Company Return on Investment* (New York: Faulkner, Dawkins & Sullivan, Inc., November, 1972).

The Financial Reporting Problem

The dissatisfaction of investors and other financial analysts with corporate financial reports is evident from the following selected remarks:

If accountants want to continue to enjoy a role in the investment management process, they should prepare to focus their energies on supplying whatever data a workable theory of security valuation requires, rather than defending the present ritual.[12]

Congress has become increasingly alert to the lack of uniformity in accounting rules and to the deleterious effects this situation can have on the legislature's attempts to write laws.[13]

It is going to be difficult to detect from 1973 financial reports whether a company's fundamentals are deteriorating since there are many accounting, operating, and financial gimmicks that management can use in the short-run to hide the effect on profits of a deterioration in fundamentals.[14]

The federal securities acts have gone a long way toward eliminating fraudulent or purposely misleading financial statements. However, the Equity Funding case proves that fraudulent financial reports have not been entirely eliminated, and it must be remembered that some small and intrastate firms are exempt from federal reporting requirements. Investors do have to depend on the certification of corporate reports by outside accountants as protection from inadequate reporting and fraudulent practice.

Inadequate Disclosure vs. Lack of Uniformity

For some years a battle has raged over whether the information problem is largely one of "inadequate disclosure" or one of "lack of uniformity" in corporate reporting. Disclosure problems certainly exist, but the Securities & Exchange

---

12 J. L. Treynor, "The Trouble with Earnings," *Financial Analysts Journal*, No. 28 (September–October, 1972), p. 43.

13 "Who Will Set CPA Rules?" *Dun's Review* (September 1976), p. 62. Reprinted with the special permission of *Dun's Review*, September 1976. Copyright 1976. Dun & Bradstreet Publications Corporation.

14 David F. Hawkins, "Accounting Dodos and Red Flags—A Guide to Reading 1973 Annual Reports," *Financial Executive* (May, 1974), p. 84.

Commission (SEC) is exerting considerable effort to assure full, accurate, and adequate disclosure of material corporate financial information. Sufficient information should be given, either in the body of the report or in footnotes, to facilitate comparisons among firms using alternative accounting techniques. Admittedly, the cost of gathering and reporting this additional information would have to be weighed against its usefulness in performing a sound analysis. Where adjustments are relatively easy and necessary for useful comparison, sufficient information should be given for adjustment from the method used to other acceptable methods. Footnotes, explanations, and qualifications to the annual reports taken by the accountants for preceding years should be repeated in current annual reports and in comparative statements to the extent that they continue to be of significance. Differences between net income reported to stockholders and that reported to the Internal Revenue Service should be explained. The analyst should not be required to spend time and effort searching SEC filings and old reports to gather the information necessary to interpret the data currently reported. Unfortunately, these suggestions have not been uniformly adapted by accountants.

Accountants should prepare statements that are useful to the user. Users desire statements that are reliable and informative for the purpose of appraising the financial strength and profitability of the firm and for making interfirm comparisons. Users are not so much interested in a past accounting of stewardship as in developing a base useful for projecting earnings, dividends, and financial strength. What is needed is disclosure of *material* information necessary for proper evaluation of a corporation's securities, not greater disclosure per se. Under SEC regulations, S-X-Rule 1-02 states, "The term 'material' when used to qualify a requirement for the furnishing of information as to any subject, limits the information required to those matters on which an average prudent investor ought reasonably be informed." Rule 3-06 goes beyond this to say, "The information required with respect to any statement shall be furnished as a minimum requirement to which shall be added such further material information as is necessary to make the required statements, in the light of the circumstances under which they are made, not misleading."[15] A mere proliferation of details may only make sifting out the really significant information more difficult. As G. K. Chesterton pointed out, "The best place to hide a leaf is in a forest."

Absolute uniformity in accounting data should not be expected or sought. The complex and varied nature of business operations and a rapidly changing economy suggest a need for flexibility in reporting. Firms should be allowed to continue choosing among generally accepted accounting principles, but they

---

15 William Holmes, "Materiality—Through the Looking Glass," *Journal of Accountancy* (February, 1972), p. 45.

should also be required to disclose in dollar amounts the impact on net income and balance sheet values of the accounting alternative chosen.

The analyst has the responsibility to interpret the information and recognize economic reality, assuming the facts are fully and accurately disclosed. Accountant and management should seek to present the information in the form most useful to users. Reports should not be so prepared that only a very experienced professional analyst can dig out, rearrange, and adjust published figures by interpretation of notes to financial statements and other supplementary information to make them useful.

Summary

The function of security analysis is to determine the best relative values and portfolio composition at any point in time. This requires the investor to screen and classify financial assets on the basis of quality (financial risk) and then, in terms of intrinsic values. The necessary screening process has become more practical since the introduction of computers and computer banks of corporate financial information.

The investor must understand the differing concepts of risk underlying fundamental analysis as compared with the portfolio selection models and that modern portfolio theory has added a new and important dimension to the problem of security selection. Historically, this has not been considered in the fundamental analysis approach to security selection. Therefore, the material in this chapter recommends an integration of the two approaches.

Security analysis deals with both qualitative and quantitative data. Qualitative factors are subjective. All projections are qualitative, for they strictly are subjective, although expressed in quantitative terms. It is important to remember that the future always is uncertain and that projections only can be stated in terms of probabilities.

In analyzing quantitative accounting data, investors will use ratio analysis, which facilities comparison of meaningful components of financial statements. Once ratios are calculated, they must be interpreted in absolute terms and in terms of trends, which involves certain subjective judgments. In any case, the underlying factors that have resulted in the ratios and their trends are most important as a basis for assessing the future prospects of the firm.

In spite of the great improvement in financial reporting, there still exist problems of inadequate disclosure and lack of uniformity in reporting financial data. The SEC, the Financial Analysts Federation, and the American Institute of Certified Public Accountants, as well as committees of the stock exchanges and the National Association of Security Dealers, are working cooperatively for continuing improvement in the area of financial reporting.

CHAPTER 3

Security Valuation: The Cornerstone of Fundamental Analysis

The objective of fundamental analysis is to screen and classify financial assets in terms of investment quality (an assessment of risk) and expected return. Security analysts utilize expectations for the economy in the aggregate and for industry groupings (product line analysis) as a basis for forecasting profits, dividends, and possibly a future stock price for an individual security, which allows calculation of an intrinsic value and expected return. This information is an important factor used by knowledgeable investors in deciding whether to buy, hold or sell a particular security.

Intrinsic value of an asset reflects investors' expectations about future cash flows that will be generated by means of acquisition of that asset. It is a forecasted value that is likely to be quite different than current market price. Moreover, intrinsic value estimates for a given security could differ among individuals since the personal projection of future cash flows and risk could differ.

An important point to recognize is that under conditions of uncertainty intrinsic value estimates can never be precise. They merely provide a yardstick against which to measure current prices on the basis of expectations for future economic and other events. Such estimates are no more accurate than the expectations underlying them. Still, a standard is necessary and useful, even if it is only a loose one, to serve as a check on the reasonableness of estimations that underlie the selection of securities.

Expectation, Uncertainty, and Valuation Theory

Investors, acting individually or with others through institutions, invest in order to increase wealth. An investor should seek the highest level of expected return for any given level of risk. However, expectations about future events can be based only in part on known facts, and in part on forecasts that are subject to uncertainty. The interest payments which are supposed to be made on a corporate or municipal bond, for example, may be counted among the known facts; but, whether or not such future commitments will be met will be determined, at least in part, by chance factors.

Forecasts which underlie financial decisions are continually reassessed, whether implicitly or explicitly, and securities that trade in organized markets are "revalued" accordingly. According to Keynes, "Our knowledge of the factors which govern the yield of an investment some years hence is usually very slight and often negligible."[16] It is important, therefore, not to make the assumption of perfect certainty when creating valuation estimates.

The Time Value of Money

The time value of money is a phenomenon common to all valuation approaches. This concept will therefore be developed at the outset. An investor commits a given sum of money, foregoing present consumption, in exchange for the promise of a future stream of benefits. A dollar to be received today, however, is worth more than one to be received at some future date because.

1. The risk that a dollar due to be received at a future date may not be received would be avoided were it forthcoming immediately.
2. A dollar in hand could earn a return in each period it is available, leading to an increase in investor wealth.

The timing of cash flows, therefore, is highly important in determining the expected return from an investment.

---

16 John M. Keynes, *The General Theory of Employment, Interest Money* (New York: Harcourt Brace, 1936).

Future Values and Compound Interest

The process by which interest earns interest upon itself is called *compounding*. Table 3–1 shows the effect of interest compounding at an annual rate of eight percent on an initial balance of $1,000 over a five year period. Note the growing importance of interest earned on interest through reinvestment. For long-term bonds, for example, the interest-on-interest component may amount to over half the total return received by an investor, depending on the reinvestment assumptions that are made.[17]

Table 3–1   The Annual Effect of Compounding at Eight Percent Over a Five-Year Period

Year	Initial Balance	Interest on Principal	Interest Earned on Reinvested Interest	Total Interest Earned	Year-End Balance
1	$1,000.00	$80.00	0	$ 80.00	$1,080.00
2	1,080.00	80.00	$ 6.40	86.40	1,166.40
3	1,166.40	80.00	13.31	93.31	1,259.71
4	1,259.71	80.00	20.78	100.78	1,360.49
5	1,360.49	80.00	28.84	108.84	1,469.93

The process of interest compounding may be represented compactly in equation form as follows:

$$TV_t = A_0(1+r)^t, \tag{3.1}$$

where

TV_t = the terminal value at time t,

A_0 = the cash flow at time $t = 0$, or the invested principal,

r = the periodic interest rate,

t = the number of interest periods for which compounding takes place.

---

17 Sidney Homer and Martin L. Leibowitz, *Inside the Yield Book*, New York Institute of Finance (Englewood Cliffs, N.J.: 1972), pp. 21–22.

Thus, were $1,000 placed in an eight percent interest-bearing account compounded annually, assuming no withdrawals were made during the period, balances for the first and second years corresponding with those shown in Table 3–1 may be calculated as follows:

$$TV_1 = \$1,000(1 + .08)^1 = \$1,080.00;$$

$$TV_2 = \$1,000(1 + .08)^2 = \$1,166.40.$$

Compound return is a more potent growth force than investors sometimes realize. At a compound growth rate of eight percent, for example, a $1,000 principal would double approximately every nine years. Thus, $1,000 would grow to $8,000 in about 27 years, $50,540 in about 50 years, and $2,550,749 in 100 years. As one wit has said, "Thrift is a marvelous virtue in one's ancestors." The annual rate available on high-quality bonds generally exceeded eight percent during the 1970s, surpassing 15 percent in 1981, and then falling back toward, but not below, the eight percent level after 1981.

Present Value

Suppose that a security whose par value is $1,000 is retired at the end of one year with a single lump-sum payment of $1,080 and that there are no payments on the security in the interim. Also assume that the actual per annum yield on an ordinary passbook account in a bank is eight percent. Let us disregard the tax implications for the moment. If the market price of the security were $1,000 or more, the investor would be at least as well off putting the money in the bank at eight percent. The present value of a single payment to be received at some future point in time, t, may be obtained as follows:

$$PV_t = A_t \times \left[\frac{1}{(1+r)^t} \right], \qquad (3.2)$$

where

A_t = cash flow at time t,

r = the discount rate or opportunity cost.

Present value, in the sense of Equation (3.2) is an amount of money, A_0, which, if it were on hand today and invested at a compound rate (r) would grow to equal the future payment (A_t) by the end of time period T. For example, substituting into Equation (3.2):

$$PV_t = A_t \left[\frac{1}{(1+r)^t} \right]$$

$$= \frac{\$1,080}{(1+.08)^1}$$

$$= \$1,000.$$

Given the alternative provided by an ordinary passbook account whose effective yield is eight percent, one should not pay more than $1,000 for this security.

Present value tables are presented at the end of this chapter. In Equation (3.2) the present value of any cash flow A_t is obtained by multiplying that cash flow by the quantity:

$$PV_\$ = \frac{1}{(1+r)^t} \qquad (3.3)$$

This quantity is the present value of *one dollar* forthcoming at time t. The present value of a one-dollar cash flow, $PV_\$$, will vary, depending on the discount rate r and the timing of that cash flow t. The present value table shows the present value of $1 for various combinations of the discount rate and the timing of cash flow. For example, assume that a financial instrument promised to pay you $1,360.00 four years from now, and you believe you could earn 10 percent in alternative uses of the money with equivalent risk. What is the maximum price you should be willing to pay for this instrument today? Using Table 3–A in the appendix [or Equation (3.3)], we find that the present value of $1 received four years from now is .683 (68.3 cents). The maximum price one should pay, therefore, is $928.88 (.683 × $1,360). This will assure earning the required 10 percent compunded annual return over the four years, assuming the payment of $1,360.00 is actually received.

Contracts and Annuities.   Suppose that a contract involved a stream of cash flows, A_t t = 1, 2,..., T (the number of years to maturity), which represent payments of various amounts for T periods beginning at time, t=1. The present value of a series of cash flows is simply the sum of the present values associated with each cash flow:

$$PV = \sum_{t-1}^{T} A_t \left[\frac{1}{\left(1+r\right)^t} \right], \tag{3.4}$$

An *annuity* is a special form of contract whose payment stream, A_t, $t=1,2,...,T$, consists of payments, A_{cD}, which are the same from one period to the next. If we substitute the constant A_c for the variable A_t in Equation (3.4), the constant factors out, and the result simplifies as follows:

$$PV = A_c \left[\sum_{t-1}^{T} \frac{1}{\left(1+r\right)^t} \right], \tag{3.5}$$

Equation (3.5) defines the present value of an annuity which offers a constant payment, A_c, where the appropriate discount rate is r. In the special case where the constant payment is $Ac = \$1.00$, the constant A_c drops out of Equation (3.5) and we obtain:

$$PV_\$ = \left[\sum_{t-1}^{T} \frac{1}{\left(1+r\right)^t} \right], \tag{3.6}$$

Equation (3.6) defines the present value of a one-dollar annuity to be received for T periods, beginning at the end of period $t = 1$, where the discount rate is r. The present value of *any* annuity, of course, will vary, depending on the variables A, T, and r.

Table 3-B presented in the chapter appendix is an annuity table which sets out the present value of a one-dollar annuity for various combinations of the discount rate r and time periods T. For example, suppose an investor wished to know the present value of $1 to be received one year from today, assuming eight percent compounded annually could be earned in alternative uses of the money. Using Equation (3.3) the present value is:

$$PV_\$ = \frac{1}{\left(1+r\right)^t} = \frac{1}{\left(1+.08\right)} = .92593 .$$

The present value of $1 to be received each year for the next three years, assuming eight percent can be earned in alternative uses of the funds, is determined by adding the present values of each individual receipt, as determined from Table 3-A in the chapter appendix:

$$PV_1 = \quad .926$$

$$PV_2 = \quad .857$$

$$PV_3 = \quad \underline{.794}$$

Present value of series = $2.577

If $850 is expected each year for three years rather than $1, the present value of such a series can be calculated by multiplying $850 × 2.577, or the present value is $2,190.45. We could, therefore, say we would not be willing to pay more than $2,190.45 for a security that offered a cash flow of $850 a year for three years, if we believed we could earn eight percent compounded annually in investments of equivalent risk.

Perpetuities.   While all bonds in the United States have a maturity date, the British Consuls are perpetual bonds. A consul pays interest to perpetuity to whoever happens to own it, but the principal is never repaid.

The present value of a consul at any moment in time is equal to the net present value of all interest payments due into perpetuity and may be expressed as follows:

$$PV = A_c \left[\sum_{t=1}^{\infty} \frac{1}{(1+r)^t} \right], \tag{3.7}$$

where A_c is the constant interest payment and r is the discount rate.

The calculation of this present value is simplified by exploiting the fact that the summation in Equation (3.7) has a limit:

$$PV = \frac{A_c}{r} \tag{3.7a}$$

Equation (3.7a) may be used in actual computations. For example, the maximum price an investor, who could earn nine percent on alternative investments of equivalent risk, would pay for at six percent, $1,000 par Consul would be $666.67 ($60/.09).

Bond Valuation

The basic idea underlying all valuation approaches is the present value concept. Let us first consider the valuation of a bond since it is somewhat easier than valuing common stock. The value of a bond can be defined as the total present value of all interest payments plus the present value of the return of principal upon maturity. The amount of each interest payment, the time pattern in which they will be paid, and the face value of the bond are specified in a bond contract.

It is important to understand that, when purchasing bonds, investors seek a yield that is commensurate with alternative possible uses of funds. The yields desired by investors change over time as the supply of and the demand for loanable funds change. Bond prices also change over time, reflecting changing desired yields and other market phenomena.

Yield to Maturity

The yield to maturity on a bond is that discount rate which equates the purchase price of a bond to the present value of the cash inflows. This is merely the internal rate of return, r^*, which is defined in the following identity:

$$\sum_{t=0}^{T} \frac{A_t}{\left(1 = r^*\right)^t} = 0, \tag{3.8}$$

where A_t is the cash flow for period t, whether it be a net cash outflow or inflow, and T is the last period in which a cash flow is expected.

To illustrate, suppose that a $1,000 par bond has five years remaining to maturity, a four percent coupon rate, and interest that is payable semiannually. If market conditions are such as to require a six percent yield to maturity, we see from Table 3-2 that the bond would sell for $914.70 (which is the present value of the future cash inflows). Since cash flows are received semiannually, they are not discounted at the six percent annual rate, but at one-half the annual rate.

Bond yield tables eliminate the necessity of performing laborious calculations such as that illustrated in Table 3–2. Table 3–3 shows the various prices required to offer given yields to maturity for a four percent coupon bond maturing in five years. The number in the body of the table represents a percentage of par value. For example, a five-year, four percent coupon bond should sell at 91.47

Table 3–2   Determination of Present Value of a Four Percent Coupon, $1,000 Par, Five-Year Bond When Six Percent Yield to Maturity is Desired

Period	Cash Flow	Present Value Factor at Three Percent	Present Value of Cash Flow
1	$ 20	.970874	$ 19.418
2	20	.942596	18.852
3	20	.915142	18.303
4	20	.888487	17.770
5	20	.862609	17.252
6	20	.837484	16.750
7	20	.813092	16.262
8	20	.789409	15.788
9	20	.766417	15.328
10	1,020	.744094	758.976
Sum of present values			$914.699

Note: Three-place present value tables, both for the present value of $1 received at the end of year and for $1 received annually at the end of each year for n years, are presented in an appendix at the end of this chapter. Six-place accuracy for discount factors was used in the example to minimize rounding error.

percent of par value to yield six percent to maturity, or at a price of $914.70 for a $1,000 par bond.

Computer programs are also available that will make the illustrated calculations, and some hand-held calculators are programmed to make these calculations.

The Reinvestment Assumption.   Yield to maturity calculations assume that all interim cash flows are reinvested at the yield to maturity rate. This can be illustrated by noting that if $914.70 were invested at a six percent rate compounded semiannually for five years, it would grow to $1,229.28. Alternatively, a receipt of $20 every six months for five years, assuming receipts are reinvested at six percent compounded semiannually over the five-year period, plus $1,000 at the end of the fifth year, would also result in a wealth position of $1,229.28 at the end of the period, as shown in Table 3-4.

The realized yield on a bond held to maturity will in most instances be quite different from the yield to maturity calculated at purchase due to changing money market conditions and reinvestment rates over the life of the bond. If the $20-semi-annual interest payments in the previous illustration were reinvested at less than the assumed six percent annualized rate, the realized yield would be less than six

Table 3-3 Coupon Yield Tables, Four Percent Coupon

Yield				Years and Months				
	4–9	4–10	4–11	5–0	5–3	5–6	5–9	6–0
2.00	109.02	109.17	109.32	109.47	109.92	110.37	110.81	111.26
2.20	108.07	108.21	108.34	108.48	108.88	109.28	109.67	110.07
2.40	107.14	107.26	107.38	107.50	107.85	108.20	108.54	108.89
2.60	106.21	106.32	106.42	106.52	106.83	107.13	107.43	107.73
2.80	105.30	105.39	105.47	105.56	105.82	106.08	106.33	106.59
3.00	104.39	104.46	104.54	104.61	104.82	105.04	105.24	105.45
3.20	103.50	103.55	103.61	103.67	103.83	104.01	104.17	104.34
3.40	102.61	102.65	102.69	102.74	102.86	102.99	103.11	103.23
3.60	101.73	101.76	101.79	101.82	101.89	101.98	102.06	102.14
3.80	100.86	100.87	100.89	100.90	100.94	100.98	101.02	101.06
4.00	100.00	100.00	100.00	100.00	100.00	100.00	100.00	100.00
4.20	99.14	99.13	99.12	99.11	99.06	99.03	98.98	98.95
4.40	98.30	98.27	98.25	98.22	98.14	98.06	97.98	97.91
4.60	97.46	97.42	97.38	97.35	97.22	97.11	96.99	96.89
4.80	96.63	96.58	96.53	96.48	96.32	96.17	96.02	95.87
5.00	95.81	95.75	95.68	95.62	95.43	95.24	95.05	94.87
5.10	95.40	95.33	95.27	95.20	94.98	94.78	94.57	94.38
5.20	95.00	94.92	94.85	94.78	94.54	94.32	94.10	93.88
5.30	94.60	94.51	94.43	94.36	94.10	93.87	93.62	93.39
5.40	94.20	94.11	94.02	93.94	93.67	93.41	93.15	92.91
5.50	93.80	93.70	93.61	93.52	93.23	92.96	92.68	92.42
5.60	93.40	93.30	93.20	93.11	92.80	92.52	92.22	91.94
5.70	93.01	92.90	92.80	92.69	92.37	92.07	91.76	91.46
5.80	92.61	92.50	92.39	92.28	91.95	91.63	91.30	90.99
5.90	92.22	92.10	91.99	91.88	91.52	91.19	90.84	90.52
6.00	91.83	91.71	91.59	91.47	91.10	90.75	90.39	90.05
6.10	91.44	91.32	91.19	91.07	90.68	90.31	89.94	89.58
6.20	91.06	90.93	90.79	90.66	90.26	89.88	89.49	89.12
6.30	90.68	90.54	90.40	90.26	89.85	89.45	89.04	88.65
6.40	90.29	90.15	90.01	89.87	89.43	89.02	88.60	88.20
6.50	89.91	89.76	89.62	89.47	89.02	88.59	88.16	87.74
6.60	89.54	89.38	89.23	89.08	88.61	88.17	87.72	87.29
6.70	89.16	89.00	88.84	88.69	88.21	87.75	87.28	86.84
6.80	88.79	88.62	88.46	88.30	87.80	87.33	86.85	86.39
6.90	88.41	88.24	88.08	87.91	87.40	86.91	86.42	85.95
7.00	88.04	87.87	87.70	87.53	87.00	86.50	85.99	85.50
7.10	87.67	87.49	87.32	87.14	86.60	86.09	85.56	85.07
7.20	87.31	87.12	86.94	86.76	86.20	85.68	85.14	84.63
7.30	86.94	86.75	86.57	86.38	85.81	85.27	84.72	84.20
7.40	86.58	86.38	86.19	86.00	85.42	84.86	84.30	83.76
7.50	86.22	86.02	85.82	85.63	85.03	84.46	83.88	83.34
7.60	85.86	85.65	85.45	85.25	84.64	84.06	83.47	82.91

Table 3–3 (continued)

Yield	Years and Months							
	4–9	4–10	4–11	5–0	5–3	5–6	5–9	6–0
7.70	85.50	85.29	85.08	84.88	84.26	83.66	83.06	82.49
7.80	85.14	84.93	84.72	84.51	83.87	83.26	82.65	82.06
7.90	84.79	84.57	84.36	84.14	83.49	82.87	82.24	81.65
8.00	84.44	84.21	83.99	83.78	83.11	82.48	81.84	81.23
8.10	84.09	83.86	83.63	83.41	82.74	82.09	81.44	80.82
8.20	83.74	83.50	83.28	83.05	82.36	81.70	81.04	80.41
8.30	83.39	83.15	82.69	82.69	81.99	81.32	80.64	80.00
8.40	83.04	82.80	82.57	82.33	81.62	80.93	80.24	79.59
8.50	82.70	82.45	82.21	81.98	81.25	80.55	79.85	79.19
8.60	82.36	82.11	81.86	81.62	80.88	80.17	79.46	78.79
8.70	82.02	81.76	81.51	81.27	80.51	79.80	79.07	78.39
8.80	81.68	81.42	81.17	80.92	80.15	79.42	78.69	77.99
8.90	81.34	81.08	80.82	80.57	79.79	79.05	78.30	77.60
9.00	81.00	80.74	80.48	80.22	79.43	78.68	77.92	77.20
9.20	80.34	80.06	79.79	79.53	78.71	77.94	77.16	76.43
9.40	79.68	79.39	79.12	78.84	78.01	77.22	76.42	75.66
9.60	79.02	78.73	78.45	78.17	77.31	76.50	75.68	74.90
9.80	78.37	78.08	77.78	77.50	76.62	75.78	74.95	74.15
10.00	77.73	77.43	77.13	76.83	75.93	75.08	74.22	73.41

Source: Reproduced from *Expanded Bond Values Table*, Publication #83, p. 299. Copyright 1970, Financial Publishing Company, Boston Massachusetts.

percent upon maturity. Of course, if interest payments were reinvested at a rate higher than six percent, realized yield would exceed six percent upon maturity. If a bond is not held to maturity, of course, the realized yield may again be quite different since the reinvestment period has changed and the price at which the bond was sold could be quite different from face value.

Rising interest rates after purchase of a bond would allow reinvestment at higher rates than assumed by the yield to maturity calculation but would cause the price of the bond to fall, resulting in a lower terminal value if sold before maturity. A decline in quality (as perceived in the market) after purchase would also result in a fall in price, other things being equal. Therefore, an investor is subject to "price risk" when interest rates rise after purchase or quality of the bond declines. If interest rates fell after purchase or quality improved, of course, the result would be precisely the opposite.

The reinvestment assumption has other important implications, as when selecting among discount, par, and premium bonds. When rising interest rates are anticipated, an investor should prefer premium or par bonds since their coupon

Table 3–4   An Illustration of the Reinvestment Assumption

Period	Cash Received and Reinvested	Terminal Value of $1 Invested for T Years	Terminal Value
1	$ 20	$(1.03)^9$	$ 26.097
2	20	$(1.03)^8$	25.337
3	20	$(1.03)^7$	24.599
4	20	$(1.03)^6$	23.882
5	20	$(1.03)^5$	23.186
6	20	$(1.03)^4$	22.511
7	20	$(1.03)^3$	21.855
8	20	$(1.03)^2$	21.218
9	20	$(1.03)^1$	20.600
10	1,020	1	1,020.000
Total			$1,229.285

rates will be higher than those on discount bonds of equivalent quality. Under these conditions, and investor seeks to maximize the current interest receipts so as to obtain more to reinvest at rising rates. On the other hand, when interest rates are expected to decline, deep discount bonds would be attractive. A large part of the total yield for a deep discount bond is represented by the accumulation (excess of face value over purchase price) received upon maturity, which will not have to be reinvested at falling rates.

Yield to Call.   A call clause gives the issuing corporation the right, at its discretion, to require that the bonds be submitted for payment prior to maturity at a designated price. Corporations will only exercise the call privilege when they can refinance at lower interest cost, which can adversely affect the bondholder's economic interest since reinvestment of the funds received will have to be at the lower prevailing rates.

Accordingly, a sophisticated investor will consider both the yield to maturity and the yield assuming the bond is called when evaluating callable bonds. Actually, neither the yield to maturity or the yield to call can be considered accurate measures of the yield that will be realized from holding a bond for two reasons. First, both measures assume reinvestment of cash flows to the terminal date used at the calculated yield rate which is not likely to match actual experiences (the reinvestment assumption previously discussed). Second, the yield to call does not recognize what will happen to the proceeds after the bond is called and prior to maturity. Thus, it cannot be directly compared with calculated yields to maturity for other bonds. Still, they offer a reasonable estimate of potential realized yield for comparative purposes, and can be calculated on a "what if" basis to consider future reinvestment rates and the date of call which are uncertain.

A yield to call is defined as that discount rate that equates the present value of the promised cash flow to the assumed date of call (coupon payments plus call price) to the market price. To illustrate, assume that 10 percent bonds issued by corporation X are callable after five years at $1,050 per bond. The bonds currently sell at par and thus yield 10 percent to maturity. If the bonds are called at the earliest call date, they would pay $50 semiannually for the five years and $1,050 at the end of the fifth year. A trial and error approach and a hand-held computer can be used to determine the yield to call through an interactive process. The calculated yield to call for the above bond is about 10.2 percent.

Approximating Net Yield to Maturity.   When bond yield tables and calculators equipped for present value calculations are not readily available, an approximation of the net yield to maturity is provided by

$$ YTM = \frac{C + \dfrac{F - P}{T}}{\dfrac{F + P}{2}}, \qquad (3.9) $$

where
  YTM = net yield maturity,
  C = annual dollars paid in interest
  F = face or par value of the bond,
  P = selling price of the bond,
  T = number of years to maturity.

For a four percent, $1,000 bond purchased at $914.70, with five years remaining to maturity, we obtain

$$ YTM = \frac{40 + \dfrac{1000 - 914.70}{5}}{\dfrac{100 + 914.70}{2}} = \frac{57.06}{957.35} = 0.59602 , $$

according to this approximation. This approximation could serve as a beginning point for a trial and error approach when calculating a yield to maturity or a yield to call.

Conclusions Concerning Bond Yields and Prices

Under conditions of perfect certainty, the value of a bond (or any other investment asset) is the present value of all anticipated cash flows. Bond prices change from time to time, reflecting changing market conditions and quality ratings for individual bonds. Bond prices vary inversely, moreover, with each change in minimum required yield.

Yield to maturity calculations assume reinvestment of all cash flows at the yield to maturity rate. This explains the advantage of discount over par or premium bonds for an investor who expects interest rates to decline over the time a bond will be held, as a part of the return on a discount bond is fixed and thus would not be subject to reinvestment at a lower interest rate. If interest rates are expected to increase over time, by contrast, premium bonds would have an advantage. One's expectation concerning future interest rates, therefore, is an important consideration when purchasing bonds (or any security), and the accuracy of interest rates assumptions is crucial when valuing bonds.

Stock Valuation

Under conditions of certainty, a stock's intrinsic value, as with a bond, would be the discounted present value of all future cash flows. Stocks (preferred or common), however, offer no legal commitment to pay dividends or return principal as bonds do, and thus the valuation of future cash flows is more complicated. The stream of income that will flow to stockholders is highly uncertain and depends on corporate success and the outcome of other chance events. As noted earlier, an intrinsic value can never be precisely determined. The systematic use of valuation theory, however, should serve an important purpose as a check on the reasonableness of current market price when considering the purchase or sale of a stock.

Historical Background

The stock market crash in 1929, which by 1932 culminated in a 90 percent decline in the Dow Jones Index, stimulated efforts to develop a theory of stock valuation. The development of formal stock valuation approaches seems to have begun in 1930 when Robert F. Weiss stated that "the proper price of any security, whether a stock or a bond, is the sum of all the future income payments discounted at the current rate of interst in order to arrive at present value."[18]

Samuel Elliot Guild[19] was the first to present a series of tables based on the present value approach for the purpose of measuring intrinsic value. Guild's approach was an ad hoc approach that assumed the following:

1. The average rate at which company earnings would grow over the time period in question.

2. The dividend-earnings ratio that would prevail for the stock at the end of the holding period selected.

3. The price-earnings ratio that would prevail for the stock at the end of the holding period selected.

4. The internal rate of return or yield required by the investor.

Guild's objective was to provide an investor with a simple procedure for calculating the maximum price, given a set of known parameters, that would be commensurate with a specified rate of return.[20]

John Burr Williams[21] was the first to provide a comprehensive and rigorous foundation on which the intrinsic value of a stock could be defined. While Williams's contribution was singularly important to the development of a modern theory of security valuation, it suffered from at least one serious shortcoming: No account was taken by Williams of uncertainty regarding either future cash flows, one's knowledge about these flows, or the likelihood that the appropriate discount rate would not remain constant over the holding period assumed for the stock.[22]

---

18 R.F. Weiss, *Investing for True Value*, Barron's, September 8, 1930.

19 S.E. Guild, *Stock Growth and Discount Tables* (Boston: Financial Publishing Co., 1931).

20 For expansions of the Guild tables utilizing a present value approach and incorporating more sophisticated assumptions, see R.M. Soldofsky and J.T. Murphy, *Growth Yields on Common Stocks: Theories and Tables*, Rev. ed. (Iowa City: Bureau of Business and Economic Research, State University of Iowa, 1964); W. Scott Bauman, *Estimating the Present Value of Common Stocks by the Variable Rate Method*, Monograph (Ann Arbor: Bureau of Business Research, The University of Michigan, 1963); and N. Molodovsky, C. May, and S. Chottiner "Common Stock Valuation: Theory and Tables," *Financial Analysts Journal* (March–April, 1965), pp. 104–112.

21 J.B. Williams *The Theory of Investment Value* (1938; reprint ed., Amsterdam, The Netherlands: North Holland Publishing Co., 1964).

22 See F.H. Knight, *Risk, Uncertainty and Profit* (London School of Economics and Political Science, Series of Reprints of Scarce Tracts, No. 16, 1933).

These shortcomings must always be kept in mind when using intrinsic value calculations. Multiple intrinsic values can be calculated to allow for a range of assumptions, and these calculations will serve to usefully test the reasonableness of current market prices.

Present Value Approaches

Asset values, as recorded on a balance sheet, are not utilized in stock valuation theory. Accounting values (original cost less accumulated depreciation) tell us little about the current worth of a company. The liquidation value of a firm's assets is also of little significance since liquidation will usually occur only when serious financial difficulties have been encountered.

An investment asset has *value* because an owner anticipates receiving future cash flows from it. The value of an asset, therefore, depends on the size of the future cash flows generated, the time pattern over which they are to be received, the risk involved, and the rate that could be earned in alternative uses of the funds. What is important, therefore, is current expectation concerning the cash flows, and not what was paid to acquire an asset at some time in the past.

Dividend-Capitalization Models.   A corporation is granted a charter into perpetuity, and the presumption is made that it will be in existence for an infinite period. Therefore, the current value of a stock should represent the discounted present value of the dividend payments that would be forthcoming over that infinite time horizon. This relationship is expressed by the equation:

$$PV = \sum_{t=1}^{\infty} D_t \left[\frac{1}{(1+k)^t} \right],$$ (3.10)

where
D_t = the dividend per share in period t,
k = the market return appropriate to a pure equity stream, or the discount rate.

Where the dividend payment is to be made into perpetuity at a constant rate (the no-growth case), Equation (3.10) simplifies to

$$PV = \frac{D^3}{k},$$ (3.10a)

which defines the present value of a perpetuity.

Book Value versus Intrinsic Value.   The no-growth assumption would apply to a firm whose capital (C) and the rate of return earned on that capital (r) remained constant, further assuming that the firm paid all profits as dividends in the year earned. Total profits of the firm could be defined as (rC). The value of the firm's stock would then equal

$$V_0 = \frac{rC0}{\left(1+k\right)} + \frac{rC0}{\left(1+k\right)^2} + \cdots + \frac{rC0}{\left(1+k\right)^\infty}$$

$$V_0 = \frac{rC0}{k}$$

Although this model is unrealistic, it does provide interesting insight into the relation between book value of the firm (C_0) and intrinsic value (V_0). If $r = k$, then book value (C_0) equals intrinsic value (V_0). If r is greater than k, however, intrinsic value (V_0) will exceed book value. This conclusion is quite reasonable since the firm is assumed to earn a higher rate on new investment than that required by the market. On the other hand, if r is less than k, intrinsic value (and, therefore, market value) will be less than book value.

Not surprisingly, therefore, stocks typically sell at a price different from book value. A firm is not likely to earn a return on new investment exactly equal to the market-required return for investment in its stock over any extended period of time.

A growth firm, in terms of the above logic, can be defined as a firm earning a higher rate of return on new investments ($\hat{r}$) than market-required return for investment in its stock (k). A declining firm would be one where $k > r$.

Growth Models.   To assume that dividend payments could be constant into perpetuity is unrealistic. Dividends do change over time, reflecting corporate success or failure and market factors. Stocks are usually purchased with the anticipation of corporate success and dividend growth, and models have been developed by Gordon[23] and Lerner and Carleton[24] which incorporate a constant growth assumption. A constant growth assumption may itself be questionable but

---

23 M.J. Gordon, *The Investment, Financing and Valuation of the Corporation* (Homewood, Ill.: Richard D. Irwin, 1962).

24 Eugene M. Lerner and Willard T. Carleton, *A Theory of Financial Analysis* (New York: Harcourt, Brace & Worlds, 1966).

can be considered in the sense of an estimated long-run average growth for purposes of generating an intrinsic value estimate.

Let the dividend received on a particular stock at time $t = 0$ be D_0 (the current dividend). Suppose that dividends will grow at a constant rate, g, forever. The dividend at any future point in time, t, therefore, is simply:

$$D_t = D_0(1+g)^t. \tag{3.11}$$

Substituting Equation (3.11) into Equation (3.10) and simplifying we obtain

$$PV = D_0 \left[\sum_{t=1}^{\infty} \frac{(1+g)^t}{(1+k)^t} \right]. \tag{3.12}$$

Provided that the discount rate, k, is larger than the growth rate, g, it can be shown that Equation (3.12) is mathematically equivalent to[25]

$$PV = \frac{D_1}{k-g}, \tag{3.13}$$

where D_1 is the dividend to be received at time $t = 1$, or at the end of one holding period.

Discounting Dividends Rather Than Earnings.   Earnings not paid out in dividends are retained. When retained earnings are invested in profitable projects, the added earnings produce opportunities for higher future dividends. A present value approach, therefore, considers the earnings potential that results from the reinvested earnings by taking account of the future dividends generated. It would be double counting to discount both present earnings and future dividends that result from earnings retention.

Implicit Consideration of Capital Gains.   A shareholder who sells his or her stock might well realize capital gain as well as receiving dividends. Capital gains are considered in the above growth model, consistent with the assumed dividend growth rate and constant discount rate. To illustrate, assume Firm A pays a $1 dividend at the end of the first year of holding the stock (D_1), and dividends are expected to grow at a constant rate of eight percent. Further assume that opportu-

---

25 For proof see Lerner and Carleton, ibid., pp. 105–108.

nity cost of a particular investor is 14 percent. The intrinsic value of Firm A stock at this moment according to equation (3.13) is

$$PV_a = \frac{D_1}{k-g} = \frac{1}{.14-.08} = \frac{1}{.06} = \$16.67$$

Let us determine the present value of the stock five years from now, utilizing the same growth and discount rate assumptions:

$$PV_{a_5} = \frac{D_6}{k-g}.$$

The expected dividend at the end of year five (D_6) is

$$D_6 = \$1(1+g)^5 = \$1(1.08)^5 = \$1(1.46933) = \$1.46933 .$$

The value of Firm A stock at the end of year five would, therefore, be

$$PV_{a_5} = \frac{D_6}{k-g} = \frac{\$1.46933}{14-.08} = 24.488.$$

Discounting the expected cash flows generated by holding the stock for five years, we arrive at a consistent present value of $16.67, as calculated below:

End of Period	Cash Flow Dividend	Cash Flow Sales Price	Discount Factor	
1	1.0000	—	.87719	0.87719
2	1.0800	—	.76947	0.83103
3	1.1664	—	.67497	0.78729
4	1.2597	—	.59208	0.74584
5	1.3605	24.4888	.51937	13.42535
Total Present Value				16.66667

We have ignored the impact of taxes in the above calculations, which will be introduced in our discussion of a finite holding period below.

Dividend Policy and Stock Valuation.   Miller and Modigliani argued that the value of a firm is not affected by the dividend policy of that firm in a world without taxes or transaction costs.[26] Let us illustrate this argument in terms of a dividend growth valuation model.

Consider a firm that expands its capital (C) each year by retaining a portion of earnings (b). Profit for this firm can be defined in terms of the rate earned on capital (r) or as rC_0. Retained earnings would then equal brC_0. Capital one year hence would equal capital at the beginning of the year (C_0) plus retained earnings brC_0. The rate of growth in capital can then be expressed as

$$g = \frac{C_1 - C_0}{C_0} = \frac{[C_0 + brC_0] - C_0}{C_0} = \frac{brC_0}{C_0} = br. \tag{3.14}$$

The rate of growth in dividends, in accordance with the above assumptions, also equals br:

$$g = \frac{D_1 - D_0}{D_0} = \frac{[(1 - b)r(C_0 + brC_0)] - [(1 - b)rC_0]}{(1 - b)rC_0} \tag{3.15}$$

$$= (1 + br) - 1 = br$$

Now, we restate equation (3.13) in terms of earnings per share (e) and an assumed dividend payout ratio ($1 - b$).

$$V_0 = \frac{e_1(1 - b)}{k - br}, \quad \text{since } g = br. \tag{3.16}$$

If one further assumes that the firm exactly earns the rate required by the market on new investments in accordance with capital budgeting literature ($k = r$), the valuation equation can be restated as follows:

$$V_0 = \frac{e_1(1 - b)}{k - bk} = \frac{e_1(1 - b)}{k(1 - b)} = \frac{e_1}{k} \tag{3.16a}$$

Under these assumptions, dividend policy is irrelevant (it has no effect on the valuation of the firm) since b cancels out.

The above conclusion obviously does not follow when r and k differ or when taxes and transaction costs are considered. Ross, moreover, points out that a firm is valued on the basis of the *perceived* stream of cash flow that an investment in

---

26 M. Miller and F. Modigliani, "Dividend Policy, Growth and the Valuation of Shares," *The Journal of Business* (October, 1961), pp. 411–433.

that firm will generate, and that changes in dividend policy could well alter the market's perceptions[27] and thus affect the firm's valuation. For example, if the dividend were reduced, the market might well interpret this reduction as implying a reduction in future profitability, resulting in the sale of shares and downward pressure on market price and intrinsic value estimations. The relation between k and r does appear to be the critical variable when trying to assess the likely impact of dividend policy changes on stock values.

Finite Horizons and Valuation.   Investors have the opportunity to sell their stock at any time and likely perceive of their investment horizons as limited to some finite period. A model that assumes an infinite horizon would not, therefore, serve as a very useful basis for stock selection or as a check on the reasonableness of estimations that enter into portfolio selection.

A limited holding period model, by contrast, assumes a sale of the stock being valued at the end of an assumed holding period. The present value, in this context, is the sum of the present values associated with the dividends received during a holding period, plus the present value of the sales price at the end of the holding period:

$$PV = \sum_{t=1}^{T}\left[\frac{D_t}{(1 + k)^t}\right] + \frac{P_T}{(1 + k)^T}, \tag{3.17}$$

where P_T is the expected sales price. Equation (3.17) can be rewritten in terms of earnings per share as follows:

$$PV = C_0 l \sum_{i=1}^{T}\frac{(1 + g)^t}{(1 + k)^t} + \frac{C_0 M_c(1 + g)^T}{(1 + k)^T}, \tag{3.17a}$$

where
    C_0 = current earnings per share,
    g = the anticipated compound annual growth rate of earnings per share,
    l = the proportion of earnings paid out as dividends in each holding period,

---

27 S.A. Ross, "The Determination of Financial Structure: The Incentive-Signaling Approach," *The Pell Journal of Economics* (Spring 1977), pp. 23–40.

$M_c =$ the multiplier applied to earnings per share in the terminal year to determine selling price,

$k =$ the appropriate discount rate.

Equations (3.17) and (3.17a) can be modified to account for the effects of taxation. To illustrate, suppose that

1. A stock is purchased at year-end 1978 at $95 per share;
2. Dividend income is taxed at a 50 percent rate and capital gains at an effective rate of 20 percent (in accordance with capital gains tax law in effect prior to the Tax Reform Act of 1986);
3. Earnings per share at the time of purchase are $9.50, and are expected to grow at a compound annual rate of six percent;
4. The company pays out 55 percent of earnings in the form of dividends each year;
5. The stock will be sold at the end of the third year, and a price–earnings ratio of 15 is expected to apply to the stock at the time of sale;
6. A rate of eight percent after taxes is available in alternative investment opportunities felt to be of equivalent risk.

Based on these assumptions, the present value of the stock is found to be $130.40, by means of the following sample calculation:

Year	EPS	Dividends	After-Tax Dividend	After-Tax Proceed from Sale	Present Value Factor at Eight Percent	Present Value of Cash Flow
1978	9.50					
1979	10.07	5.54	2.77		.926	2.565
1980	10.67	5.87	2.94		.857	2.520
1981	11.31	6.22	3.11	154.72*	.794	125.317
Present Value of Stock						130.402

* The expected selling price of $169.65 (15 X 11.31) less the capital gains tax of $14.93([74.65(capital gain) ×.4×.5])

The model described by Equation (3.17a) may be used in sensitivity analysis; that is, the estimates of C_0, g, k, and T can be varied one at a time, or in combination, to determine the sensitivity of the valuation estimate to changes in these parameters. The model does not require a constant growth rate or discount rate assumption. The problem for the analyst is determining the expectations stated in

1 through 6 above. The analytical framework developed in the remainder of the book is utilized to develop such expectations.

Growth Duration. The longer one projects an above-average growth rate for dividends and earnings, the higher will be the present value of the stock as calculated by any of the models discussed above. There is always some combination of growth rate and growth period that will justify any current market price. This point is made nicely by an illustrative valuation of IBM stock by Williamson.[28] In 1968 IBM sold at about $320 per share; 1967 earnings were $5.80 per share, and dividends were $2.17 per share. Consistent with recent growth, Williamson predicted earnings per share of $7 for 1968. He initially forecast a 16 percent earnings growth rate for 10 years, followed by indefinite growth of two percent and a dividend payout rate of 40 percent, which were in line with experience for IBM over the previous 10 years. Using a discount rate of seven percent, he calculated an intrinsic value of $172.94. Noting that this represented about one-half of the current market value, Williamson said, "It does not seem sensible to predict only 10 years of above-average growth for IBM, so I extended my growth forecast to twenty years." Now the intrinsic value came to $432.66— well above the market. When a 10 percent discount rate was substituted for the seven percent rate, and a growth rate of 16 percent for twenty years, however, Williamson found an intrinsic value of only $205.73.

Clearly, a growth model is quite sensitive to changes in the parameters included. The illustration shows the importance of not being carried away by enthusiasm that may prevail from time to time in the market and the tenuous nature of intrinsic value estimates.

Limitation of Dividend Valuation Models. The models discussed to this point are all subject to a number of simplifying assumptions that limit the accuracy of intrinsic value estimates. These limitations are briefly summarized as follows:

1. The intrinsic value estimate is no more accurate than the estimates of earnings and dividends underlying that valuation. Experience suggests that earnings growth rates can vary markedly over time, and firms do change their dividend policies. The problem of forecasting earnings and dividends will be discussed in more depth later in the book.

---

28 J. Peter Williamson, *Investments: New Analytic Techniques* (New York: Praeger, 1971), pp. 155–159.

2. The discount rate (k) is typically held constant for the period covered by the model. In actuality, required market rates change over time, and the risk-class of a given firm may also change. In either situation, the assumption of a constant (k) would not be valid. The discount rate chosen should represent what the investor could earn in alternative instruments of equivalent risk. It is the required return of the investor.

3. Either earnings growth is assumed into perpetuity, or a terminal value representing the expected sales price of the stock at some predetermined time is made. The declining present value of far distant streams does lessen the importance of errors in the estimation of such streams when a hold into infinity is assumed. However, the difficulty lies in imagining how accurate estimates can be made over such long horizons. When a finite holding period is assumed, the question arises as to how one determines that holding period in advance. Even if the holding period could be estimated accurately, one still faces the difficult problem of estimating the market value of the stock at the end of the holding period.

4. Growth is assumed to be financed through retained earnings. This assumption ignores the possible use of debt, new stock issues, and other sources of funds that could finance growth in assets and earnings.

5. Constant growth rate assumptions are often used. The rate then supposedly represents an average compound growth expected over the holding period. There is the danger of relying too much on the past when estimating this growth rate, especially when the firm has experienced high recent growth than can rarely be sustained indefinitely. This point is illustrated in the discussion of the valuation of IBM stock above.

6. After-tax cash flows could be estimated by assuming the tax bracket rate that will be applicable to the investor for each annual holding period. The appropriate tax bracket will depend, however, on the total income of the investor and tax deductions available, not just investment income. Such estimates are, of course, subject to error.

One would not, therefore, anticipate a high degree of accuracy in intrinsic value estimates when the inherent limitations of the valuation models are considered. The models do serve to clarify the relationship between the key factors that affect stock valuation, however. They also offer a way of studying the reasonableness of the assumptions that seem to underlie market values at a given point in time thereby providing a constant framework for relative comparisons of securities. The importance of valuation efforts lies more in the discipline and organized structure it provides for making buy and sell decisions than in the numbers generated.

Price-Earnings Ratios

A price-earnings ratio, as typically reported, is simply the result of dividing the current market price of a company's common stock by the most recent twelve months' earnings per share. The ratio reflects what a perspective investor must currently pay to buy one dollar of reported earnings of the company.

Price-earnings ratios can change daily as market price changes and should not be mistaken as indicators of intrinsic value. They do suggest the esteem in which a company is held by the market at a moment of time, but are not indicative of whether or not the stock is overpriced based on assumptions about future earnings, risk and opportunity costs as are estimates of intrinsic value.

Price-earnings ratios may, in fact, give a distorted view of relative value due to different accounting techniques that may be used by different firms, thereby making reported earnings noncomparable.[29] Also, a price-earnings ratio may be temporarily high because earnings are currently low and the market expects a return to higher earnings levels. Moreover, price-earnings ratios reflect *historical earnings* while the investor is concerned with future earnings.

Price-Earnings Ratios and Valuation

Some practicing analysts seem to prefer using a modified price-earnings ratio as a multiplier of earnings to generate an intrinsic value estimate, rather than present value techniques.[30] In this approach, earnings are represented by an estimated average future earning per share, often referred to as "normalized earnings per share." Normalized earnings per share (e_n) has been defined as the "level of net income which would prevail currently if the economy were experiencing mid-cyclical conditions."[31] The determinations of normalized earnings per share, therefore, involves a consideration of the earnings experience of a firm over a

---

29 We will have a good deal to say about problems of accounting techniques and noncomparability of earnings later in this book.

30 R.A. Bing, "Survey of Practitioners' Stock Evaluation Methods," *Financial Analysts Journal*, 26, No. 2 (May–June 1971) pp. 55–60.

31 Volkert S. Whitbeck and Manown Kisor, Jr., "A New Tool in Investment Decision Making," *Financial Analysis Journal* Vol. 19, No. 3 (May–June 1963), p. 57.

previous business cycle and an evaluation of current and expected market and cost conditions. In effect then, it involves the same earnings forecasting efforts that would be needed to generate present value estimates.

The multiplier (P/e_n) is primarily determined by the riskiness of the firm and the expected rate of growth in earnings. It is often assumed that the Dow-Jones Industrial Average represents a cross-section of stocks with average risk and growth prospects and the stock under study is given a multiplier that would be higher than the average for that index if it has higher than average growth prospects unless the higher growth is coupled with substantially greater risk.

An estimate of intrinsic value is then provided as follows:

$$V_o = e_n \, (P/e_n)$$

Those who favor this approach feel that the serious limitations underlying the earnings and dividend forecasts required by present value techniques make such calculations not worth the effort. It must be remembered, however, that the P/E multiplier approach is merely a short-cut method where the impact of growth, risk and dividend policy is supposedly captured in one statistic (Pe_n). The real benefit gained in the valuation effort is the assessment of those underlying factors affecting value in an organized way, not the valuation estimate itself. The writer, therefore, believes that the present value approach should be used.

Statistical Approaches to Estimating Intrinsic Value

The valuation formula for an assumed constant growth model, as already developed, can easily be converted to a price-earnings form by dividing both sides of the equation by earnings as follows:

$$P = \frac{D}{(k-g)}$$

therefore $P/E = \dfrac{D/E}{k+g}$.

Differing price–earnings ratios among companies should, therefore, be explainable in terms of differing dividend policies (D/E), growth rates (g), or risk adjusted market required returns (k). Several authors have attempted to use statistical techniques, namely multiply regression analysis to estimate the appropriate price-earnings ratio at a moment in time for these varying forces.[32]

Whitbeck and Kisor, for example, obtained estimates of dividend payout ratios, earnings growth rates and the variation (standard deviation) of those earnings growth rates (a proxy for risk) from selected security analysts for 135 stocks. They then used multiple regression techniques to define the average relationship between each of these variables and price-earnings ratios as of June 8, 1962. They found that each of the three variables studied had the expected sign and appeared to be significant. The regression results were as follows:

$$\text{Theoretical P/E Ratio} = 8.2 + 1.5 \text{ (Growth Rate)}$$
$$+ 6.7 \text{ (Dividend Payment Ratio)}$$
$$- .2 \text{ (Standard Deviation)}$$

The usefulness of the model was tested by computing the theoretical P/E ratio for each individual stock based upon their projected dividend payments, earnings variability and growth, and then classifying the stocks into overvalued and undervalued stocks in terms of a comparison of their actual and theoretical P/E ratios. It was found that the undervalued group consistently outperformed the S&P 500 on the basis of rate of return over four quarters, while the overvalued group consistently underperformed the S&P 500. The results were encouraging.

Unfortunately, the Whitbeck-Kisor, and other such statistical models built upon regression techniques, have been plagued by instability in the regression coefficients over time and have also been sample sensitive. For this reason, the models have not been widely used by practitioners. The idea is interesting, but forecasting ability of the models have not been established. We can only encourage further research in this area for the present.

Summary

Stock valuation efforts represent an attempt to uncover the relationships that exist among the variables which affect the prices of financial assets, and to provide a systematic way of considering these forces relative to current market price when selecting financial assets for a portfolio. The central idea underlying present value approaches is that a security is worth the discounted present value of all future cash flows generated through its purchase.

---

32 For example, see Volkert S. Whitbeck and Manown Kisor, Jr., ibid., pp. 55–62; or Burton G. Malkiel and John G. Cragg, "Expectations and the Structure of Share Prices," American Economic Review, 60, No. 4 (September 1970), pp. 601–617.

Some practitioners prefer using a price-earning multiplier and forecasted earnings to generate intrinsic value estimates. The price-earning multiplier approach is, however, merely a short-cut method where the impact of growth, risk and dividend policy is supposedly captured in that multiplier.

It is important to recognize that under conditions of uncertainty intrinsic values can never be precise. Valuation models provide a systematic approach for assessing the impact of changing economic and company factors through their effect on earnings, dividend policies, and risk on the prices of financial assets. It is the understanding gained in the analysis that is important and useful, not the intrinsic value estimate in and of itself. We will be concerned with developing the information needed to effectively utilize valuation models to study these underlying relationships during the remainder of this book.

APPENDIX TO CHAPTER 3

Table 3–A Present Value of $1 Received as the End of the Year

Years Hence	1%	2%	4%	6%	8%	10%	12%	14%	15%	16%	18%
1	0.990	0.980	0.962	0.943	0.926	0.909	0.893	0.877	0.870	0.862	0.847
2	0.980	0.961	0.925	0.890	0.857	0.826	0.797	0.769	0.756	0.743	0.718
3	0.971	0.942	0.889	0.840	0.794	0.751	0.712	0.675	0.653	0.641	0.609
4	0.961	0.924	0.855	0.792	0.735	0.683	0.636	0.592	0.572	0.552	0.516
5	0.951	0.906	0.822	0.747	0.681	0.621	0.567	0.519	0.497	0.476	0.437
6	0.942	0.888	0.790	0.705	0.630	0.564	0.507	0.456	0.432	0.410	0.370
7	0.933	0.871	0.760	0.665	0.583	0.513	0.452	0.400	0.376	0.354	0.314
8	0.923	0.853	0.731	0.627	0.540	0.467	0.404	0.351	0.327	0.305	0.266
9	0.914	0.837	0.703	0.592	0.500	0.424	0.361	0.308	0.284	0.263	0.225
10	0.905	0.820	0.676	0.558	0.463	0.386	0.322	0.270	0.247	0.227	0.191
11	0.896	0.804	0.650	0.527	0.429	0.350	0.287	0.237	0.215	0.195	0.162
12	0.887	0.788	0.625	0.497	0.397	0.319	0.257	0.208	0.187	0.168	0.137
13	0.879	0.773	0.601	0.469	0.368	0.290	0.229	0.182	0.163	0.145	0.116
14	0.870	0.758	0.577	0.442	0.340	0.263	0.205	0.160	0.141	0.125	0.099
15	0.861	0.743	0.555	0.417	0.315	0.239	0.183	0.140	0.123	0.108	0.084
16	0.853	0.728	0.534	0.394	0.292	0.218	0.163	0.123	0.107	0.093	0.071
17	0.844	0.714	0.513	0.371	0.270	0.198	0.146	0.108	0.093	0.080	0.060
18	0.836	0.700	0.494	0.350	0.250	0.180	0.130	0.095	0.081	0.069	0.051
19	0.828	0.686	0.475	0.331	0.232	0.164	0.116	0.083	0.070	0.060	0.043
20	0.820	0.673	0.456	0.312	0.215	0.149	0.104	0.073	0.061	0.051	0.037
21	0.811	0.660	0.439	0.294	0.199	0.135	0.093	0.064	0.053	0.044	0.031
22	0.803	0.647	0.422	0.278	0.184	0.123	0.083	0.056	0.046	0.038	0.026
23	0.795	0.634	0.406	0.262	0.170	0.112	0.074	0.049	0.040	0.033	0.022
24	0.788	0.622	0.390	0.247	0.158	0.102	0.066	0.043	0.035	0.028	0.019
25	0.780	0.610	0.375	0.233	0.146	0.092	0.059	0.038	0.030	0.024	0.016
26	0.772	0.598	0.361	0.220	0.135	0.084	0.053	0.033	0.026	0.021	0.014
27	0.764	0.586	0.347	0.207	0.125	0.076	0.047	0.029	0.023	0.018	0.011
28	0.757	0.574	0.333	0.196	0.116	0.069	0.042	0.026	0.020	0.016	0.010
29	0.749	0.563	0.321	0.185	0.107	0.063	0.037	0.022	0.017	0.014	0.008
30	0.742	0.552	0.308	0.174	0.099	0.057	0.033	0.020	0.015	0.012	0.007
40	0.672	0.453	0.208	0.097	0.046	0.022	0.011	0.005	0.004	0.003	0.001
50	0.608	0.372	0.141	0.054	0.021	0.009	0.003	0.001	0.001	0.001	

Table 3–A (continued)

Years Hence	20%	22%	24%	25%	26%	28%	30%	35%	40%	45%	50%
1	0.833	0.820	0.806	0.800	0.794	0.781	0.769	0.741	0.714	0.690	0.607
2	0.694	0.672	0.650	0.640	0.630	0.610	0.592	0.549	0.510	0.476	0.444
3	0.579	0.551	0.524	0.512	0.500	0.477	0.455	0.406	0.364	0.328	0.290
4	0.482	0.451	0.423	0.410	0.397	0.373	0.350	0.301	0.260	0.226	0.198
5	0.402	0.370	0.341	0.328	0.315	0.291	0.269	0.223	0.186	0.156	0.132
6	0.335	0.303	0.275	0.262	0.250	0.227	0.207	0.165	0.133	0.108	0.088
7	0.279	0.249	0.222	0.210	0.198	0.178	0.159	0.122	0.095	0.074	0.059
8	0.233	0.204	0.179	0.168	0.157	0.139	0.123	0.091	0.068	0.051	0.039
9	0.194	0.167	0.144	0.134	0.125	0.108	0.094	0.067	0.048	0.035	0.026
10	0.162	0.137	0.116	0.107	0.099	0.085	0.073	0.050	0.035	0.024	0.017
11	0.135	0.112	0.094	0.086	0.079	0.066	0.056	0.037	0.025	0.017	0.012
12	0.112	0.092	0.076	0.069	0.062	0.052	0.043	0.027	0.018	0.012	0.008
13	0.093	0.075	0.061	0.055	0.050	0.040	0.033	0.020	0.013	0.008	0.005
14	0.078	0.062	0.049	0.044	0.039	0.032	0.025	0.015	0.009	0.006	0.003
15	0.065	0.051	0.040	0.035	0.031	0.025	0.020	0.011	0.006	0.004	0.002
16	0.054	0.042	0.032	0.028	0.025	0.019	0.015	0.008	0.005	0.003	0.002
17	0.045	0.034	0.026	0.023	0.020	0.015	0.012	0.006	0.003	0.002	0.001
18	0.038	0.028	0.021	0.018	0.016	0.012	0.009	0.005	0.002	0.001	0.001
19	0.031	0.023	0.017	0.014	0.012	0.009	0.007	0.003	0.002	0.001	
20	0.026	0.019	0.014	0.012	0.010	0.007	0.005	0.002	0.001	0.001	
21	0.022	0.015	0.011	0.009	0.008	0.006	0.004	0.002	0.001		
22	0.018	0.013	0.009	0.007	0.006	0.004	0.003	0.001	0.001		
23	0.015	0.010	0.007	0.006	0.005	0.003	0.002	0.001			
24	0.013	0.008	0.006	0.005	0.004	0.003	0.002	0.001			
25	0.010	0.007	0.005	0.004	0.003	0.002	0.001	0.001			
26	0.009	0.006	0.004	0.003	0.002	0.002	0.001				
27	0.007	0.005	0.003	0.002	0.002	0.001	0.001				
28	0.006	0.004	0.002	0.002	0.002	0.001	0.001				
29	0.005	0.003	0.002	0.002	0.001	0.001	0.001				
30	0.004	0.003	0.002	0.001	0.001	0.001					
40	0.001										

Table 3–B Present Value of $1 Received Annually at the End of Each Year for N Years

Years (N)	1%	2%	4%	6%	8%	10%	12%	14%	15%	16%	18%
1	0.990	0.980	0.962	0.943	0.926	0.909	0.893	0.877	0.870	0.862	0.847
2	1.970	1.942	1.886	1.833	1.783	1.736	1.690	1.647	1.626	1.605	1.566
3	2.941	2.884	2.775	2.673	2.577	2.487	2.402	2.322	2.283	2.246	2.174
4	3.902	3.808	3.630	3.465	3.312	3.170	3.037	2.914	2.855	2.798	2.690
5	4.853	4.713	4.452	4.212	3.993	3.791	3.605	3.433	3.352	3.274	3.127
6	5.795	5.601	5.242	4.917	4.623	4.355	4.111	3.889	3.784	3.685	3.498
7	6.728	6.472	6.002	5.582	5.206	4.868	4.564	4.288	4.160	4.039	3.812
8	7.652	7.325	6.733	6.210	5.747	5.335	4.968	4.639	4.487	4.344	4.078
9	8.566	8.162	7.435	6.802	6.247	5.759	5.328	4.946	4.772	4.607	4.303
10	9.471	8.983	8.111	7.360	6.710	6.145	5.650	5.216	5.019	4.833	4.494
11	10.368	9.787	8.760	7.887	7.139	6.495	5.988	5.453	5.234	5.029	4.656
12	11.255	10.575	9.385	8.384	7.536	6.814	6.194	5.660	5.421	5.197	4.793
13	12.134	11.343	9.986	8.853	7.904	7.103	6.424	5.842	5.583	5.342	4.910
14	13.004	12.106	10.563	9.295	8.244	7.367	6.628	6.002	5.724	5.468	5.008
15	13.865	12.849	11.118	9.712	8.559	7.606	6.811	6.142	5.847	5.575	5.092
16	14.718	13.578	11.652	10.106	8.851	7.824	6.974	6.265	5.954	5.669	5.162
17	15.562	14.292	12.166	10.477	9.122	8.022	7.120	6.373	6.047	5.749	5.222
18	16.398	14.992	12.659	10.828	9.372	8.201	7.250	6.467	6.128	5.818	5.273
19	17.226	15.678	13.134	11.158	9.604	8.365	7.366	6.550	6.198	5.877	5.316
20	18.046	16.351	13.590	11.470	9.818	8.514	7.469	6.623	6.259	5.929	5.353
21	18.857	17.011	14.029	11.764	10.017	8.649	7.562	6.687	6.312	5.973	5.384
22	19.660	17.658	14.451	12.042	10.201	8.772	7.645	6.743	6.359	6.011	5.410
23	20.456	18.292	14.857	12.303	10.371	8.883	7.718	6.792	6.399	6.044	5.432
24	21.243	18.914	15.247	12.550	10.529	8.985	7.784	6.835	6.434	6.073	5.451
25	22.023	19.523	15.622	12.783	10.675	9.077	7.843	6.873	6.464	6.097	5.467
26	22.795	20.121	15.983	13.003	10.810	9.161	7.896	6.906	6.491	6.118	5.480
27	23.500	20.707	16.330	13.211	10.935	9.237	7.943	6.935	6.514	6.136	5.492
28	24.316	21.281	16.663	13.406	11.051	9.307	7.984	6.961	6.534	6.152	5.502
29	25.066	21.844	16.984	13.591	11.158	9.370	8.022	6.983	6.551	6.166	5.510
30	25.808	22.396	17.292	13.765	11.258	9.427	8.055	7.003	6.566	6.177	5.517
40	32.835	27.355	19.793	15.040	11.925	9.779	8.244	7.105	6.642	6.234	5.548
50	39.196	31.424	21.482	15.762	12.234	9.915	8.309	7.113	6.661	6.246	5.554

Table 3–B (continued)

Years Hence	20%	22%	24%	25%	26%	28%	30%	35%	40%	45%	50%
1	0.833	0.820	0.806	0.800	0.794	0.781	0.769	0.741	0.714	0.690	0.667
2	1.528	1.492	1.457	1.440	1.424	1.392	1.361	1.289	1.224	1.165	1.111
3	2.106	2.042	1.981	1.952	1.923	1.868	1.816	1.696	1.589	1.493	1.407
4	2.589	2.494	2.404	2.362	2.320	2.241	2.166	1.997	1.849	1.720	1.605
5	2.991	2.864	2.745	2.689	2.635	2.532	2.436	2.220	2.035	1.876	1.737
6	3.326	3.167	3.020	2.951	2.885	2.759	2.643	2.385	2.168	1.983	1.824
7	3.605	3.416	3.242	3.161	3.083	2.937	2.802	2.508	2.263	2.057	1.883
8	3.837	3.619	3.421	3.329	3.241	3.076	2.925	2.598	2.331	2.108	1.922
9	4.031	3.786	3.566	3.463	3.366	3.184	3.019	2.665	2.379	2.144	1.948
10	4.192	3.923	3.682	3.571	3.465	3.269	3.092	2.715	2.414	2.168	1.965
11	4.327	4.035	3.776	3.656	3.544	3.335	3.147	2.752	2.438	2.185	1.977
12	4.439	4.127	3.851	3.725	3.606	3.387	3.190	2.779	2.456	2.196	1.985
13	4.533	4.203	3.912	3.780	3.656	3.427	3.223	2.799	2.468	2.204	1.990
14	4.611	4.265	3.962	3.824	3.695	3.459	3.249	2.814	2.477	2.210	1.993
15	4.675	4.315	4.001	3.859	3.726	3.483	3.268	2.825	2.484	2.218	1.995
16	4.730	4.357	4.033	3.887	3.751	3.503	3.283	2.834	2.489	2.216	1.997
17	4.775	4.391	4.059	3.910	3.771	3.518	3.295	2.840	2.492	2.218	1.998
18	4.812	4.419	4.080	3.928	3.786	3.529	3.304	2.844	2.496	2.219	1.999
19	4.844	4.442	4.097	3.942	3.799	3.539	3.311	2.848	2.496	2.220	1.999
20	4.870	4.460	4.110	3.954	3.808	3.546	3.316	2.850	2.497	2.221	1.999
21	4.891	4.476	4.121	3.963	3.816	3.551	3.320	2.852	2.498	2.221	2.000
22	4.909	4.488	4.130	3.970	3.822	3.556	3.323	2.853	2.498	2.222	2.000
23	4.925	4.499	4.137	3.976	3.827	3.559	3.325	2.854	2.499	2.222	2.000
24	4.937	4.507	4.143	3.981	3.831	3.562	3.327	2.855	2.499	2.222	2.000
25	4.948	4.514	4.147	3.985	3.834	3.564	3.329	2.856	2.499	2.222	2.000
26	4.956	4.520	4.151	3.988	3.837	3.566	3.330	2.856	2.500	2.222	2.000
27	4.964	4.524	4.154	3.990	3.839	3.567	3.331	2.856	2.500	2.222	2.000
28	4.970	4.528	4.157	3.992	3.840	3.568	3.331	2.857	2.500	2.222	2.000
29	4.975	4.531	4.159	3.994	3.841	3.569	3.332	2.857	2.500	2.222	2.000
30	4.979	4.534	4.160	3.995	3.842	3.569	3.332	2.857	2.500	2.222	2.000
40	4.997	4.544	4.166	3.999	3.846	3.571	3.333	2.857	2.500	2.222	2.000
50	4.999	4.545	4.167	4.000	3.846	3.571	3.333	2.857	2.500	2.222	2.000

PART II

FUNDAMENTAL ANALYSIS

CHAPTER 4

Analysis of the Economy and Stock Price Aggregates

Fundamental analysis begins by determining the state of the economic environment and the implications of that environment for investment decisions. Growth is the focal point when analyzing equity investments, since growth in earnings and cash flow is expected to provide the basis for growth in dividends and stock prices.

The dividend yield on common stocks often is substantially lower than the current yield that can be obtained through long-term commitments, such as bonds. Accordingly, a stock can only be a desirable investment if one expects the growth in stock price to more than cover the gap in bond current yields and stock dividend yields. It is important, therefore, that the analyst form some judgment as to future long-term secular growth of the economy and its major components, and also an opinion concerning the cyclical outlook for the economy.

Economic and demographic analysis provides a background for industry and company analysis. Economic analysis also provides a background for estimating levels of interest rates and the long-term trend of price-earnings ratios. The analyst also would hope to spot sectors of the economy that appear to offer better than average profit opportunities and relate that information to specific companies. For example, in the 1950s and sell the stock of Botany which produced business type suits mainly purchased by the middle-aged group. This proved to be a highly profitable decision.

The future is unlikely to be a mirror of the past, but reviewing the past offers an understanding of the interaction among important variables and forms a base for making projections. We will, therefore, first review the long-term past record, in an effort to overcome illusions sometimes held by investors whose judgment often is the result of their own relatively short experience.

Analysis of the Economy

Investment performance is associated intimately with the economic activity of the nation. Stocks typically perform well when the economy is strong and prosperous. Not all industries and companies prosper equally, and the investor eventually must assess the impact of a changing economic environment on particular companies.

Underlying Determinants of the Level of Economic Activity

The broadest measure of economic activity is the Gross National Product statistics (GNP),which represent the value of the aggregate amount of goods and services produced in a national economy. The GNP can be viewed as an aggregate sales index, since the marketplace is the touchstone for measuring value.

Changes in the level of the GNP can be studied by considering the four basic variables underlying the level of economic activity listed below:

1. The anticipated growth of the employed labor force.
2. The trend in average number of hours worked per week.
3. The trend in output per hour worked, which is an indicator of labor productivity.
4. The change in the price level.

The first three factors determine the anticipated change in the real GNP, while the price level factor relates the analysis to the current GNP.

The above framework typically underlies GNP forecasting models, and has been used by Lacy Hunt in his *CM&M Economic Commentary*. The commentary forecasted a 2.5 percent annual growth rate for the spring quarter 1987 for real GNP, and noted that two main factors supported that projection. "First, the index of aggregate hours worked rose at a 2.2 percent annual rate. Only a modest 0.3 percent rate of increase in productivity is needed in order for our GNP forecast to be achieved. This is well within recent experience. Productivity rose at a 0.4 percent annual pace in the first quarter and by an average 0.6 percent in 1985 and 1986. Second, with April and May data already reported, industrial production apparently gained at a 2.2 percent rate in the second quarter versus a better 3.2 percent rate in the first quarter."[33]

---

33 Lacy H. Hunt, *CM&M Economic Commentary*, "Outlook Update," CM&M Group, Inc., New York, July, 1987.

Investors can review well-known GNP prediction models in terms of their underlying assumptions for the basic variables, as done above.

The Long-Term Record of Economic Growth. Real GNP has grown at a 2.92 percent compound annual growth rate from 1929 through 1985 and GNP in current dollars grew at a 6.73 percent rate over the same time period (see Table 4–1). Growth rates were a bit higher from 1960 through 1985, with real GNP growing at a 3.10 percent rate and current GNP growing at an 8.53 percent rate. Table 4–1 also shows that the growth rate for industrial production, as measured by the Federal Reserve Board Index, has consistently been higher than the growth rate for real GNP, and also it is true that cyclical fluctuations have been much wider for industrial production than for real GNP. Moreover, the cycles in industrial production have been much closer in amplitude to cycles in corporate profits than the cycles of GNP. Therefore, the cycles of industrial production may have greater significance to an investor than the cycles of GNP which are so often referred to in the newspaper. Table 4–2 contrasts the industrial production and GNP cycles.

Business Cycles and the Investor

Cyclical patterns and trends are as important to the investor as are longer secular trends. Actually, the business profits and stock market cycles since 1961 appear to have been major factors causing many investors to question the desirability of investment in common stocks in the late 1970s and early 1980s. For example, an investment in a portfolio of common stocks in 1968 that behaved as did the Standard & Poor's composite stock index would have shown a loss in 1969, 1970, 1971, 1974, 1975, 1977, and 1978. The portfolio would have grown at a compound annual rate of only 3.83 percent over the 17-year period ending at year-end 1985. In view of the high inflation experienced during the 1970s, this was not an exciting performance. Stock prices did begin to rise sharply in late 1985, however, rewarding the patient investor. Market indexes reached new records in 1987, reaching 2600 for the Dow-Jones industrial Index by September 1987. Interest in common stock investment was again strong, as we experienced one of the longest continued economic growth periods in our history (66 months since the trough of November 1982) by June 1988.

The length of particular business cycles has varied, as shown on Table 4–3. Each cycle reflects particular characteristics that determines its length—it is useful to examine past cycles. Many economists might have had a better forecasting record had they considered the average length of past cycles--three-year mini-

---

**Table 4–1   Growth Rates for Gross National Product (GNP) and
Industrial Production Selected Periods**

Compound Growth Rate In

| Years | Gross National Product | | Federal Reserve Board Index of Industrial Production (%) |
	Real (%)	Current Dollar (%)	
1929–1985	2.92	6.73	N.A.
1933–1985	3.86	8.55	N.A.
1939–1985	3.55	8.56	4.56
1960–1985	3.10	8.53	3.81
1960–1980	3.29	8.69	4.08
1960–1975	3.26	7.83	3.75
1960–1970	3.79	7.02	4.86
1960–1965	4.62	6.47	6.25
1980–1985	2.31	7.88	2.77

Source: Growth rate calculations were based on data included in Table B–1 and B–2, pp. 253 and 254 of the *Economic Report of the President*, January, 1986.

---

mum, five-year maximum. The mean length of the 30 cycles, 1854–1986, either from trough to trough or peak to peak was 51 months.

Since the 1930s there have been only three expansions that exceeded five years in length. The 1938–45 period reflected World War II and should be considered an aberration. The 1961–69 expansion was peculiar in that the stated expansion included a mini-recession in 1967 that ended a 1961–1966 corporate profits expansion of 83 percent, even though the economic expansion continued to December 1969. Corporate profits after taxes did not exceed the 1966 level until 1972, a major factor explaining the poor stock market performance during the period 1966–1971. Therefore, of significance to investors, the profits recovery and expansion that began in the first quarter, 1961 ended in 1966 (5 years), not in 1969. The stock market discounted and signaled in advance this major profits change when it declined 27 percent in 1966. The stock market declined an additional 37 percent from December 1968 to May 1970, in anticipation of the 1970 decline in corporate profits. The current historically long economic expansion continues as of June 1, 1988 and was recognized by rapid growth in stock prices even though profits peaked in 1984. Stock prices did, however, fall sharply in October 1987.

In summary the probabilities appear strong that a full cycle based on profit expectations will last at least three years but not much over five years. The market

Table 4–2   Business Cycles and Cycles of Industrial Production

	Business Cycles			Industrial Production		
		Duration (Months)				Duration (Months)
Trough	Peak	Peak to Peak		Trough	Peak	Peak to Peak
	Jan. 1893				Mar. 1892	
1. June 1894	Dec. 1895	35		1. Oct. 1893	Nov. 1895	44
2. June 1897	June 1899	42		2. Sept. 1896	June 1900	55
3. Dec. 1900	Sept. 1902	39		3. Oct. 1900	July 1903	37
4. Aug. 1904	May 1907	56		4. Dec. 1903	May 1907	46
5. June 1908	Jan. 1910	32		5. May 1908	Mar. 1910	34
6. Jan. 1912	Jan. 1913	36		6. Jan. 1911	Jan. 1913	34
7. Dec. 1914	Aug. 1918	67		7. Nov. 1914	May 1917	52
8. Mar. 1919	Jan. 1920	17		8. Mar. 1919	June 1920	32
					Feb. 1920	
9. July 1912	May 1923	40		9. Apr. 1921	May 1923	39
10. July 1924	May 1926	41		10. July 1924	Mar. 1927	46
11. Nov. 1927	Aug. 1929	34		11. Nov. 1927	July 1929	28
12. Mar. 1933	May 1937	93		12. July 1932	May 1937	34
13. June 1938	Feb. 1945	93		13. May 1938	Nov. 1943	78
				No Trough	July 1948	
14. Oct. 1945	Nov. 1948	45		Determined		
15. Oct. 1949	July 1953	56		14. Oct. 1969	July 1953	60
16. May 1954	Aug. 1957	49		15. Apr. 1954	Feb. 1957	43
17. Apr. 1958	Apr. 1960	32		16. Apr. 1958	Jan. 1960	35
18. Feb. 1961	Dec. 1969	116		17. Feb. 1961	Sept. 1969	116
19. Nov. 1970	Nov. 1973	47		18. Nov. 1970	Nov. 1973	50
20. Mar. 1975	Jan. 1980	74		19. Mar. 1975	Mar. 1979	64
21. July 1980	July 1981	18		20. Jan. 1980	July 1981a	28
22. Nov. 1982				21. Nov. 1982		

Source: *Business Conditions Digest* (January 1987).

discounts expected changes in the trend and level of corporate profits, not economic cycles per se, however, and profit expectations became strong after 1985. A continued economic expansion may not mean a continued profit expansion, however, and the economy faced major problems in 1987. Large trade deficits adversely affect many trade-sensitive industries. Local areas heavily

Table 4–3 Business Cycles Expansions and Contractions in the United States, 1854–1986

Business cycle reference dates		Duration in Months			
		Contraction		Cycle	
		(Trough from previous peak)	Expansion (Trough to peak)	Trough from Previous Trough	Peak from Previous Peak
Trough	*Peak*				
December 1854 ...	June 1857	...	30	...	...
December 1858 ...	October 1860	18	22	48	40
June 1861 ...	April 1865	8	46	30	54
December 1867 ...	June 1869	32	18	78	50
December 1870 ...	October 1873	18	34	36	52
March 1879 ...	March 1882	65	36	99	101
May 1885 ...	March 1887	38	22	74	60
April 1888 ...	July 1890	13	27	35	40
May 1891 ...	January 1893	10	20	37	30
June 1894 ...	December 1895	17	18	37	35
June 1897 ...	June 1899	18	24	36	42
December 1900 ...	September 1902	18	21	42	39
August 1904 ...	May 1907	23	33	44	56
June 1908 ...	January 1910	13	19	46	32
January 1912 ...	January 1913	24	12	43	36
December 1914 ...	August 1918	23	44	35	67
March 1919 ...	January 1920	7	10	51	17
July 1921 ...	May 1923	18	22	28	40
July 1924 ...	October 1926	14	27	36	41
November 1927 ...	August 1929	13	21	40	34
March 1933 ...	May 1937	43	50	64	93
June 1938 ...	February 1945	13	80	63	93
October 1945 ...	November 1948	8	37	88	45
October 1949 ...	July 1953	11	45	48	56
May 1954 ...	August 1957	10	39	55	49
April 1958 ...	April 1960	8	24	47	32
February 1961 ...	December 1969	10	106	34	116
November 1970 ...	November 1973	11	36	117	47
March 1975 ...	January 1980	16	58	52	74
July 1980 ...	July 1981	6	12	64	18
November 1982		16	...	28	...

Table 4-3 (continued)

Business cycle reference dates	Contraction (Trough from previous peak)	Expansion (Trough to peak)	Cycle Trough from Previous Trough	Cycle Peak from Previous Peak
Average, all cycles:				
1854–1982 (30 cycles)	18	33	51	[1]51
1854–1919 (16 cycles)	22	27	48	[2]49
1919–1945 (6 cycles)	18	35	53	53
1945–1982 (8 cycles)	11	45	56	55
Average peacetime cycles:				
1854–1982 (25 cycles)	19	27	46	[3]46
1854–1919 (14 cycles)	22	24	46	[4]47
1919–1945 (5 cycles)	20	26	46	45
1945–1982 (6 cycles)	11	34	46	44

Note: Underscored figures are the wartime expansions (Civil War, World Wars and II, Korean war, and Vietnam war), the postwar contractions, and the full cycles that include the wartime expansions: [1]29 cycles, [2]15 cycles, [3]24 cycles, and [4]13 cycles.

Source: U.S. Department of Commerce, Bureau of Economic Analysis, *Business Conditions Digest*, January 1987, p. 104.

dependent on the oil and gas industry are suffering the consequences of a decline in world oil prices and real interest rates were relatively high. There were good fundamental reasons for a sharp break in stock prices in October 1987.

The fact that the stock market typically has reached bear market lows every four calendar years (not every 48 months) in 1949, 1953, 1957–58, 1962, 1966, 1970, 1978, and 1982 reflects the constant repetition of the business and profits cycle recurring on the average of every three to five years. The anticipated behavior of corporate profits is the important variable.

Corporate Profits

Corporate after-tax profit data goes back only to 1929. For earlier data we must use figures that link Cowles Commission earnings per-share data to Dow-Jones Industrial Average or Standard & Poor's stock indexes. The long-term record of growth for corporate profits, GNP, and stock prices is portrayed in Table 4–4.

Over very long periods of time, corporate profits have grown at a faster pace than real GNP, though at a slower rate than current dollar GNP. Corporate profits, after the inventory valuation and capital consumption adjustments have declined consistently as a percentage of current dollar GNP during the past World War II period, as shown in Table 4-5. Furthermore, the record of corporate profits has been much more erratic than that of GNP and industrial production statistics.

There have been only four five-year periods of strong corporate earnings growth measured on a before-tax basis, during the years 1910–1986. Earnings rose

Table 4-4   Growth in Corporate Profits, GNP, and Stock Prices: Compound Annual Growth Rates, 1871–1985

	GNP and Profit Data			
Years	Current Dollar GNP (%)	Real GNP (%)	Current Dollar Profits, All U.S. Corporation	Cowles Commission Earnings Linked to Dow-Jones Industrial Average Earnings Per Share (%)
1871–1929	6.10	4.0	N.A.	2.4
1871–1980	6.31	3.6	N.A.	3.0
1929–1977	6.20	3.1	4.6	3.7
1929–1980	6.55	3.1	5.5	3.5
1933–1980	8.54	4.1	a	8.8
1933–1985	8.55	3.9	a	a
1970–1985	9.56	2.6	9.2	7.2

	Stock Price Data		
	Dow-Jones Industrial Average (%)	Current Dollars	
Years		Standard & Poor's 500 (%)	Standard & Poor's 400 (%)
1871–1929	N.A.	N.A.	N.A.
1871–1980	N.A.	N.A.	N.A.
1929–1977	3.9	3.9	4.5
1929–1980	10.9	3.0	3.6
1933–1980	11.4	5.5	6.2
1970–1985	3.8	5.5	5.7

ªProfits were negative in 1933. Therefore, no meaningful calculation is possible.

83 percent between 1925 and 1929, helping to fuel the strong growth in stock prices during that period. Profits then fell sharply during the Depression of the 1930s and did not recover to the 1929 level until 1947–48. Corporate profits grew slowly during the period 1947–48 through 1960–61, rising only from $31.8 billion in 1948 to $39.5 billion in 1961, or at a compound annual rate of 1.7 percent per year. Profits then rose at a compound annual rate of 12.2 percent to $70.3 billion dollars during the five year period ending in 1966, fueling a sharp rise in stock prices. Corporate profits then fluctuated around the 1966 level until 1973 when before-tax profits rose to $96.9 billion from only 65.6 billion in 1971. Profits continued to rise sharply after 1973 reaching a high of $195.8 billion in 1979 (a compound annual growth rate of 12.4 percent). Corporate profit growth has slowed since 1979, and dropped sharply in 1982. Profit growth resumed after 1982, and stock prices rose to new records in 1987. The market appeared to anticipate a drop in future profit growth in October 1987, and, as previously suggested, fundamental factors supported such concern.

Common Stock Price Performance

Common stock prices trended downward during the period 1881–1898, reflecting flat corporate earnings. During the period 1899–1906 stock prices rose, reflecting a significant rise in corporate earnings. The stock price index then did not rise above its 1906–09 level until the 1925–29 bull market sixteen years later, reflecting higher wartime earnings during the 1915–20 period. It then took twenty-five years before the price index reached its 1929 level in 1954. While investors may be correct in the long-run, that may be too long a time for purposes of realistic investment decisions. In the sixteen years from 1950 to 1966, stock prices rose spectacularly: Dow-Jones Industrial Average, 160 to 1000 and the Standard & Poor's 400 (425) Industrials 16 to 100.

History soon proved that the rapid growth in stock prices during the 1950–66 period would not be sustained. During the 1968–1981 period stock prices tended to move up and down around a horizontal trend line. An upward trend began again in 1982 and continued, with some downward interruptions into early 1987, before falling calamitously in October 1987. Stock prices also have become increasingly volatile, resulting in increased risk, especially where liquidity is important. This must be considered when planning a portfolio.

Table 4–5 Corporate Profits and Gross National Product (GNP), 1948–1986

Year	GNP	Corporate Profits Before Taxes $	Corporate Profits Before Taxes % of GNP	All U.S. Corporations After Taxes $	All U.S. Corporations After Taxes % of GNP
1948	261.6	31.8	12.2	20.0	7.7
1949	260.4	24.9	9.6	15.6	6.0
1950	258.3	38.5	13.3	21.6	7.5
1951	333.4	39.1	11.7	17.9	5.4
1952	351.6	33.8	9.6	16.0	4.6
1953	371.6	34.9	9.4	16.4	4.4
1954	372.5	32.1	8.6	16.4	4.4
1955	405.9	42.0	10.4	21.8	5.4
1956	428.2	41.8	9.8	21.8	5.1
1957	451.0	39.8	8.8	20.7	4.6
1958	456.8	33.7	7.4	17.5	3.8
1959	495.8	43.1	3.7	22.4	4.5
1960	515.3	39.7	7.7	20.5	4.0
1961	533.8	39.5	7.4	20.1	3.8
1962	574.6	44.2	7.7	23.5	4.1
1963	606.9	48.9	8.1	26.2	4.3
1964	649.8	55.4	8.5	31.4	4.8
1965	705.1	65.2	9.3	38.0	5.4
1966	772.0	70.3	9.1	40.8	5.3
1967	816.4	66.5	8.2	38.6	4.7
1968	892.7	73.1	8.2	39.5	4.4
1969	963.9	69.6	7.2	36.2	4.1
1970	1,015.5	57.0	5.6	29.8	3.6
1971	1,102.7	65.6	6.0	35.6	3.2
1972	1,212.8	76.8	6.3	43.0	3.6
1973	1,359.3	96.9	7.1	56.7	4.2
1974	1,472.8	107.2	7.3	65.0	4.4
1975	1,598.4	109.2	6.8	67.7	4.2
1976	1,782.8	138.3	7.8	85.4	4.8
1977	1,990.5	160.5	8.1	100.6	5.1
1978	2,249.7	182.1	8.1	115.0	5.1
1979	2,508.2	195.8	7.8	126.2	5.0
1980	2,732.0	181.8	6.7	114.8	4.2
1981	3,052.6	181.5	6.0	117.6	3.9
1982	3,166.0	129.7	4.1	83.4	2.6
1983	3,405.7	159.3	4.7	99.9	2.9
1984	3,765.0	189.3	5.0	114.9	3.1
1985	3,998.1	170.3	4.3	103.8	2.6
1986	4,208.5	171.7	4.1	96.1	2.3

Source: Corporate profits with inventory valuation and capital consumption adjustments. *Economic Report of the President*, January 1987, pp. 258, 624.

Price-Earnings (P/E) Ratios

Price-earnings (P/E) ratios are calculated by dividing current market price per share by the latest twelve months earnings per share. They indicate the amount investors are willing to pay for each currently reported dollar of earnings. Mean price-earnings ratios for the period 1947–1985 are reported in Table 4–6.

Price-earnings ratios rose to relatively high levels during the 1958–1972 period, suggesting market confidence in future corporate growth and expectations of relatively low levels of risk for stock investors. Beginning in 1973, P/E ratios declined sharply to 1947–1951 levels and remained at the lower levels through 1981. Interestingly, while earnings per share for the corporations included in the Dow-Jones Industrial Average rose approximately 87 percent from the 1966 average level, it never rose more than five percent above its February 1966 level of 1000 through 1981 and actually was only at 870 in December 1981.

Not much attention should be paid to the very high P/E ratio for the Dow-Jones Industrial Average Industrials in 1982. The Dow-Jones Industrial Index rose from 875 in 1981 to 1046.54 in 1982, though twelve month earnings were to drop to 9.15 per share in 1982 from 113.71 in 1981. Earnings rose to more normal levels in 1983 and continued to a high in 1986.

Price-earnings ratios rose sharply after 1982 reaching an average level of 18.2 for the first two quarters of 1987, further supporting the sharp rise in stock prices experienced after 1982 and especially in 1986 and 1987. The relatively high P/E ratios suggested caution, and culminated in the sharp stock price fall in October 1987. Price-earnings ratios were still at relatively high levels at the time of writing this book.

Valuation Logic and Aggregate P/E Ratios.   Our study of valuation in Chapter 3 taught us that the value of any financial asset is the capitalized value of earnings, which provides the cash flows that are discounted. Investors can be said to have determined value by multiplying a capitalization rate (P/E ratio) by earnings. This raises the question, however, as to why P/E ratios vary so much from year-to-year (see Table 4–6).

In Chapter 3, we showed that a present value dividend model could be converted into a price-earnings model of the following form:

$$P/E = \frac{D/E}{K-g}$$

The explanation for differing price–earnings ratios over time and among companies can be sought, therefore, by exploring the following three variables:

1. The dividend payout ratio D/E, or dividends divided by earnings.

Table 4–6   Mean Price-Earnings (P/E) Ratios, 1947–1986

Year	Dow-Jones Industrial Average	Mean P/E Ratios Standard & Poor's 400 (425)	Standard & Poor's 500
1947	9.3	9.2	9.5
1948	7.8	6.5	6.4
1949	7.7	6.1	7.2
1950	7.0	6.3	7.2
1951	9.7	8.9	9.7
Average 1948–1951	8.3	7.4	8.0
1952	11.1	10.2	11.1
1953	10.1	9.6	9.9
1954	12.1	10.7	13.0
1955	12.1	11.3	12.6
1956	14.7	14.0	13.7
1957	13.0	13.6	11.9
Average 1952–1957	12.2	11.6	12.0
1958	18.3	17.3	19.1
1959	18.3	17.3	17.7
1960	19.4	17.9	17.8
1961 Peak-Mean	21.1	20.4	22.4
1962	17.2	16.8	17.2
1963	17.2	17.1	18.7
1964	17.9	17.7	18.6
1965	16.9	16.8	17.8
1966	15.1	15.2	14.5
1967	16.1	16.9	18.1
1968	15.3	17.3	18.0
1969	15.3	17.3	15.9
1970	14.4	16.4	18.0
1971	15.9	17.9	17.9
1972	14.3	20.0	18.9
Average 1958–1972	16.9	17.4	18.0
1973	10.7	16.6	15.9
1974	7.4	10.3	10.0
1975	9.7	10.6	10.2
1976	9.7	12.8	12.2
1977	9.4	10.1	9.8

Table 4-6 (continued)

	Mean P/E Ratios		
Year	Dow-Jones Industrial Average	Standard & Poor's 400 (425)	Standard & Poor's 500
1978	7.1	9.1	8.7
1979	6.7	8.3	7.9
1980	7.9	8.3	8.0
1981	7.7	9.0	8.7
1982	114.4	8.4	8.1
1983	17.4	13.6	12.6
1984	10.7	11.5	10.8
1985	16.1	12.0	11.5
1986	16.4	17.7	16.5

2. The risk adjusted market required rate of return on a stock or group of stocks (K). This represents the return required by investors to purchase the given stock or group of stocks.
3. The expected growth rate of dividends for the stock (g).

Historical data concerning dividend payout ratios is available, but the other two factors are more difficult to assess

Determining (K): The Required Rate of Return.   It is generally agreed that three basic factors determine the required rate of return (K); the risk-free rate of return demanded in that economy, the expected rate of inflation, and a risk premium. The risk-free rate reflects the basic time value of money assuming no probability of default and no inflation. Logically, the real risk-free rate should be determined by the real growth rate of the economy, which in turn is a function of underlying investment opportunities and the funds and resources available to take advantage of such opportunities. The real growth rate of the U.S. economy generally has ranged from about 2.5 percent to 4.5 percent, and would likely be stable over long periods of time since the basic factors that determine real growth are slow to change.

The expected rate of inflation, however, can vary markedly from period to period, affecting the value of financial assets through its effect on K. The higher the expected rate of inflation, the higher will be K. Estimation of the expected rate of inflation is, therefore, also a critical factor affecting stock prices.

Determining (g): The Growth Rate of Dividends.   Growth in dividends is determined by the growth of earnings, though the dividend growth rate also would be affected by changes in the dividend payout ratio. Growth in earnings can be studied by analyzing its underlying determinants.

While gross revenues (mainly sales) are the basic source of funds to a corporation, there may be revenue growth without a correlated growth in earnings. Costs may rise faster than sales prices, as has occurred in many industries at times since 1966. We must concentrate, therefore, on growth in earnings as the base supporting rising equity values.

Investors typically concentrate on earnings per share when analyzing profitability, which is considered a more meaningful basic statistic for investment analysis than aggregate earnings. Growth in total dollar earnings may not translate into growth in earnings available to support share value. In fact, earnings per share could fall as reported earning after taxes rose, because of an increase in the number of shares outstanding that exceeded the percentage increase in reported earnings (earnings dilution). Growth in earnings per share can be the result of either growth in the rate of return on stockholders' equity or growth in the total equity per share (book value per share), or both, as shown below, where EAC equals "earnings available to common stockholders" (earnings after taxes less preferred dividends):

$$\frac{EAC}{Common\ Equity} \times \frac{Common\ Equity}{Number\ of\ Shares} = \frac{EAC}{Number\ of\ Shares}$$

Over any extended period of time there must be an increase in total invested capital to provide increases in earnings per share. Simply to generate an increased rate of return on a more or less stable capital base would be unusual. Growth in book value per share is the result of either earnings retention or the sale of additional stock at prices in excess of book value. American corporations have, on average, raised about two-thirds of funds used through earnings retention. A fast growing corporation will, therefore, typically offer a low dividend payout ratio and conversely, a high earnings retention rate.

It can be shown, using valuation models, that the rate of growth in earnings per share is the product of the rate of return earned on owners' equity times the proportion of earnings retained. This does assume, however, that past rates earned on owners' capital can at least be maintained. Moreover, it implies that if corporations in the aggregate (say in terms of the Dow-Jones Industrial Average or the Standard & Poor's Indexes) retain 45 percent of earnings on average and earn 11-1/2 percent on owner's equity on average, earnings per share will grow for this group at about 5.18 percent per year (.45 x .115). This relationship is sometimes referred to as the sustainable rate of growth for a firm.

Return on owners' equity can be further analyzed by observing the following relationships:

$$\frac{EAC}{Total\ Assets\ (TA)} \times \frac{Total\ Assets\ (TA)}{Owner's\ Equity} = \frac{EAC}{Owners'\ Equity}$$

Thus, the two basic determinants of return on owners' equity are the return on total assets and the proportion of assets financed by owners as opposed to creditors funds.

Finally, we can usefully observe that return on total assets has two basic determinants:

$$\frac{EAC}{Net\ Sales} \times \frac{Net\ Sales}{Total\ Assets} = \frac{EAC}{Total\ Assets}$$

Let us now use the framework we have developed to assess the basic factors affecting the growth of dividends.

Dividend and Profit Growth Analysis.   Dividend growth can be expected to relate to a firm's earning growth over time. Accordingly, we have presented data for the basic factors underlying earnings growth for the Standard & Poor's 400 Stocks in Table 4-7. Total asset data was not available prior to 1976, limiting the data gathered.

Steady increases in book value per share over the period studied have supported earnings per share growth. Retention of earnings per share is the factor most commonly leading to increases in book value per share. The retention rate for all U.S. corporations was about 47–50 percent during the years 1965–72, and it seems reasonable to assume this also was true for the Standard & Poor's 400 Stocks. Beginning in 1973, the retention rate increased to the 57–63 percent range, and stayed in that range until 1981. The retention rate then dropped sharply after 1981, but the impact of this drop is somewhat mitigated by the sharp decrease in the inflation rate for the U.S. economy. The drop in retention rate, in and of itself, could suggest lowered business confidence in the prospects for future investment and slower profit growth in the future. This drop had not discouraged investors prior to September 1987 as stock prices rose to new records but in October 1987 the Dow-Jones Index fell by over 30 percent in a week. Negative factors such as the trade deficit, the U.S. government deficit, and rising interest rates coupled with programmed trading took its toll.

Equity and asset turnovers tend to increase during inflation. The equity turnover did rise sharply to relatively high levels during the 1970s and early 1980s

Table 4–7 Factors Unerlying Earnings Per Share and Dividend Growth, 1965–1985

Year	Return on Owner's Equity (EAC/OE)(%)	Book Value Per Share (OE/# of Shs.)	Return on Asset Invests (EAC/TA)(%)	Leverage Factor (TA/OE)(%)	Equity Turnover (Sales/OE)(%)	After-Tax Profit Margin (EAC/Sales)(%)	Turnover & Assets (Sales/TA)(%)	Retention Rate (%)
1965	12.64	43.50			1.85	6.82		
1966	12.88	45.59			1.94	6.64		
1967	11.76	47.78			1.92	6.12		
1968	12.27	50.21			2.02	6.07		
1969	11.86	51.70			2.10	5.65		
1970	10.28	52.65			2.09	4.92		
1971	10.80	55.28			2.14	5.04		
1972	11.71	58.34			2.21	5.30		
1973	14.15	62.84			2.37	5.96		
1974	14.17	67.81			2.69	5.28		
1975	12.11	70.84			2.61	4.63		
1976	13.91	76.26	66.64	2.09	2.58	5.42	1.23	60.3
1977	13.91	82.21	65.94	2.11	2.65	5.27	1.25	58.3
1978	14.50	89.34	66.73	2.17	2.74	5.30	1.26	59.1
1979	16.29	98.71	73.92	2.20	2.88	5.68	1.31	63.3
1980	14.65	108.33	65.43	2.23	2.96	4.95	1.32	59.2
1981	14.12	116.06	63.20	2.24	2.91	4.87	1.29	57.9
1982	10.82	118.60	47.05	2.31	2.74	3.96	1.18	45.5
1983	11.78	122.32	51.38	2.28	2.66	4.41	1.16	50.0
1984	13.98	123.99	57.95	2.37	2.92	4.75	1.23	58.2
1985	11.34	126.20	43.87	2.53	2.91	3.85	1.15	48.5

EAC = Earnings Available to Common Shareholders   OE = Owner's Equity   TA = Total Assets

Source: Author's calculations based on data provided in the *Financial Summary* published by Compustat Services Inc, Volume 6, Denver, Colorado, Standard & Poor's 400 Composite, November 6, 1986.

when inflationary pressures were strong. Fortunately equity turnovers remained high during the period 1982–1985, though inflation fell. Firms are using their equity capital efficiently, at least in an historical sense. The rise in equity turnover is encouraging, but it must be noted that it occurred during one of our longest, continuous economic expansions on record. Firms may find it difficult to maintain such turnovers in the face of intense foreign competition and a possible slow down in the economy.

After-tax profit margins fell sharply after 1979 to almost one-half of what they were in 1965. This is an adverse factor for investors. The question is, is the drop permanent or only fleeting? One could hypothesize that rising union power and increased foreign competition had permanently reduced profit margins. National income data does suggest a real transfer from the corporate sector to government and individual sectors of the economy over the past decade. It is interesting to note that Kessel and Alchian found that the average increase in equity was greater for firms with lower wage ratios.[34] The relative importance of wages to total costs is worth considering when analyzing a firm, especially if inflation is anticipated. It is important to note, however, that the inflation rate fell sharply in the 1980s. Real returns, therefore, were not falling as fast as the dropping margin would suggest.

Professor Reilly examined the relationship between profit margins for the Standard & Poor's 400 stocks and the rate of inflation as measured by the Consumer Price Index for the period 1960–82.[35] The correlation was –0.60. He also considered the annual percentage changes in the two series and the correlation was – 0.11. One would expect profit margins to fall as inflation rose and vice-versa. This did not work out in the 1970s, but the margin did fall sharply in 1985 when the rate of inflation had fallen. Inflation is bad for stocks since it brings about rising interest rates, a rising K, and therefore falls in stock values.

An increase in oil prices in mid-1987, rising wholesale prices, federal deficits, pressure on interest rates, and intense foreign competition all suggest that one cannot anticipate a rise in margins in the near term. This is adverse for investors.

On the other hand, the relatively low inflation rate in mid-1987, the markedly increased inflow of foreign funds to our financial markets, and the continuing economic expansion should affect stock prices favorably. One cannot, however, be confident that inflow of foreign funds will not slow down and possibly leave

34 R.A. Kessel and A.A. Alchain, "The Measuring and Validity of the Inflation-Induced hag on Wages Behing Prices," *American Economic Review*, 50, No. 1, March, 1960, pp. 43–66.

35 Frank K. Reilly, *Investment Analysis and Portfolio Management*, 2nd Edition (Chicago: The Dryden Press, 1985) p. 387.

Figure 4–1 Short-Term Interest Rates: Money Market Discount Rate, Effective Date of Change; All Others, Quarterly Averages

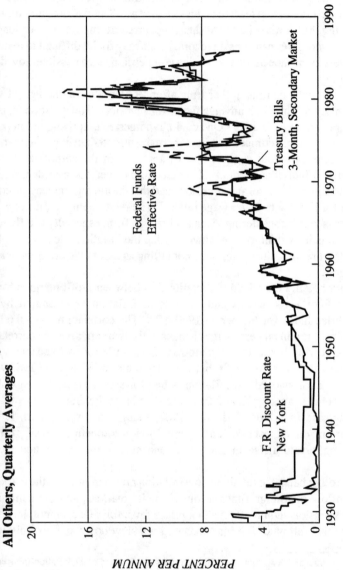

Source: 1986 Historical Chart Book, Board of Governors of the Federal Reserve System, Washington, D.C., p. 98.

Figure 4-2 Long-Term Bond Yields, Quarterly Averages

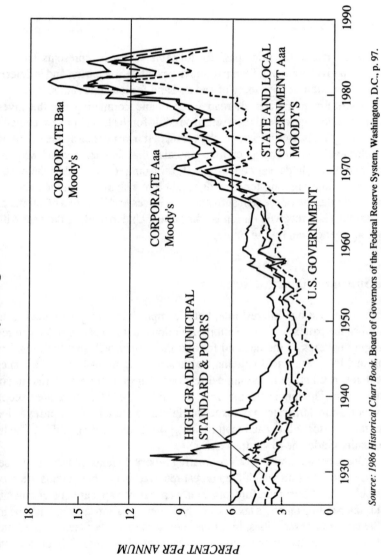

Source: 1986 Historical Chart Book, Board of Governors of the Federal Reserve System, Washington, D.C., p. 97.

the U.S. stock market if the dollar continues to fall and the trade and government deficits are not corrected.

Interest Rates

An interest rate is the price paid for loanable funds. It represents the required return, at a given moment, for a particular type of debt security, and is determined by the interaction of the supply of and demand for loanable funds.

There are numerous alternatives available competing for the investor's dollar. Investors seek the highest return possible for the level of risk accepted when committing funds. It is important, therefore, that investors be aware of the pattern of yields available at any given time, and also that they understand why interest rates, and other yields, vary over time. If, for example, one makes the mistake of investing heavily in long-term bonds just before a sharp rise in the general level of interest rates, he or she will suffer serious losses both in terms of capital and/or the current yield received on funds committed. Understanding the past will help develop a better feel for the future.

The Structure of Interest Rates

There is not just one interest rate, but a complex structure of interest rates that describes the pattern of interrelations of various maturities and risks, and reflects changing patterns in the demand for and the supply of loanable funds. Typical short and long-term yield patterns are shown in Figure 4–1 and 4–2. Generally, all interest rates move in the same direction, with short-term rates moving over a wider range. The longer the maturity, the higher the rate. There are exceptions, however. Short-term rates have exceeded intermediate-term rates and even longer-term rates. Also, within each maturity category quality ratings differ. The higher the quality grade, the lower the rate.

One must be careful when comparing reported yields on tax-exempt securities with securities on which the interest received is taxable. Yields are reported on a before-tax basis; therefore, tax-exempt securities appear to offer much lower yields. Depending on one's tax bracket, however, the after-tax yield may be higher on the tax-exempt securities. Investors should use after-tax yields, based on their particular tax status, when making investment decisions. Call protection and marketability also affect interest rate patterns.

In periods of economic growth, yields on lower quality debt issues tend to move closer to yields on high grade issues. In periods of economic contraction the yield on low and high grade issues tend to move further apart. This narrowing and widening of the yield spread can be observed in Figure 4–2. This change in yield patterns generally has been explained in terms of changes in investor psychology that take place over the economic cycle. The optimism that is generated during a long economic upswing is thought to cause investors to become less concerned about financial or default risk, while the pessimism associated with recessions is thought to have the opposite effect. This suggests investors could profit by emphasizing acquiring more risky bonds during an economic downswing when the added yield offered to take the higher risk is at a peak, and then concentrate on selecting high quality securities at or near the peak of the economic cycle. One should watch the changing risk premiums over time and keep the patterns in mind when selecting bonds.

Interest rate patterns reflect demand and supply factors at work in the financial markets. The higher the demand, given a fixed supply of funds, the higher the level of rates, and vice-versa. The demand curve for loanable funds is subject to greater volatility than is the supply curve and is more important in establishing rates. Salomon Brothers and Bankers Trust of New York publish excellent annual studies of the demand and supply factors and forecast changes for the next year.

The Federal Reserve and Interest Rates

The Federal Reserve in carrying out its policy decisions enters the market on either the demand or supply side, thereby affecting interest rates especially in the short-term markets. In periods of strong economic expansion, the Fed is likely to be worried about rising inflationary pressures. Demand for available funds tends to rise sharply during an expansion and is likely to exceed the supply of funds available, leading to rising rates. The Fed tends to restrict growth in the money supply during such a period to combat inflationary pressures. Conversely, in periods of economic contraction demand for funds tends to fall, and the Fed typically is allowing the money supply to grow, leading to falling interest rates.

A major reason why interest rates for different maturity categories may move temporarily in different directions is that there are different supply and demand forces operative in the various segments of the financial market. Funds do not always move easily from one maturity category to another. Moreover, the Fed tends to concentrate its actions in the short end of the market, leading to greater volatility for shorter maturities.

Expectations of future rates are quite important when planning investment policy.

Historical Record of Interest Rates and Prices of Debt Instruments

In our chapter on valuation we showed that bond prices and interest rates will vary inversely. Figure 4–3 shows the long-term secular trends that have developed in interest rates since 1925. Actually, there have bene three major secular trends since 1900:

1. From 1900–1920 a secular rise in interest rates and corresponding decline in bond prices occurred.
2. From 1920–46 a secular decline in interest rates and corresponding rise in bond prices occurred.
3. From 1946–1981 a secular rise in interest rates and corresponding decline in bond prices was experienced.

Since 1981, we have experienced a sharp drop in the general level of interest rates and accordingly bond prices have risen.

Prior to the 1920s an absolute low for bond yields in the United States was reached in 1899, when the average yield of municipal bonds (New England) and prime corporate bonds fell to between 3.07 and 3.20 percent. From 1899 to 1920 bond yields rose substantially to 5.56 percent by May 1920.

Bond yields were at 5.50 percent in May 1930 and fell to 2.3 percent in April 1946. The yields on U.S. Government securities, however, were maintained by pegging operations conducted by the Federal Reserve during World War II, and we can learn little from this pattern. The problems that arose with the pegging operations suggest that we would not undertake such operations again, unless we were involved in a major war.

The period of 1946–1981 was a period of secular rise in interest rates, interrupted only temporarily during various economic recessions that occurred. Interest rates surpassed all previous highs, going above 16 percent in both long and short-term markets by 1981. The sharp upswing in rates from 1978 to 1981 was accompanies by a sharp rise in the inflation rate, which reached double-digit levels. A relatively restrictive monetary policy was adopted by the Fed, and large Federal budget deficits were incurred helping explain the sharp rise in interest rates. Inflation expectations are an important determinant of the level of interest rates. Interest rates fell sharply after 1981, leading to gains for bond investors.

Generally, higher yields can be found in the secondary markets (in which previously issued bonds are traded) when bond prices generally are rising, and in the new issues market when bond prices are declining. This occurs because price adjustments usually are reflected first in new issues. Inventories of bonds tend to grow in dealers' hands during declining markets (rising yields), and new issue prices are adjusted quickly downward to assure sale and avoid burdensome inventory levels. At the same time, most dealers are hesitant to mark down inventoried bonds unless the market shows real evidence of further deterioration. In rising markets, sales are brisk and dealers have no hesitancy to raise prices on new issues.

Nominal and Real Interest Rates

To represent cost or return, interest rates should be related to the rate of change in prices. One who has earned a total return of 14 percent from an investment in debt securities during a given year when the price level rose 10 percent has a net increase of only four percent in the purchasing power of the portfolio. The 14 percent return is referred to as the nominal rate of interest, while the four percent gain in purchasing power is referred to as the real rate of interest.

The real rate of interest and the rate of inflation, therefore, jointly determine the nominal rate of interest. The real rate of interest may be estimated by subtracting from the quarterly rate on three-month Treasury bills the quarterly percentage increase in the price level. Investors should concentrate on and be influenced by expected real rates of return when making investment decisions.

The real rate of interest has been volatile over the last two decades. The real rate is likely to decrease during recessions because there is a substantial amount of unused capital available and, therefore, a low return to capital. The real rate is likely to increase during periods of economic growth since capital is employed intensively and there is a need to expand the capital base. *Unexpected changes* in the rate of inflation can also cause changes in the real rate. If financial markets expect a rising rate of inflation in the future, they will increase the nominal rates demanded for funds to maintain real returns. When unexpected changes occur, however, nominal interest rates will not initially correctly reflect the changes. For example, an unexpected increase in the inflation rate will tend to cause real rates to fall.

The real rate of interest, therefore, can be volatile, reflecting both changes in the strength of the economy and faulty inflationary expectations. The real rate tends to be low during recessions and high during periods of economic strength.

The Term Structure of Interest Rates

The term structure of interest rates seeks to explain the interrelationships between yield and maturity. A pattern of yield differentials that exists between securities that differ only in regard to maturity defines a particular yield structure. Risk or taxability are other factors that can cause yield differentials to exist.

The yield structure on U.S. Government securities is not affected by differences in financial risk or taxability, and is, therefore useful as a proxy for constructing a yield curve at a moment in time. The yield curves so constructing are represented in Figure 4–3, and show the diversity that has been experienced in the market. Why do these disparate configurations occur?

The May 1967 curve is a classic example of an upward sloping curve that occurs typically in a recessionary period when interest rates are low. This shape can be explained in terms of expectations as to the future course of interest rates. When short-term rates are expected to rise in the future, it is desirable to stay short to facilitate reinvesting at the rising rates. Borrowers would prefer to invest long-term, locking in what they believe will prove to be relatively low rates. Demand for funds is concentrated, therefore, in the long-end of the market, while the supply of funds moves toward the short-term market, explaining the rising curve. Risk considerations also would suggest a rising curve, since as maturity increased, price volatility increases, and so does the possibility of unexpected adverse events.

A declining curve was present in December 1969. Such a curve tends to exist when rates are at relatively high levels and interest rates are expected to decline. Borrowers then prefer to borrow short to refinance as rates fall, thereby concentrating demand in the short-term end of the market. Lenders prefer to lend long to lock in what they feel ar historically high rates. Thus short-term rates rise to long-term levels. Moreover, high rates typically occur when the economy is strong, and the Fed will likely be restricting the money supply through operations in the short end of the market.

The humped back curve, May 1970 tends to occur when interest rates are high and about to retreat to more normal levels. A flat yield curve, June 1965, rarely exists over any period of time. It is a transitional structure usually followed by higher interest rates.

Money Supply Data

It is agreed that money and monetary policy influence economic activity, although the degree and direction of the influence is still controversial.

Figure 4–3   Yield Structure on U.S. Government Securities

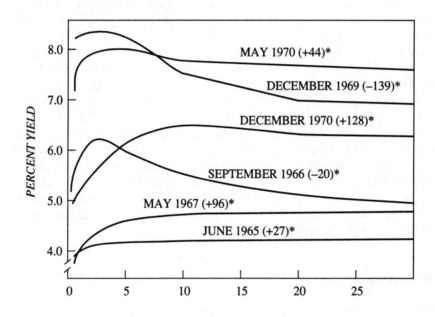

Monetarists stress the importance of control of the money supply in controlling output, employment, and inflation. They point out that changes in the growth of the money supply are highly correlated with changes in the rate of total spending.[36] Other economists argue that in the long run the level of the money supply affects prices, but has no sustained effects on output.

The Fed is the main institution determining and implementing monetary policy using the following tools: (1) open market operations, which is the buying and selling usually of short-term government securities that affects the level of bank reserves and therefore the money supply; (2) changes in reserve requirements; and (3) changes in the discount rate which is the rate at which banks can borrow from the Fed. Investors should, therefore, be interested in Fed policy and statements made by the Fed. Publications of the Saint Louis Federal Reserve Bank are an excellent source of monetary data.

Several studies have found that money supply changes lead stock prices.[37] there is evidence, however, supporting the contention that the market anticipates changes in monetary growth, which means that investors cannot use past changes in the money supply to plan purchases and sales of securities.[38] The investor can utilize monetary data to develop a feel for the trend of the economy and interest rates rather than to pinpoint market action. This is useful, however, for purposes of developing profit expectations.

Inflation and Common Stock

Persistent increases in the cost of living since World War II seriously have reduced the purchasing power of funds committed to fixed-income securities,Security;fixed-income savings accounts, or idle cash balances. Common stocks often are suggested as an inflation hedge, based on assumed continued growth in corporate earnings and dividends and, therefore, the value of common stocks. In an effort to review the effectiveness of common stocks as an inflation hedge, Table 4–8 contrasts the change in price, earnings per share, and dividends per share for the Standard & Poor's 500 stock Index against that of the Consumer Price Index (CPI) over the period 1933–1986.

Table 4–8 shows that stock prices rose substantially more than did the CPI over the entire period studied, and dividends paid also rose substantially more.

---

36 The discussion is based on Lawrence K. Roos, "An Insider is View of Innovations and Monetary Policymaking: Implications for the Economy," *The CFA Study Guide I*, 1984 (Charlottesville, Va.: The Institute of Chartered Financial Analysts) pp. 114–119.

37 For example, see Kenneth Homa and Dwight Jaffe, "The Supply of Money and Common Stock Prices," *The Journal of Finance*, December, 1971.

38 Michael Rozoff, "The Money Supply and the Stock Market-The Demise of a Leading Indicator," *Financial Analyst Journal*, September–October, 1975.

Table 4–8   Growth in Stock Prices, Earnings Per Share, and Dividends—Standard & Poor's 500 Stocks: Selected Periods, 1933–1986

Years	Year-End Price	Earnings Per Share	Dividends Per Share	Consumer Price Index
		Standard & Poor's 500 Stocks		
1933	10.10	0.44	0.44	38.8
1935	13.43	0.76	0.47	41.1
1940	10.58	1.05	0.67	42.0
1945	17.36	0.96	0.66	53.9
1950	20.41	2.84	1.47	72.1
1955	45.48	3.62	1.64	80.2
1960	58.11	3.27	1.95	88.7
1961	71.55	3.19	2.02	89.6
1965	92.43	5.19	2.72	94.5
1966	80.33	5.55	2.87	97.2
1967	96.47	5.33	2.92	100.0
1970	92.15	5.13	3.14	116.3
1975	90.19	7.96	3.68	161.2
1976	107.46	9.91	4.05	170.5
1977	95.10	10.89	4.67	181.5
1980	135.76	14.82	6.16	246.8
1982	122.55	12.64	6.87	289.1
1984	167.24	16.64	7.53	311.1
1985	210.68	14.63	7.90	322.2
1986	242.17	14.48	8.28	328.4
		Compound Annual Growth Rates		
1933–1986	6.18	6.80	5.69	4.11
1945–1986	6.64	6.84	6.36	4.51
1950–1986	7.11	4.63	4.92	4.30
1960–1986	5.64	5.85	5.72	5.16
1967–1986	4.96	5.40	5.64	6.46
1970–1982	2.40	7.80	6.74	7.88
1980–1986	10.13	–0.39	5.05	4.88
1970–1977	0.76	11.35	5.83	6.56
		Percentage Change		
1933–1986	2298	3191	1782	746
1945–1986	1295	1408	1155	509
1960–1986	317	343	325	270
1967–1986	151	172	184	228
1975–1986	169	82	125	104
1980–1986	79	–0.3	34	33
1970–1982	33	137	119	149
1970–1975	–0.2	55	17	39

Common stocks, on average, did offer an effective inflation hedge over the entire time period, in fact offering substantial growth in real wealth.

However, the rise in stock prices during the period 1967–1986 did not compensate for the loss in purchasing power suggested by the CPI but would do so if growth in dividends is allowed for. Moreover, stocks did not offer an effective hedge when 1970 is the base year. An analysis such as this is deficient on two accounts. First, a stock average is not a realistic proxy for an individual or many institutional portfolios. Second, the CPI may not represent the effect of inflation on a particular individual or a particular institution.

The early states of an inflationary period commonly are marked by large increases in the supply of money and credit, and thus by relatively low interest rates. Prices tend to rise faster than the money supply, reflecting inflationary anticipations, and the real supply of money then begins to decline. Interest rates rise sharply. The resulting tight liquidity situation and high interest rates are reflected in lower values for many financial assets, especially those offering fixed payouts to the holders. However, once the inflation rate begins to level off or starts to decline, even though prices continue to rise, stocks should begin to show more favorable price rises in line with expected growth in earnings and dividends. Thus, stocks perform poorly during an accelerating phase of inflation (e.g., the 1970–1980 period), but may more than offset the effects of inflation, provided that corporate profits and dividends grow at a rate exceeding the average rate of inflation.

Alchian and Kessel[39] stress the importance of whether the firm is a net monetary debtor or creditor in evaluating its prospects for serving as an effective inflation hedge. A *monetary asset* is defined as an asset whose market value is independent of changes in the price level, such as money, accounts and notes receivable, and fixed-income securities that were purchased. A *monetary liability* is defined as a liability whose amount is independent of changes in the price level—i.e., denominated in dollars and payable in terms of the contractual amount no matter what happens to the price level during the time the debt is owed. Therefore, while banks are large debtors and would tend to gain during an inflationary period by repaying these debts with depreciated dollars, they are even larger creditors and lose when repaid with depreciated dollars. Therefore, on average, bank stocks have not proven to be good inflation hedges. Also, banks are characterized by large amounts of labor per dollar of invested capital, and wage costs for banks have tended to rise faster during inflationary periods than have the prices charged for bank services.

---

39 Armen A. Alchian and Reuben A. Kessel,"Redistribution of Wealth Through Inflation," *Science*, Vol. 130, No. 3375 (September 4, 1959), pp. 535–539.

In summary, an accelerating period of inflation is not good for stock prices. Restrictive monetary and fiscal policies used to restrain inflationary pressures lead to relatively high interest rates, reduced real demand, and lower volumes of output. While unemployment often results, organized labor is able to increase dollar wage costs, and unit production costs tend to increase. Competition and political pressure make it difficult to raise prices sufficiently to maintain nominal, let alone real, profit margins, and corporate profits tend to decline in real terms. History does suggest that when inflation rates slow down appreciably, stock prices move up substantially from lows recorded during the height of the inflation. When and if inflation rates recede, future returns on stocks are likely to be a function of corporate earnings and dividend growth, which in turn depends on the ability of corporations to earn an adequate return on invested capital. Notice the poor performance of the stock price index during the high inflation years of 1967–1977.

CHAPTER 5

Financial Statements: A Basic Raw Material of Fundamental Analysis

A tendency toward an underlying continuity in business affairs makes the financial record, as portrayed in accounting reports, the logical point of departure for the projections needed for valuation estimates and risk analysis. Accounting reports call attention to the problems and the opportunities that confront an enterprise. Accounting has been defined as "the process of identifying, measuring, and communicating economic information to permit informed judgments and decisions by users of the information."[40]

Four major financial statements, useful for investment analysis, are outputs of the accounting system: (1) the balance sheet; (2) the income statement; (3) the statement of owners' equity (or retained earnings); and (4) the statement of changes in financial position. These statements and accompanying text are the main source of financial information for persons outside the business organization. They attempt to summarize in three or four pages the activities of a business over a specified period of time (the income statement, statement of changes in financial position, and statement of owners' equity), and the financial position at a moment

---

40 Charles J. Woelfel, Ezra Solomon and John J. Pringle, *Introduction to Accounting and Finance* (Malvern, P/o, American Institute for Property and Liability Underwriters, 1978), p. 7.

in time (the balance sheet). The statements portray where the firm is currently, and the operating results for the accounting period by which the firm arrived at this position.

One must recognize, however, that accounting language has many dialects. Words may not have the same meaning when used in accounting as in non-accounting usage. For example, value as applied to long-life assets in accounting is historical costs less amounts recovered through charges to the income account, not current market value, replacement value, or liquidation value of that asset. Also, judgment often plays an important role in determining accounting values. Moreover, the rules that underlie the keeping of accounting records have changed over time in response to a changing society. One must, therefore, exercise caution when making comparisons of accounting data through time or between companies.

Accounting Principles

The word *principle* has been defined as "a general law or rule adopted or professed as a guide to action; a settled ground or basis of conduct or practice."[41] The most authoritative source of accounting principles is the set of opinions of the Accounting Principles Board of the American Institute of Certified Public Accountants (AICPA). Also, the Financial Accounting Standard Board (FASB) issues from time to time Statements of Financial Accounting Standards, which represents authoritative expressions of generally accepted accounting principles. The financial reports of most companies of any substantial size are examined by certified public accountants who apply these principles. The SEC also is an authoritative source of accounting principles, and their pronouncements generally have been consistent with the Opinions of the Accounting Principles Board. Finally, some accounting principles have gained acceptance through widespread use.

Accounting principles do not, however, prescribe exactly how each detailed event should be recorded. Acceptable alternatives often are available for recording an event, such as L.IF.O. or F.I.F.O. L.IF.O. for determining inventory costs, allowing judgment on the part of the accountant in reporting data. An analyst, accordingly will not know the precise meaning of all the items on the financial statements without determining which of the equally acceptable possibilities has been selected for reporting purposes. Absolute uniformity in accounting data, over time or between firms, should not be assumed. The complex and varied nature of

---

41 AICPA, *Accounting Terminology Bulletin*, No. 1, p. 9.

business operations and a rapidly changing economy suggest a need for flexibility in reporting, which is offered within the framework of principles developed for accounting.

Basic Concepts

Basic concepts that underlie the preparation of financial statements, and are the foundation on which accounting principles were built, are reviewed below.

The Money Measurement Concept

A standard of measure is needed to bring financial transactions together in a meaningful way. It would not be useful to present a list of the pounds of raw material in inventory, the number of trucks owned, the acres of land owned, and the number of buildings owned. We need a way of expressing these things in terms that reflect value and claims that can be added and subtracted. The monetary unit becomes the common denominator allowing us to express the combined value of the many different assets and to measure the effect of operating policies on the well-being of the firm and its shareholders.

Adopting the money measurement concept does impose a severe limitation on accounting reports. For example, while changing laws, aggregate economic events, a strike, or the health of the firm's president all affect the future market value of a company, they are not recorded or accounted for specifically in the financial statements of that company. An analyst must seek information not found in the accounting reports to lend meaning to an investment analysis.

The usefulness of accounting data is reduced seriously when the value of money is fluctuating. Sales and profits could increase in dollars during an inflationary period, when in terms of purchasing power the business is suffering real losses. We shall discuss inflation adjusted accounting data and other implications of inflation for investment analysis at appropriate places in this book.

The Business Entity Concept

Accountants prepare statements for business entities, which are separate and distinct from the owners of that entity. At times analysts may be interested in something larger than the business entity. For example, a creditor can sue and collect from an individual's personal assets for a business debt, where that individual is the proprietor or a partner in the business. While the accounting records and statements would reflect only the business transactions, the creditor certainly could be interested in the personal assets of the principals.

A corporation is, by definition, a legal entity separate from the owners (stockholders). One corporation, however, might own a large block of stock of another corporation, and a share of stock in that company really shares in a broader interest than the individual corporate entity. The accountant may combine the businesses for accounting purposes and present a set of what are called consolidated financial statements.

The Going Concern Concept

Accounting assumes that a business will continue to operate for an indefinite period of time. The accountant, therefore, does not attempt to measure current worth of the business. The accountant views himself or herself as a financial historian. Acquired but unused resources are shown not at their current value to a buyer, but rather at cost.

The success or failure of a business only can be determined by accumulating all transactions from the opening of the business until its liquidation. It would not, however, be feasible to await liquidation to judge the success or failure of current operating policies. While accounting for the success or failure of a business in midstream carries inaccuracies with it, since many transactions and commitments will be incomplete on any given date chosen, an attempt must be made. The going-concern convention recognizes this need.

Analysts must understand that a great deal of estimation enters into the process of preparing periodic accounting reports, introducing uncertainty into the interpretation of these reports. Some examples of the estimates necessary are:

1. The determination of the cost of inventory used in the production process and the valuation of inventory not yet used.
2. An estimation of possible losses that will be encountered in the collection of receivables or of other loss reserves.
3. The life and salvage value of assets, underlying the determination of depreciation expense.
4. The method to be used in estimating depreciation expense.
5. The extent of future warranty claims.

As noted above, assets typically are entered in the accounting records at the price paid to acquire them, thereby assuring objective determination of value. This historical cost is the basis for all subsequent accounting for the asset.

The worth of an item obviously may change over time, and the values recorded for assets in the balance sheet, do not therefore reflect current worth, or what an asset could be sold for. One cannot value a business by looking at the total value listed for assets in the balance sheet. A capitalization of the net earnings these assets generate, as estimated in the income statement, would form a more useful basis for estimating the current value of a business. Actually, valuation of a firm is related more usefully to cash flows generated through the investment of funds than to reported accounting profits.

Cost values for assets often are systematically reduced over the estimated life of a long-term asset for balance sheet purposes by processes called *depreciation, depletion,* or *amortization.* At the same time, that portion of historical cost charged as depreciation, depletion, or amortization expense of the current period is deducted from net total revenues to determining profit in the income statement. Also, if a long-term expenditure (such as the prepayment of five years of premiums for an insurance policy) is made, the expenditure would be set up as the value of the asset in the balance sheet, and one-fifth of that amount would be recognized each year for five years as insurance expense in the income statement. All expenditures are not expenses for purposes of determining net income. Thus, cash flow and reported profit are two different things.

Note that if a company pays nothing for an item, that item usually will not appear in the accounting records. Thus, the knowledge, contacts, and skill of employees, and the good reputation of the company may be important assets to that company and have real value if that company were sold, but they do not appear on the financial statements since a cost has not been incurred. As another example, the death of a key executive could have an important effect on the value of that company's stock. The accounting records, however, will not be affected by this event.

The Dual-Aspect Concept

Accounting is governed by the principle of double-entry bookkeeping; the duality of every business transaction. All assets of the business are owned (claimed) by someone, either owners or creditors. Regardless of the number of transactions the firm engages in, this duality and balance prevails at all times. This duality is expressed in the basic accounting equation:

1. A liability is incurred, thereby increasing creditors' claims.
2. Ownership claims increase, since they were the source of the funds used to make payment.
3. Another asset was disposed of and is the source of the funds used in payment.

The duality of the transaction is clear.

   To illustrate, assume a firm were created, borrowed $25,000 from a bank and sold common stock for $50,000. The firm's balance sheet would then appear as follows:

Assets		Liabilities and Equity	
Cash	$75,000	Bank Loan	$25,000
		Owners' Equity:	
		Common Stock	$50,000
	$75,000	Total	$75,000

   Now assume that $25,000 is used as a downpayment to acquire a building costing $100,000, with the remaining $75,000 borrowed through a mortgage loan. Further assume $25,000 is used to acquire inventory, that the firm intends to resell. The balance sheet will now appear as follows:

Assets		Liabilities and Equity	
Cash	$15,000	Bank Loan	$25,000
Inventory			
(at cost)	25,000	Mortgage Loan	75,000
Building	100,000	Total Debt	$100,000
		Owners' Equity	
		Common stock	50,000
	$150,000		$150,000

   Finally, let us assume that one-half of the inventory is sold for $20,000 in cash. Actually, revenues and expenses for a given accounting period are recorded separately, and the net effect of these items, in terms of the profit earned or loss incurred, is transferred to the retained earnings account on the balance sheet. We will, unrealistically, assume that no costs were incurred in generating the $20,000 of revenue, other than the cost of the inventory. We will not even recognize depreciation of the building for purposes of this illustration. We merely want to highlight the relation between the income statement and the balance sheet as reflected through changes in the retained earnings account. It would be useful to attempt to create the new balance sheet (the correct figures appear below).

Assets		Liabilities and Owners Equity	
Cash	$ 45,000	Bank Loan	$ 25,000
Inventory			
(at cost)	12,500	Mortgage Loan	75,000
Building	100,000	Total Debt	$100,000
		Owners Equity	
		Common Stock	50,000
		Retained Earnings	7,500
	$157,500		$157,500

Full Disclosure

Accountants are required to disclose all the facts that would have significant influence on the judgment of a user of their reports. Accounting policies must be disclosed in the footnotes to the annual report, such as the inventory costing system used or the handling of a pension plan. Analysts should read and digest the footnotes before beginning to analyze the financial statements.

When an accounting method is used that departs from the official position of the Financial Accounting Standards Board, that departure must be disclosed along with justification for using the method chosen.

Accountants are expected to summarize and highlight key information in their reports. The full disclosure concept can be violated by excessive disclosure.

Accrual Basis

Accounting records typically are kept on an accrual rather than a cash basis. Under an accrual system, revenue is recognized when earned and expenses are recognized when incurred, rather than when cash is received or expended. The use of the accrual basis requires a number of adjustments at the end of the accounting period. For example, the determination of the amount of prepaid interest to remain in the balance sheet account and the amount to be recognized as expense during the current accounting period. Also, expenses that have been incurred during the current accounting period, but will not be paid until the next accounting period, must be recognized in the year in which those expenses were incurred. This would be accomplished by making a year-end adjustment entry debiting wages expense (an expense in the income statement) and crediting accrued wages payable (a must be recognized in the year in which those expenses were incurred. This would be accomplished by making a year-end adjustment entry debiting wages expense (an expense in the income statement) and crediting accrued wages payable (a current liability in the balance sheet). Accordingly, reported profits and cash flow are two different things. Since users of statement are interested in both, the accountant prepares an income statement and then a summary cash flow statement.

Consistency

The consistency doctrine requires that the same treatment be given to comparable transactions from period to period. This allows users to compare accounting data and reports over time and study trends. For example, if a firm has chosen to use the F.I.F.O. inventory costing system in the past, it is expected to continue using that system in the future.

At times a particular company does have a need to change a particular accounting method. Such a change can be made, but the justification for the change must be disclosed along with an explanation of the effects of the change on the financial statements. The justification and the explanation of effects is presented in the footnotes to the financial statements in the year in which the change occurs. Firms are not required to repeat this information in future years, which could mislead a user of the statement attempting to make comparisons through time. Accordingly, if an unusual change in data occurs between two given years, it is desirable to review the financial reports of the years involved to determine if a change in accounting methods occurred.

Accounting for Inflation

Business people, financial analysts, and accountants have long realized that traditional financial statements prepared on the historical cost basis for measuring income and asset values produce misleading results when prices are changing. The inflation rate in the United States prior to the 1970s was relatively low, however, and many felt that the year-to-year changes in accounting data brought on by such inflation were insignificant and could best be estimated by the analyst.

The late 1970s was marked by unprecedently high inflation rates for the United States that led to strong pressures for change that would result in reporting inflation-adjusted data in annual company reports. The SEC (Accounting Series Release 190) in 1976, for the first time, required the nation's largest non-financial corporations to report in their 10-K filings estimates of the extent to which undervaluation of inventory and plant and equipment resulted in understatement of expenses and overstatement of profit in the income statement. Although not a comprehensive restatement of financial data to reflect the impact of inflation, the data generated were believed to offer a more useful suggestion of true earning power by many analysts.

Financial Accounting Standards Bulletin No. 33 (adopted September 1979) required the disclosure in annual reports of two different types of inflation-adjusted financial data by publicly held corporations with total assets of more than $1 billion or inventories and property and equipment valued at $125 million. Inflation-adjusted data and its limitations are discussed in much greater detail in Chapter 7, after the subjects of depreciation and inventory accounting are more fully developed.

Consolidated Statements

Practically all large corporations are holding companies with subsidiaries and/or affiliates. A subsidiary is a corporation controlled by a parent company, the latter owning at least 50 percent of the voting stock of the subsidiary. To file a consolidated tax return, the parent must own at least 80 percent of the voting and non-voting common stock of the subsidiary. The definition of an affiliate is not so precise. An affiliate includes corporations that are controlled effectively even though there is less than a 50 percent ownership.

Consolidated statements view all the companies involved as though they were a single entity. Accordingly, all assets, liabilities, and earnings or losses are combined with corresponding items in the financial statements of the parent company, after elimination of all intercompany transactions. Where the parent owns less than 100 percent of the subsidiary's common stock, the minority interest of outsiders is recognized in an owners' equity account.

Why Consolidate?   When income statements are not consolidated, only the dividend income from subsidiaries is included in the parent's balance sheet. When no dividends are received, therefore, there is no recognition of subsidiary earnings in the income statement of the parent company, resulting in understatement of the income in which the stockholders of the parent company have an interest.

To illustrate, assume Company X reports net earnings of $2,000,000 for the year and has $500,000 shares of common stock outstanding. Company X has therefore earned $4 per share. Further, assume that Company X owns 100,000 shares of the 150,000 shares of common stock of Company Y, and that Company Y earned $3 per share for the year. If Company Y paid no dividends for that year, none of its earnings would be reflected in an unconsolidated statement for Company X. Actually, two thirds of the $450,000 of earnings of Company X, or $300,000, belong to Company X. Company X could, after all, have required Company Y to pay a dividend since it effectively controls Company Y. The analyst should therefore recognize that an investor in Company X has interest in earnings of $4.60 per share (the $300,000 spread over the 500,000 shares) not $4 per share.

Extent of Consolidation.   The annual report indicates whether statements are consolidated and the extent of their consolidation. It may state that "all subsidiaries are consolidated," or "all subsidiaries are consolidated except X financial subsidiary," or "all domestic subsidiaries are consolidated, but not foreign subsidiaries." Financial subsidiaries, even if owned 100 percent, often are not included in a consolidation because they have a large debt-to-equity ratio, which could make debt appear excessive on an operating parent's consolidated statement. A finance company, because of the liquid nature of its assets, is assumed to be able to safely carry a higher debt-to-equity ratio.

Reasons for not consolidating a subsidiary, other than the debt problem relative to consolidating a finance subsidiary, might be:

1. Where control was felt to be temporary, such as when the parent expects to dispose of the stock of the subsidiary in the near future.
2. Where there is uncertainty as to income, such as with foreign subsidiaries facing restrictions on conversion and repatriation of funds. Future taxes on repatriations also inject an uncertainty.

Basic Methods for Accounting for Ownership in Other Corporations

Three methods may be used to account for ownership in a subsidiary:

1. Consolidated Financial Statements.
2. Equity Method.
3. Cost Method.

Consolidation and the Equity Method differ in the details recorded in the financial statements. Under the Equity Method the investment in a subsidiary initially is recorded at cost.[42] The carrying amount in subsequent statements is adjusted to recognize the investor's share of the earnings or losses of the subsidiary. Dividends received, for example, reduce the carrying amount of the investment. APB Opinion No. 18 requires that in applying the Equity Method, any difference between the cost of an investment and the investor's equity in the net assets of the invested at the date of the investment be accounted for as if the invested were a consolidated subsidiary. Accordingly, the cost of investment would first be allocated to the investor's share of the invested's net identified assets and liabilities on the basis of the fair value. Only excess of the cost of the investment over the sum of the amounts so allocated should be amortized over a period not to exceed forty years as a reduction of the amount recognized each period by the investor as its equity in the earnings or losses of the invested.

Under the Cost Method, the investment in a subsidiary is recorded at cost and income is recognized only if it is received by the parent as dividend distributions.

Limitations of Consolidated Statements.   The major limitations of consolidated statements is their failure to report distinct information about the assets, liabilities, revenues, and expenses of the separate companies included in the consolidation. The individual statements for the separate entities that have been consolidated usually are not reported separately. Forecasting would be facilitated by showing the independent statements of the entities so as to reflect the varied resources and activities and prospects of the several entities that have been combined.

Moreover, ratio analysis based on consolidated statements can deceive the analyst, since non-homogeneous groupings often are reported. For example, a loss operation could be counter-balanced by a profitable on in a given year, when neither has strong prospects for the future. Earning power could then be over-estimated.

Business Combinations

Acquisitions, mergers, and consolidations are common occurrences today. Two conflicting approaches have been developed to account for such events, the "pooling of interest" and "purchase" approaches.

---

42 APB (Accounting Principles Board) Opinion No. 18 covers the procedures that should be followed in applying the Equity Method.

Under the *pooling of interests* method, the former ownership interests continue (pooling assumes an exchange of voting securities) and assets and liabilities of the constituents are carried on the statement of the combined entity at their recorded accounting values. The *purchase method*, views the combination as the acquisition by one entity of another. Assets and liabilities are recorded at cost, which is based on fair values at the date of acquisition (not recorded accounting costs). Moreover, the pooling method picks up income of the constituents for the entire fiscal period in which the combination occurs, while under the purchase method the acquiring entity picks up the income of the acquired entity only from the date of acquisition.

Analysts should recognize that the rationale that accountants use in distinguishing pooling of interests from purchase combinations often may not be relevant to the analyst attempting to determine true recurring earnings. Room for abuses and loose interpretations are present under accounting rules when accounting for business combinations.[43] For example, broad latitude is possible in applying the rules of valuation and appraisal that can lead to understatement of asset values and concomitantly the understatement of costs and overstatement of income as those assets are depreciated.

Professors Briloff and Engler illustrate the effects of the pooling method by considering the companies shown in Table 5–1.[44]

Table 5–1   Data Highlighting Significant Effects of the Pooling Method (Millions of $)

Name of Acquiring and Pooled Company (Year of Acquisition)	Market Value of Share Issued in Acquisition	Book Value of Acquired Company	Unrecorded Value and Assets
Pepsico, Inc. and Taco Bell (1978)	$ 139	$ 36	$ 103
General Electric Co. and Utah International, Inc. (1976)	$2,130	$640	$1,490

---

43 Professor Abraham J. Briloff illustrates many of the potential abuses in articles first appearing in 1967 in the *Financial Analysts Journal* and *Barrons*.

44 A.J. Briloff and C. Engler, "Accountancy and the Merger Movement: A Symbiotic Relationship," *The Journal of Corporation Law*, Fall, 1979.

Had the above acquisitions been recorded on the purchase basis, the acquiring companies would have reflected substantially higher values for the assets acquired. Accordingly, future costs related to the depreciation or amortization of those assets would have been substantially higher, leading to lower reported profits. Ratios used in analyzing profitability, liquidity, and long-term solvency would, therefore, be significantly different if the pooling approach, rather than the purchase method, were used.

Interim Reports

Analysts must recognize the seasonal nature of corporate income when reviewing quarterly, semi-annual, or nine-month statement data. An analyst could be misled badly if he or she merely multiplies quarterly figures by four- or six-month figures by two to represent a year. When there is an important seasonal element it would be estimated by reviewing past years' data, and current data should be adjusted accordingly.

Moreover, an analyst must recognize that corporations usually make adjustments only at the end of the year. These adjustments, therefore, are not reflected in interim statements.

Introduction to the Basic Financial Statements

Useful approaches for analyzing the data offered in each of the four major statements will be developed in Chapters 6 through 11. At this point, we briefly review the structure and content of each statement, using the 1987 Annual Report of DuPont for illustrative purposes.

The Consolidated Income Statement

Table 5–2 reproduces the income statement as it appeared in the 1987 Annual Report for DuPont. Total expenses incurred in operating the company are broken into major expense categories and the total ($27,132 billion in 1987) is deducted from total revenues generated in a given year ($30,792 billion in 1987) to determine "Earnings Before Taxes." Note that taxes other than income taxes were deducted as an expense category for purposes of determining the earnings before income taxes. Income taxes are then deducted to determine "Net Income," which

Table 5–2   Financial Statements—Consolidated Income Statement (Dollars in millions, except per share)

	1987	1986	1985
Sales	$30,468	$27,148	$29,483
Other Income	324	273	382
Total	30,792	27,421	29,865
Cost of Goods Sold and Other Operating Charges	17,150	15,129	17,898
Selling, General and Administrative Expenses	2,716	2,350	2,077
Depreciation, Depletion and Amortization	2,225	2,119	1,796
Exploration Expenses, Including Dry Hole Costs and Impairment of Unproved Properties	459	550	561
Research and Development Expense	1,223	1,156	1,144
Interest and Debt Expense	435	438	513
Taxes Other Than on Income	3,085	2,656	2,282
Gains from Sales of Businesses	(161)	(140)	(27)
Loss on Restructuring of Investments	—	178	226
Early Retirement Program Expense	—	—	200
Total	27,132	24,436	26,670
Earnings Before Income Taxes	3,660	2,985	3,195
Provision for Income Taxes	1,874	1,447	2,077
Net Income	$1,876	$1,538	$1,118
Earnings Per Share of Common Stock	$ 7.39	$ 6.35	$ 4.61

Source: E.I. DuPont de Nemours and Company, *1987 Annual Report*, p. 26.

is earnings after income taxes. The net income represents the earnings available to common stockholders for purposes of determining earnings per share.

Investors often seek more detail than is provided in a summary income statement. Additional information can be gained from the notes to the financial statements, investment manuals (such as *Standard & Poor's, Moody's,* and *Value Line*), and analyses prepared by brokerage firms and other investment professionals. Practicing analysts may visit companies to gain additional data. We will suggest a general format useful for purposes of analyzing the income statement in Chapter 6.

For example, the *1987 DuPont Annual Report* offers sales and operating income data by major industry segments and by geographical areas for 1987, 1986, and 1985. Moreover, the performance of each industry segment during the 1987 year and contrasted to 1986 and its outlook are discussed separately in an early section of the report. This information would be useful when attempting to forecast revenues and profits. It is important to remember that financial statements report on past history, while it is the future success and profitability of the company that will determine the success of an investment in that company.

The footnotes to the financial statements also discuss the accounting policies adopted by DuPont and offer details on particular debt securities outstanding. Selected financial data adjusted for the effects of changing prices also is contained in the report.

The Balance Sheet

Note that assets are listed in the Balance Sheet (Table 5–3) in order of their liquidity. Liquidity refers to the length of time it normally takes to convert assets to cash through revenue generating operations. Typically, cash acquired by a company is invested in inventory and plant and equipment. The inventory is then sold on credit terms becoming accounts receivable, at a price that includes recovery of all costs including depreciation of plant and equipment and a profit. As receivables are collected, we are back to cash, which can be used to maintain the productive base of the company, replenish inventories needed in the production process, and finance growth through profits.

An appropriate balance of liquid versus relatively non-liquid assets is needed. If an excess of liquid assets is held, the opportunity for profit is sacrificed. An inadequate amount of liquid assets, however, may lead to an inability to pay bills and bankruptcy.

Liabilities are listed in the order in which they must be paid. The stockholders equity represents residual claims on assets. The amount shown ($14,244 billion in 1987) need never be paid by the firm to anyone. It represents the owners' claim on assets, calculated on the basis of the original cost of those assets less charges to the income account to date (or book value). The amount of liabilities relative to the amount of equity for a firm is important to analysts, as it is an indicator of risk and leverage.

The Consolidated Statement of Stockholders' Equity

A potential stockholder would have interest in what caused the changes in Stockholders' Equity from year-to-year. For example, did an increase in stockholders' equity result from the sale of new stock or from the retention of earnings? The statement of stockholders' equity (Table 5–4) answers questions of this type.

**Table 5–3   Financial Statements—Consolidated Balance Sheet
(Dollars in millions)**

December 31	1987	1986
Assets		
Current Assets		
Cash and Marketable Securities	$ 756	$ 584
Accounts and Notes Receivable	4,376	3,771
Inventories	4,342	4,253
Prepaid Expenses	479	352
Total Current Assets	9,953	8,960
Property, Plant and Equipment*	33,400	31,859
Less: Accumulated Depreciation,		
Depletion and Amortization	17,546	16,162
	15,854	15,697
Investment in Affiliates	541	469
Other Assets	1,861	1,607
Total	$28,209	$26,733
Liabilities and Stockholders' Equity		
Current Liabilities		
Accounts Payable	$ 2,422	$ 2,346
Short-Term Borrowings and Capital Lease Obligations ...	1,641	1,625
Income Taxes	388	183
Other Accrued Liabilities	1,689	1,482
Total Current Liabilities	6,140	5,636
Long-Term Borrowing	3,018	3,227
Capital Lease Obligations	84	89
Other Liabilities	1,827	1,669
Deferred Income Taxes	2,801	2,648
Minority Interests in Consolidated Subsidiaries	95	90
Stockholders' Equity (See page 28)	14,244	13,374
Total	$28,209	$26,733

* Includes oil and gas properties accounted for by the successful efforts method of accounting.

Source: E.I. DuPont de Nemours and Company, 1987 Annual Report, p. 27.

Stockholders' Equity is broken into four separate accounts: preferred stock, common stock, paid-in capital, and retained earnings. Preferred stock has a preference as to dividends at a stipulated rate that must be paid in any given year, before any dividends may be paid to the common stockholders. Also, preferred stock typically has a preference to funds generated in the sale of company assets in the event of liquidation of the company. Most preferred stocks do not share in company earnings beyond their preference dividend and, therefore, do not have the growth potential associated with common stock.

Table 5–4   Financial Statements—Consolidated Statement of Stockholders' Equity (Dollars in millions, except per share)

	1987	*1986*	*1985*
Preferred Stock, without par value—cumulative 23,000,000 shares authorized; issued at December 31:			
$4.50 Series—1,672,594 shares (callable at $120) ..	$ 167	$ 167	$ 167
$3.50 Series—700,000 shares (callable at $102) ...	70	70	70
	237	237	237
Common Stock, $1.66 2/3 par value; 300,000,000 shares authorized; issued at December 31: 1987—238,833,676; 1986—239,978,627; 1985—240,636,707	398	400	401
Additional Paid-In Capital			
Balance at Beginning of Year	4,535	4,492	4,455
Common Stock			
Issued for Acquisition	—	42	—
Issued in Connection with Compensation and Benefit Plans	57	38	37
Repurchased and Retired	(37)	(37)	—
Balance at End of Year	4,555	4,535	4,492
Reinvested Earnings			
Balance at Beginning of Year	8,202	7,529	7,142
Net Income	1,786	1,538	1,118
	9,988	9,067	8,260
Preferred Dividends	(10)	(10)	(10)
Common Dividends (1987—$4.40; 1986—$3.05; 1985—$3.00)	(792)	(734)	(721)
Total Dividends	(802)	(744)	(731)
Common Stock Repurchased and Retired	(132)	(121)	—
Balance at End of Year	9,054	8,202	7,529
Total Stockholders' Equity	$14,244	$13,374	$12,659

Source: E.I. DuPont de Nemours and Company, *1987 Annual Report*, p. 28.

Stock accounts, preferred or common, typically are kept at par value, which has no relation to current market value of the stock. Note that DuPont has a par value of $1.66 2/3 per share while the common stock sold at over $80 per share in June 1988. When stock is sold originally by the company at a price in excess of par value, the additional payments are credited to paid-in capital. In June 1988 the market value of the 238,833,676 shares of DuPont common stock outstanding as of December 31, 1987 would have approximately $20 billion dollars (238,833,676 × $85/sh), well in excess of the approximately $5 billion shown in the capital stock and paid-in capital accounts of DuPont. It is important to recognize that accounting values do not represent market values.

The retained earnings account is the summation of all earnings of DuPont since the company first began to operate less all dividends paid out to stockholders and all charges made directly to the retained earnings account rather than to the income account. The amount shown for 1987 ($9,054 billion), however, has already been invested in the assets listed on the balance sheet. It is not a cash fund that could be used to pay dividends or expand operations.

Statement of Changes in Financial Position

This statement (Table 5–5) often is referred to as the statement of sources and uses of funds or a cash flow statement. It shows how funds were obtained by the company during the year and how these funds were used. It is constructed by determining changes in balance sheet accounts from the prior year to the year being studied and adjusting this data for fund flows that can be identified but are not accounted for accurately by balance sheet changes.

The statement is designed to answer the following types of questions:

1. How much of required capital to support continuing operations and growth was the firm able to generate internally and what amount did the firm have to raise in the money and capital markets?
2. How has the firm invested funds generated through operations and access to the money and capital markets?
3. Were externally raised funds in the form of equity or debt?
4. Has the firm been building up liquid assets to support an expanded level of operations or is it becoming less liquid?
5. Is the output of the company selling well or is it building up in inventory?
6. Are receivables being collected on time?

Table 5-5 Financial Statements—Consolidated Statement of Changes in Financial Position (Dollars in millions)

	1987	1986	1985
Cash and Marketable Securities at Beginning of Year	$ 584	$ 583	$ 674
Cash Provided by Operations			
Net Income	1,786	1,538	1,118
Depreciation, Depletion and Amortization	2,225	2,119	1,796
Increase in Deferred Income Taxes—Noncurrent	153	305	716
Dry Hole Costs and Impairment of Unproved Properties	272	372	347
Loss on Restructuring of Investments	—	178	226
Early Retirement Program Expense	—	—	200
Other Noncash Charges and Credits—Net	132	5	(15)
Cash Flow from Operations—Before Changes in Working Capital	4,568	4,517	4,388
Changes in Working Capital*			
Decrease (Increase) in Current Assets			
Accounts and Notes Receivable	(605)	273	(230)
Inventories	(89)	(380)	(81)
Prepaid Expenses	(127)	24	(5)
Increase (Decrease) in Current Liabilities			
Accounts Payable	76	(204)	105
Income Taxes	205	(248)	(139)
Other Accrued Liabilities	207	(125)	47
Increase in Working Capital	(333)	(660)	(303)
Net Decrease (Increase) in Working Capital from Major Acquisitions and Sales of Businesses	96	(110)	—
Increase in Working Capital—Excluding Major Acquisitions and Sales of Businesses	(429)	(550)	(303)
Cash Provided by Operations	4,139	3,967	4,085
Dividends Paid to Stockholders	(802)	(744)	(731)
Investment Activities			
Capital Expenditures			
Additions to Property, Plant and Equipment	(3,035)	(2,737)	(3,046)
Investment in Affiliates	(177)	(202)	(33)
Major Acquisitions			
Working Capital	—	(149)	—
Other Net Assets	—	(1,032)	—
After-Tax Proceeds from Sales of Businesses	447	179	21
Miscellaneous—Net	(88)	(136)	(306)
Cash Used for Investment Activities	(2,853)	(4,077)	(3,364)

Table 5–5 (continued)
Financing Activities

Increase in Short-Term Borrowings and Capital Lease Obligations	16	902	121
Changes in Long-Term Borrowing and Capital Lease Obligations			
Increases	115	642	237
Reductions	(329)	(610)	(478)
Increase (Reduction) in Borrowing and Capital Lease Obligations	(198)	934	(120)
Common Stock			
Issued for Acquisition	—	43	—
Issued in Connection with Compensation and Benefit Plans	58	40	039
Repurchased and Retired	(172)	(162)	—
Cash Provided by (Used for) Financing Activities	(312)	855	(81)
Cash and Marketable Securities at End of Year ..	$ 756	$ 584	$ 583
Increase (Decrease) in Cash and Marketable Securities	$ 172	$ 1	$ (91)

* Excluding Cash and Marketable Securities, and Short-Term Borrowings and Capital Lease Obligations.

Source: E.I. DuPont de Nemours and Company, *1987 Annual Report*, p. 29.

CHAPTER 6

Analysis of the Income Statement: General Approach and Revenue Analysis

For many years, major emphasis has been placed on the income statement—not only in the case of common stock analysis—but also in the case of bonds, private placements, and preferred stock analysis. The margin of safety for fixed income security holders is provided by a corporation's earnings and cash flow. The value of the business reflects the amount that can be earned on the invested capital and the cash flow generated by that firm. Therefore, the analyst must determine a true earnings base of recurring earnings from which growth and volatility of earnings and dividends may be projected. All a common stockholder can receive from an investment are dividends and/or capital appreciation. Both are dependent on future earnings—and expectations by investors of future earnings and dividends.

Information Provided By the Income Statement

Security analysts seek information from the income statement in answering the following questions:

1. What is the true recurring earnings base that serves as a starting point for generating useful projections of future performance?

2. How has the company performed over a relatively long time horizon (ten years of data often are studied to encompass a business cycle), and in the recent past? What factors underlie the revenue and cost trends exhibited?
3. Is earnings growth consistent or is the company in decline? Does the earnings patterns from year-to-year display significant variability? If so, what causes this variability?
4. How does the company being analyzed compare with the earnings growth of the economy and the industry in which it participates? How does the company compare with competitors, in terms of revenue, cost behavior, and profitability?
5. Does the company appear to have good control of costs?

The focal point of common stock analysis is on growth and profitability of the firm.

Income Statement Structure

The most fundamental accounting principal applied to the income statement is that which requires the matching of revenues and expenses. As we discussed in Chapter 5, revenue is recognized when it is realized, not when the cash is received. The matching concept requires the recognition of all costs that are associated with the generation of the revenue reported in the income statement. Many subjective judgments are required of accountants in matching costs and revenues, leading to potential limitations of an analysis and possibly misleading conclusions if not properly considered by the analyst.

Income Statement Format

Balance sheet format is standardized in annual reports, but this is not true for the income statement. An analyst will find it useful to recast the income statement he wishes to study in the general form suggested in Table 6–1. Hopefully, more detailed information actually will be available, such as the major expense items making up the total of cost of goods sold, and that detail should be shown in the recast statements.

Table 6-1 Analytic Format for Income Statement

Major Divisions	Comments
Gross sales and revenue	Sometimes not given.
Sales return and allowances and cash discount	Sometimes not given.
Net sales or revenues	Often the first item in the income statement. SEC requires a breakdown of profits for each industry segment for which sales comprise ten percent of the total. Also a breakdown of sales and earnings by broad geographic areas outside the United States.
Other income	Listed here in the AICPA* recommended form; but if it is material and nonrecurring, it is preferable to list below under extraordinary items.
Cost of goods sold	Rarely broken down into its components. It is useful to have detail on the components.
Gross profit	Net sales less cost of goods sold.
Gross profit margin	Percentage of gross profit to sales calculated by analyst.
Selling expenses	Promotion, selling, and distribution expenses.
General administrative expenses	Salaries, wages, office supplies, insurance, taxes other than income taxes, etc.
Profit from operations	Percentage of sales; operating profit margin calculated by analyst.
Profit from operations-margin Other income	Nonoperating income such as dividends and interest income typically are listed here. When it is regular and recurring in nature, the AICPA recommends showing it where indicated above; but if the items are substantial, analysts prefer that it be located here in the statement.
Other expenses	Nonoperating expenses such as bond interest, note interest, amortization, and bond discount.
Income before income taxes	Federal and foreign income taxes.
Income taxes	
Income before extraordinary items	
Extraordinary income and extraordinary expenses	Usually nonrecurring items of material amount, net of applicable income tax. Major items should be explained.
Net income	
Net income–profit margin	
Net profit divided by sales	
Retained earnings at beginning of year	

Table 6–1 (continued)

Cash dividends on common stock	Also preferred dividends if any.
Cash dividends as percentage of net income	Payout ratio.

Retained earnings at end of year
Per share of common stock:
   Income before extraordinary items
   Extraordinary items net of taxes
   Final net income
   Dividends

---

* AICPA (American Institute of Certified Public Accountants).

A spreadsheet of the company's income statements for about ten years should be prepared to develop a feel for trends, revenue, and cost behavior over time.[45] Ten years is long enough to include a complete economic cycle. The spreadsheet can be entered in a computer, using Lotus 1,2,3 or a similar spreadsheet program, to facilitate analysis.

The analyst should determine and enter true recurring earnings for each year in the spreadsheet, which may be different than reported earnings. The analyst must reorganize and adjust for possible lack of uniformity in the accounting data when preparing such a spreadsheet (e.g., changes in methods used for reporting inventory), to assure comparability of data.

Analysis of Key Items on the Income Statement

The determination of net income involves two basic steps: (1) revenues attributable to the period reported must be separated from those that would be credited properly to other periods, and (2) the costs that were incurred in generating these revenues must be determined directly or by assignment to income statement accounts. The remainder of this chapter and chapters 7 and 8 are devoted to an analysis of the major items that require careful attention by the analyst. The

---

45 Standard & Poor's Compustat tapes contain income statements data and useful ratios covering many years for a large selection of companies. This data could facilitate preparation of spread sheets.

relationship between items in the income statement usually is explored by means of ratio analysis, which will be discussed separately in Chapter 10.

Recognition of Revenue

Under the accrual system, the rules governing recognition of revenues appear straightforward. The rules, however, are subject to exceptions and a variety of interpretations that could mislead an analyst. For example, a profit is deemed to be realized when a sale is made, unless a serious question exists about the collectability of the resulting receivable. The judgment as to the noncollectability of a receivable may, however, be based on conservative or liberal assumptions. Not all banks agreed on the collectability of loans to Third World countries in 1987, and the extent of loan loss reserves set up for such loans can vary from bank to bank. Since the charge made to set up a loan loss reserve (or a bad debts reserve for a corporate receivable) reduces reported income of the period, reported profits by individual banks may not be comparable in terms of judging relative efficiency or future profitability.

The Focus Points of Analysis

Analysts have long stressed growth in demand for a company's products as important to successful investment. Growth in earnings power, not sales per se, is the desired objective. Cost behavior, therefore, is important. Continued growth in profits over long periods of time, however, is not likely unless sales are growing. Cost economies usually are not repeated on a yearly basis.

The aim of sales analysis is to project revenues for possibly the next three to five years as a basis for generating cost and profit expectations. When studying historical revenue data the analyst should be concerned with the size, trend, composition, and underlying determinants of those revenue patterns.

For the purposes of developing future sales forecasts, the analyst could:

1. Calculate the compound growth rate in sales over a period of about ten years, to insure including the effects of the business cycle.
2. Calculate a standard deviation around the average of the above data to assessing the stability of revenue patterns over time.
3. Observe the resistance of company sales to negative economic and other factors.

4. Assess the major factors underlying the sales pattern observed.

Footnotes and discussion in the body of the financial report may offer information useful in estimating the physical sales volume. The analyst also can adjust reported sales data by utilizing a price index, such as the Consumer Price Index (CPI). An index adjustment will not generate physical volume figures, but the approximations of physical patterns generated can be useful.

Market Share Analysis

Analysts typically compare the sales patterns for a given company with those of its principal competitors and appropriate aggregate data (such as GNP data). Charting can be a helpful tool.

For purposes of growth comparisons, one should use semilogarithmic scaled graph paper. Arithmetic scaled paper can give misleading results, since equal space on a chart reflects equal absolute quantities, not rates of growth. Semilogarithmic scaled paper represents equal percentage change (not absolute) by equal space changes. Growth is best measured in terms of percentage change, to avoid differing base problems, not absolute change.

For example, assume sales for Firm A grew from $1 million to $10 million over a ten-year period, while sales for Firm B grew from $90 million to $100 million over the same time period. If sales are charted on arithmetic scale paper, two parallel lines are shown suggesting no difference in growth. Obviously Firm A had had a much larger relative growth (25.9 percent compound annual growth rate for Firm A compared to about a 1.6 percent compound annual growth rate for Firm B). Charting on logarithmic scaled paper would clearly show this, since the space from 1 to 10 is much deeper than the space from 90 to 100.

The slope of the sales line on a semilogarithmic scaled chart and the changing character of that slope indicates the stability or the accelerating or decelerating nature of the demand for the company's products.

Sales Growth and Input–Output Analysis

Above average sales growth for a company usually is predicated on expected rapid growth of the industry in which the company operates. A company may, however, accomplish above average growth by gaining an increased share of total industry demand. Forecasting end-use demand for a company's products is therefore useful.

The heart of any really sophisticated system of forecasting demand on the basis of past demand–supply relationships rests on input–output tables. Input–output tables indicate how much each industry requires of the production of each other industry in order to produce each dollar of its own output. The various industrial subdivisions are listed both vertically and horizontally, similar to an intercity mileage chart on a road map. The individual inputs into a given industry are read vertically, while the industry's dollar sales to other specific industries are read horizontally. The U.S. Department of Commerce publishes these tables on an infrequent basis in the *Survey of Current Business*.

Product mix and market share data can be important in spotting a growth company. For example, it was agreed in the 1970s that semiconductor producers emphasizing transistors would have a slower growth rate than those whose major product was integrated circuits. Moreover, those integrated circuit producers who specialized in devices that were particularly applicable to computers could be expected to grow more rapidly.

Trends and Common Size Statements

Common size statements can be useful for purposes of analyzing trends and the changing relationship between financial statement items. In a common size statement, all items in that statement are expressed as a percent of a base figure. For example, all items in each year's income statement could be presented as a percentage of net sales. By reviewing several years of such statements one could observe changes in the relative importance of cost items, and how cost items vary as sales change.

Horizontal analysis is also a useful tool. In horizontal analysis, each item in the income statement is expressed as an index number calculated by dividing a given year's number by the number of a base year. Data on automobile companies is utilized to illustrate the process in Table 6–2. Net operating revenues increased by 76 percent from 1975 to 1981 for General Motors. This may sound impressive, until one notes that GNP increased 91 percent over the same time period. In other words, sales for General Motors grew at a rate below the economy average during this time period, no doubt reflecting the rapid rise in sales of foreign car companies. During the period 1975–85, General Motors was the only U.S. automobile company to equal or exceed the growth of GNP. Interestingly it is Ford Motor Company that adapted most effectively to changing demand and supply conditions in the automobile market in recent years. Table 6–2 would not have suggested this. Remember, the key to successful investing is looking ahead.

Table 6–2 Horizontal Analysis of Operating Revenues for Automobile Companies

Company	Millions of $							Index Number (1975 = 100)						
	1975	1980	1981	1982	1983	1984	1985	1975	1980	1981	1982	1983	1984	1985
American Motors	2,552.6	4,039.9	2,588.9	2,878.4	3,271.7*	4,212.5	4,039.9	100	158	101	113	128	165	158
Chrysler	11,598.4	9,225.3	10,821.6	10,044.9**	13,240.4	19,572.7	21,255.5	100	80	93	87	114	169	183
Ford	24,009.1	37,085.5	38,247.1	37,067.2	44,454.6	52,336.4	52,774.4	100	154	159	154	185	218	220
General Motors	35,724.9	57,728.5	62,698.5	60,025.6	74,581.5	83,889.8*	96,371.6**	100	162	176	168	209	235	270
Gross National Product (Billions of Dollars)	1,598.4	2,732.0	3,052.6	3,166.0	3,401.6	3,774.7	3,988.5	100	171	191	198	213	236	250

* Data includes discontinued operations

** This year's data reflect an acquisition or merger

Source: Company data obtained from Standard & Poor's Industry Surveys, Autos–Auto Parts, Basic Analysis October 30, 1986 (Section 2), Page A95. GNP, data obtained from *Statistical Abstract*, 1987.

We also could have contrasted growth of unit sales for individual car companies against growth in the total number of cars sold in the United States, emphasizing real growth by means of index numbers. One also could observe the reaction of sales of particular companies to changes in the general economic environment through horizontal analysis.

Installment Sales

Many companies recognize the entire profit for an installment sale when the sale is made, assuming the company is reasonably certain it will be paid. Certain types of sales may, however, result in periodic installment payments which could stretch over several years (e.g., a land development company). One could then raise the question as to the number of payments that would have to be received before the buyer has a sufficient stake to make continued payments relatively certain. The American Institute of Certified Public Accountants (AICPA) has issued standards governing the accounting for installment sales, but some companies may follow practices that are more conservative than the required standards while other companies follow only the minimally acceptable standards.

For tax purposes, companies typically report only actual income as payment is received. The effective tax rate, therefore, calculated for the company by dividing taxes paid by net income may well be lower than the applicable corporate rate would suggest. In other words, profits reported to stockholders typically are higher than the profits reported to the IRS when installment sales are involved. It would be helpful if corporations provided an estimate of the deferred taxes, and made adequate provisions for uncollectable receivables arising through installment sales.

Conglomerates and Sales Breakdowns

Analysts of diversified businesses face the problem of separating and understanding the impact that the different individual segments of the business have on the operational results of a firm. Opportunities for growth will vary among the different product lines, and this must be taken into account when forecasting sales and profitability. Analysts require information that is broken down to represent homogeneous groupings whose characteristics are similar in terms of growth potential, variability, and risk. A sample of the type of such a breakdown by DuPont is shown in Table 6-3.

Table 6-3 Industry Segment Information

1987	Agricultural and Industrial Chemicals	Biomedical Products	Coal	Fibers	Industrial and Consumer Products	Petroleum Exploration and Production	Petroleum Refining Marketing and Transportation	Polymer Products	Consolidated
Sales to Unaffiliated Customers[1]	$3,979	$1,266	$1,770	$5,261	$3,284	$2,066	$9,031[2]	$3,811	$30,468
Transfers Between Segments	575	7	58	91	63	1,066	305	135	—
Total	$4,554	$1,273	$1,828	$5,352	$3,347	$3,132	$9,336	$3,946	$30,468
Operating Profit	$ 708	$ 44	$ 234	$1,019	$ 383	$ 882	$ 154	$ 587	$ 4,011
Provision for Income Taxes	(270)	4	(80)	(462)	(142)	(782)	—	(240)	(1,972)
Equity in Earnings of Affiliates	25	—	3	67	(59)	—	23	2	61
After-Tax Operating Income	$ 463[3,4]	$ 48	$ 157	$ 624	$ 182	$ 100[6]	$ 177[7]	$ 34[3]	$ 2,100[8]
Identifiable Assets at December 31	$2,889	$1,417	$2,629	$3,502	$2,649	$5,080	$4,066	$2,874	$25,106[9]
Depreciation, Depletion, and Amortization[10]	$ 307	$ 85	$ 195	$ 334	$ 162	$ 900	$ 153	$ 249	$ 2,456
Capital Expenditures[11]	$ 323	$ 127	$ 127	$ 501	$ 279	$ 932	$ 213	$ 444	$ 3,035

Table6–3 (continued)

1986	Agricultural and Industrial Chemicals	Biomedical Products	Coal	Fibers	Industrial and Consumer Products	Petroleum Exploration and Production	Petroleum Refining Marketing and Transportation	Polymer Products	Consolidated
Sales to Unaffiliated Customers[1]	$3,396	$1,150	$1,501	$4,786	$2,839	$1,926	$7,893[2]	$3,657	$27,148
Transfers Between Segments	538	5	38	63	81	902	318	158	—
Total	$3,934	$1,155	$1,539	$4,849	$2,920	$2,828	$8,211	$3,815	$27,148
Operating Profit	$ 347	$ 123	$ 189	$ 946	$ 297	$ 389	$ 623	$ 471	$ 3,385
Provision for Income Taxes	(128)	(32)	(59)	(447)	(100)	(448)	(227)	(207)	(1,648)
Equity in Earnings of Affiliates	22	—	(3)	43	(28)	—	18	2	54
After Tax Operating Income	$ 241[2]	$ 88[13]	$ 130	$ 542[14]	$ 169[15]	$ (59)[16]	$ 414[1]	$ 266	$ 1,791[8,18]
Identifiable Asset at December 31	$2,954	$1,197	$2,700	$3,061	$2,440	$5,169	$3,904	$2,724	$24,149[9]
Depreciation, Depletion and Amortization[10]	$ 394	$ 63	$ 154	$ 319	$ 133	$ 960	$ 136	$ 261	$ 2,489
Capital Expenditures[11]	$ 310	$ 95	$ 136	$ 443	$ 263	$ 781	$ 233	$ 399	$2,737

Table 6–3 (continued)

1985	Agricultural and Industrial Chemicals	Biomedical Products	Coal	Fibers	Industrial and Consumer Products	Petroleum Exploration and Production	Petroleum Refining Marketing and Transportation	Polymer Products	Consolidated
Sales to Unaffiliated Customers[1]	$3,396	$1,150	$1,501	$4,786	$2,839	$1,926	$7,893[2]	$3,657	$27,148
Transfers Between Segments	480	1	18	24	50	1,299	627	106	—
Total	$3,868	$1,017	$1,535	$4,507	$2,830	$4,758	$10,088	$3,485	$29,483
Operating Profit	$(176)	$61	$188	$345	$284	$2,128	$434	$269	$3,533
Provision for Income Taxes	125	—	(57)	(131)	(98)	(1,804)	(177)	(97)	(2,239)
Equity in Earnings of Affiliates[19]	18	—	—	29	(5)		18	1	61
After-Tax Operating Income[19]	$ (33)[20]	$61	$ 131	$ 243	$ 181	$ 324	$ 275	$ 173	$ 1,355[8]
Identifiable Assets at December 31	$2,364	$ 747	$2,559	$2,686	$1,909	$5,706	$4,196	$2,835	$23,002[9]
Depreciation, Depletion and Amortization[10]	$277	$57	$ 145	$ 260	$ 119	$ 786	$ 123	$ 228	$ 2,059
Capital Expenditures[11]	$332	$82	$ 129	$ 351	$ 257	$1,113	$ 289	$ 392	$ 3,046

[1] Sales of refined petroleum products of $8,126 in 1987, $7,018 in 1986, and $8,701 in 1985, exceeded 10 percent of consolidated sales.
[2] Excludes crude oil and refined product exchanges and trading transactions.
[3] Agricultural and Industrial Chemicals includes $31 gain and Polymer Products includes $69 gain from side of U.S. high density polyethylene business and related ethylene facilities.
[4] Includes gain of $31 from sale of a chlorine and caustic soda production facility.

[5] Includes $28 write-off inactive coal mines.
[6] Includes $28 charge for abandonment of marginal domestic producing properties and $14 write-off of previously capitalized exploratory well costs; also reflects $45 benefit from settlement of certain sales contracts.
[7] Includes $29 benefit from adjustment of prior year tax provisions.
[8] The following reconciles After-Tax Operating Income to Net Income:

	1987	1986	1985
After-Tax Operating Income	$2,100	$1,791	$1,355
Interest and Other Corporate Expenses			
Net of Tax*	(314)	(253)	(237)
Net Income	$1,786	$1,538	$1,118

*Includes interest and debt expense and other corporate expenses such as exchange gains and losses, minority interests in earnings of consolidated subsidiaries, and amortization of capitalized interest. Also includes $40 charge in 1987 and $13 charge in 1986 for debt restructurings.

[9]The following reconciles Identifiable Assets to Total Assets:

	1987	1986	1985
Identifiable Assets at December 31	$25,106	$24,149	$23,002
Investment in Affiliates	541	469	280
Corporate Assets	2,562	2,115	1,858
Total Assets at December 31	$28,209	$26,733	$25,140

[10]Includes depreciation on research and development facilities, impairment of unproved properties and, in 1986 and 1985, depreciation reflected in loss on restructuring of investments.

[11]Excludes investment in affiliates.

[12]Includes charge of $76 associated with the planned dismantlement of chlorocarbons and chloralkali facilities, partially offset by gains of $31 on the sale of the company's 50 percent interest in Condea Chemi GmbH, a German affiliate, and $13 on the sale of the sodium silicates business.

[13]Includes gain of $15 from sales of technology.

[14]Includes gain of $30 on the sale of the "Reemay" and U.S.-based "Typar" businesses.

[15]Includes benefit of $12 on withdrawal from the commercial propellants business.

[16]Includes $45 benefit from adjustment of prior year tax provisions partly offset by a $35 write-off of an investment in a petroleum concession in the Gulf of Suez.

[17]Includes $45 benefit from adjustment of prior year tax provisions.

[18]Includes $54 reduction due to the Tax Reform act of 1986.

[19]Includes Early Retirement Program expense as follows:

Agricultural and Industrial Chemicals	$24
Biomedical Products	8
Coal	(4)
Fibers	49
Industrial and Consumer Products	18
Petroleum Exploration and Production	(14)
Petroleum Refining, Marketing and Transportation	(13)
Polymer Products	31
Total	$99

[20]Includes loss of $66 attributable to the withdrawal from the company's investment in Syngas Company and the shutdown of an associated methanol plant, loss of $22 due to the shutdown of an ethylene production unit, and loss of $32 on disposition of DuPont Canada's interest in Petrosar Limited.

See Industry Segment Reviews for a description of each industry segment. Products are transferred between segments on a basis intended to reflect as nearly as practicable the "market value" of the products.

Source: E.I. DuPont de Nemours and Company, 1987 Annual Report, pp. 38 & 39.

The 1987 DuPont Annual Report also offered seven pages of discussion, reviewing past performance of each industry segment shown in Table 6–3 and comments on the outlook for each segment. DuPont also offered data covering capital expenditures, investment, employment, sales, net income, and net assets by major geographic areas in its 1980 annual report, but such data was not offered in the 1987 report.

The degree of disclosure of product line breakdown varies widely among companies. There are numerous difficulties, including problems of allocating overhead and interdivisional transfer pricing, in preparing such data. Moreover, management is reluctant to divulge information that might help competitors.

SFAS14[46] was issued by the Financial Accounting Standard Board (FASB) in 1976, establishing disclosure requirements concerning information about operations in different industries, foreign operations, and major customers. Companies are required in their annual reports to offer breakdowns of significant segments in terms of revenues, operating profit, and identifiable assets. Also, method of accounting for transfer pricing and cost allocations are to be disclosed. A segment is significant if sales, operating profit, or identifiable assets are ten percent or more of the combined accounts for all of a company's industry segments.

While disclosure of information on business segments is helpful, one must recognize the many judgments necessary for preparing such data, which limit its usefulness. Cost allocations often are arbitrary, and there are no generally accepted principles governing such allocations. Information on business segments must be treated as highly qualitative, and one must not attribute undue accuracy to such data.

Calculating Growth Rates

Analysts typically calculate compound annual growth rates, based on the logic of compound interest, when studying long-term trends in sales and other variables. A compound annual growth rate is that rate, which if applied each year for a given number of years to a beginning balance, will cause the balance to grow to the ending known value. Relatively inexpensive hand calculators, such as the Texas Instrument Business Analyst II, will make such calculations.

One should always use a compound annual growth rate for time series, rather than a simple average growth rate. A simple average growth rate typically will overstate the growth experienced. To illustrate, assume sales for a given company

46 SFAS14, "Financial reporting for Segments of a Business Enterprise."

calculated can be misleading. If distortion is feared, one might average data to determine the beginning and ending numbers, adjust any given year's data to a more "normal" level, or determine the rate based on regression analysis where all data is utilized.

Regression Analysis

Regression analysis is a valuable statistical technique that can yield useful insights when used properly. We can only introduce the subject in this book, and suggest that those not familiar with the tool review a statistics textbook.

Regression analysis can be used to examine the relationship between variables, either in a cross-sectional or a time series analysis. An analyst, for example, could assess the strength of the relationship between disposable personal income and a company's sales, in a simple regression analysis. The correlation coefficient generated is a measure of the degree of association between the dependent and independent variables. Moreover, the regression line developed through such an analysis could be used as a beginning framework for generating a sales forecast. Actually, in generating a sales forecast more than one independent variable might be used in the regression analysis (multiple regression). Curvilinear and multiple regression techniques may provide better forecasts if the relationship is not linear, or depends on more than one independent variable.

As one becomes more sophisticated in analysis, the cost increases may or may not justify the added expenditure of time and money. Also, underlying relationships can change markedly over time. Computers eliminate the need for manual calculations, however, and make the mathematical work simple.

Nonrecurring Items

Net income should reflect all operating items related to the current period, with segregation and disclosure of extraordinary and nonrecurring items. Nonrecurring gains and losses arise for reasons outside the regular course of business and are not expected to be repeated in future years. Therefore, nonrecurring revenues should not be included in a forecast of future revenues. Events which occurred in past years that can result in nonrecurring income are tax adjustments and/or tax forgiveness, litigation and claims and/or renegotiation, an accounting charge or change in accounting estimates, or a prior period adjustment such as could result from foreign currency translations and adjustment. A sale of assets also could result in nonrecurring revenues, since a company does not often sell productive assets gains and losses arise for reasons outside the regular course of business and are not expected to be repeated in future years. Therefore, nonrecurring revenues should not be included in a forecast of future revenues. Events which occurred in past years that can result in nonrecurring income are tax adjustments and/or tax forgiveness, litigation and claims and/or renegotiation, an accounting charge or change in accounting estimates, or a prior period adjustment such as could result from foreign currency translations and adjustment. A sale of assets also could result in nonrecurring revenues, since a company does not often sell productive assets such as plant and equipment. Another example would be the proceeds of life insurance policies on key company officers. Where possible, the results of nonrecurring events should be placed in the year in which the event occurred to better understand year-to-year changes in revenues and income. For example, a tax refund received in 1987 for overpayment of 1986 and 1985 taxes should be handled by restating the revenues, costs, and income for 1986 and 1985. The adjustment is necessary to properly review trends over time. Of course, if the nonrecurring items are small, it is not necessary to make such adjustment.

Discontinuation of a product line or sale of a segment of the business can result in a large magnitude nonrecurring item. The discontinuation or sale may well be the result of unprofitable operation in that segment of the business, and may include large termination benefits for employees. The effect on the future operations of the company must be analyzed carefully.

Industry Analysis and Performance

While a broad holding of stocks (such as those included in the Standard & Poor's 400 Index) would have recorded little or no capital gains over various time periods after 1966, a portfolio invested in selected industry grouping could have shown excellent performance. Of the 46 Moody's Industry Groups shown in Table 6–4, about half did as well or better than the published market averages over the period 1957–59 to February 1981.

A firm's profits typically are affected by economy-wide factors (e.g., interest rates and price level fluctuations), and by factors specific to the product line or industry areas in which the firm operates, and by factors specific to the firm itself (e.g., quality of management and locational factors). Therefore, a part of the revenues and earnings of a corporation is determined by industry forces.

Table 6–4   Moody's Index of Market Price Trends of Industry Groups, 1957–1959 to February 1981 (1957–1959=100)

Industry	Approximate Increase to 1980	Moody's Feb. 1981
1. Oil service	39X	3,924.9
2. Electronics	8¼–8¾X	883.4
3. TV radio broadcasting		827.3
4. Cosmetics	7¼–7¾X	769.0
5. Soft drinks		723.4
6. Drugs	6½X	645.8
7. Cigarettes		549.1
8. Printing and publishing		522.7
9. Machinery and equipment	5–5½X	513.4
10. Machine tools		502.5
11. Business equipment		500.3
12. Liquor		411.9
13. Railroad equipment		396.9
14. Aerospace		394.8
15. Oil	3¾–4X	390.3
16. Apparel		381.7
17. Soap		371.9
18. Railroads		335.3
19. Airlines		330.6
20. Insurance—property and casualty		313.0
21. Farm equipment		303.8
22. Foods	2¾–3½X	295.4
23. Natural gas		280.0
24. Automotive equipment		278.5
25. Insurance—life		251.4
26. Appliances		249.5
27. Nonferrous metals		247.4
28. Building materials	2–2½X	246.6
29. Banks		237.4
30. Retail stores		231.0
31. Electrical equipment		218.5
32. Textiles		196.7
33. Finance companies		170.2
34. Containers		162.1
35. Paper and products		156.6
36. Chemicals		145.6
37. Grocery chains	1–1¾X	140.2
38. Service companies		127.1

Industry Growth and the "Life Cycle"

Some writers, notably Julius Grodinsky[47] drew a rough parallel between industry growth and the human life cycle. They point out that when new industries are born, there often is a rush by many companies to enter the field in this period of initial and rapid growth. This is followed by a shakeout period with only a relatively few survivors and by a continuing period of strong growth, although the rate of growth is slower than in the initial period. Grodinsky described these first two periods as: (1) the pioneering stage, and (2) the expansion stage. Finally, industries are expected to stop growing, either living a relatively stable existence for an extended period of time or dying.

Grodinsky pointed out the great risk of selecting stocks in the pioneering stage, where little information about participants may be available. There is little or no past record to guide investors, or aid in preparing future projections. Some suggest participating in the pioneering stage buying stocks of many companies in the new industry, thereby spreading the risk. Grodinsky and the author feel the average investor is better served by concentrating on companies whose major product lines are in the second or third stage (especially the second stage). Moreover, we believe this analysis, while useful, must be brought into context with security price. Many stocks during the second phase (the growth phase) may sell at relatively high price-earnings (P/E) ratios that more than discount their growth potential.

An Illustrated Revenue Analysis

An industry analysis lays the basis for analyzing company performance and future revenue prospects. A well-prepared analysis of Deere and Company dated January 1981, constructed by Mr. Jerry Anderson, while at Sanford C. Bernstein & Co., Inc.is used with permission of that company for illustrative purposes.

The report began with historical and forecasted data for the United States Agricultural Tractor market as shown in Tables 6–5 and 6–6. Continued growth in the 40 p.t.o. (power-take-off, the standard measure for agricultural tractor horsepower in the United States) was forecast, as well as continued expansion of the four-wheel drive segment. While the under 40 p.t.o. segment was expected to expand rapidly over the forecast period, 1984–85 was expected to represent a peak in unit sales, as a fall-off in replacement demand was anticipated after that peak

---

47 Julius Grodinsky, *Investments* (New York: The Ronald Press, 1953), Part II.

Table 6-5 United States Agricultural Tractor Market—Industry Unit Sales

U.S. Horsepower Classification	1979	1980E	1981E	1984E
Under 30	41,820	38,015	42,000	53,800
30–39	7,477	6,725	7,600	9,690
40–49	17,055	16,300	16,575	16,975
50–59	12,632	11,850	12,550	13,710
60–69	14,788	12,700	13,100	12,700
70–79	6,790	5,565	6,525	6,695
80–89	11,460	9,510	11,150	11,480
80–99	2,275	1,910	2,175	2,250
100–119	15,022	12,150	14,400	15,085
120–139	25,910	20,600	23,800	23,500
140–159	11,407	9,475	10,600	10,925
160–179	4,728	3,925	4,450	4,885
Over 180	5,468	4,825	5,200	6,540
Total Two-Wheel Drive	176,832	153,650	170,125	188,235
170–199	4,944	4,550	5,350	6,565
200–249	4,926	4,100	4,625	5,535
250+	1,585	1,650	1,685	2,155
Total Four-Wheel Drive	11,455	10,400	11,660	14,255
Total Market	188,287	164,050	181,785	202,490

Source: Farm & Industrial Equipment Institute and Bernstein estimates. Sanford C. Bernstein & Co., Inc., New York, *Deere & Company*, January, 1981, p. 18.

Table 6-6 Summary—Agricultural Tractor Market—Industry Model Mix Analysis and Forecast

	1979	1980E	1981E	1984E
Under 40 p.t.o. Horsepower	26.18%	27.27%	27.28%	31.36%
40–99 p.t.o. Horsepower	34.53	35.25	34.15	31.51
100–139 p.t.o. Horsepower	21.74	19.97	21.01	19.05
Over 140 p.t.o. Horsepower	11.47	11.11	11.14	11.04
Total Two-Wheel Drive	93.92%	93.60%	93.58%	92.96%
Four-Wheel Drive	6.08%	6.40%	6.42%	7.04%
Total U.S. Market	100.00%	100.00%	100.00%	100.00%

Source: Bernstein estimates. Sanford C. Bernstein & Co., Inc., op. cit., p. 19.

was reached. The under 40 p.t.o. market was dominated by Japanese manufacturers at the time of preparing the report, because of cost advantage and a paucity of U.S. manufacturing capacity for small diesel engines.

Deere's Industrial Position and Strategic Orientation

Among domestic manufacturers, Deere was believed to be the leader in every major segment of the two- and four-wheel drive tractor market. Under 40 p.t.o. tractors were sourced from Yanmar, a Japanese vendor, and this source was considered safe for the future.

Deere's strategy for continued market leadership and penetration was based on two elements: (1) product quality, and (2) low-cost manufacture. Deere also

Table 6–7   Research & Development Expenditures as a Percentage of Sales

Fiscal Year	Deere & Company	Allis-Chalmers	Caterpillar Tractor	Clark Equipment	International Harvester	Massey-Ferguson
1977	3.8%	3.4%	3.8%	1.2%	2.7%	1.9%
1978	3.7	3.4	3.6	1.3	2.6	1.6
1979	3.8	3.0	3.7	1.5	2.6	1.5
Three-Year Average	3.8	3.3	3.7	1.4	2.6	1.7
1979 Dollar Expenditure (mil.)	$188.1	$58.9	$283.0	$26.3	$217.8	$44.3

Source: Corporate reports and Bernstein estimates. Sanford C. Bernstein & Co., Inc., op. cit. p. 22.

maintained a highly efficient and regarded network of retail dealers, considered one of its greatest competitive advantages. Deere, at the time of the report, was thought to be the industry's lowest cost producer of agricultural tractors in the domestic market. Financial plans were prepared and appeared to offer adequate and reasonable cost financing for purposes of carrying out the strategies. Research and development also was considered to be a vital part of the company's overall strategy. Deere was spending a larger percentage of sales revenues on research

Table 6–8   Two-Wheel Drive Agricultural Tractors, Estimated Domestic Market Share—1979

Company	40–99 H.P.	100–140 H.P.	Over 140 H.P.	Total Market
Allis-Chalmers	2%	2%	2%	6%
J. I. Case	3	3	2	8
Deere & Company	14	14	17	35
Ford Motor Company	9	2	0	11
International Harvester	8	7	4	19
Massey-Ferguson	9	1	1	11
White Motor	2	2	1	5
Other	4	1	0	3
Total	51%	32%	17%	100%

Source: Bernstein estimates. Sanford C. Bernstein & Co., Inc., op. cit., p. 23.

Table 6–9   Four-Wheel Drive Agricultural Tractors, Estimated Domestic Market Share—1979

Company	Estimated Market Share
Allis Chalmers	7%
J. I. Case	14
Deere & Co.	29
Ford Motor Company	1
International Harvester	18
Massey-Ferguson	2
White Motor	5
Versatile	8
Steiger[a]	16
	100%

[a]Includes only those units marketed under the Steiger brand name.

Source: Bernstein estimates. Sanford C. Bernstein & Co., Inc., op. cit., p. 23.

and development than its major competitors at the time of the report, as shown in Table 6–7.

Table 6–10   United States Agricultural Tractor Market, Deere & Company Unit Sales

U.S. Horsepower Classification	1979E	1980E	1981E	1984E
Under 30	6,600[1]	6,045[1]	6,720[1]	9,145[1]
30–39	n/m[1]	100[1]	380[1]	725[1]
40–49	3,000[2]	2,895[2]	2,910[2]	2,970[2]
50–59	2,275[2]	2,135[2]	2,225[2]	2,435[2]
60–69	2,390	2,050	2,100	2,055
70–79	3,250	2,645	3,065	3,145
80–89	4,475[2]	3,710[2]	4,350[2]	4,705[2]
90–99	2,150	1,815	2,020	2,025
100–119	5,300	4,280	5,150	5,505
120–139	12,250	9,735	11,305	11,515
140–159	5,650	4,690	5,300	5,680
160–179	0	0	0	0
Over 180	3,250	2,895	3,225	4,185
Total Two-Wheel Drive	50,590	42,995	48,750	54,090
170–199	1,150	1,160	1,470	1,935
200–249	2,200	1,845	1,990	2,490
Over 250	0	0	0	110
Total Four–Wheel Drive	3,350	3,005	3,460	4,535
Total Market	53,940	46,000	52,210	58,625

[1]Comprises models sourced from Yanmar.
[2]Comprises units sourced from the Deere & Company factory in Mannheim, Germany.

Source: Bernstein estimates. Sanford C. Bernstein & Co., Inc., op. cit., p. 26.

Market Penetration Forecast

Table 6–8 and 6–9 compare Deere's market position in 1979 with its competitors. Table 6–10 shows Deere's 1979 and projected penetration in the U.S. market for agricultural tractors.

In the under 40 p.t.o. segment Deere was expected to increase its share on the strength of new product introductions substantially. Limited gains were expected in the 40–99 p.t.o. and 100–139 p.t.o. segments, because of market and competitive factors. Both the 40–99 p.t.o. and 100–139 p.t.o. segments were expected to decline in relative importance to the entire market and Deere was expected to direct its attention elsewhere. Also, competitors were in the process of introducing new, more competitive models in these markets.

A significant increase in market share for Deere was expected in the four-wheel drive segment of the market based on introduction of a new model and the relieving of capacity constraints.

The North American market for combine harvesters was believed to be in a mature phase. Total unit sales were expected to decline by about 1.0% per year over the 1979–84 forecast period. The same trends that were influencing the agricultural tractor market were felt to be operative in the combine harvester market—namely, the increase in size of the average farm and farmers' need for productivity improvements to offset inflationary cost increases. Estimates were prepared for unit sales, both of rotary and conventional combines for the North America and export markets and for Deere's share of these markets. Moreover, Deere was expected to introduce a new large size rotary combine after 1984, following the next expected domestic agricultural equipment market cycle decline. During the interim, efforts of major competitors to concentrate on the rotary end of the market should enable Deere to further its penetration of the conventional combine market.

Deere entered the construction and industrial equipment market for two reasons: (1) this market typically has a cycle that does not coincide with the agricultural equipment cycle, and (2) manufacturing both types of equipment provides an increased opportunity for vertical integration into the manufacture of a variety of shared components. Deere was working to increase product line depth and breadth via progressive new product introductions and to take advantage of market segmentation. Deere was expected to expand its market share and experience revenue growth and profitability in this area of operations.

Historical and Forecast Summary

Each segment discussed above was analyzed extensively in this 123-page report. The report includes 91 tables and analyzes both revenues and costs by plant location and geographical areas. We are only summarizing the approach for illustrative purposes. The report concludes by presenting year-by-year forecasts by manufacturing plant, a historical and forecasted consolidated income statement, a forecasted balance sheet, and a forecasted cash flow statement. Since we are interested in revenues analysis, the historical and forecasted income statement is presented as Table 6–11.

The revenue estimates developed consider the basic five factors suggested by Michael Porter[48] somewhat modified and enlarged—namely:

1. The threat of new entrants to the major markets served by Deere.
2. The threat posed by substitute products or services.
3. The possible new entry of products by the company under analysis.
4. The rivalry among existing firms serving the markets important to Deere, and Deere's present and expected position in those markets.
5. Deere's strategy for maintaining its leadership position in their market and their financial and other abilities to carry out these strategies.
6. The position in the life-cycle analysis approach of the major product lines of Deere.

We will postpone discussing cost estimates developed in this report until a framework for cost analysis has been developed. At that time, we will not only discuss cost and profit estimates, but offer a valuation estimate for Deere as of January 1981, using a dividend capitalization model.

---

48 Michael Porter, *Competitive Strategy: Techniques for Analyzing Industrial and Competitors* (New York: The Free Press, 1980).

Table 6–11 Deere & Company Consolidated Income Statement—Historical and Forecast ($ Million)

	1973	1974	1975	1976	1977	1978	1979	1980E	1981E	1984E
Total Sales	$2,003.0	$2,495.1	$2,955.2	$3,133.8	$3,604.0	$4,155.0	$4,933.1	$5,304.0	$6,263.3	$9,239.9
Interest & Miscellaneous Income	$ 45.7	$ 43.5	$ 39.5	$ 49.2	$ 56.3	$ 74.4	$ 81.8	$ 80.0	$ 87.7	$ 129.3
Foreign Exchange Gain	1.6	4.3	0.0	0.3	0.0	0.0	0.5	0.0	0.0	0.0
Total Revenues	$2,050.3	$2,542.9	$2,994.7	$3,183.3	$3,660.3	$4,229.4	$5,015.4	$5,384.0	$6,351.0	$9,369.2
Cost of Goods Sold	1,479.5	1,932.5	2,273.3	2,316.2	2,686.9	3,142.3	3,794.6	4,207.2	4,898.4	7,139.9
Gross Profit	$ 523.5	$ 562.6	$ 681.9	$ 817.5	$ 917.1	$1,012.7	$1,138.5	$1,096.8	$1,364.9	$2,100.0
Selling, General & Administrative	$ 189.5	$ 223.5	$ 274.6	$ 316.2	$ 347.6	$ 377.5	$ 444.4	$ 508.0	$ 572.9	$ 774.4
Research & Development	73.9	86.1	98.0	108.4	137.5	155.0	188.1	201.5	248.0	361.1
Operating Income	$ 260.1	$ 253.0	$ 309.3	$ 392.9	$ 432.0	$ 480.2	$ 506.1	$ 387.3	$ 544.0	$ 964.5
Interest Expense	$ 27.4	$ 34.9	$ 67.4	$ 56.8	$ 63.5	$ 86.4	$ 95.5	$ 183.5	$ 162.1	$ 238.0
Foreign Exchange Loss	0.0	0.0	17.2	0.0	13.6	53.9	0.0	0.0	0.0	0.0
Miscellaneous Expense	4.8	4.8	5.2	4.4	3.2	4.3	3.8	5.0	6.5	10.0
Total Expense	$1,775.1	$2,281.8	$2,735.7	$2,802.0	$3,252.4	$3,819.4	$4,526.6	$5,105.2	$5,887.9	$8,523.4
Pretax Income	$ 275.2	$ 261.1	$ 259.0	$ 381.3	$ 407.9	$ 410.0	$ 489.0	$ 278.8	$ 463.1	$ 845.8
Income Taxes	121.1	112.3	103.7	165.4	181.9	184.5	214.9	117.6	208.4	380.6
Net Income	$ 154.1	$ 148.8	$ 155.3	$ 215.9	$ 226.0	$ 225.5	$ 274.1	$ 161.2	$ 254.7	$ 465.2
Equity Income	$ 14.4	$ 15.5	$ 23.8	$ 25.7	$ 29.6	$ 39.3	$ 36.5	$ 45.6	$ 45.0	$ 79.0
Net Income	$ 168.5	$ 164.3	$ 179.1	$ 241.6	$ 255.6	$ 264.8	$ 310.6	$ 206.8	$ 299.7	$ 544.2
Net Per Share—Primary	$ 2.88	$ 2.78	$ 3.01	$ 4.04	$ 4.24	$ 4.38	$ 5.12	$ 3.34	$ 4.72	$ 8.50
Net Per Share—Fully Diluted	$ 2.88	$ 2.78	$ 2.98	$ 3.89	$ 4.07	$ 4.20	$ 4.90	$ 3.27	$ 4.72	$ 8.50

Source: Corporate reports and Bernstein estimates.

CHAPTER 7

The Income Statement: Cost of Goods Sold and Related Cost Items

Many income statements offered by firms today separate the results achieved through regular operations from those produced by nonoperating and/or extraordinary activities of the company. Moreover, expenses often are classified by functions, e.g., the cost to produce and sell goods, selling expenses, administrative expenses, and other expenses. This facilitates year-by-year comparisons of key expense categories and forecasting efforts.

We will concentrate on items affecting the cost of goods sold in this chapter, ending with a discussion of inflation adjusted accounting data. The analysis of other expense items will be covered in Chapter 8.

Cost of Goods Sold

At the moment that net income is increased by revenues derived from the sale of a product, it is also decreased by the costs associated with producing that product. If one thinks of a cashier in a supermarket, it is not difficult to understand that it would not be feasible to record the cost at the same time as sales value is running up for every item sold.

Accountants determine the total cost of goods sold for a period by a process of deduction. The value of inventory on hand at the beginning of the period is added to that acquired during the period to determine the total cost for all goods available for sale. Those units still on hand at the end of the period obviously were not sold. Accordingly, the value of goods on hand at the end of the period is determined by means of a physical inventory and subtracted from the costs of goods available for sale to determine the cost of goods sold figure used in the income statement.

Inventory Valuation and Price Level Changes

Inventory, in accordance with accounting standards should be valued "at cost or market, whichever is lower." Application of this rule, however, requires the determination of cost.

If prices were constant, the determination of cost of goods sold would be simple. Prices to acquire units of inventory do change, however, and one must determine which particular units were sold to match costs and revenues. To illustrate the problem, assume the data shown below.

	Number of Units	Cost Per Unit	Total Cost
Beginning inventory	140	$12	$1,680
Purchase, February 26	70	18	1,260
Purchase, June 13	70	22	1,540
Purchase, September 28	70	28	1,960
Purchase, December 12	70	35	2,450
Available for Sale	420		$8,890
Units Sold	220		
Units in Ending Inventory	200		

How are the units sold and those in ending inventory valued? The two most widely used methods for assigning these costs are First-in-First-Out (F.I.F.O.) and Last-in-First-Out (L.I.F.O.).

F.I.F.O. Method.   The F.I.F.O. method is based on the assumption that the first merchandise acquired is the first merchandise sold. The ending inventory, therefore, consists of the most recently acquired goods. This method may be adopted by any business, regardless of whether or not the actual physical flow of inventory corresponds to the assumption of selling the earliest acquired goods first. The key to calculating the cost of goods sold is determination of the value of the ending inventory of 200 units that was determined by physical count. The value of the ending inventory is $5,730. Calculated as follows:

70 units purchased December 12	$2,450
70 units purchased September 28	1,960
60 units purchased June 13 (@ $22/unit)	1,320
200 units	$5,730

Cost of goods sold is $3,160 calculated as follows:

Beginning Inventory	$1,680
Plus Purchases	7,210
Cost of Goods Available for Sale	$8,890
Less Ending Inventory	$5,730
Cost of Goods Sold	$3,160

L.I.F.O. Method   Under this method, the most recently acquired goods are assumed to be sold first, and the ending inventory consists of "old" goods acquired through the earliest purchases. Such a flow assumption seems to match the actual flows in the oil industry, for example, since oil enters the storage tanks at the top and this newest oil is drawn first as oil is taken from the tank.

For purposes of measuring income the flow of costs may be more significant than the actual flow of goods. L.IF.O. seems realistic in this context since costs stated in more current dollars are matched against revenues stated in relatively current dollars.

The value of the ending inventory under the L.IF.O. method is $2,760 calculated as follows:

140 units, beginning Inventory	$1,680
60 units, February 26 Purchase	1,080
200 units	$2,760

Cost of Goods Sold is $6,130 calculated as follows:

Beginning Inventory	$1,680
Plus Purchases	7,210
Cost of Goods Available for Sale	$8,890
Less Ending Inventory	2,760
Cost of Goods Sold	$6,130

Comparison of Costing Methods.   Assuming that net sales for the period were $13,200, the gross profit as reported under each of the above methods is shown below:

	F.I.F.O.	L.I.F.O.
Net Sales	$13,200	$13,200
Less Costs of Goods Sold	3,160	6,130
Gross Profit	$10,040	$ 7,070

It is apparent that during a period of rising prices the use of L.IF.O. will result in lower reported profits and, therefore, the firm will incur a lower income tax liability than under F.IF.O. If prices were to fall, than the firm using F.IF.O. would report the lower profits and higher cost of goods sold. Current tax laws practically allow any business firm to adopt L.IF.O., regardless of the actual flow of goods through the firm, and many firms have adopted the method since the 1950s. A firm that uses L.IF.O. for financial reporting purposes also must use that system for tax purposes.

Profits appear to be more volatile when F.IF.O. rather than L.IF.O. costing is used to determine ending inventory values. This occurs because F.IF.O. accounting tends to cause inventory profits to be added to regular operating profits when prices are rising since current cost is not matched with current revenue. The opposite will occur during a recession, thus increasing volatility. Where selling prices are less flexible than new material prices, however, profits may not be more volatile under F.IF.O. than under L.IF.O.

It is agreed that profits are overstated in real terms by F.IF.O. (or average cost) as opposed to using the L.IF.O. system during an inflationary period. This is because "old" inventory costs that do not reflect current replacement costs are matched against revenues stated in current dollars that fully reflect current selling prices. It is important to understand that a significant portion of reported net income of companies using the F.IF.O. method may be inventory profits that will melt away as inventory must be replaced in the future.

Finally, L.IF.O. could show illusory profits if a firm does not replenish inventory in a given year and digs into the "old" cost L.IF.O. reserve to meet sales at current prices. The firm will have to restock eventually at the higher current replacement cost, causing a sharp decline in future profits. This can occur, for example, when a firm faces an extended strike by employees and attempts to continue sales from existing inventory.

Expenditures Included in Inventory

Management has a great deal of flexibility in determining what expenses will be capitalized in the inventory accounts and which expenses will be written off directly as cost of the period. For example, if the personnel department was housed in the building used for administrative staff, the expenses associated with its operation are likely to be written off directly as part of administrative expense. If the personnel department staff were housed in an operating plant, at least part of the expenses of its operation are likely to be capitalized in the inventory account. A liberal interpretation of the question of capitalizing versus expensing such costs could improve reported income for a given period. Moreover, different decisions as to whether to capitalize in the inventory account or directly expense could distort comparability of reported income data between companies or through time.

Decreasing Cost Industries

In a decreasing cost industry, such as semiconductors and possibly computers, L.I.F.O. will report higher profits during a period of rising prices, rather than F.I.F.O. Since the reporting of lower profits saves taxes, it is not surprising to note that in 1984 only 38 percent of firms in those industry groups used the L.I.F.O. method.

Adjusting Non-Comparable Inventory Data

Where inventories are not a significant asset, the analyst need not be overly concerned about differences in inventory costing systems through time for a company or when comparing different companies. In many cases, however, misleading conclusions may be drawn if the analyst is not careful to adjust when different systems are used.

The footnotes to the financial statements, unfortunately, rarely facilitate an accurate adjustment, unless a company has just switched from one method to the other. Where a company has changed inventory costing methods, they must report the dollar and cents impact on inventory, cost of goods sold, taxes and profits in the financial report of that year. This data need not be repeated, however, in future annual reports. When contrasting two companies using different inventory costing methods, the analyst can only subjectively adjust the data of one to the system used by the other company. Sometimes analysts assume that the gross profit margin percentages would have been the same if the companies had used the same inventory costing procedures, to facilitate an adjustment. This is not a useful technique, however, since this will wash out differing efficiencies between companies that the analyst is looking for.

FASB Statement No. 33[49] requires that large corporations disclose what it would cost to replace their inventories at year-end and what their cost of goods sold would be if computed using current replacement cost at the date of sale. This

---

[49] Financial Accounting Standards Board Statement No. 33, "Financial Reporting and Changing Prices" (Stamford, CT, 1979).

data can help the analyst better frame reasonable adjustments where two companies use different inventory costing systems.

For comparative purposes, either the L.IF.O. or F.IF.O. firm could be adjusted to the system used by the other firm. We have indicated above our preference for L.IF.O. reporting on the grounds that this system reports more meaningful profit data. Therefore, it would seem best to adjust the firm using F.IF.O. to the L.IF.O. approach. Unfortunately, one is likely to find that available information facilitates adjustment of the L.IF.O. company to a F.IF.O. basis, using current replacement cost information.

Data for the Maytag Company in Table 7–1, as prepared by Cottle, Murray and Block, illustrate the adjustment process, based on recognizing that L.IF.O. inventory plus L.IF.O. reserve equals F.IF.O. inventory.

Balance Sheet Effects

Finally, it is important to recognize that the choice of an inventory costing system also affects the balance sheet. A period of sustained inflation tends to cause assets to be valued in the balance sheet at amounts substantially below their current replacement cost, especially when the L.IF.O. costing system is used. This occurs because inventory is carried at "old" costs to acquire, which deviate more and more from current replacement cost as the inflation continues. Accordingly, a company using L.IF.O. may have a low current ratio relative to a company using F.IF.O. when the liquidity of the two companies is the same.

Changes in Inventory Accounts

It can be interesting to note how each of the three basic inventory accounts change over time. For example. assume one noted that Raw Materials Inventory was declining while Finished Goods Inventory was increasing. This could be favorable, if it meant that the firm was increasing the holdings of finished goods to meet rising demand and decreasing the supply of raw materials to reflect new efficiencies in the inventory handling and production process. It could suggest increasing difficulty in selling finished goods and adjustment of the raw materials inventory position to bring it in line with falling demand, which would be an unfavorable scenario.

Table 7–1   Illustrative Adjustment of Selected Data from the 1985 Annual Report of Maytag Company to a F.I.F.O. Approach (Millions of Dollars)

	1985	1984
1. L.I.F.O. reserve	37.3	39.1
2. Inventories (L.I.F.O.)	78.5	77.7
3. Total = F.I.F.O. Inventories	115.8	116.8
4. Cost of Sales	432.9	421.5
5. Stockholders' Equity (L.I.F.O.)	256.6	228.9
6. Stockholders' Equity (F.I.F.O.)	276.7	250.0
7. Net Income (L.I.F.O.)	71.8	63.1
8. Net Income (F.I.F.O.)	70.8	

F.I.F.O. Stockholders' Equity = [(1 - tax rate) x (L.I.F.O. reserve)] + L.I.F.O. Stockholders' Equity. The tax rate was 46% at the time of this example.

F.I.F.O. net income = [(1985 LIFO reserve - 1984 L.I.F.O. reserve) x (1 – tax rate)] + 1985 L.I.F.O. net income.

Source: S. Cottle, R. Murray and F. Black, *Graham and Dodd's Security Analysis*, 5th Edition, (New York, McGraw-Hill Inc., 1988) pp. 206–207.

Depreciation

Depreciation of production facilities would be a cost entering into the determination of cost of goods sold, but depreciation of sales office space properly would be shown as a selling expense. Depreciation may, therefore, affect the determination of several major subdivisions of the income statement.

Depreciation accounting is a system of accounting which aims to distribute the cost...of tangible capital assets, less salvage (if any) over the estimated useful life of the unit (which may be a group of assets) in a systematic and rational manner. It is a process of allocation (of cost), not of valuation. Depreciation for the year is the portion of the total charge under such a system that is allocated to the year. Although the allocation may properly take into account occurrences during the year, it is not intended to be a measurement of the effect of all such occurrences.[50]

Because the accounting charge for depreciation does not represent a corresponding outlay of cash, some investors and analysts have implied that deprecia-

---

50 "Review and Resume," *Accounting Terminology Bulletin* No. 1 (New York: American Institute of Certified Public Accountants, 1953), p. 25.

tion is not a real expense by using the terms "cash earnings per share" or "cash flow earnings per share" and have even substituted these terms for "net earnings per share." Strong criticism of this position by the AICPA, the NYSE, and the Financial Analysts Federation sharply has reduced the use of these terms in brokerage houses and annual corporate reports.

Since fixed assets, particularly plant and equipment, represent such a substantial outlay, it would be impractical to write them off entirely as an expense charged against the income of the year in which they are purchased, especially since benefits from their use will be received over an extended period. Furthermore, as soon as it is purchased, a fixed asset begins to depreciate. To ignore this fact would be to experience a gradual loss of capital without any reflection on the books of account. Accountants consider the original cost of a fixed asset to be a prepaid expense that must be amortized during the service life of the asset by regular periodic charges to the depreciation expense account. After deduction of the annual charge, the remaining amount is the unamortized cost; but in no way, except by coincidence, does this amount represent the economic value of the asset at that time.

Basis for Depreciation–Replacement Value vs. Original Cost

Inflation, which has long been a problem, has led many to advocate a policy of substituting replacement cost for original cost as the basis for determining depreciation charges in the income statement. Corporate management especially has been vocal in this regard. The basic function of depreciation charges is to amortize the cost of a capital asset over its useful life. Management is concerned with a second function: providing the funds needed for replacement of assets after they have worn out or become obsolete technologically. Depreciation charges do not provide a company with cash. However, they are tax deductible and they do protect cash generated by sales operations from the burden of taxes.

When replacement costs have risen far above original cost, prudent business management must recognize this capital erosion and set aside the additional funds necessary to continue a business in operation. Such funds must be provided from retained earnings, because the income tax laws do not recognize the inflation situation. Income taxes must be paid on the capital lost through inflation, which makes the problem of maintaining a company's capital doubly difficult.

Other countries (e.g., the Netherlands, Chile, and Brazil) with more rapid inflation than the United States, have changed their tax laws in various ways, to prevent the gradual liquidation of capital investment through payment of income taxes on capital eroded by inflation; asset values are raised yearly and depreciated on the new values.

A change to replacement cost would change fundamental concepts of accounting, since it would represent a breaking away from the basic idea that balance sheet and expense accounts are based on monetary cost and not on economic values. The cost basis of measurement has the advantages of: (1) uniformity of interpretation of the values to be entered in the balance sheet and the charges to be entered in the income account, and (2) objectivity. Accountants question whether a system based on an attempt to measure replacement values, with its loss of objectivity, has additional advantages that more than offset the advantages of the cost basis. Other questions are raised, such as whether the assets are replaced with like assets or superior ones that justify part of the higher cost, whether the assets will in fact be replaced as technology changes, and whether current or future customers should pay for the replaced equipment.[51]

In June 1969 the AICPA issued APB Statement No. 3, "Financial Statement Restated for General Price Level Changes." This statement, which still reflects the AICPA thinking at this writing, is quoted in part as follows:

> The Board believes that general price-level financial statements or perti-
> nent information extracted from them present useful information not available
> from basic historical-dollar financial statements. General price-level informa-
> tion may be presented in addition to the basic historical statement but should
> not be presented as the basic statements.[52]

This view was reiterated by the AICPA in its "Fundamental Statement" published in October 1970.

Magnitude of Depreciation

Two major reasons why investors and analysts need to devote so much attention to depreciation are: (1) the magnitude of depreciation, and (2) the leeway that management can exercise in reporting depreciation—that is, the lack of uniformity in reporting depreciation in published reports. The magnitude of depreciation is evident when it is related to corporate profits as is done in Table 7–2. This table shows that depreciation in absolute terms has risen from $4.7 billion annually in

---

51 See *Accounting Research Bulletin* No. 43, published in 1953 for both the majority view and the dissenting view of a special committee appointed by the AICPA.

52 APB Statement No. 3, "Financial Statement Restated for General Price Level Changes," *Journal of Accountancy* (September 1969), pp. 62–68.

Table 7-2 Absolute Importance of Depreciation and Relative Importance of Cash Flow[a] of All U.S. Corporations (Billions of Dollars), 1946–1986

Year	(1) Capital Consumption Allowances (Depreciation Only)	(2) Capital Consumption Adjustment	(3) Capital[b] Consumption Allowances Including Capital Consumption Adjustment	(4) Profits Before Taxes	(5) Profits Tax (Income Tax Liability)	(6) Profits After Taxes	(7) Total Cash Flow I Capital Consumption (Depreciation Only) Plus Net Profits After Taxes (Col 1 + 6)	(8) Undistributed Profits (Profits After Dividends)	(9) Net Cash Flow II Capital Consumption Allowances (Depreciation Only) Plus Undistributed Profits (Col 1 + 8)	(10) Capital Consumption Allowances (Depreciation Only) As % of Cash Flow II (Col 1/9)
1946	4.7	2.7	7.4	24.6	9.1	15.5	20.2	9.9	14.6	32.2
1947	5.8	3.4	9.2	31.5	11.3	20.2	26.0	13.9	19.7	29.4
1948	7.0	3.9	10.9	35.2	12.4	22.8	29.7	15.7	22.7	30.8
1949	8.0	3.8	11.8	28.9	10.2	18.7	26.7	11.5	19.5	41.0
1950	8.8	4.0	12.8	42.6	17.9	24.7	33.5	15.9	24.7	35.6
1951	10.3	4.6	14.9	43.9	22.6	21.3	31.6	12.8	23.1	44.6
1952	11.5	4.5	16.0	38.9	19.4	19.5	31.0	10.7	22.2	51.8
1953	13.2	4.1	17.3	40.5	20.3	20.2	33.4	11.5	24.7	53.4
1954	15.0	3.2	18.2	38.1	17.6	20.5	35.5	11.4	26.4	56.8
1955	17.4	2.1	19.5	48.4	22.0	26.4	43.8	16.1	33.5	51.9
1956	18.9	3.0	21.9	48.6	22.0	26.6	45.5	15.5	34.4	54.9
1957	20.9	3.3	24.2	46.9	21.4	25.5	46.4	14.0	34.9	59.9
1958	22.0	3.4	25.4	41.1	19.0	22.1	44.1	10.8	32.8	67.1
1959	23.6	2.9	26.5	51.6	23.6	28.0	51.6	15.8	39.4	59.9
1960	25.2	2.3	27.5	48.5	22.7	25.8	51.0	13.0	38.2	66.0
1961	26.6	1.8	28.4	48.6	22.8	25.8	52.4	12.5	39.1	68.0

Table 7-2 (continued)

Year										
1962	30.5	-1.2	29.3	53.6	24.0	29.6	60.1	15.2	45.7	66.7
1963	32.5	-2.1	30.4	57.7	26.2	31.5	64.0	16.0	48.5	67.0
1964	34.5	-2.8	31.7	64.7	28.0	36.7	71.2	19.4	53.9	64.0
1965	37.5	-3.8	33.7	75.2	30.9	44.3	81.8	25.2	62.7	59.8
1966	40.6	-3.9	36.7	80.7	33.7	47.0	87.7	27.6	68.2	59.5
1967	44.1	-3.7	40.4	77.3	32.5	44.8	89.0	24.7	68.8	64.1
1968	48.1	-3.7	44.4	85.6	39.3	46.3	94.3	24.2	72.3	66.5
1969	52.9	-3.5	49.4	83.5	39.7	43.8	96.7	21.2	74.1	71.4
1970	56.6	-1.5	55.1	71.5	34.5	37.0	93.6	14.1	70.7	80.1
1971	60.9	-0.3	60.6	82.0	37.7	44.3	105.2	21.3	82.2	74.1
1972	67.9	-2.5	65.4	96.2	41.4	54.8	122.5	30.0	97.9	69.4
1973	73.8	-1.9	71.9	115.8	48.7	67.1	140.9	39.3	113.1	65.3
1974	81.7	2.9	84.6	126.9	52.4	74.5	156.2	43.6	125.3	65.2
1975	88.7	12.2	100.9	123.5	50.2	73.3	162.1	41.0	129.7	68.4
1976	97.1	14.7	111.8	156.9	64.7	92.2	189.2	56.4	153.5	63.3
1977	104.7	7.2	111.9	171.7	69.2	102.5	207.2	61.4	166.1	63.0
1978	136.4	13.5	149.9	203.6	83.0	120.6	257.0	86.3	222.7	61.2
1979	155.4	15.9	171.3	225.0	87.6	137.4	292.8	102.5	257.9	60.3
1980	175.4	17.2	192.6	214.4	82.3	132.0	307.4	94.6	270.0	65.0
1981	206.2	16.8	223.0	209.3	81.2	128.1	334.3	77.3	283.5	72.7
1982	222.0	1.1	223.1	152.4	59.2	93.2	315.2	38.8	260.8	85.1
1983	231.2	33.2	264.4	178.4	75.8	102.6	333.8	39.6	270.8	85.4
1984	256.6	41.0	297.6	205.4	93.6	111.8	368.4	44.7	301.3	85.2
1985	268.2	58.1	326.3	191.3	91.8	99.5	367.7	30.2	298.4	89.9
1986	280.3	56.6	336.9	202.0	103.5	98.5	378.8	22.3	302.6	92.6

[a]In 1976 the Bureau of Economic Analysis of the U.S. Department of Commerce completed a benchmark revision of the National Income and Product accounts. The depreciation measure included in the NIPAs of the revision is based on current-cost valuation and the straightline depreciation formula. The new measure of depreciation will not be appropriate for all uses. For example, in studies of the effects of tax policies, the old measure probably would be required. Accordingly, in addition to the new series, the NIPAs will continue to show tax return-based depreciation for corporations and non-farm sole proprietorships and partnerships. Also, several variants based on consistent accounting will be provided regularly in the Survey of Current Business so that users can judge the effects of depreciation formulas, service lives, and valuations and, if they desire, substitute an alternative for the NIPA measure.

[b]The adjustment of the previous estimates of capital consumption allowances to the new basis and the associated changes in the profit-type incomes, which are net of capital consumption allowances, is accomplished by a new entry labeled capital consumption adjustment. This entry equals the previous measure of capital consumption (based on tax return information) less the new measure (based on consistent accounting and valued in current prices).

Source: U.S. Department of Commerce, various issues of Survey of Current Business.

1946 to $280.3 billion for 1986. Furthermore, in relative terms, depreciation as a percentage of Cash Flow I (depreciation plus net profits) ranged between 46 percent and 58 percent between 1960 and 1986, and depreciation as a percentage of Cash Flow II (depreciation plus undistributed profits after dividends) ranged between 59 percent and 93 percent in the same period. The major uses of cash flow are for:

1. Corporate dividends and debt amortization, including sinking fund payments;
2. Required increases in working capital; and
3. Capital budget programs, repurchase of company securities, etc.

In broad terms, cash flow represents the basic protection offered investors for both dividends and debt service requirements, including sinking funds and amortization.

Methods of Reporting Depreciation

Although corporate laws and accounting principles require that corporations make some charge for depreciation, corporate management is permitted numerous alternatives in the manner in which it amortizes the cost of fixed assets over their useful life on its books and in published reports.

The straight-line method provides for the regular distribution of the original cost of fixed assets, less their estimated salvage value, over their estimated service lives. In addition to the straight-line method of depreciation, the Internal Revenue Code permitted two other depreciation methods: the declining-balance method and the sum-of-the-years-digits method in a 1954 tax revision.

The declining-balance method permits a taxpayer to use a rate of depreciation, not exceeding twice the straight-line rate, on the original cost (unadjusted for salvage value) less accumulated depreciation. The Code permits a taxpayer to change at any time from the declining-balance method to the straight-line method since charging all original cost as depreciation under the declining-balance method is impossible arithmetically. The straight-line rate would be based on a realistic estimate of the remaining life of the property at the time of the switch.

The sum-of-the-years-digits method is somewhat more complicated. The annual depreciation deduction is calculated by applying a changing fraction to the original cost of the property less the estimated salvage value. The numerator of the fraction is the number of useful years of life remaining for the property, what it will be in the first year, in the second year, etc. The denominator is the factorial sum of the estimated useful life of the property and may be calculated by using Equation (7.1) below:

$$D = N \frac{(N + 1)}{2}$$ (7.1)

where D = the denominator of the fraction used to calculate the annual depreciation charge

N = the number of years of useful life of the asset for a fixed asset with an estimated life of five years the fractions used would be 5/15, 4/15, 2/15, and 1/15

The annual depreciation charges under the three depreciation methods are contrasted in Table 7–3. Obviously, the reported earnings for a given year would be different if companies did not use the same depreciation method, and therefore would not be comparable unless adjustments were made.

Accelerated Cost Recovery System (ACRS)

Prior to 1981 taxpayers could compute depreciation using either: (1) the facts and circumstances method, or (2) the Class Life System. These methods gave taxpayers great flexibility in calculating depreciation, and led to possible abuse by tax authorities.

The Economic Recovery Tax Act of 1981 substantially revised the method of computing depreciation by introducing the ACRS, which is still used today.

Table 7–3   Annual Depreciation Charge for a Fixed Asset Costing $1,000 with No Expected Salvage Value and an Estimated Useful Life of Five Years

Year	Straight-Line Method	Declining-Balance Method	Sum-of-the-Years Digits Method
1	$200	$400	$333.33
2	200	240	266.67
3	200	144	200.00
4	200	108*	133.33
5	200	108*	66.67

*It is assumed that the taxpayer switched to straight-line depreciation in the fourth year.

Taxpayers have virtually no choice under this system in selecting a useful life for depreciation property and salvage value is ignored. The Tax Reform Act of 1986 provided less liberal write-offs, especially of real estate, but retained the ACRS approach. The shorter depreciable lives mandated by ACRS do introduce another factor that can cause taxable income to differ from reported accounting income

Table 7–4   Accerated Cost Recovery System (ACRS)

ACRS Class and Method	ADR Midpoint	Special Rules
3-year, 200% declining balance	4 years or less	Includes some race horses. Excludes cars and light trucks.
5-year, 200% declining balance	More than 4 years to less than 10	Includes cars and light trucks, semiconductor manufacturing equipment, qualified technological equipment, computer-based central-office switching equipment, some renewable and biomass power facilities and research and development property.
7-year, 200% declining balance	10 years to less than 16	Includes single-purpose agricultural and horticultural structures and railroad track. Includes property with no ADR midpoint.
10-year, 200% declining balance	16 years to less than 20	None.
15-year, 150% declining balance	20 years to less than 25	Includes sewage treatment plants, telephone distribution plants and comparable equipment for two-way voice and data communication.
20-year, 150% declining balance	25 years or more	Excludes real property with ADR midpoint of 27.5 years or more. Includes municipal sewers.
27.5-year, straight-line	N/A	Residential rental property.
31.5-year, straight-line	N/A	Nonresidential real property.

Source: *Tax Reform 1986*, Arthur Anderson & Company, 1987, p.112.

since different depreciating methods may be used for purposes of preparing financial statements and tax returns.

The new system relies on pre-1981 Asset Depreciation Range (ADR) guidelines. Assets are assigned to one of six categories, or to one of two classes of real property as shown in Table 7–4.

Flow-Through Method and Normalizing Method of Reporting Depreciation

Since 1954 most corporations have reported publicly on a straight-line basis to stockholders, while taking advantage of the rapid amortization permitted under the Code for tax purposes. Until fiscal 1968, income statements in annual reports of numerous corporations reported depreciation by the flow-through method, which annually flows through the full tax savings to net income. However, other corporations reported depreciation by the normalizing method, making a charge in the income account equivalent to the tax savings and thus washing out the benefits of the tax savings as far as final net income in their published income statements. In statements the charge for deferred taxes usually is included in the total item entitled "Federal Income Taxes."

In December 1967 the AICPA stated categorically that the deferred method of tax allocation should be followed.[53] An exception to insistence on the deferred method would be allowed for regulated companies like public utilities where particular regulatory authorities may require the use of flow-through accounting.

Those who favor normalizing state that the use of rapid amortization for tax purposes will result in lower taxes being paid in the earlier years of the life of the assets than under the straight-line method because of higher depreciation charges, but that in later years depreciation will be less than straight-line rates; taxes will therefore be higher than in the earlier years. Total taxes for the entire life of the assets should be the same under either straight-line for tax purposes or rapid amortization for tax purposes. Therefore, tax savings are temporary and deferred until later years of lower depreciation charges. Those holding this viewpoint, including the AICPA and the SEC, therefore wish to eliminate any effect of tax savings on net income in the earlier years of the asset's life.

Those who have advocated the flow-through method, including numerous state public utility commissions (not the SEC), have argued that as long as a

---

53 "Accounting for Income Taxes," Opinions of the Accounting Principles Board No. 11 (New York: American Institute of Certified Public Accountants, 1967).

company is regularly expanding and purchasing fixed assets, the new assets will have the advantage of rapid amortization, therefore offsetting the declining depreciation on older assets. The lower taxes paid in the earlier years, therefore, are not deferred to later years, but payment will be deferred indefinitely. Therefore, there will be a constantly increasing "deferred taxes" account on the balance sheet.

Although depreciation is a real expense, it does not involve an outlay of cash in the period charged; therefore, the sales revenues allocated to the depreciation charges do represent a tax-protected source of funds to the business enterprise. While the total depreciation charged over the life of the asset is not affected by the method used, the greater amounts of revenues protected in early years by the declining-balance method and sum-of-the-years-digits method have a higher present value than funds that might be protected in later years. Rapid amortization is similar to an interest-free loan from the Treasury Department. Generally firms do not have access to other sources of funds with no greater risk or cost than the funds provided by depreciation. Therefore, acquiring an increased amount of funds through depreciation tends to lower the cost of capital to the firm.

Adequacy of Depreciation Charges

Depreciation charges often are substantial, and the estimates made have a material effect on the reported profits or loss of a given year. Profits are overstated when depreciation charges understate the actual using up of assets during the productive process. Depreciation charges can be understated by increasing the estimated life of the asset beyond that over which the asset is useful economically, or overstating salvage value. For example, several American airlines extended the depreciable life of their aircraft between 1968 and 1970, thereby reducing annual depreciation expense and increasing reported earnings at a time when airline earnings generally were depressed.

Accountants cannot know in advance how long an asset will last or what its salvage value will be. The depreciation expense charged in the income statement is a rough estimate of cost and does not allow for the effects of inflation. Determining the adequacy of depreciation charges is difficult. The following tests are suggested:

1. The consistency of the rate of depreciation charged over time can be explored by studying depreciation as a percentage of gross plant assets and sales over an extended period of time.

2. Depreciation rates of a given company should be compared to those utilized by similar companies.

A study by Price Waterhouse found that current cost depreciation exceeded historical cost depreciation by 37 percent in 1980 and averaged 31 percent from 1980 to 1983.[54] This suggests that income, based on historical accounting, has been overstated, as there was inadequate provision for replacement of fixed assets. Analysts should keep this in mind when reviewing the adequacy of depreciation charges and comparing income data.

Depletion

The depletion allowance, for tax purposes, represents recognition of the fact that operations of companies with wasting assets result in a decrease in the value of their natural resources as these are used up. Depletion is the accounting term applied to the amortization of the cost of exhaustible natural resources such as minerals, metals, and standing timber.

Wasting Asset Companies

The majority of wasting asset companies, such as mining companies, depreciate their fixed assets through cost depreciation charges to a depreciation expense account. However, for their wasting assets they use percentage depletion accounting. Also, these wasting asset companies have large expenditure and development costs. A comparative cash flow analysis, because of heavy depletion charges and encompassing special tax treatment for these development costs, is as essential as

---

54 Price Waterhouse & Co., *Inflation Accounting*, New York, 1981.

net income analysis for wasting asset companies and has been used for such companies for many years.[55]

Percentage Depletion Method

This method[56] differs from normal depreciation methods, and therefore from the cost amortization method, in that allowable depletion charges are based on gross income instead of on the cost of reserves. Percentage depletion is used only for income tax purposes, not for financial statements made available by the company to the public. Percentage depletion is calculated by multiplying the allowable percentage for the particular mineral in question by the gross income from the property, but it is limited to 50 percent of the taxable or net income from the property. The gross income under Treasury regulations is not the same as the gross income of the taxpayer as defined in other sections of the Internal Revenue Code. Rather, according to the Treasury, it must be calculated separately. It is the amount for which the mineral is sold if the sale takes place in the vicinity of the property in the form in which the mineral is sold by basic producers; or it is the calculated value at the basic state of production in case it is sold later at a more advanced state, for example, after processing.

Exploration and Related Costs

Under the Internal Revenue Code, the taxpayer has the choice of accounting for exploration costs not in excess of $400,000 by either (1) charging them off currently as incurred, or (2) considering them as a deferred charge to be deducted proportionately as the extracted minerals that result from the exploration are sold.

---

55 On the companies' own books and for public reporting purposes on charges for depletion, they deduct that percentage of the cost of the natural resource property which the mineral (or the resource) extracted bears to the total resource content. This is known as the "units-of-production" method. This method is also applied to calculate the depreciation on equipment, such as cars, where their service life is governed by the same factors.

56 Sec. 613. Percentage Depletion—Internal Revenue Code General Rule—In the case of mines, wells, and other natural deposits listed in subsection (b) the allowance for depletion under Section 611 shall be the percentage, specified in subsection (b), of the gross income from the property, excluding from such gross income an amount equal to any rents or royalties paid or incurred by the taxpayer in respect of the property. Such allowances shall not exceed 50 percent of the taxpayer's taxable income from the property computed without allowance for depletion. In no case shall the allowance for depletion under Section 611 be less than if computed without reference to this section (i.e., not less than the cost method).

All such expenditures may be capitalized. Any excess exploration costs must be capitalized. Such deductions are in addition to depletion allowances, but they must be considered when the taxpayer is calculating net income to determine the 50 percent limitation for percentage depletion.

Exploration and Development Costs—Gas and Oil

Partly due to public resentment against the big oil companies, effective January 1, 1975, the percentage depletion allowance for gas and oil wells (with certain exceptions) was repealed. The repeal affected all tax years after 1974. The 1975 Energy Policy and Conservation Act directed the Securities and Exchange Commission to come up with oil and gas industry accounting standards by December 22, 1977. The Financial Accounting Standards Board held a four-day hearing in New York on March 30, 31, April 1 and 4, 1977, on financial accounting for the extractive industries. There was almost even division between those who wanted the full-cost method and those who wished the successful-efforts method. On July 19, 1977, the FASB proposed (FASB No. 19) that the successful-efforts method be used "for financial statements for fiscal years beginning after June 15, 1978...(and the standards) to be applied retroactively through the restatement of financial reports for prior periods.[57]

Smaller oil and gas firms objected strongly to FASB No. 19, and the Department of Energy suggested that companies that had been using the full-cost method could reduce their exploration activities because of the unfavorable earnings impact associated with successful-efforts accounting. The SEC then issued three Accounting Series Releases, adopting both a form of the successful-efforts approach and a full-costing approach, and suggesting a yet-to-be-developed method (reserve recognition accounting).[58]

---

57 Peter B. Roche, "Successful-Efforts Method for Reporting Oil and Gas Search Costs Backed by Panel," *The Wall Street Journal*, July 20, 1977, p. 8.

58 See "Adoption of Requirements for Financial Accounting and Reporting Practices for Oil and Gas Producing Activities," *Accounting Series Release No. 253* (Washington, D.C.: SEC, August, 1978); "Requirements for Financial Accounting and Reporting Practices for Oil and Gas Producing Activities," *Accounting Series Release No. 257* (Washington, D.C.: SEC, 1978); and "Oil and Gas Producers Full Cost Accounting Practices," *Accounting Series Release No. 258* (Washington, D.C.: SEC, 1978).

Depletion and Depreciation Reserves Distributed to Stockholders

Unfortunately, the income tax regulations confuse the status of depreciation and depletion reserves that are accumulated. These regulations state that "a distribution made from (charged to) a depletion or depreciation reserve based on the cost or other basis of the property, instead of being charged to retained earnings, will not be considered as having been paid out of the earnings of the property." Therefore, such distributions to stockholders are not taxable as ordinary dividends. However, the regulations clearly state that such reserves are "not a part of surplus out of which ordinary dividends may be paid." Such distributions are considered to be liquidating dividends because they represent a return of capital and not a distribution of earnings. Numerous tax-exempt dividends result, and prior to 1972 this was the major reason for the tax-exempt status to the recipient of a portion of dividends paid by many public utility companies.

Amortization of Intangibles

In addition to the major noncash charges for depreciation and depletion in the income statement, the amortization of intangibles such as goodwill, patents, and trademarks represents noncash charges in the income account.

Intangible Assets

The following statements are pertinent to the classification and amortization of intangible assets:

Intangible assets are classified in APB Opinion No. 17, Par. 12 as follows:

(a) Those having a term of existence limited by law, regulation, or agreement, or by their nature (such as patents, copyrights, leases, licenses, franchises for a fixed term and goodwill as to which there is evidence of limited duration);

(b) Those having no such limited term of existence and as to which there is, at the time of acquisition, no indication of limited life (such as goodwill generally, going value, trade names, secret processes, subscription lists, perpetual franchises, and organization costs.[59]

---

59 "Inventory of Generally Accepted Accounting Principles for Business Enterprises," *Accounting Research Study No. 7* (New York: American Institute of Certified Public Accountants, 1965), p. 54.

When a corporation decides that a type (b) intangible may not continue to have value during the entire life of the enterprise, it may amortize the cost of such intangible by systematic charges against income despite the fact that there are no present indications of limited existence or loss of value which would indicate that it has become type (a) and despite the fact that expenditures are being made to maintain its value.[60]

The problem of determining the time over which the values recognized for intangibles are consumed is a difficult one, and differing judgments can lead to noncomparability of reported income data by different companies.

Goodwill. Goodwill, and the accounting for goodwill has become important to analysts with the tremendous merger movement that has occurred since World War II. The costs of acquisitions often have been well in excess of the book value of the assets acquired, and a balancing item of goodwill has been added in the balance sheet. The AICPA requires that the item of goodwill be amortized annually as a charge against income over a period of not more than forty years. Since firms may write-off choosing any time span within the forty-year period, profit comparability can be distorted.

Capitalizing Versus Expensing

Expenditures for items where the benefits are expected to be received over a period longer than one year typically are capitalized (recorded in asset accounts) and the total recorded depreciated or amortized over the life of the asset. Where the benefit is expected to be received within a year, the cost of the item is directly charged to an expense account and fully reduces reported profit of that year. Many items are not easily labeled as short- or long-term, and some companies may capitalize a given item while other companies expense it. This can lead to non-comparability of reported profits.

Capitalized Items and Deferred Expense Items

There are numerous items that a corporation may expense in its tax return but capitalize in its published balance sheet. Many companies have followed a similar

---

60 Ibid., p. 155.

procedure in regard to advertising and promotional expenses. Analysts are cynical about capitalization and deferral of expense items.[61] cushioned its decline in profits by deferring to later years the costs of training pilots, mechanics, and ground crews to handle new equipment. Estimates were that such deferrals of expenses amounted to $9 to $10 million. The analyst must make adjustments, increasing reported expenses and decreasing reported profits for these and similar expense items that should be expense in the current year rather than deferred to later years.

Other items that are capitalized in annual reports, but expensed in tax returns, are intangible drilling costs of oil and natural gas producers and exploration and development expenses of mining companies. These all raise a problem for the analyst attempting to place different companies on a comparable base.

Another item that must be mentioned is interest charged to construction credit, which is capitalized by public utility companies in their published statements but is expensed in their income tax reports. This item will be examined in detail in Chapter 12.

One further item should be mentioned because it is often capitalized in published balance sheets while being expensed in tax reports to the IRS. This is the item of cost applicable to "start-up" and related expenses for new plants. The analyst may decide that if the company is regularly expanding, capitalizing such expenses in the company's published reports is justifiable. This item will almost always be expensed in the tax report. The reverse item is cost of plant closing, which should be reported separately before extraordinary items.

FASB Number 33: Inflation-Adjusted Data

Financial Accounting Standards Bulletin No. 33 required the disclosure in annual reports of two types of inflation-adjusted data by publicly held corporations with total assets of more than $1 billion, or whose inventories and property, plant, and equipment are valued at more than $125 million dollars. Each of the types of inflation-adjusted data is discussed briefly below. This data was required from 1979 through 1986 but became voluntary in 1987. Many companies still provide estimates.

Constant Dollar Data.   Constant dollar data is derived by restating historical accounting data in dollars of current purchasing power. The historical stated

---

61 When companies defer items that more properly should be currently expensed, the result is higher reported profit. For 1968 United Air Lines cushioned its decline in profits by deferring to later years the costs of training pilots, mechanics, and ground crews to handle new equipment. Estimates were that such deferrals of expenses amounted to $9 to $10 million. The analyst must make adjustments, increasing reported expenses and decreasing reported profits for these and similar expense items that should be expense in the current year rather than deferred to later years.

accounting value is multiplied by a fraction, the numerator of which is the current consumer price index for urban items and the denominator the index that prevailed at the date related to the amount being restated. For example, assume an asset was acquired for $15,000 on January 1, 1975. It would be restated in terms of December 31, 1980, dollars as follows:

$$\frac{1980 \text{ Index}}{1975 \text{ Index}} \times \$15,000 = \text{Cost of the asset in terms of 1980 dollars}$$

$$\frac{261.5}{161.2} \times \$15,000 = \$24,333$$

Raising the value of a depreciable asset affects the income statement as well as the balance sheet, since depreciation expense also would be increased, thereby lowering reported profits.

The actual preparation of constant dollar financial statements is more complex than illustrated above. To restate historical statements, one must distinguish between monetary and nonmonetary items. A monetary item is cash or any claim receivable or payable in a specified number of dollars. When the price level rises, each dollar purchases less in terms of real goods and services. A holder of monetary assets, therefore, loses in real terms since the number of dollars will remain fixed. Nonmonetary assets tend to behave in the opposite manner, since the number of dollars that can be obtained through sale of such assets tends to rise during inflation. It is preferable, therefore, to hold nonmonetary assets rather than monetary assets during a period of inflation. The value of nonmonetary assets is raised accordingly, as in the illustration above, to recognize the rising value; the purchasing power loss of monetary assets also must be recognized.

One who incurs monetary liabilities gains when prices rise, since the obligations are repaid with dollars of lesser purchasing power than those acquired when the obligation was assumed. Index adjustments are, therefore, also made to recognize such gains, and the gain on monetary liabilities is offset against the loss on monetary assets to determine whether the firm had a net gain or loss on monetary items.

Constant dollar adjustments do provide objectively and consistently determined estimates from company to company on the impact of inflation. This enhances comparability of such data. Unfortunately, however, such estimates can be misleading. Constant dollar data assumes that the impact of inflation falls equally on all firms and classes of assets and costs, which is not correct. Using a single index to adjust the historical data of all firms would hide the effects of changing technology, supply and demand shifts that may well be related to the inflation phenomena, and the impact of successful or unsuccessful management in meeting the problem brought on by inflation. In short, one could say that such data are better than nothing, assuming the user understands their limitations. In all cases, such data should be used with caution.

Current Value Data

Proponents of this approach are interested in what the business is worth now rather than historical past accounting values. They argue the value of assets should be stated in terms of the present value of the future receipts these assets can be expected to generate or as the cost of replenishing the assets at today's prices. The latter method is used by most firms to prepare supplementary current value inflation-adjusted data in accordance with requirements of FASB No. 33.

Such estimates seem more useful than index number-adjusted data, but they also suffer serious analytical drawbacks. The differing impact of inflation on firms and classes of assets and costs is estimated. The computation of current value or cost, however, is subjective since many assets do not have a ready market price and might be replaced with a different type of asset or not replaced at all. Accounting rules do allow considerable flexibility in determining current value estimates, and certainly comparing data prepared by different companies will be difficult. In short, the accuracy of current cost estimates is open to serious question. Still, the estimates of management offer possible insights into the impact of inflation on business firms that were not available formerly to analysts.

Tables 7–5 and 7–6 offer an illustration of the reporting of inflation-adjusted data by E.I. DuPont Company. The income reported after inflation adjustments is less than one-half of the income reported on a historical cost basis. The higher effective tax rate is incurred by the company when inflation-adjusted data are considered. Finally, note that inflation-adjusted earnings per share (constant dollars) did not cover the dollar dividend paid per share in 1980. This has important cash flow implications, as well as showing that profits are overstated significantly on an historical cost basis.

Table 7–5   E.I. DuPont Company—Comparative Historical Dollar, Constant Dollar, and Current Cost Income Statements, 1980 (Dollars in Millions)

	As Reported in the Primary Statements (Historical Dollars)	General Inflation (Average 1980 Constant Dollars)	Adjusted for Changes in Specific Prices 1980 Current Costs)
Sales	$13,652	$13,652	$13,652
Other Income	149	149	149
Total	13,801	13,801	13,801
Cost of Goods Sold and Other Operating Charges	10,293	10,420	10,437
Selling, General, and Administrative Expenses	1,466	1,466	1,466
Depreciation and Obsolescence	804	1,156	1,109
Interest on Borrowings	110	110	110
Total	12,673	13,152	13,122
Earnings Before Income Taxes and Minority Interests	1,128	649	679
Provision for Income Taxes	402	402	402
Earnings Before Minority Interests	726	247	277
Minority Interests in Earnings of Consolidated Subsidiaries	10	10	10
Income from Continuing Operations	$ 716	$ 237	$ 267
Effective Income Tax Rate	36%	62%	59%
Gain Attributable to Holding Net Monetary Liabilities		$ 85	$ 85
Income Including Gain Attributable to Holding Net Monetary Liabilities	$ 716	$ 322	$ 352
Increase in Value of Inventories and Net Plants and Properties Held During the Year			
Measured in Constant Dollars			$ 1,290
Measured by Current Costs*			1,050
Excess of Constant Dollar Over Current Cost Increase			$ 240

*At December 31, 1980, current cost of inventories was $3,300, and current cost of plants and properties, net of accumulated depreciation and obsolescence, was $8,281.

Source: 1980 Annual Report of E.I. DuPont.

Table 7–6   E.I. DuPont Company—Comparison of Selected Financial Data in Historical Dollars, Constant Dollars, and Current Costs* (Millions in Dollars, Except Per Share; All Constant Dollar and Current Cost Data in Average 1980 Dollars)

	1980	1979	1978	1977	1976
Sales					
Historical Dollars	13,652	12,572	10,584	9,435	8,361
Constant Dollars	13,652	14,272	13,368	12,830	12,103
Income from Continuing Operations					
Historical Dollars	716	939	787	545	459
Constant Dollars	237	620	585	522	421
Current Costs	267	554			
Earnings Per Share from Continuing Operations					
Historical Dollars	4.83	6.42	5.39	3.69	3.10
Constant Dollars	1.55	4.21	3.97	3.50	2.81
Current Costs	1.76	3.75			
Effective Income Tax Rate	36%	37%	41%	44%	44%
Historical Dollars	62%	50%	54%	52%	55%
Constant Dollars	59%	53%			
Current Costs					
Gain Attributable to Holding Net Monetary Liabilities	85	102	109	109	77
Earnings per Share Including Gain Attributable to Holding					
Net Monetary Liabilities	4.83	6.42	5.39	3.69	3.10
Historical Dollars	2.13	4.92	4.73	4.25	3.34
Constant Dollars	2.34	4.46			
Current Costs					
Excess of Constant Dollar Over Current Cost Increase in Value of Inventories and Net Plants and Properties	240	—	—	—	—
Stockholders' Equity at Year End	5,690	5,312	4,760	4,317	4,030
Historical Dollars	10,251	10,273	9,832	9,491	9,203
Constant Dollars	10,365	10,585			
Current Costs					

Table 7–6 (continued)

Debt Ratio (%) at Year End	21%	20%	22%	26%	27%
Historical Dollars	12%	12%	14%	17%	19%
Constant Dollars	12%	12%			
Current Costs					
Dividends Paid Per Common Share					
Historical Dollars	2.75	2.75	2.42	1.92	1.75
Constant Dollars	2.75	3.12	3.05	2.61	2.53
Market Price per Common Share at Year End	42.00	40.38	42.00	40.13	45.04
Historical Dollars	40.11	43.34	51.09	53.21	63.78
Constant Dollars	246.8	217.4	195.4	181.5	170.5

Average DPI-U (1967 = 100)

*Current cost data have not been developed for years prior to 1979.

Source: 1980 Annual Report of E.I. DuPont.

CHAPTER 8

Analysis of the Income Statement: Operating Expenses and Other Items

Selling, administrative, other expenses and taxes must be deducted from gross profit, and other income added, to determine net income. These expenses are not identifiable specifically with or assigned to production. Some costs may be included here because they are difficult to allocate; it is, therefore, possible that a part of some of these expense items should affect production costs.

Operating Expense

The main classifications under operating expenses in the income statement are selling, general, and administrative expenses. Expenses related to storing and displaying merchandise for sale, advertising, sales salaries, and delivery costs are the main items included under selling expenses. General and administrative expenses include: costs related to the operation of the general offices, costs of the accounting department, costs of the personnel office, and the costs of the credit and collections department. Certain expenses may be listed separately under operating expenses, including depreciation, depletion and amortization, maintenance and repair expenses, research and development (R & D) expenses, rental expenses, costs of exploration, and employee benefit payments (mainly pension costs), though they should have been part of the determination of cost of goods sold.

The analyst should calculate each of the listed expenses as a percentage of sales, as is done in preparing common size statements, which were discussed in Chapter 6. This will highlight the changing importance of expense items, trend patterns, and how costs relate to sales activity. A useful comparison also can be made between the behavior of individual expense items relative to sales, both over time and with industry composite figures.

Maintenance and Repairs

The significance of maintenance and repair costs will vary with the amount invested in plant, equipment, and productive activity. These costs typically are composed of both fixed and variable elements. While it is useful to look at their behavior in relation to sales, one should not make much of this comparison—a consistent relationship with sales is not to be expected. Also, it is useful to look at annual maintenance and repair costs in relation to total plant and equipment. Unfortunately, maintenance and repair expense is not always presented separately in the financial statements.

These costs are discretionary and can be postponed within limits. Unfortunately, management may be tempted to postpone needed maintenance and repairs when revenues are falling to maintain the level of income reported to stockholders. This can lead to continued future deterioration in profits. The analyst should assure himself/herself that reasonable amounts are being spent to maintain competitive facilities.

Inadequate maintenance and repairs can shorten the useful lives of assets, thereby invalidating depreciation expense charges, which are related to useful life estimates.

Rental Expenses

A large number of corporations have chosen to lease rather than purchase assets. Lease rental costs, therefore, can become important expense items. Where a long-term lease is involved, the resulting rental expense can be characterized as a required series of payments over many years that include elements of both principal amortization and interest expense. To an important extent, the payment requirements on a long-term lease are equivalent to fixed charges incurred when debt is utilized to acquire an asset, and the fixed charge obligation of a lease can force a company into financial difficulties just as readily as can fixed charges on funded or other debt.

An analyst should determine the future minimum lease payments required, both for capital leases and operating leases, and relate the payment requirements to expected cash flow to ensure that the firm has not over-committed itself.

Exploratory Expenses

Exploratory expenses, including intangible drilling and development costs, are a major expense item for oil, gas, and mining companies. Many companies charge off exploration costs currently, arguing that the future benefits are too uncertain to justify capitalizing such expenditures. Some companies, however, capitalize all development costs and amortize them over future periods. This can create a noncomparability problem when assessing the profitability of two companies using the different techniques.

For example, Standard Oil of California sold at a price-earnings ratio of about 12.5 during the years 1954–56, while Amerada Petroleum sold at a price earnings ratio of about 25. One could ask, why were investors willing to pay twice as much for a dollar of reported earnings of Amerada? The answer seems to lie solely in the way intangible drilling costs were handled.

Amerada chose to expense all such costs in the year incurred. Standard Oil of California chose instead to capitalize such costs and write them off over the life of the leasehold, which was then averaging ten years. Amerada reported a net income ranging from twenty-two to twenty-four million dollars over the years 1954–56 and also reported intangible drilling costs ranging from twenty-five to twenty-seven million dollars over the same years. If one were to convert Amerada data to the system used by Standard Oil of California they would report only about one-tenth of the intangible drilling costs actually reported each year. This would double reported profits, and the price earnings ratios based on the adjusted data would then be about the same. It seems the market did make such adjustments.

Full-Cost Versus Successful Effort Methods

We discussed the full-cost and successful efforts methods in Chapter 7. These methods now govern accounting in the oil and gas industry. Under the successful efforts method the costs associated with unsuccessful attempts to find gas and oil are charged immediately against earnings while the costs associated with success-ful drillings are capitalized. Full-cost accounting capitalizes all exploratory expenses and amortizes them as the resources actually are produced. A growing company doing a large amount of exploration will report lower earnings under the doing a large amount of exploration will report lower earnings under the successful efforts method (similar to Amerada above) and probably appear more volatile.[62]

Pension Costs

Pension plans come in a variety of shapes, sizes, and formats. Let us first distinguish between defined contribution and defined benefit plans.

A defined contribution plan is one in which the firm's contribution rate is fixed—usually in terms of covered wages and salaries. Once a company has made the required contribution, it has no liability for additional payments. The recognition of the required contribution as expense, therefore, assures proper recognition of pension costs in the income account.

A defined benefit plan, by contrast, "is one where the benefits are established in advance by formula and the employer contributions are treated as variable."[63] The estimation of the size of the pension obligation is difficult and subject to great uncertainty in terms of what the company actually will be obligated to pay in the future. Approximately 90 percent of plans today are of the defined benefit type.

Under a defined benefit plan the employer's commitment is to fund a future benefit, often defined in terms of the last three to five years of salary. The required annual contribution to the plan is not fixed, but is being redefined constantly in terms of changing wage rates, earnings rates of the fund, and other variables. Whether or not present employees will live long enough to collect benefits, how long they will collect benefits, the future salary rate that will determine benefit levels, and the earnings rate that will be experienced on pension plan assets, has been estimated to lead to defendable pension plan expense estimates that could be as much as five times as large as others. The required annual contribution to the plan is not fixed, but constantly is being redefined in terms of changing wage rates, the earnings rate of the fund and other variables.

---

62 For example, when Texaco switched to the "successful efforts" method in 1975, estimates were that full-cost accounting had increased reported profits by $500 million over the preceding ten years.

63 Dan M. McGill, *Foundations of Private Pensions* (Homewood, Ill.: Richard D. Irwin; 1975), p. 98.

Accounting for Defined Benefit Plans

When a firm establishes a defined benefit plan, it commits itself to two undetermined costs: (1) past service costs that arise because of contracted obligations to employees for years served before either the founding of a plan or a change in the plan, and (2) current period costs as required by the plan. APB Opinion 8 and FASB Statement No. 87 (issued in December 1985) are the basic guides to accounting for pension costs.

APB Opinion 8 establishes both a floor and ceiling in terms of items that must be included when determining pension costs. This leaves, however, a large area for different cost determinations by different companies. Moreover, there appeared to be little uniformity in the information covering pension plans and costs provided in footnotes, and often far too little detail for purposes of evaluating the reasonableness of the annual charge actually made by a company. Footnotes typically provided information covering the actuarial present value of vested and nonvested accumulated plan benefits, the plan's assets at market value and the interest assumption used. No information was available concerning salary projections or the age distribution of the work force, an important component of ultimate liability.

SFAS 36 required that accumulated benefits be disclosed in annual reports. Accumulated benefits are the amount workers would be entitled to if they stopped working for the company at the date of the financial statements. Statement 87 requires a more suitable number for an ongoing firm, the estimate of benefits earned for services rendered to date based on future pay rates—not today's level. Moreover, it requires all companies to use the "projected unit credit" actuarial cost method. This method includes salary progression estimates that would result from inflation, promotion, and productivity gains. Also limitations are placed on the freedom to select actuarial assumptions.

Finally, current accounting requirements call for amortization of prior service costs and of actuarial gains and losses over the remaining service lives of the existing employees rather than the 30 or 40 years write-off period that had been used typically. Statement 87 should result in more realistic and comparable pension plan cost estimates among companies. Still, an analyst must recognize two things when evaluating pension charges and pension plans:

1. A defined benefit plan places an uncertain constraint on the future earnings of a firm in terms of the amount available to owners and managers.
2. Reported profits can be distorted in a comparative sense because of different assumptions used in determining annual charges, both over time and between companies.

Actuarial Funding Formulas

These formulas are driven by two primary variables:

1. The interest rate assumption, which represents the annual rate of return that the actuary expects the pension fund assets to earn.
2. The wage assumption, which represents the annual rate at which covered wages are expected to grow.

The higher the interest rate assumption and the lower the wage growth assumption, the smaller will be the reported unfunded pension liability and the lower the required company contribution. In actuality, the setting of these assumptions is more art than science, making it difficult to compare pension costs between firms and to judge the adequacy of the costs charged for funding purposes.

Prior Service Charges

Accounting views prior service costs as an expense that should be spread over subsequent years, even though the liability could be immediate. The analyst should include such charges as an ordinary charge against income and such charges should not be run through the inventory accounts. These charges will require regular cash disbursements by the company to the pension plan in the future and represent a constraint on future income growth.

Impact of Inflation

In a world of uncertain future inflation rates and changing social patterns, the benefit package that a firm is required to fund is difficult to define precisely before the fact. The purpose of a pension program is to provide not merely so many unadjusted dollars of income at retirement, but rather an amount that is sufficient to fund some target standard of living for the retiree. This will be reflected in union bargaining and wage scales upon which the benefits are based.

Each generation is blessed with the task of funding the promises and/or miscalculations of the previous generation. In order for one generation of producers and wage earners to subsidize a previous one, in the form of benefits improvements, output must be growing at a rate that is sufficient to fund the resulting benefits. If output (and firm income) does not grow at the required rate, just two alternative possibilities remain: (1) the pension system must renege, or (2) there must be a continuous relocation of wealth flowing from producers to nonproducers and denigration in the claim that producers have on the fruits of their own labor or capital. In the face of declining worker productivity in the 1970s, declining birth rates and increased life expectancies, investors have ample justification for concern with the effect of pension plan obligations on their future well being.

An analyst must consider the elasticity of demand for a firm's products and the resulting ability to pass on rising costs related to inflation and improved benefits. Rising pension claims act as a constraint on future firm income and, therefore, deserves careful analysis.

Termination of a Pension Plan and Risk Profiles

The Employment Retirement Income Security Act (ERISA, 1974), provides that the sponsor of a plan who terminates that plan at a time when pension fund assets are not sufficient to fund that portion of vested benefits that are guaranteed by the Pension Benefit Guarantee Corporation (PBGC), is liable to PBGC up to a limit of 30 percent of net worth.[64] This "converted employer pension obligations from gratuities to corporate liabilities enforceable at law."[65] Accordingly, ERISA changed the risk profile of firms that offered pension plans. Market risk profiles will be higher:

1. The more closely related future benefit levels are to inflation related variables.
2. The narrower a firm's equity cushion.
3. The narrower the spread between marginal revenue and cost.
4. The more variable the firm's total revenue function.
5. The higher the degree of statistical relationship between a firm's total revenue function and the status of business conditions in general.

An investor should require a higher potential return for a firm that has a higher risk profile, and avoid firms where the risk exceeds his capacity to accept.

Firms may, and have, terminated pension plans where the value of the assets in the pension fund exceeded the level of guaranteed benefits plus .3 times the

---

64 Modifications of the act to increase this limit have been considered, but Congress has not taken action to date.

65 Treynor, Patrick Regan and William Priest, *The Financial Reality of Pension Funding Under ERISA* (Homewood, Il.: Dow Jones–Irwin, 1976) p. VII.

market value of the firm's equity. The firm, under these conditions, can walk away from its pension liabilities and gain assets. PBGC must make up the deficit. This part of the law may well be changed in the future. Two studies have shown positive returns to shareholders around the time of such a termination.[66]

Other Employee Benefits

Accounting requires the disclosure of the costs of past employment benefits (OPEB). The costs of health and life insurance benefits are the main components of these costs, and such benefits usually continue after an employee reaches retirement and often include the spouse and children. These costs are potentially large and should receive careful consideration in terms of the liability they create and their impact on future income.

These costs typically are accounted for on a pay-as-you-go basis; this could substantially underestimate future liability and place a constraint on income. Cottle, Murray and Block recommend multiplying the annual expense reported by a company by a factor between 10 and 15 (with the factor rising with age of the work force), to estimate the balance sheet liability.[67] They feel this reasonably estimates the liability over the working lives of the employees and allows for inflation.

Research and Development Costs

Research and development costs are difficult to properly account for because:

1. The ultimate results are highly uncertain.
2. The long time that can occur between the initiation of a research project and the determination of its ultimate success or failure.

Such expenditures are often substantial and must be considered when analyzing current income and forecasting future profits.

---

66 J. Van Der Heis, "The Effect of Voluntary Terminations of Oversized Defined Benefit Pension Plans on Shareholder Wealth," *The Journal of Risk and Insurance* (1987), and M. J. Alderson and K. C. Chan, "Excess Asset Reversions and Shareholder Wealth," *Journal of Finance* (March, 1986).

67 Sidney Cottle, Roger Murray, and Frank Block, *Graham and Dodd's Security Analysis*, 5th Ed. (New York: McGraw-Hill Book Company, 1988), p. 193.

FASB Statement Number 2 concludes that, subject to certain exceptions, all Research and Development (R & D) costs should be charged to expense in the year incurred. This does seem to conflict with the accounting principle of matching costs and revenues since it does not match the expenses with the potential future benefits the firm hopes to generate.

The analyst should attempt to judge the success of past R & D expenditures and the likelihood of future successes when evaluating a firm. It is the future that is of importance when evaluating a common stock, and accounting for R & D expenses is not helpful in this regard. Evaluation of the potential future success generated by R & D outlays requires information on the types of research performed, the outlays by category, the technical feasibility of projects being undertaken, the quality of the research staff, and it is useful to know the company's success-failure experience in the past.

Interest Expense

Interest costs generally are expensed, when incurred, except in the case of public utilities and industries, such as real estate.

Interest related to construction may be capitalized by public utilities. Utilities cannot include funds raised for purposes of planned construction while those funds are a part of current assets in their rate base, on which they are permitted to earn a fair rate of return. These funds for construction also must be excluded from the rate base. If the matter were left at that point, the utilities would be paying the cost for the funds, but would not be permitted to capitalize the interest costs on funds raised for construction, prior to the time that useful fixed assets are available and added to the rate base.

Investors should realize that the interest charged to construction credit items is temporary in nature, and will disappear as soon as the funds actually are invested in fixed assets. Ideally, as soon as this occurs, the company will begin to earn a fair return on the additional plant and equipment, and the additional earnings will replace the amount that was added previously to earnings for interest charged to construction credit. It is, however, a noncash item and the situation may not be ideal.

Assume that the interest charged to construction credit items was equal to $0.25 per share this year as part of total reported earnings of $2.25 ($2 per share being earned on the old property). Next year the item is lost. If earnings on the old property rise by 8%, then earnings on the old property would rise from $2 per share $2.16 per share. If no additional earnings flow from the new property the earnings per share will be reported as $2.16 next year versus $2.25 this year. If earnings on new property were $0.09 per share then earnings per share would be reported as $2.25 in each year. If earnings per share on the new property exceed $0.09 per share, then an increase in earnings per share, compared to last year, will be reported. An analyst must consider this item when forecasting income and for purposes of deciding whether or not management's expansion plans were desirable for the owners. This item also must be considered when calculating interest or fixed charges coverage ratios, as we will discuss in Chapter 11.

Break-Even Analysis and Leverage

Cost analysis is concerned with the relationship between sales, costs, and profits. The analyst wants to know how costs vary as sales and output levels change and the effect of those variations on the profitability of the firm.

A framework known as break-even analysis has been developed to explore those relationships. It is based on classifying costs into fixed and variable cost categories. Fixed costs are those that do not change with changes in the level of output. Variable costs are those that change as the level of output changes. For example, the preparing of the plates for each page of this book are a fixed cost, since the total cost will be the same whether one book is printed or five thousand books are printed. The paper used is a variable cost that will tend to vary directly and proportionately with the number of books produced.

An Illustrative Break-Even Analysis

The break-even point is that level of output at which neither a profit is earned or a loss incurred. This could only occur where total revenues equal total costs. To illustrate, let us assume that the sales price for a unit of product sold by the firm is $5 and that fixed costs total $2,000, while variable costs are $2 per unit and vary in direct proportion with changes in the level of output. Under these conditions the firm will break-even if it sells 666⅔ units calculated as follows when X equals the number of units at break-even:

$$\text{Total Revenues} = \text{Total Costs}$$

$$\text{Total Revenues (R)} = \text{Fixed Costs (F)} + \text{Variable Costs (V)}$$

$$\$5X = \$2000 + \$2X$$

$$\$3X = \$2000$$

$$X = 666\tfrac{2}{3} \text{ Units}$$

Figure 8–1   Illustrative Straight-Line Break-Even Chart

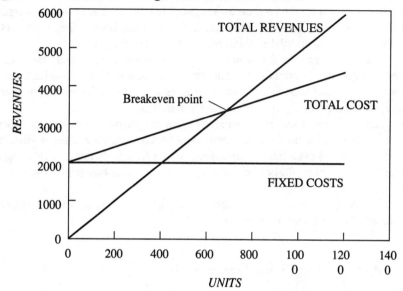

This can also be represented in a diagram (see Figure 8–1).

Only after a company moves beyond the break-even point does it realize a profit, and the break-even point is, therefore, important.

Limitations of Break-Even Analysis

The above illustration assumed that all costs could be classified as either fixed or directly and proportionally variable throughout time.

First, there are costs that are semivariable, that is they are fixed over a certain range of outputs and then vary. In the long-run, all costs are probably variable since plant scale can be changed. Therefore, break-even estimates built on the basis of a simplified analysis could only be useful, even in the estimating sense, over limited time periods. A straight-line will not represent a semivariable cost, as it assumes a constant rate of change. An example of a semivariable cost might be the cost associated with a generator used to produce electric power. That cost could be fixed up to a certain number of units of output (capacity for that generator) and then rise sharply as a new generator must be brought on line to continue to expand output.

Second, the sales price was assumed constant no matter how many units were assumed sold. A firm might have to lower price to sell additional units, and a straight line would not then represent the change in total revenues as sales changed. Some type of curve, based on the elasticity of demand for the firm's products, would likely represent total revenue behavior as sales change.

The total cost curve also would be represented more realistically by a curve than a straight line. Economies of scale are likely to cause total cost to increase at a decreasing rate at least to the point of diminishing returns. Moreover, as noted above, all costs probably are variable in the long-run.

Finally, break-even analysis requires that the variable components of expense be separated from the fixed component. Accounting data is not segregated in this fashion and even internal management of a firm finds this a difficult task. An outside analyst could only crudely approximate such breakdowns based on past experience.

Still, the break-even framework can be useful if its limitations are recognized and its applications kept in proper perspective.

Some Applications of Break-Even Analysis

Leverage is present whenever a firm has fixed costs. Once a firm develops a volume of sales that is sufficient to cover its fixed costs, further increments in sales will result in a more than proportionate increase in profitability. However, this is a two-edged sword. If sales fall below the break-even level, profits will fall more than in proportion to the drop in sales. A firm that has a high proportion of fixed costs is then risky when an analyst fears an economic downturn and interesting if an economic expansion is expected.

Also, the higher the level of fixed costs relative to variable costs the higher the break-even point, but the greater the rate of profit increase once sales exceed the break-even level. Moreover, a company with a higher degree of operating leverage could appear to be an exceptional growth company in a booming economy. The sharp increase in earnings could, however, be temporary and rapidly disappear in a cyclical economy. If one observed the increase in profits without reference to leverage of the firm, they could draw an incorrect conclusion about the long-run profitability of the firm.

Contribution Margin

The contribution margin is what remains of the sales price after deducting variable cost per unit. It is important as fixed costs must be met from this margin before a profit can be earned. From our break-even illustration above, the contribution margin is $3 per unit. If sales exceed 666⅔ units (the break-even point), profits will expand at a rate of $3 per unit sold. This, of course, is based on the oversimplification that straight line assumptions can be utilized. Such assumptions, while not accurate, may provide useful ballpark estimates.

Keep in mind that changes in sales mix or the efficiency of a firm will result in a different profit change for a given sales volume estimate than the profit margin would suggest. Still a useful estimate may be obtained at minimum cost by using straight line assumptions, and the analyst can vary that estimate subjectively to allow for greater reality.

An Illustrative Cost Analysis

For illustrative purposes, we return to our review of an analysis of Deere & Company issued by Sanford C. Bernstein & Co., Inc. in January, 1981. We discussed their analysis and forecast of revenues at the end of Chapter 6. We will review their analysis of costs and their profit forecasts in this chapter, and suggest a valuation for the stock that could have been prepared based on the data generated in the report.

"The key to a financial analysis of Deere & Company is an understanding of the company's revenues and cost structure for either a single product line or a group of closely associated product lines. As the factories are treated as profit centers, manufacturing costs specific to each factory may be estimated." Further, the costs and profitability generated by the sales branches, as a total group, may be estimated."[68] The analyst chose to separate costs into fixed and variable components, and use these estimates with revenue estimates to review past profit contribution and forecast future profit contribution for each major cost center. The analyst did have the advantage of detailed data gathered in field visits that would not necessarily be part of the annual report.

---

68 Sanford C. Bernstein & Co., Inc. Report, (New York, 1981), p. 106.

The Waterloo Tractor Works

Let us review the study of and forecasts for a particular cost center, namely the Waterloo Tractor Works. Revenues expected to be generated by this plant were forecast based on the data presented in Chapter 6. The estimates for selected years are presented in Table 8–1.

Fiscal 1980 results were expected to reflect the dampening effects of cyclical economic conditions as well as other adverse factors, such as the Soviet grain embargo. Fixed costs were expected to rise in reaction to both inflationary trends in personnel costs and higher levels of depreciation and amortization. The expectation of higher levels of depreciation and amortization were based on expected capital expenditures designed to expand capacity and enhance manufacturing efficiencies. While the expected increase in fixed costs would raise the break-even point, it would also increase the degree of operating leverage. Increased operating leverage would accelerate profit growth as long as sales were expanding; and decrease profits if sales declined. Accordingly, operating profit margins were

Table 8–1   North American Agricultural Tractors—Waterloo ($ million)

	1979E	1980E	1981E	1984E
Net Sales	$1,020.0	$1,021.7	$1,288.0	$1,840.0
Direct Labor	33.0	33.2	41.9	59.8
Direct Materials	480.0	485.3	618.2	883.3
Variable Manufacturing Overhead	112.0	127.6	146.3	207.1
Total Variable Manufacturing Costs	$ 625.0	$ 646.1	$ 806.4	$1,150.2
Variable SG&A-Allocated	$ 20.0	$ 21.4	$ 25.8	$ 33.7
Total Variable Costs	645.0	667.5	832.2	1,183.9
Variable Profit	375.0	354.2	455.8	656.4
Fixed Manufacturing Overhead	112.0	124.5	144.4	211.6
Fixed SG&A-Allocated	68.0	71.6	86.3	112.8
Total Fixed Costs	$ 180.0	$ 196.1	$ 230.8	$ 324.4
Operating Profit[1]	$ 195.0	$ 158.1	$ 225.0	$ 332.0

[1]Before allocation of net miscellaneous items.

Source: Bernstein estimates, Bernstein Report, op. cit., p. 34.

expected to show a sharp decline in 1980 to about 15.53 and then rise to about 17.5% in 1981.

Total variable costs were expected to rise by 12.9% per year over the forecast period (1980–1984), mainly because of a rise in direct material cost, the largest component of variable costs, and also in direct labor costs. Rises in revenues after 1980 are expected to offset these cost increases, keeping the relationship between total operating costs and sales steady.

Consolidated Income Statement

An historical and forecasted consolidated income statement was presented in Table 6–11 in Chapter 6. This statement was prepared on the basis of the data gathered and analyzed for each major cost center. For example, the forecasts for 1984 by cost center and for the total company are presented in Table 8–2. The following highlights of the financial forecasts were noted in the report[69]:

1. Return on investment was expected to recover strongly from 1980s depressed level, but to remain below the levels achieved in the 1973–1979 period. The analysis of return on investment is summarized in Table 7–3. This is a useful check on the reasonableness of the assumptions underlying their forecasts. The erosion of return relative to 1973–79 derives from expected continued pressure on net margins in North American operations.

2. Return on equity is forecast to recover to just under 19% by 1984, modestly above the 17.7% recorded in fiscal 1979, but generally below the returns achieved during most of the 1970s.

3. Total dividend payments are projected to rise by 14.2% per year through 1984 as shown below[70]:

Period	Earnings Per Share	Dividends Per Share	Payout Ratio
1980	3.27	1.875	57.3%
1981	4.72	2.050	43.4%
1982	6.00	2.300	38.3%
1983	7.50	2.600	34.7%
1984	8.50	3.000	35.3%

---

69 Sanford C. Bernstein & Co., Inc., op. cit., p. 100–101.

70 Sanford C. Bernstein & Co., Inc., op. cit., p. 102.

Dividends per share were $1.55 in 1979 and $0.66 in 1973. The report then noted that "if economic conditions are such that our earnings and cash flow projections are not realized, dividend growth will be reduced accordingly." The report also noted that management felt strongly that financial leverage should be constrained to protect current debt ratings, even if dividend growth is reduced as a result. Still, the author of the report felt the dividend projections were reasonable.

4. The earnings retention rate was expected to fall below that in the 1970s when it reached a high of 75.6%. Capital expenditure programs were expected to be maintained, however.

An Illustrative Valuation Model

We will use the limited hold present value valuation framework, assuming a five-year hold ending at year-end 1984, for purposes of preparing a suggested valuation of Deere & Company stock as of January, 1981. The following data is required to calculate intrinsic value for the stock:

1. Expected earnings per share and dividends per share over the period 1980–84. These estimates are provided above, as prepared by the analyst.
2. The expected tax rate for the investor. We will assume an effective rate for calculation purposes of 50% (the top bracket rate at that time) for ordinary income and 25% for capital gains. Note that intrinsic values would be different for different investors, depending on their tax circumstances.
3. The opportunity cost for the investor. There are several approaches suggested in the investment literature for estimating this variable. We will review these approaches below and arrive at an estimated discount rate.
4. The price at which an investor might have expected to sell the stock at the end of 1984. We will estimate this variable by multiplying expected earnings per share for 1984 by the price-earnings ratio we might have expected to exist at that time. Development of this estimate also will be discussed below.

Estimating the Appropriate Discount Rate

A common stock is a desirable purchase when an investor believes that the expected return generated from holding that stock exceeds the return required by

Table 8–2 Deere & Company—Fiscal 1984 Forecast ($ Million)

	Waterloo	Har-vester Works	Imple-ment & Other	Con-struc-tion & Indus-trial	Total North American Manu-facturing	Mann-heim	Zwei-brucken & Other	Total Overseas Manu-facturing	Total Deere & Company
Net Sales	$1,840.3	$1,157.0	$2,672.0	$1,772.0	$7,441.3	$ 986.1	$ 812.5	$1,798.6	$9,239.9
Direct Labor	59.8	52.1	100.2	88.6	300.7	49.3	35.7	85.0	385.7
Direct Materials	883.3	538.0	1,456.2	779.7	3,652.2	43.0	414.4	907.4	4,564.6
Variable Manufacturing Overhead	207.1	167.8	340.0	265.8	980.6	140.5	126.1	266.6	1,247.2
Total Variable Manufacturing Costs	$1,150.2	$ 757.9	$1,896.4	$1,134.1	$4,938.5	$ 682.8	$ 576.2	$1,259.0	$6,197.5
Variable SG&A Allocated	$ 33.7	$ 21.1	$ 48.9	$ 32.5	$ 136.3	$ 18.1	$ 14.9	$ 32.9	$ 169.2
Total Variable Costs	$1,183.9	$ 779.0	$1,945.3	$1,165.5	$5,074.8	$ 700.9	$ 591.1	$1,291.9	$6,366.7
Variable Profit	$ 656.4	$ 378.0	$ 726.7	$ 605.5	$2,366.5	$ 285.2	$ 221.4	$ 506.7	$2,873.2

Table 8–2 (continued)

	Waterloo	Har-vester Works	Imple-ment & Other	Con-struc-tion & Indus-trial	Total North American Manu-facturing	Mann-heim	Zwei-brucken & Other	Total Overseas Manu-facturing	Total Deere & Company
Fixed Manufacturing Overhead	$ 211.6	145.2	$ 360.7	$ 290.8	$1,008.4	$ 167.6	$ 117.5	$ 285.1	$1,293.5
Fixed SG&A Allocated	112.8	70.9	163.8	107.6	456.2	60.4	49.8	110.3	566.4
Total Fixed Costs	$ 324.4	$ 216.1	$ 524.5	$ 399.4	$1,464.5	$ 228.1	$ 167.3	$ 395.4	$1,859.9
Operating Profit[1]	$ 322.0	$ 161.9	$ 202.2	$ 206.1	$ 902.1	$ 57.1	$ 54.1	$ 111.2	$1,013.3
Net Miscellaneous Items									136.1
Unallocated SG&A									31.3
Equity Income									0.0
Pretax Income									$ 848.8
Taxes									380.6
Net Inc-Consol Group									$ 465.2
Equity Income									79.0
Net Income									$ 544.2
Earnings Per Share									$ 8.50

[1]Operating profits before allocation of net miscellaneous items.

Note: Totals may not add due to rounding.

Source: Corporate reports and Bernstein estimates. Bernstein Report, op. cit., p. 110.

Table 8–3 Deere & Company—Analysis of Return on Investment and Capital Self-Sufficiency[1]

	Net Margin[2]	× Capital Turnover[3]	= Return on Investment	+ Effect of Financial Leverage	= Return on Equity	× Retention Rate	= Reinvestment Rate	− Growth in Operating Investment	= Equity Capital Required as % of Equity Base[4]
1973	9.2%	1.75	16.1%	6.9%	23.0%	75.6%	17.4%	1.3%	16.1%
1974	7.4	2.15	15.9	3.8	19.7	72.1	14.2	24.4	(10.2)
1975	7.4	2.05	15.2	5.5	20.7	69.7	14.4	23.7	(9.3)
1976	8.7	1.68	14.6	5.7	20.3	74.3	15.1	10.3	4.8
1977	8.1	1.83	14.8	3.7	18.5	71.6	13.3	21.3	(8.0)
1978	7.5	1.74	13.1	3.6	16.9	68.0	11.5	10.5	1.0
1979	7.4	1.87	13.8	3.9	17.7	68.2	12.1	10.7	1.4
1980E	5.8	1.82	10.6	0.0	10.6	45.2	4.8	34.9	(30.1)
1981E	6.2	1.59	9.9	4.3	14.2	55.5	7.9	4.5	3.4
1984E	7.3	2.01	14.7	4.1	18.8	64.7	12.2	11.4	0.8

[1] All data based on beginning year balances.

[2] Pre-interest expense net of related taxes.

[3] Based on operating capital as defined in Table 84.

[4] Represents amount of equity, stated as a percentage of prior year net worth, needed to maintain constant capital ratios; positive number implies a reduction in financial leverage.

Source: Corporate reports and Berstein estimates, Berstein Report, op, cit., p. 117.

the investor for the level of risk represented for that stock. It is an opportunity cost concept, based on answering the question what could the stockholder earn on alternative investments of equivalent risk.

The Discounted Cash Flow Approach

One approach suggested in the literature is based on a manipulation of the hold into perpetuity valuation model as follows:

$$P = D_1/k - g$$

where P = The intrinsic value estimate for the stock.

D_1 = The dividend expected to be received at the end of the first holding period.

g = The compound annual growth rate expected for dividends.

k = The appropriate discount rate.

Accordingly:

$$k = D_1/P + g$$

The expected dividend at the end of the first one year holding period is relatively easy to estimate. Current market price of the stock at the time the estimate is being prepared could be logically used for *P*. The difficulty is estimating *g*. Two possible ways of estimating *g* are suggested below and related to the analyst's forecasts:

1. The historical growth rate for *g* could be used if earnings and dividend growth rates have been relatively stable in the past. Total dividends paid grew at 15.6% compound annual rate from 1973 through 1980. Over a ten-year period, ending in 1984, however, our analyst estimated the earnings growth rate as 11.5%, and felt that the growth rate could slow to 9%, assuming a GNP growth of 9% (3% real and 6% inflation), with the profitability estimate given. This could suggest a 10% growth estimate, assuming constancy in the dividend pay-out ratio. Remember, our purpose is more to illustrate the valuation process than to develop accurate estimates for Deere & Company.

2. Retention Growth. The basic valuation model into perpetuity can be used to show that in the model,

$$g = br$$

where g = The growth rate expected for dividends.

    b = The retention rate for the firm, calculated by dividing dividends per share by earnings per share.

    r = The rate of return earned on owner's equity.

For steady state profitability assumptions (average for the cycle), the analyst's projections would lead to the following:

$$g = (.65)\,(.177) = .115$$

This rate often is called the sustainable growth rate for a firm. Since it is higher than the historical estimate above, yet in line with a ten-year period, we would raise our growth rate expectation to 11–11.5%. Based on our work above we would suggest calculating intrinsic value using an 11% discount rate.

The Capital Asset Pricing Model Approach

The literature also suggests using the Capital Asset Pricing Model Approach for estimating k. First, one would have to estimate a risk-free rate. The 90-day Treasury bill rate is often suggested as a proxy for the risk-free rate. The T-bill rate, however, varies markedly over time and is not truly riskless when one considers the need to roll over funds. Practitioners often use as a base rate the rate on long-term Treasury bonds rather than a risk-free rate, since common stocks are long-term securities, and treasury bonds rates are more stable. Also, long-term bonds reflect an opportunity cost an investor certainly would want to exceed, to accept the added risks associated with purchasing common stocks.

Brigham and Gapenski[71] note that Merrill Lynch publishes on a regular basis a forecast based on discounted cash flow methodology for the expected return on the market. They suggest subtracting the current long-term Treasury bond rate from Merrill Lynch's current market forecast to determine implied market risk premiums. To illustrate, assume that Merrill Lynch's reported expected return on the market at the end of 1980 were 20%, and the Treasury bond rate were 11%. The implied market risk premium would then be 9%. We would then determine the beta for Deere & Company and multiply it by the risk premium to estimate k. Assuming the beta for Deere & Co. were 1.2, then k would equal 10.8%. This would strengthen using a g of 11% rather than 11.5%.

---

71 Eugene Brigham and Louis Gapenski, *Financial Management: Theory and Practice*, 5th Ed. (New York: The Dryden Press, 1988), p. 226.

One must remember, however, that we are trying to estimate investor's expectations (not necessarily those of Merrill Lynch), and professional analysts other than Merrill Lynch may have different market expectations. We, therefore, did not press to get accurate forecasts for 1980 since we are more interested in illustrating the methodology than in valuing Deere & Co.

Estimating the Sales Price for the Stock

A market price for a stock can be said to equal earnings per share times the price earnings ratio at any given time. The report on Deere provided us with estimates of earnings and dividends per share that we will assume we accept as reasonable. We still must estimate the appropriate price earnings ratio that we feel will prevail by year-end 1984. This estimate should be based on past history, our future expectations and the market conditions we expect for year-end 1984. The average annual price-earnings ratio varied between seven and eight during the years 1972 through 1979 and rose to 9.5 in 1980. The favorable expectations suggested in the report could justify an expectation of 10 in a price-earnings ratio for year-end 1984 as of January 1981. The actual price-earnings ratio was higher as earnings expectations for this report were not realized. Let us assume a price-earnings ratio of 10, since we are estimating as of January 1981.

The Valuation Model

Based on the assumptions noted above, we would have determined an intrinsic value of $53.53 for Deere & Company calculated as shown in Table 8-4. These calculations also assume the investor receives the 1981 dividends and all dividends in succeeding years including 1984.

The intrinsic value estimate would have suggested purchasing the stock. Graham and Dodd, however, suggested a margin of at least 40% for intrinsic value over purchase price to cover forecasting errors. The margin here is only 13.89% (53.53 – 47/47), and a purchase would not have been suggested if their rule had been applied. We suggest requiring a margin of at least 30% before purchasing a stock, and would not, therefore, have recommended purchase as of January 1981. The analyst's expectations were not realized since the stock sold at about $40 per share by year-end 1984, and earnings per share actually had fallen rather than rose. Our decision not to purchase, even with the favorable information developed in the research report, would have been a correct one. Currently, however, the stock is again in favor with institutional investors, and rated highly in terms of timeliness by Value Line in a 1988 report.

Table 8–4   Calculation of Intrinsic Value for the Common Stock of Deere & Company as of January 1981

Year	Earnings Per Share	Dividends Per Share	After Tax Dividend	Discount Factor @11%	Present Value of Dividends
1980	$3.27	—	—	—	—
1981	4.72	2.050	1.025	.9009	.9234
1982	6.00	2.300	1.150	.8116	.9333
1983	7.50	2.600	1.300	.7312	.9506
1984	8.50	3.000	1.500	.6587	.9881

Present Value of Expected Dividends   3.7954

Plus Present Value of Sales Price:

Expected Sales Price =   8.5 × 10   = $85.00

Expected Capital Gains

($85.00 – Purchase Price*) = $47.00

Expected Capital Gains Tax   ($85.00 – 47.00) (.25)   = (9.50)

$75.50

Present Value of Realized Cash Inflow   (75.50 × .6587)   = $49.7318

Intrinsic Value Estimate   = $53.5272

*Average Price for January, 1981.

CHAPTER 9

Balance Sheet Analysis

It has long been recognized that for most corporations there is little correlation between the earning power value of a stock and its book value and between economic and market value of assets and their book value. Most investors and analysts pay little attention to book value, in terms of valuing a business, except in the case of (1) financial corporations if stated asset values are assumed to be close to realizable market values; (2) public utilities because they are entitled (although not guaranteed) to earn a fair return on the fair value of assets used in the public service; and (3) on occasion, natural resource companies.

After World War II and until the 1970s less and less attention had been paid to balance sheet analysis, we believe less attention than should have been paid. While it is true that the value of a business and particularly of its owner's equity rests largely on earning power and its quality, inadequate liquidity or an over-burdensome debt can prevent future growth and possibly lead to bankruptcy. Corporate liquidity did shrink sharply in the 1970s, as shown by the fall in liquidity ratios in Figure 9–1. The ratio of liquid assets to short-term market debt and debt maturity ratios had fallen to historic lows by 1980.

Inflation would encourage a sharp curtailment in liquidity since a holder of monetary assets loses during such a period. Moreover, firms would want to avoid holding excess liquid assets, since they could be losing profits that could have been gained by more effectively investing these assets. Still, the sharp drops in corporate liquidity during this period make corporations more vulnerable to a recession. Investors should carefully monitor these developments in relation to firms whose securities they are reviewing for potential purchase.

Balance Sheet Disclosure

Investors must understand what balance sheets demonstrate. One examines a balance sheet to determine the company's current financial position, the amount and nature of invested capital, the sources of invested capital, the proportionate

Figure 9–1 Cyclical Pattern of Debt Financing, Liquidity Ratios, and Debt Maturity Ratios for Nonfinancial Business Corporations

a. Cyclical Pattern of Debt Financing

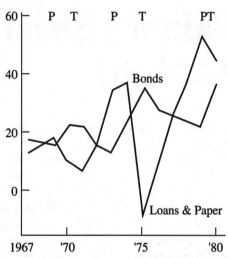

Taxable Bonds vs. Loans and Paper, Annual Net
Increases in Amounts Outstanding, $Billions.

b. Liquidity Ratios   c. Debt Maturity Ratios

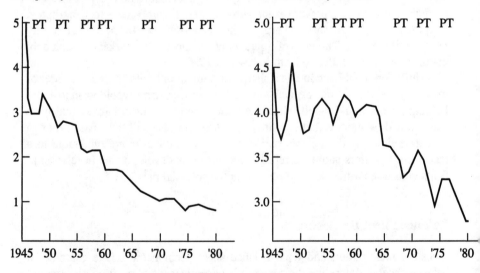

Liquid Assets to Short-Term Market Debt   Long-Term Market Debt to Short-Term
                                               Market Debt

Note: P (Peak) and T (Trough) Represent N.B.E.R. Reference Cycle Peaks and Troughs.

Source: H. Kaufman, J. McKean, and D. Foster, *1981 Prospects for Financial Markets* (New York: Salomon Brothers, December 8, 1940), p. 7.

division of corporate capitalization, and, with the income statement, the rate of return earned on total assets, on total capitalization, and on stockholders' equity.

Balance Sheet Values

The word "value" is used in accounting to describe the figure at which an asset or liability is carried in the accounts, although the amount may represent something different than "value" as the word is used ordinarily. Accounting is based predominantly on cost, and assets usually are carried at cost or some modification of cost. For example, accountants report the original cost of fixed assets on the balance sheet, less amortization of that cost over the useful life of the asset. Inventories will reflect the cost to purchase the items included, unless current market value falls below that cost. Accounting values, therefore, are not intended to represent current market value, replacement value, or liquidation value of assets.

Accounting values are book values which signifies only the amount at which an item is stated in accordance with the accounting principles related to the item. The term *book value* also is used to represent the total owner's equity shown in the balance sheet; book value per share is the owners' equity divided by the number of shares outstanding. Book value per share should not be thought of as an indicator of economic worth.

Balance Sheet Information Sought by Analysts

Balance sheet is a technical accounting term. "In this view, a balance sheet may be defined as a tabular statement or summary of balances (debt and credit) carried forward after an actual or constructive closing of books of account kept according to principles of accounting.[72] This is as far as accountants are willing to go. The investor must expect neither more nor less than this. A balance sheet does not purport to list economic or investment values, which are related more to cash flow and earning power of a firm.

The major types of information that the analyst seeks from the balance sheet are as follows:

1. The sources of funds that have been used to acquire the corporate assets:

---

72 Accounting Research Study No. 7 (New York: American Institute of Certified Public Accountants, 1965), p. 226.

(a) The long-term funds invested by creditors (bondholders, private placement noteholders, equipment trust noteholders, etc.), by preferred stockholders and by common stockholders. In the case of common stockholders, it includes earnings retained in the business (not paid out as dividends) and capital in excess of par.

(b) The short-term funds supplied by banks, commercial paper houses, factors and trade creditors, etc.

On the basis of the above information, the investor can calculate the proportion of invested capital contributed by creditors, preferred stockholders, and common stockholders and can determine such ratios as long-term debt to stockholders' equity. It is worthwhile for the investor to calculate the market value of the corporation's securities and the ratios of each component to the total capitalization so calculated. In this calculation par value often is used for bonds and preferred stock, but market value is used for common stock: hence the term "total capitalization with common at market" (number of shares times market value).

2. The strength of the corporation's working capital position as indicated by the various working capital ratios. These ratios indicate the corporation's assumed ability to meet current liabilities, which are expected to be paid with current assets.

3. The assets of the corporation, which indicate the sources of the corporation's income and the manner in which capital was invested, as well as providing a base for assessing the adequacy of total assets and the mix of assets to support expected levels of operation.

4. Data for an analysis of the balance sheet combined with an analysis of the income statements to indicate:

(a) The amount and the rate of return on total long-term capitalization (an excellent test of corporate management).

(b) The rate of return on total assets.

(c) The rate of return on the stockholders' equity.

(d) A check of the retained earnings account in the balance sheet with the earnings reported over a period of years in the income statement. [Retained earnings at the beginning of the period plus earnings (less losses) for the entire period less dividends paid should give the total in the retained earnings account at the end of the period, except for charges or credits made directly to the retained earnings account that may not have been recorded in any income statement but that should have been disclosed in annual reports.]

In essence, the balance sheet when combined with income statement data offers a basis for a long-term study of earning power relative to asset mix and financial structure.

We will discuss the ratios mentioned above in much greater detail in Chapter 11.

Assets Section of the Balance Sheet

In considering assets in the balance sheet as offsets to the liabilities and capital, the analyst must recognize what asset figures really mean. The analyst should not be under the illusion that these offsets to liabilities and capital represent reliable estimates of economic value, except to some extent in the case of current assets; and, even in this case, book figures may be far removed from economic values, especially in the case of inventories.

Current Assets—Working Capital

Current assets of a business (also called circulating assets or working assets) represent its working capital. The character of a borrower's working capital has been of prime interest to grantors of credit; and bond indentures, credit agreements, and preferred stock agreements commonly contain provisions restricting corporate actions that would effect a reduction or impairment of working capital (and would impair ability to satisfy debt requirements). Such restrictions can affect future financing possibilities of a firm, growth and dividend paying capacity thereby affecting the common stockholders' interest. Net working capital is represented by the excess of current assets over current liabilities and identifies the relatively liquid portion of total enterprise capital that constitutes a margin or buffer for meeting obligations within the ordinary operating cycle of the business.

For accounting purposes the term *current assets* is used to designate cash and other assets or resources commonly identified as those that are expected to be realized in cash or sold or consumed during the normal operating cycle of the business. Thus, the term comprehends in general the following resources:

1. Cash available for current operations and items that are the equivalent of cash;
2. Inventories of merchandise, raw materials, goods in process, finished goods, operating supplies, and ordinary maintenance material and parts;

3. Trade accounts, notes, and acceptances receivable;
4. Receivables from officers, employees, affiliates, and others, if collectable in the ordinary course of business, usually within a year;
5. Installment or deferred accounts and notes receivable if they conform generally to normal trade practices and terms within the business;
6. Marketable securities representing the temporary investment of cash; and
7. Prepaid expenses such as insurance, interest, rents, taxes, unused royalties, current paid advertising service not yet received, and operating supplies.

The ordinary operations of a business involve a circulation of capital within the current asset group. Expenditures are accumulated as inventory cost. Inventory costs, on sale of the products, are converted into trade receivables and ultimately into cash again. The average time intervening between the acquisition of materials or services entering this process and the final cash realization constitute an operating cycle.

Cash and Cash Equivalent Items

Cash equivalent items include temporary investments of currently excess cash in short-term, high-quality investment media such as Treasury bills and Banker's Acceptances. There is little or no chance of loss in the event these items had to be liquidated.

Sometimes cash and cash equivalent items are segregated arbitrarily and not included in current assets. If such segregated items have been excluded from current assets and if these items are, in fact, subject to the full control of management and not required to be segregated by regulations or contract agreements, the analyst should add them back to the current assets.

The firm is likely to operate a pension fund and that pension fund could have cash items. We would not, however, consider these cash items as current assets. The company may be able to capture some or all of these assets through an "asset reversion" (where pension fund assets are excess), but such a process requires approval of the Pension Benefit Guarantee Corporation and typically is subject to long delays. The firm does not have ready access to this cash for corporate purposes.

Receivables

Receivables, less any allowance for doubtful accounts, are included as current assets on the grounds that the firm intends to convert them to cash in the ordinary operating cycle of the business. Receivables, accordingly, may be included as a current asset when the payment period runs beyond a year, as with installment sales discussed below. This must be kept in mind when judging the firm's ability to pay current liabilities.

The analyst must consider the nature of the receivables in terms of the characteristics of the industry and the company's business. The analyst should determine whether the receivables are proportionately larger than normal in respect to current assets for the type of business and whether the deductions for estimated doubtful accounts are reasonable in terms of industry averages and firm experience. Schedule VIII of a firm's 10-K filing with the SEC offers useful information for purposes of evaluating the adequacy of the reserve for doubtful accounts of a firm, especially when compared with other firms operating in the same industry. Any information on the average age of receivables and trends in this respect is significant. Receivables turnover ratios (discussed in Chapter 11) are a useful analytical tool.

Installment Sales and Receivables

Various methods are used in accounting for installment sales. The following two methods are the most important:

1. Consider each collection on installment sales as both a recovery of cost and a return of profit to the same extent as the ratio of cost and profit at the time the sale was consummated. Such installment sales are only taken up as income and considered as income for tax purposes in the period in which the receivables are actually collected.
2. Consider the full amount of installment sales as ordinary sales for the period in which the sales are first consummated, although income taxes will not be paid until the receivables actually are collected. In such cases the analyst should make an estimate of the income taxes to be paid when the receivables are collected and should deduct these taxes from the receivables on the balance sheet.

The estimate for doubtful or uncollectible accounts must be reasonable in relation to receivables in the case of installment sales, and this is true if profits on installment sales are taken into income in the period that the sales are accomplished rather than when receivables are collected. If a corporation sells its installment notes to banks or finance companies, it should note whether they have been sold outright or on a "recourse basis." In the latter case, the corporation has a contingent liability, which usually is not shown in the balance sheet but is included as a footnote. The analyst must consider the size of these contingent liabilities and the likelihood of the contingency materializing in the light of industry and company experience and the character of the receivables.

Inventories

The analyst should, where possible, calculate inventory turnover. Unfortunately, a definitive ratio usually can be achieved by outside analysts only through an examination in terms of annual figures, dividing cost of goods sold by average inventory. Ideally, with respect to seasonal business, monthly sales at cost would be the most relevant, but annual figures are often the only ones available to investors.

Recessions, generally characterized as inventory recessions, result from excessive inventory build-ups during the previous expansion and require working down. Wide fluctuation in the price structure has heretofore caused severe inventory problems; but the advent of computer controls combined with economic and market analysis has somewhat reduced the inventory problem. Still, in certain industries excessive inventories and inventory price fluctuations can cause serious financial problems as in 1974 and 1975. Inventories in the following expansion were more tightly controlled.

The analyst also must consider the implications of F.I.F.O. and L.I.F.O. inventory accounting as applied to analysis between companies and over a period of years for the same company if company reports do not provide actual figures indicating the effect of a change from F.I.F.O. to L.I.F.O. or vice versa.[73] One must be careful to make appropriate adjustments when comparing two firms, one of which uses L.I.F.O. while the other uses F.I.F.O. The firm using L.I.F.O. will report a lower profit and inventory than the firm using F.I.F.O. when there are no real differences.

Our study of the L.I.F.O. inventory costing technique in Chapter 6 showed that the inventory stated on the balance sheet is likely to include old costs, which would not reflect current market values. We suggest, therefore, that the analyst

---

73 See discussion of Inventory Accounting in Chapter 6.

add back the L.IF.O. reserve to assets before calculating a current ratio, return on owners' equity or assets, or an inventory turnover. When projecting the likely profit margin for next year, however, it is better to keep the inventories on a L.IF.O. basis since reported profit is then closer to economic or real profit.

Long-Term Investments—Noncurrent Assets

One of the noncurrent classifications applicable to assets is that of investments. Investments owned by business enterprises include shares of stock, bonds, and other securities, mortgages and contracts receivable, life insurance policies on the lives of officers that designate the company as beneficiary, and special funds to finance plant expansion or to retire long-term debt. Temporary investments are classed as current assets. Only long-term holdings of securities are classified as investments.

A basic accounting position on the reporting of long-term investments and noncurrent assets is quoted below.

Long-term investments in securities should be carried at the lower of aggregate cost or market. When market quotations are available, the aggregate quoted amounts (and information as to whether aggregate cost or market is the carrying amount) should be disclosed. Investments in affiliates should be segregated from other investments.[74]

Fixed Assets

Fixed assets consist of land, plant, and equipment reported at cost less depreciation, i.e., amortization of cost. The process of depreciation is the process of amortization of cost over the estimated life of the asset and is in no sense a process of valuation, as discussed in Chapter 6.

The economic value of fixed assets is their earning power, which bears no necessary relationship to the amount at which they are carried in the books. In most cases, the going-concern value and the replacement value of fixed assets in recent years are well in excess of the amount at which the fixed assets are recorded in the company's books of account, as evidence by the willingness of acquiring companies to pay 1 $\frac{1}{2}$ times book value or more in recent years.

---

74 Quoted from Accounting Research Study No. 7, pp. 259–260, and APB Opinion No. 18, except for changes made by FASB Statement No. 12 (December 1975).

Since it has been permissible to use one set of accounting rules when reporting to the IRS and another when reporting to stockholders, in the mid 1970s there was overreporting of profits to stockholders. By 1979 underdepreciation is said to have amounted to almost a fourth of pretax profits in reports to stockholders and about half of that in reports to the IRS. Many said that the estimating of replacement costs might have the advantage to corporations of showing the IRS that the corporations' real profits didn't merit present taxes.

Wasting Assets

Natural resources are wasting assets. They are exhausted physically through extraction and, except for timber, they are irreplaceable. Until these resources are extracted from the land, they are classified as fixed assets; once they have been extracted, they are classified as inventories until sold.

Accepted practice in accounting for natural resources is as follows:

When the presence of a natural resource is discovered subsequent to acquisition of the property, or when the extent of the deposit is determined to be materially more extensive than previously assessed, it is accepted practice to reconsider previous allocations of aggregate cost.

The search for new resources is a continuing endeavor.... This endeavor necessitates large outlays for exploration, options, lease bonuses, advance royalties, abstract and recording fees, geological and geophysical staff expenses, and so forth. Even when the most advanced geological and geophysical technology is used to predict reserves, there is no assurance that resource deposits in paying quantities will be located, or that once located, the original estimates of the deposit will hold up. The uncertainty characteristic of extractive industries presents difficult problems and cost determination and allocation. It is accepted practice either to capitalize or expense the outlays mentioned above; but the majority practice is to capitalize the costs that are readily identifiable with the successful acquisition of specific resources in paying quantities and to expense the others.[75]

---

75 Accounting Research Study No. 7, p. 258.

Intangibles

Intangibles that appear in the balance sheet come from two sources: (1) intangible assets purchased outright, and (2) intangible assets developed initially in the regular course of business. Such assets have no physical existence and depend on future anticipated benefits for their value.

Intangibles purchased outright are intangibles (such as goodwill) that have been acquired in exchange for an issue of securities, for cash, or for other considerations. The AICPA stated in APB Opinion No. 17 (1970) that the costs of all intangible assets, including those arising from a "purchase" type of business combination, should be recorded as assets and should be amortized by systematic charges to income over estimated benefit periods, the period of amortization not to exceed forty years.

Goodwill has been important in recent years as the result of the multitude of mergers and other acquisitions that have taken place. The acquiring corporation often pays more than book value of the assets acquired, and the difference is recorded as goodwill under the purchase of assets method. As explained earlier, the use of the "pooling of assets" method has been discouraged by AICPA pronouncements.

There may be intangible assets developed in the regular course of the business—for example, as the result of research and development or of advertising and promotion. With respect to research and development, the author of an AICPA-published study has stated that "the most practical treatment is to charge these expenditures to expense currently, for it is usually difficult to determine in advance the benefit that may result in future periods."[76] This position was adopted officially by the AICPA in Statement of Financial Accounting Standards No. 2. With respect to advertising costs incident to developing consumer preference for trademarks, tradenames, brand names, and brands, this author also has stated: "It is, however, impossible to delineate the portion of advertising costs that have expired in the production of current revenue from the portion that may be applicable to the future. Treatment as current expense is, therefore, accepted practice."[77]

The questionable liquidity value of intangibles has led to the suggestion that such assets be eliminated from total assets and owner's equity when studying capital structure. These assets, however, may be among the most valuable owned by the enterprise, and it, therefore, seems inadvisable to eliminate them from

---

76 Accounting Research Study No. 7, pp. 265–266.

77 Ibid., p. 266.

consideration in a financial analysis. Goodwill, for example, should be supported by superior earning power and this can be looked for. The accountant's value for intangibles in a balance sheet are highly questionable, but one should assess whether values beyond the physical assets of a business exist when assessing its common stock.

Liabilities and Capital Sections of the Balance Sheet

The balance sheet furnishes information on the amount of funds raised from creditors, both short- and long-term obligations, and from owners (including retained earnings). Investors should analyze the long-term capitalization of the corporation (long-term debt plus owners' equity), by means of ratios, to indicate the degree of financial leverage being utilized by the corporation and rates of return being earned on capitalization. Short-term obligations should be analyzed in terms of the current assets and cash flow factors from which payment must come.

Current Liabilities

Current liabilities designate obligations that must be paid within one year from the date of the balance sheet. The current liability classification, however, is not intended to include a contractual obligation falling due at an early date that is expected to be refunded, or debts to be liquidated by funds that are carried in noncurrent asset accounts.[78] Liquidation of such liabilities reasonably could be expected to require the use of current assets or the creation of other current liabilities. Current liabilities are therefore related to current assets when assessing the possibility that the firm will experience liquidity problems. The ratios used in such an analysis are discussed in Chapter 11.

Long-Term Debt

This section consists of long-term obligations such as bonds, private placement notes, equipment obligations, and term and time bank loans, the latter generally with maturities of one to eight years. The amounts that appear on the balance sheet

---

78 See "Restatement and Revision of Accounting Research Bulletins," *Accounting Research Bulletin* No. 43, pp. 21–23, and amendment by SFAS No. 6 (May 1975), for a detailed and specific item-by-item discussion of the accounts included as current liabilities.

generally can be assumed to state accurately the amount of long-term obligations currently outstanding. Notes to financial statements will furnish additional information about the debt contracts, such as restrictive clauses against charges to retained earnings for dividends and officers' salaries. Such restrictions are important to common stockholders, since they can limit financing opportunities to support growth and dividend payments.

Leases

In the post-World War II period, leasing has become a major method of financing the use of property and equipment; annual rentals under leases run into billions of dollars. Leasing differs in technique, although often not in substance, from conventional purchase of assets.

FASB Statement No. 13 contains guidelines, which became effective January 1, 1977, for classifying leases and accounting and reporting standards for each class of lease.

Before the FASB issued Statement 13 during 1976, the IRS had ruled on May 5, 1975, that a lessor had to have at least 20 percent equity in the property leased in order to have the owner privilege of the investment credit. At that time the SEC was requiring only footnote disclosure of lease obligations in financial statements. When Statement 13 called for capitalization on the balance sheet, the debt-to-equity ratio of companies making use of leasing was greatly affected. For this reason Statement 13 permitted companies that had leases already in existence four years (until December 31, 1980) before requiring capitalization. However, in the spring of 1977 the SEC proposed requiring immediate retroactive application of FASB Statement No. 13 to existing leases in reports for fiscal years ending on or after December 1977. This was in the belief "that most of the data will have to be accumulated by the end of this year under other requirements and should be available at that time for restatement purposes."[79] If a company had difficulty resolving its restrictive clause problems, and therefore could not comply with requirements, it was to disclose that fact.

According to FASB Statement No. 13 leases are classified as (1) capital leases, or (2) operating leases. Operating leases are those that the lessor will reacquire to lease again. They are to be accounted for as rental expense to the lessee and as rental income to the lessor.

Capital leases are defined under the following criteria:

---

79 See SEC Section of News Report, *Journal of Accountancy* (May, 1977), pp. 20–22.

1. The lease transfers ownership of the property to the lessee by the end of the lease term.
2. The lease contains a bargain purchase option.
3. The lease term is equal to at least 75 percent of the estimated economic life of the leased property. This criterion does not apply if the beginning of the term falls within the last 25 percent of the total estimated life.
4. The present value of the minimum lease payments at the beginning of the lease term equals 90 percent of the fair value of the leased property, less any related investment tax credit retained by the lessor.
5. If the lease meets any of these criteria, it must be capitalized by the lessee on the balance sheet as an asset and an obligation. If it doesn't meet any of these criteria, it is an operating lease and needn't be capitalized, according to the statement.[80]

Unfunded Pension Reserves—Past Service Cost

When a corporation establishes a pension fund, it accepts two costs: (1) past service costs that have not been funded, and (2) current pension costs based on current payrolls. Pension costs and especially legislation to require vesting of pensions were discussed in Chapter 8.

The problem as far as the balance sheet is concerned is that of past service costs—the unfunded pension costs covering the period prior to the inauguration of the pension plan. These funds were not set aside previously but would have been funded if a pension plan had been in effect. The amount of these unfunded pension costs often is substantial and in the case of large corporations may amount to several billion dollars.[81] The article states that Investors Management Sciences, Inc., recorded, in their survey of 1976 corporate pension liability, that General Motors had $7.3 billion in unfunded past/prior service costs and $3 billion in unfunded vested benefits. IMS's survey covered 1,644 companies. These unfunded pension costs are a liability of the corporation. However, many pension fund agreements provide that annual payments to amortize unfunded pension costs may be skipped in years of poor earnings, sometimes for as many as three consecutive years.

---

80 Quoted directly from FASB section of News Report, *Journal of Accountancy* (January 1977), p. 7.

81 See "Unfunded Pension Liabilities: A Growing Worry for Companies," *Business Week* (July 18, 1977k), pp. 86–88.

However, the Accounting Principles Board of the AICPA stated that a major objective of Opinion No. 8 was to eliminate inappropriate fluctuation in recorded pension costs. It stated that "costs should not be limited to the amounts for which the company has a legal liability." The principles involved are that the pension cost accounting method should be applied consistently from year to year and that the amount recognized for past pension service costs should be relatively stable from year to year.[82] Opinion No. 8 does not require that certified statements disclose the amount of unfunded or otherwise unprovided for past or prior service costs. However, the SEC does require such disclosure.

It is certainly true that the unfunded cost is to a degree a fluctuating type of liability and therefore should not have to be incorporated as a liability on the balance sheet proper. However, the requirement by the AICPA that the amount of the annual past pension service cost (amortized) should be stable from year to year should place the analyst on notice that the liability for past service costs is a liability that should be amortized in a relatively stable manner.

Preferred Stock Equity

If the corporation has preferred stock outstanding the balance sheet will disclose the number of shares, the par or stated value per share, and the total dollar amount of the preferred stock. In the balance sheet, preferred stock is listed in the capital section along with the common stock. Although it is essentially an equity security, it is a strictly limited equity security.

The preferred stock is senior to the common stock. The amount shown on the balance sheet should represent the claim of preferred stock coming ahead of the common stock, but this is not always the manner in which it is reported. If the preferred stock has a par value or a stated value relatively close to its legal claim (for example, liquidating value) ahead of the common stock, then the balance sheet closely reflects the actual situation. However, if the stated value is only a nominal amount and is not close to the claim of the preferred stock, then the preferred stock on the balance sheet (number of shares of preferred stock times the stated value) does not reflect the true situation. In addition, there may be dividend arrears, which, while they are not liabilities of the corporation, do represent a claim senior to the common stock. However, such arrearages usually are not shown on the balance sheet but are disclosed only as a footnote thereto.

---

82 Julius W. Phoenix, Jr., and William D. Bosse, "Accounting for the Cost of Pension Plans-More Information on APB No. 8, *Journal of Accountancy* (October 1967); and "Pension Reform," *Journal of Accountancy* (May 1972), p. 76.

In summary, if the balance sheet does not reflect the preferred stock's claim properly, the analyst should reconstruct the balance sheet so that it reflects the preferred claims that are senior to the common stock.

Common Stock Equity

Because the common stock is the residual claimant to the assets and the earnings of the corporation, the common stock section of the balance sheet is divided into three separate accounts: capital stock, retained earnings (formerly earned surplus), and capital paid-in in excess of par (or stated) value (formerly capital surplus).

There is considerable lack of uniformity in the manner in which common stock (and preferred stock) is reported in the balance sheet. Many analysts feel that the trend in recent years toward highly condensed statements supported by notes to financial statements has gone too far (e.g., giving only one summary figure for capital stock). Furthermore, in spite of the opinion[83] that the term "surplus" should not be used because it has a "money in the bank" connotation that is misleading, a few corporations still use the term.

---

83   Accounting Research Study No. 7, pp. 188–190 states:

67. While the terms capital surplus and earned surplus have been widely used, they are open to serious objection.

1. The term surplus has a connotation of excess, overplus, residue, or "that which remains when use or need is satisfied" (Webster), whereas no such meaning is intended where the term is used in accounting.
2. The terms capital and surplus have established meanings in other fields, such as economics and law, which are not in accordance with the concepts the accountant seeks to express in using those terms.
3. The use of the term capital surplus (sometimes called, paid-in surplus) gives rise to confusion. If the word surplus is intended to indicate capital accumulated by the retention of earnings, i.e., retained income, it is not used properly in the term capital surplus; and if it is intended to indicate a portion of the capital, there is an element of redundancy in the term capital surplus.
4. If the term capital stock (and in some states the term capital surplus) be used to indicate capital which, in the legal sense, is restricted as to withdrawal, there is an implication in the terms surplus or earned surplus of availability for dividends. This is unfortunate because the status of corporate assets may be such that they are not, as a practical matter, or as a matter of prudent management, available for dividends.

68. In seeking terms more nearly connotative of the ideas sought to be expressed, consideration should be given primarily to the sources from which the proprietary capital

An authoritative writer[84] on accounting has suggested the following break-down of the capital section of the balance sheet, although stating that "the detail breakdown...is not ordinarily shown in financial statements."

Stockholders' equity in capital invested

Capital stock

Preferred stock–5% cumulative; par value
$100; authorized—shares; issued—shares   . . . . .
Class A preferred stock–$2.00 cumulative;
no par value, redeemable value $30; authorized
and issued—shares   . . . . .
Common stock-no par value; stated value $10;
authorized—shares; issued—shares of
which—are in treasury   . . . . .

Capital paid-in excess of park, redemption and stated
values of capital stocks

Premium on preferred stock   . . . . .
Arising from treasury stock
transactions   . . . . .
Paid-in on common stock
Retained earnings capitalized on
stock dividends   . . . .

---

was derived....

69. In view of the foregoing the committee in 1949...recommending that, in the balance-sheet presentation of stockholder's equity:

1. The use of the term surplus (whether standing alone or in such combinations as capital surplus, paid-in surplus, earned surplus, appraisal surplus, etc.) be discontinued...

3. The term earned surplus be replaced by terms which will indicate source, such as retained income, retained earnings, accumulated earnings, or earnings retained for use in the business. In the case of a deficit, the amount would be shown as a deduction from contributed capital with appropriate description. that the term "surplus" should not be used because it has a "money in the bank" connotation that is misleading, a few major corporations still are using the term on their balance sheets.

84 Ibid., pp. 191–192.

Retained earnings:

    Appropriated in amount equal to restriction
        under bank loan as to payment of dividends   . . . . .

    Unappropriated   . . . .

        Total   . . . . .

    Deduct cost of—shares of treasury stock   . . . . .

    Stockholder equity   . . . . .

CHAPTER 10

Earnings Per Share and Cash Flow Analysis

On Wall Street, a most significant figure used in reference to common stock is its earnings per share along with its correlated ratio of market price to earnings per share (the P/E ratio). Accountants and financial analysts have criticized the undue emphasis often placed on earnings per share, especially when reviewed in isolation without consideration of accounting limitations inherent in the calculation and other income statement items. Moreover, reported net income or earnings per share are not good surrogates for cash flow from operations when considering bill paying capacity and ability to finance company growth and operations.

The three major criticisms of the use of earnings per share figures by themselves are: (1) without correlation with an income statement review and analysis, it can lead to erroneous conclusions; (2) reported earnings per share may be non-comparable over time or between companies; and (3) it concentrates the investor's attention on a single figure without reference to the corporation as a whole, which would provide information on the sources and the nature of income and provide some basis for a reasonable projection of earnings and dividends. An analyst of financial statements should carefully review the income statement and adjust where needed to represent economic and comparable income over time and between firms.

Calculating Earnings Per Share

Earnings per share are calculated by dividing the earnings available to common stockholders (earnings after taxes less any required preferred stock dividends) by the weighted average number of common shares outstanding over the year for which the calculation takes place. Opinion No. 15[85] required two presentations of earnings per share when dilutive securities (convertible securities or securities with warrants) that can be used to purchase common stock are outstanding: (1) primary earnings per share and (2) fully diluted earnings per share. These latter two calculations recognize the potential for dilution of earnings per share, if the dilutive securities are utilized to acquire common stock. Moreover, Opinion 15 required that earnings per share or net loss per share must be reported separately for ordinary items, extraordinary items and total earnings.

An illustrative calculation can clarify the meaning of primary and fully diluted earnings per share. Assume a company has outstanding 20 million shares of common stock (on average) and that common equity totals $400 million in the balance sheet. Further assume that there is $400 million of 5 percent preferred stock outstanding of which $200 million is convertible into 40 million common shares. Also assume there is $400 million of 10 percent long-term debenture bonds outstanding, of which $200 million is convertible into 30 million common shares. Finally, assume this company has a profit before interest charges and income taxes of $200 million and is subject to an effective income tax rate of 50 per cent. The corporate tax rate today is lower than 50 per cent, but the aim merely is to show the impact of taxes. Primary earnings per share for a company that has no dilutive securities outstanding would be the same as the usually determined earnings per share, or undiluted earnings per share. Fully diluted earnings per share (assuming all convertible securities are converted) and undiluted earnings per share for our illustrative company are shown in Table 10–1.

Primary earnings per share is calculated on the basis of the number of common shares actually outstanding plus shares that would be issued in a conversion when the convertible instruments are considered common stock equivalents by the accountant. They would be so considered when the cash yield on such convertibles is less than $66\frac{2}{3}$ per cent of the then average AA corporate bond yield. Accordingly, in the above example, if all of the convertibles were considered common stock equivalents then primary and fully diluted earnings per share would be the same. If none of the convertibles were considered common stock equivalents, then primary earnings per share would equal undiluted earnings per share. If a part of the convertible securities were considered common stock equivalents, then primary earnings per share would fall between undiluted and fully diluted earnings per share. Though not illustrated, where options or warrants are considered to be common stock equivalents, the funds raised in their exercise are

---

85 "Earnings Per Share," Opinions of the Accounting Principles Board No. 15 (New York: AICPA, 1969).

Table 10–1   Calculation of Undiluted and Fully Diluted Earnings Per Share (Millions of Dollars)

	Undiluted		Fully Diluted
Earnings Before Interest and Taxes	$200		$200
Interest Expense* ($400 Million × .1)	40	($200 Million × .1)	20
	160		180
Taxes at 50%	80		90
Earnings After Taxes	80		90
Preferred Dividend ($400 million × .05)	20	($200 Million × .05)	10
Earnings Available to Common	60		80
Number of Shares*	20		90
Earnings Per Share	$ 3.00		$ 0.89

*The conversion of the $200 million of bonds resulted in the issue of an additional 30 million shares outstanding. The conversion of the $200 million of preferred stock resulted in the issue of an additional 40 million shares. The number of shares outstanding, therefore, increased by 70 million. Moreover, the interest expense and preferred dividends associated with instruments converted will no longer be paid and must be eliminated. This required an adjustment in taxes.

assumed to be used to purchase common stock at current market prices and retire it.

It is suggested that both primary earnings per share and fully diluted earnings per share be used when calculating an intrinsic value for a common stock. The analyst will then determine two intrinsic values and can use them as a range of potential value.

The Price-Earnings Ratio

A reported price-earnings ratio may be the current market price of the stock divided by (1) the latest available twelve months' earnings, (2) earnings projected for the next twelve months, (3) the average or midpoint of projected earnings for the next five or six years, or (4) the earnings expectation in a target year three to six years hence. The most commonly used denominator is the latest available twelve months' earnings.

P/E ratios are used commonly as indicators of relative value for various common stocks. P/E ratios can, however, give a distorted view of relative value due to different accounting techniques and definitions that may be employed by various firms or by the same firm over time, as already discussed in previous chapters. Moreover, a common stockholder is concerned with the future performance of the firm, while a P/E ratio is based on past performance. This is why estimates of future earnings are sometimes used in calculating such ratios. A P/E ratio provides only a crude indicator of relative investment merit, and must be used with great caution. Still, they do provide an indication of market expectations if earnings are properly adjusted when calculating the ratio. The higher the expected growth rate and the less the volatility of earnings, the higher the P/E ratio awarded to a firm.

Low P/E Ratio Stock Selection Approach

The low P/E approach to stock selection advocates choosing a representative group of companies from the bottom three or four deciles, or those with the lowest 30 to 40 percent of all P/E ratios. One must be careful when reviewing cyclical companies since they are likely to have very low P/E ratios when their earnings are at their cyclical peak and higher P/E ratios when their earnings are at the cyclical trough. We would suggest calculating an average of the earnings over the cycle and using this as a reference point in interpreting their P/E ratios.

Another problem arises with companies that have loss years, since a meaningful P/E ratio cannot be calculated in such years. The analyst would have to consider the future prospects of these companies when selecting stocks. Fundamental analysis and valuation, as advocated in this book, provide useful tools to aid in implementing a low P/E ratio selection approach, since they do consider the future and can handle the problems described above.

There is much support in the literature for the low price-earnings ratio approach to stock selection, as summarized briefly below:

1. Paul Miller performed a study at Drexel & Company of the price performance of the 30 Dow Jones stocks grouped by P/E ratios over the period 1937–69.[86]

    The 30 stocks were divided into two groups for each year, the ten lowest P/E ratio stocks and the ten highest. The two groups were also compared to the average for the 30 stocks. The results are summarized in Table 10–2. The low P/E stocks clearly outperformed the high P/E stocks and the Dow-Jones Industrial Average.

---

86 See B. Graham, D. Dodd and S. Cottle, *Security Analysis Principles and Technique*, 4th Ed. (New York: McGraw Hill, 1962) pp. 468–477.

Table 10–2   Average Annual Percentage Gain or Loss on the Test Issues, 1937–1969

Period	Ten Low P/E Stocks	Ten High P/E Stocks	Thirty DJIA Stocks
1937–1942	– 2.2%	–10.0%	– 6.3%
1943–1947	17.3	8.3	14.9
1948–1952	16.4	4.6	9.9
1953–1957	20.9	10.0	13.7
1958–1962	10.2	– 3.3	3.6
1963–1969	8.0	4.6	4.0

Source: Benjamin Graham, *The Intelligent Investor*, 4th ed.

2. David Dreman reported on extensive statistical studies supporting the low P/E stock selection approach in the 1979 edition of his book *Contrarian Investment Strategy*. The results of his study of annualized compound rates of return for a sample of 1251 companies (70% of which were listed on the New York Stock Exchange) over the period 1968–1977 are summarized in Table 10–3.
3. Anthony Hitschler, David Good, John Peavy, and others have published articles offering similar support.
4. The author of this book recently completed a study (unpublished at this time) covering the period 1968–1986 and using the P.D.E. Compustat tape which generated similar results to those found by David Dreman.

The above quoted studies offer strong support for the usefulness of price-earnings ratios as a screening tool in stock selection. Still, with the known limitations of such ratios, the selection process must probe much deeper using fundamental analysis and valuation efforts. The author is convinced that the best values will be found among stocks sporting relatively low P/E ratios, but careful selection must be made to weed out the stocks that sport low P/E ratios because their future is not bright and/or their risk is high.

Cash Flow Analysis

Cash flow is used typically on Wall Street, in the financial press, and in company reports to designate net earnings after taxes with depreciation, depletion and other

Table 10-3 Annualized Compound Rates of Return, August 1968–August 1977

Stocks Ranked by P/E Multiples Decile*	1 Quarter	6 Months	1 Year	3 Years	Holding Original Portfolio for 9 Years
1 (Highest P/Es)	-2.64%	-1.06%	-1.13%	-1.4%	0.33%
2	0.92	1.62	0.56	-0.28	1.27
3	0.51	0.62	1.63	0.85	3.30
4	3.06	3.42	3.31	4.87	5.36
5	2.19	4.46	2.93	5.02	3.72
6	4.84	5.33	6.70	4.82	4.52
7	7.90	6.07	6.85	5.89	6.08
8	8.83	8.24	8.56	7.78	6.35
9	11.85	8.40	6.08	7.73	6.40
10 (Lowest P/Es)	14.00	11.68	10.26	10.89	7.89

Average return of sample = 4.75%.

* Takes all stocks in study and divides them into ten groups according to the P/E ratio.

Source: David Dreman, *Contrarian Investment Strategy* (New York: Random House, 1979), p. 131.

noncash expense items of the period added back. It is important to realize, however, that depreciation and depletion (and other noncash expenses) are real expenses, even though they did not require a cash outflow in the current period. Any attempt to downgrade the importance of depreciation or depletion as an expense can lead to an erroneous conception of true corporate earning power over time. Inability to generate adequate earnings after depreciation may lead to serious financial problems and inability to replace assets as they wear out or become obsolete. Remember, one must replace the asset base that is wearing out if one is to continue to produce income.

Depreciation or depletion are often considered a source of funds (and listed as such in a cash flow or funds flow statement) in the sense that funds generated by sales are not siphoned off by depreciation or depletion since no expenditures are currently made. But a situation where there is no profit before depreciation or where there is a loss before deprecation clearly emphasizes that depreciation by and of itself is not a source of funds. Sales revenues are the basic source of all funds derived from operations.

Statement of Changes in Financial Position

Fragmentary information on sources and uses of funds and cash can be obtained from comparative balance sheets and income statements. A comprehensive picture of the cash flow of a business can only be gained, however, from a Statement of Changes in Financial Position, found in an annual report. This statement can provide information on such questions as:

1. How were the funds provided by operations, and from other sources, used in the business?
2. Where did the funds come from to maintain dividends in the face of potential losses?
3. How did the business get the funds to accomplish the debt repayment that took place during the period?
4. What were the sources of increases in working capital during the period or what uses were made of withdrawals from working capital?
5. How did the company finance a large investment project, such as Atlantic Richfield's financing its drilling for oil in the North Slope of Alaska?

Moreover, analysts forecast future fund flows under varying assumptions to assess the ability of the firm to finance its growth plans, maintain its capital base and reward owners. The "Consolidated Statement of Changes in Financial Position" for Bell South Corporation is offered for illustrative purposes in Table 10–4.

A Cash Focus

Statements of Changes in Financial Position often focus on explaining changes in working capital, but there are increasing demands that these statements focus on cash.[87] Analysts should concentrate on the nature of cash inflows and outflows to provide a better basis for assessing future cash flows. Previous chapters of this book offer numerous examples indicating that reported net income and cash flow are two different things, since the determination of net income is based on accrual accounting techniques. For example, depreciation is listed as an expense in a given year, thereby reducing reported profits, when there has been no corresponding cash outflow. Net income becomes an even less adequate surrogate for assessing

---

87 See FASB, *Statement of Financial Accounting Concepts*, No. 1, "Objectives of Financial Reporting by Business Enterprises" (Stanford, Conn., 1978).

Table 10–4 Consolidated Statements of Changes in Financial Position—Bell South Corporation

In Millions	For the Years Ended December 31,		
	1986	1985	1984
Funds from Operations:			
Net Income	$1,588.7	$1,417.8	$1,257.2
Add Expenses Not Requiring Funds Currently:			
Depreciation	1,935.6	1,802.2	1,535.8
Deferred Income Taxes	481.2	359.9	375.6
Investment Tax Credits	(69.9)	74.3	53.8
Deduct Income Not Providing Funds Currently:			
Interest Charged Construction	33.0	36.0	30.0
Total Funds From Operations	3,902.6	3,618.2	3,192.4
Less: Dividends Declared	954.6	847.1	766.0
	2,948.0	2,771.1	2,426.4
Funds from External Financing:			
Issuance of Common Stock	329.5	397.9	277.5
Increase (decrease) in Debt Due To:			
Issuance of Long-term Notes and Debentures	800.0	550.0	—
Short-term Borrowings-Net	(8.6)	(300.8)	341.4
Obligations Under Capital Leases-Net	11.7	11.3	123.2
Other	(142.2)	74.9	26.3
Total Funds from External Financing	990.4	733.3	768.4
Less: Retirement of Long-term Debt	1,350.0	45.0	—
Investment:	(359.6)	688.3	768.4
Construction Expenditures (including $33.0, $36.0 and $30.0, Respectively, of Interest Charged Construction)	(2,835.1)	(2,624.1)	(2,274.0)
Purchase of Treasury Stock	—	(184.9)	—
Affiliates and Other	(199.7)	(8.8)	(1.0)
	(3,034.8)	(2,817.8)	(2,275.0)
Changes in Working Capital * (excluding current maturities of long-term debt, notes payable and deferred income taxes)			
Accounts Receivable	2.7	59.6	(539.7)
Material and Supplies	(32.9)	(7.4)	(135.2)
Other Current Assets	(78.7)	(5.3)	(156.1)
Accounts Payable	293.1	(203.2)	160.9
Taxes Accrued	95.4	(44.5)	(11.1)
Advance Billing and Customer Deposits	25.1	29.2	17.7
Dividends Payable	27.8	19.5	194.4
Interest and Rents Accrued	(37.3)	16.4	(11.2)
Other Current Liabilities	(62.1)	128.6	8.6
	233.1	(7.1)	(471.7)

Table 10–4 (continued)
Other Changes:[*]

Deferred Charges and Other Assets	(24.4)	(18.6)	(54.0)
Other-net	179.9	(99.0)	50.9
	155.5	(117.6)	(3.1)
Increase (decrease) in Cash and Temporary Cash Investments	(57.8)	516.9	445.0
Cash and Temporary Cash Investments at Beginning of Period	1,008.1	491.2	46.2
Cash and Temporary Cash Investments at End of Period	$ 950.3	$1,008.1	$ 491.2

The accompanying notes are an integral part of these financial statements.

[*] ( ) Denotes a use of funds.

Source: Bell South Corporation, 1986 Annual Report, p. 42.

---

cash flow during inflationary periods. The gap between reported earnings and cash flow widens during inflationary periods, since a growing investment in receivables and inventories is not offset by corresponding increases in trade credit.

J.A. Largay, III, and CP. Stickney during the 1966–75 period preceding its bankruptcy.[88] They noted that financial indicators such as profitability ratios and trends, turnover ratios and liquidity ratios showed some down trends, but provided no definite clues to the company's impending bankruptcy. A study of cash flows from operations, however, revealed that company operations were causing an increasing drain on cash, rather than providing cash. This necessitated increasing use of external financing, the required interest payments on which exacerbated the cash flow drain. Cash flow analysis clearly was a valuable tool in this case.

A financially healthy firm will generate cash from operations on a consistent basis. Professor Bernstein has pointed out that, "The unsuccessful firm will find its cash drained by slowdowns in receivables and inventory turnovers, by operating losses, or by a combination of these factors."[89] The investor should look for companies that report real earnings, not those that are the result of inflation, that

---

88 J.A. Largay III and C.P. Stickney, "Cash Flows, Ratio Analysis and the W.T. Grant Company Bankruptcy," *Financial Analysts Journal*, July–August, 1980, pp. 51–54.

89 Leopold A. Bernstein, *Financial Statement Analysis: Theory, Application, and Interpretation*, 3rd ed., (Homewood, Ill: Richard D. Irwin, Inc., 1983) p. 405.

have healthy cash flows and sound reasons for assuming that these cash flows will continue in the future.

Inflation and Cash Flow

Profits reported to stockholders during inflationary periods are in part real earnings and in part illusion. If the need to replace worn out plant and equipment and inventories that were used to generate the cash inflows are considered, there may be no real profits. A real profit means that the firm has more real assets at the end of the period than when they began the period.

Richard Greene illustrates this problem effectively by contrasting Dow Chemical and Union Carbide:[90]

> Take a look, for example, at Dow Chemical and Union Carbide, two giant chemical companies. Over the four years from 1976 to 1979, Dow *showed earnings totaling about* $2.5 billion. Over the same period, Union Carbide reported cumulative earnings of some $1.8 billion. It would appear that both firms were robust money-makers in the same league.

> But, take it a step further and look at cash. Kidder, Peabody & Co. did this and, although Kidder's methodology is a bit controversial, the question is a matter of degree—not direction. Kidder came up with a number called discretionary cash flow. That's the figure representing how much money a firm has left to grow with—after taking out the amount necessary to maintain its property, plant and equipment after dividends. Companies don't really set aside money to replace equipment but ultimately they have to put out the cash—and it's not going toward growth.

> Dow's discretionary cash flow is at a healthy level with $924 million over the four year period. But Union Carbide has a different story, negative discretionary cash flow of $663 million. That means, according to Kidder, Union Carbide was paying dividends for that whole period of time with borrowed money. It was, in effect, cannibalizing its capital structure to keep the stock price up. That's not a healthy habit. But it's common among the kind of huge firms you'd think would know better.

---

90 Richard Greene, "Are More Chryslers in the Offering?" *Forbes*, February 2, 1981, pp. 69–73, as reported in William M. Bowen and Frank P. Ganucheau, *The Investor's Equation* (Chicago, Ill.: Probus Publishing Company, 1984), p. 111.

Table 10–5   Calculating Cash Flow From Operations

A. Sales
   +   Decrease (– increase) in accounts receivable
   +   Cash collections on sales
   +   Other revenues (+ or – adjustments for noncash items)
   =   Total cash collections from operations

B. Cost of Goods Sold (excluding depreciation, amortization, etc.)
   +   Increase (– decrease) in inventories
   +   Decrease (– increase) in trade payables
   +   Operating Expenses
   +   Other Expenses (including interest)
   +   Increase (– decrease) in prepaid assets
   +   Decrease (– increase) in accrued liabilities
   +   Income Tax Expense (excluding deferred taxes)
   +   Decrease (– increase) in accrued taxes
   =   Total cash outflows from operations

C. Net Cash Flows from Operations = A – B

Source: Leopold A. Bernstein, op. cit., pp. 411–413.

Calculating Cash Flow From Operations

One can estimate cash flow from operations by adding all noncash charges in the income statement (such as depreciation expense) to reported earnings after taxes, and deduct from this total all dividends paid and capital expenditures. A healthy company should show a positive total for cash flow from operations over a five-year period.

Professor Bernstein suggests a more detailed approach to calculating cash flow from operations, as shown in Table 10–5. This offers a more complete basis for analysis of cash flow, since it considers changes in working capital as well as dividends and capital expenditures and begins with sales rather than reported earnings.

Some Characteristics of "Good Companies"

Bowen and Ganucheau suggest the following list of characteristics of a "good company" for investment:[91]

1. The ability to raise prices to cover rises in costs, even in poor economic times. This requires that the company face a relatively inelastic demand. Companies that offer unique high-quality goods or services or are in oligopolistic market situations with little threat of new entry are most likely to meet this condition. One must be careful, however, since pricing power may be more than built into the price of the company's stock. Careful valuation analysis is still necessary.
2. The company shows unit, as well as dollar, growth in sales. In other words, the growth in sales is real.
3. Leverage, both operating and financial is favorable.
4. The company is able to retain a high or above average return on total assets and owners' equity.
5. Labor cost are low, in comparison to competitors.
6. Pension plans are funded adequately, and cash flow seems able to support future needs without hurting the return to owners.
7. Research and development efforts have been successful historically. For most companies, research and development expenses are not voluntary. Failure to maintain this effort often will lead to failure of the company, since the innovations introduced by competitors will cause their product and/or service offerings to become obsolete. A healthy cash flow is needed to support the research and development effort.
8. A relatively low fixed cost base, as indicated by a relatively high ratio of sales to each dollar of average gross plant value for the industry the company operates in.
9. A high earnings retention ratio that supports company growth and sustains capital during inflationary times.
10. A healthy cash flow over an extended period.

---

91 William M. Bowen IV and Frank P. Ganucheau III, *The Investor's Equation*, op. cit., pp. 122–130.

Ratio analysis, to be discussed in the next chapter, will provide a useful tool, with cash flow analysis, for purposes of assessing the degree to which a company offers the above characteristics.

CHAPTER 11

Ratio Analysis

The major function of financial statement analysis is to disclose those significant relationships demonstrated by the past and present record of a company, so that a meaningful projection of the company's future performance probabilities and financial strength may be estimated. The ratios suggested in this chapter represent relationships that analysts have found useful over many years of experience. Suggested ratios will be grouped into four basic areas for analytical purposes:

1. Profitability Ratios—These ratios break earnings per share into its basic determinants for purposes of assessing the factors underlying the profitability of the firm. They help assess the adequacy of historical profits, and to project future profitability through better understanding of its underlying causes.
2. Short-Term Solvency Ratios—These ratios assess the ability of the firm to meet debts maturing over the coming year.
3. Long-Term Solvency and Financial Leverage Ratios—These ratios assess the extent to which a firm relies on debt financing, and the ability of the firm to meet the fixed obligations brought about by debt financing.
4. Value Ratios—Ratios dealing with market price of the shares of the firm and its relations to relative value of a firm's stock.

Standards for a given ratio will vary according to operating characteristics of the company being analyzed and general business conditions; such standards cannot be stated as fixed and immutable. Experience plays an important role in setting such standards.

Profitability Analysis

Profitability ratios are utilized to explore the underlying causes of a change in earnings per share. They show the combined effects of liquidity, and asset and debt management on the profitability of the firm.

It is assumed that the analyst has made all adjustments deemed necessary to reflect comparable and true earning power of the corporation before calculating the ratios discussed below. It is important to stress that ratios are utilized to raise significant questions requiring further analysis, not provide answers. Ratios must be viewed in the context of other ratios and other facts, derived from sources other than the financial statements. We have noted that cash flow analysis provided an indication that W. T. Grant was getting into financial difficulties when typical profit ratios did not.

Underlying Cases of Growth in Earnings Per Share

Profit is the ultimate measure of success of a firm, but it must be related to total asset and owner's investment to avoid being misled. For example, assume a firm with 1,000,000 common shares outstanding earned $1,000,000 after taxes. Earnings per share, assuming only that class of common stock outstanding, would be $1 per share. Now assume the company could earn an additional $500,000 after taxes by utilizing the funds raised through selling an additional 1,000,000 common shares. While total earnings would increase, this would not be advantageous to the stockholder. There are now 2,000,000 shares outstanding, and since earnings would be $1,500,000 after taxes, earnings per share would fall to seventy-five cents per share. Return on the total owners' investment also would fall. This suggests concentrating at least initially, on earnings per share and its determinants rather than earnings after taxes.

The two basic determinants of earnings per share are the return on stockholders' equity and the book value per share, as shown by the equation below:

$$\text{Earnings Per Share} = \frac{\text{Earnings Available to Common (EAC)}}{\text{Average Number of Common Shares}} = \frac{\text{EAC}}{\text{Owners' Equity}} \times \frac{\text{Owners' Equity}}{\text{\# of Shares}}$$

Owners' equity would cancel when multiplying, and one would be left with earnings per share.

Growth in Book Value Per Share

How can a firm get growth in book value per share? There are three basic ways:

1. Retain earnings. When the firm retains earnings owners' equity increases, but there is no change in the number of common shares outstanding. This assumes that the retained earnings can be utilized as effectively as past owners' equity has been; in other words, that the return on owners' equity is at least maintained.

    The growth rate in earnings supported by retained earnings can be calculated by multiplying the rate of return earned on owners' equity by the retention rate of the firm (retained earnings divided by earnings after taxes). A firm that earns 10 percent on its owners' equity and has a retention rate of 40 percent, builds a four percent growth rate for earnings per share. To illustrate assume:

    Earnings per Share = 1
    Book Value per Share = $10
    Retention Rate = 40%

    Forty cents will be retained of each $1 earned per share, increasing book value per share to $10.40. If the firm continues to earn ten percent on the owners' capital $1 / $10), the earnings per share will rise to $1.04, or a four percent growth rate. If the rate earned on owners' capital fell because of the added production capacity, however, earnings per share could fall even with retention. For example, if return on owners' capital fell to eight percent, the earnings per share would be only 83 cents (.08 × $10.40 = $.832).

2. Buy back company stock at a price per share less than book value per share. The opportunity for a firm to do this can occur when there is a serious decline in the stock market, such as in 1974. Ford Motor and other firms did buy back shares in 1974, knowing that it would improve earnings per share for the remaining stockholders. Moreover, they believed there were not many profitable opportunities for investing the cash flow through added business assets.

3. Sell stock at a price above book value per share. Mergers can result in an increase in book value per share for the surviving company, since the book value of the acquired shares may be greater than the book value of the shares given in exchange. While it is true that book value per share has no necessary relationship to market value per share, investors should follow what happens to book value since it is an important determinant of earnings.

Some analysts suggest adding the sustainable growth rate of a firm and its dividend yield and comparing this figure when assessing various firms. The total in future years should exceed that offered by equivalent quality bonds, or why invest in the years must be greater, on a compound annual basis, than the difference between the yield offered by the bond and the dividend yield of the common stock to justify purchase of that stock. The price of a common stock is unlikely to offer the sustained rises needed if not supported by sustained earnings growth.

Return on Owners' Equity

It would be useful to review pages 33 through 40 at this point, to see a macro-application of the analytical framework we will develop for assessing returns on owners' equity. The equivalent of Table 4-7 can be prepared for a company as a basis for studying its profitability.

The two basic determinants of return on owners' equity are the return on total assets and the proportion of assets financed by owners as opposed to creditors. This is demonstrated in the equation below:

$$\frac{\text{Earnings Available to Common (EAC)}}{\text{Owner's Equity}} = \frac{\text{EAC}}{\text{Total Assets}} \times \frac{\text{Total Assets}}{\text{Owners' Equity}}$$

Stockholders are the residual claimants to the profits earned after taxes less any preferred dividends (earnings available to common). The rate earned on the stockholders' invested capital (return on owners' equity) and the behavior of the basic components determining that return, are the key criterion when selecting stocks.

Industry statistics on annual rates of profit on stockholders equity before and after federal income taxes are presented to Table 11-1. Average rates of return or stockholders' equity for all U.S. Corporations and the average profit earned per dollar of sales (the margin) are presented in Table 11-2. The figures offered can serve as crude benchmarks when studying individual companies. Remember, variations from average do not prove a firm will be a good or bad investment. They merely serve to suggest when caution and deeper investigation is necessary. Such investigation should center on likely future behavior suggested by past patterns, not merely historical experience.

Leveraged Capital Structures.   Most firms have a leverage capitalization, meaning debt has been used as a source of funds. This will cause profits and the return to owners to be much more variable than if only equity capital were used to raise funds. The effects of financial leverage are compounded by the effects of operating leverage introduced by fixed operating costs. To illustrate, assume the following data for Temple Corporation:

Table 11–1 Annual Rates of Profit on Stockholders' Equity by Division and Major Group (Percent)

Industry	Income before Income Taxes[1,2]					Income after Income Taxes[3]				
	4Q 1984	1Q 1985	2Q 1985	3Q 1985	4Q 1985	4Q 1984	1Q 1985	2Q 1985	3Q 1985	4Q 1985
All Manufacturing Corporations	16.4	16.5	17.2	15.4	13.8	11.0	10.4	10.9	9.9	9.0
Nondurable Manufacturing Corporations	15.9	17.6	16.6	18.2	13.7	10.9	11.5	10.9	11.7	8.8
Food and Kindred Products	20.4	17.9	21.5	22.6	22.9	13.6	10.9	13.1	14.2	14.7
Tobacco Manufacturers	40.8	30.7	36.7	41.0	30.8	24.9	18.8	21.5	25.3	19.1
Textile Mill Products	14.4	10.7	11.4	12.1	17.6	8.4	5.3	6.9	7.5	10.5
Paper and Allied Products	10.9	15.9	18.2	12.0	13.7	7.0	9.8	11.7	8.1	9.4
Printing and Publishing	32.9	27.4	37.0	35.3	31.4	18.6	16.6	23.1	21.0	18.0
Chemicals and Allied Products	13.2	18.3	18.9	13.3	2.0	10.4	12.5	13.5	9.2	0.8
Industrial Chemicals and Synthetics[3]	8.2	11.3	15.0	-0.2	-8.6	8.3	7.9	11.6	1.0	-6.9
Drugs[3]	27.1	29.5	26.8	28.2	11.5	19.3	20.5	18.3	19.3	7.7
Petroleum and Coal Products	11.4	14.6	6.6	14.0	10.0	8.7	10.5	5.1	9.4	7.7
Rubber and Miscellaneous Plastics Products	13.1	20.7	15.2	18.8	12.3	7.0	12.7	6.2	12.2	7.7
Other Nondurable Manufacturing Corporations	16.6	14.5	15.6	24.2	19.9	10.1	8.2	9.6	14.7	7.5
Durable Manufacturing Corporations	16.9	15.1	17.9	12.4	13.9	11.2	9.2	10.9	7.8	9.3
Stone, Clay, and Glass Products	13.9	5.9	19.7	17.2	13.6	9.6	2.3	11.6	9.7	8.2
Primary Metal Industries	-11.5	-1.6	-5.6	-5.7	-17.1	-13.9	-3.3	-7.8	-7.3	-15.4
Iron and Steel	-8.4	-5.0	-8.8	-2.9	-8.7	-11.3	-8.3	-12.3	-8.0	-10.5
Nonferrous Metals[3]	-13.9	1.0	-3.4	-7.6	-23.1	-16.0	0.3	-4.7	-6.7	-18.8

Table 11-1 (continued)

Industry	Income before Income Taxes[1,2]					Income after Income Taxes[3]				
	4Q 1984	1Q 1985	2Q 1985	3Q 1985	4Q 1985	4Q 1984	1Q 1985	2Q 1985	3Q 1985	4Q 1985
Fabricated Metal Products	18.7	16.6	19.8	14.9	13.4	11.5	10.0	11.4	9.6	7.7
Machinery, Except Electrical	17.6	10.7	15.2	13.3	16.3	12.4	7.1	10.0	8.5	11.7
Electrical and Electronic Equipment	17.8	15.8	14.9	11.8	12.2	12.2	9.9	8.7	7.0	8.2
Transportation Equipment	27.0	27.9	30.9	13.1	25.6	19.7	16.8	20.1	9.9	18.9
Motor Vehicles and Equipment[3]	29.1	30.8	34.8	12.5	26.3	22.8	18.5	23.1	10.7	20.9
Aircraft, Guided Missiles, and Parts[3]	24.8	23.9	24.3	14.8	25.0	15.9	15.0	15.1	8.9	16.2
Instruments and Related Products	18.3	17.1	18.0	13.1	6.7	12.5	11.6	12.3	9.9	6.4
Other Durable Manufacturing Corporations	15.0	15.6	21.4	20.9	18.0	8.5	8.9	12.3	12.0	10.0
All Mining Corporations[4]	-6.0	6.0	3.7	-3.5	-13.9	-8.6	2.1	3.8	-5.3	-12.1
All Retail Trade Corporations[4]	37.6	14.4	18.3	20.0	32.1	21.7	8.4	10.8	11.6	18.7
All Wholesale Trade Corporations	16.4	16.5	20.3	18.2	11.7	9.6	9.0	11.7	10.2	4.2

[1]Based on profit figures which include net income (loss) of foreign branches and equity in earnings (losses) of nonconsolidated subsidiaries, net of foreign taxes.

[2]Some of the rates in this column have been revised since their first appearance. See footnotes to Tables 1.0–47.1.

[3]Included in major industry above.

[4]Mining, wholesale, and retail trade data are representative of the quarterly results of companies in those divisions with assets over $25 million. Data for manufacturing corporations are universe estimates.

Source: Federal Trade Commission, *Quarterly Financial Report for Manufacturing, Mining and Trade Corporations*, 1987.

Table 11–2   Relation of Profit after Taxes to Stockholders' Equity and to Sales, all Manufacturing Corporations, 1947–87

Year or Quarter	Ratio of Profits after Income Taxes (Annual Rate) to Stockholders' Equity—Percent[1]			Profits after Income Taxes per Dollar of Sales—Cents		
	All Manufacturing Corporations	Durable Goods Industries	Nondurable Goods Industries	All Manufacturing Corporations	Durable Goods Industries	Nondurable Goods Industries
1947	15.6	14.4	16.6	6.7	6.7	6.7
1948	16.0	15.7	16.2	7.0	7.1	6.8
1949	11.6	12.1	11.2	5.8	6.4	5.4
1950	15.4	16.9	14.1	7.1	7.7	6.5
1951	12.1	13.0	11.2	4.9	5.3	4.5
1952	10.3	11.1	9.7	4.3	4.5	4.1
1953	10.5	11.1	9.9	4.3	4.2	4.3
1954	9.9	10.3	9.6	4.5	4.6	4.4
1955	12.6	13.8	11.4	5.4	5.7	5.1
1956	12.3	12.8	11.8	5.3	5.2	5.3
1957	10.9	11.3	10.6	4.8	4.8	4.9
1958	8.6	8.0	9.2	4.2	3.9	4.4
1959	10.4	10.4	10.4	4.8	4.8	4.9
1960	9.2	8.5	9.8	4.4	4.0	4.8
1961	8.9	8.1	9.6	4.3	3.9	4.7
1962	9.8	9.6	9.9	4.5	4.4	4.7
1963	10.3	10.1	10.4	4.7	4.5	4.9
1964	11.6	11.7	11.5	5.2	5.1	5.4
1965	13.0	13.8	12.2	5.6	5.7	5.5
1966	13.4	14.2	12.7	5.6	5.6	5.6

Table 11-2 (continued)

Year or Quarter	Ratio of Profits after Income Taxes (Annual Rate) to Stockholders' Equity—Percent[1]			Profits after Income Taxes per Dollar of Sales—Cents		
	All Manu-facturing Corporations	Durable Goods Industries	Nondurable Goods Industries	All Manu-facturing Corporations	Durable Goods Industries	Nondurable Goods Industries
1967	11.7	11.7	11.8	5.0	4.8	5.3
1968	12.1	12.2	11.9	5.1	4.9	5.2
1969	11.5	11.4	11.5	4.8	4.6	5.0
1970	9.3	8.3	10.3	4.0	3.5	4.5
1971	9.7	9.0	10.3	4.1	3.8	4.5
1972	10.6	10.8	10.5	4.3	4.2	4.4
1973	12.8	13.1	12.6	4.7	4.7	4.8
1973:IV	13.4	12.9	14.0	4.7	4.5	5.0
New Series						
1973:IV	14.3	13.3	15.3	5.6	5.0	6.1
1974	14.9	12.6	17.1	5.5	12.7	6.4
1975	11.6	10.3	12.9	4.6	4.1	5.1
1976	13.9	13.7	14.2	5.4	5.2	5.5
1977	14.2	14.5	13.8	5.3	5.3	5.3
1978	15.0	16.0	14.2	5.4	5.5	5.3
1979	16.4	15.4	17.4	5.7	5.2	6.1
1980	13.9	11.2	16.3	4.8	4.0	5.6
1981	13.6	11.9	15.2	4.7	4.2	5.1
1982	9.2	6.1	11.9	3.5	2.4	4.4
1983	10.6	8.1	12.7	4.1	3.1	4.9
1984	12.5	12.4	12.5	4.6	4.4	4.8

Table 11-2 (continued)

Year or Quarter	Ratio of Profits after Income Taxes (Annual Rate) to Stockholders' Equity—Percent[1]			Profits after Income axes per Dollar of Sales—Cents		
	All Manufacturing Corporations	Durable Goods Industries	Nondurable Goods Industries	All Manufacturing Corporations	Durable Goods Industries	Nondurable Goods Industries
1985	10.1	9.2	11.0	3.8	3.4	4.1
1986	9.5	7.5	11.5	3.7	2.9	4.6
1985:I	10.5	9.2	11.7	4.0	3.4	4.5
II	10.9	10.0	11.0	4.0	3.9	4.0
III	9.9	8.0	11.6	3.7	3.0	4.3
IV	9.3	8.6	9.9	3.4	3.1	3.6
1986:I	9.0	7.2	10.8	3.6	2.9	4.2
II	12.2	10.8	13.5	4.7	4.1	5.4
III	8.4	6.0	10.7	3.4	2.4	4.3
IV	8.5	5.9	11.1	3.3	2.2	4.5
1987:I	10.8	9.2	12.5	4.3	3.6	5.1
II	14.0	13.3	14.8	5.3	5.0	5.6
III	14.5	12.8	16.3	5.6	4.9	6.2

[1] Annual ratios based on average equity for the year (using four end-of-quarter figures). Quarterly ratios based on equity at end of quarter only.

Note—Based on data in millions of dollars

Source: Department of Commerce, Bureau of the Census

Taken from the Economic Report of the President, (Washington, D.C.: United States Government Printing Office, 1988) p. 353.

operating leverage introduced by fixed operating costs. To illustrate, assume the following data for Temple Corporation:

1. The product of the firm is sold at $3 per unit.
2. Fixed costs are $180,000.
3. Variable costs are $1.50 per unit and vary in direct proportion.
4. The firm is capitalized as follows:
   (a) $300,000—10% Debenture Bonds.
   (b) Common Equity equals $300,000 and there are 3,000 shares of common stock outstanding.
5. The firm currently is selling 160,000 units.
6. The effective income tax rate applicable to the firm is 40 percent.

The effect of a ten-percent increase in units sold and a ten percent decrease in units sold is illustrated in Table 11-3. Earnings per share rose 80 percent when sales increased ten percent, but fell by 80 percent when sales decreased by ten percent.

When the firm is levered financially, the difference between the rate of return on total capital invested and the rate of return on common stockholders' equity indicates the effect of trading on the equity.

Where favorable financial leverage exists, the rate of return on common stockholder's equity will exceed the rate earned on total invested capital. A strong firm will show favorable leverage even when the economy is experiencing a downturn, and certainly over an economic cycle.

Return on Total Assets

As shown above, return on total assets is a key determinant of the return earned on owners' equity. There are two basic determinants of the return on total assets: (1) the cents of profit generated by each dollar of sales (the margin), and (2) the dollars of sales generated on average for each dollar of assets (the turnover of assets). This is demonstrated in the equation below:

$$\frac{\text{Net Earnings}}{\text{Total Assets}} = \frac{\text{Net Earnings}}{\text{Net Sales}} \times \frac{\text{Net Sales}}{\text{Total Assets}}$$

Return on total assets and the behavior of its components offers probably the most useful statistics for studying the operating efficiency of a firm.

Table 11-3   Temple Corporation—The Determination of Earnings Per Share for the Three Levels of Sales

Units Sold		144,000	160,000	176,000
Sales		$432,000	$480,000	$528,000
Less Costs				
Fixed Costs	$180,000	$180,000	$180,000	
Variable Costs	216,000	240,000	264,000	
Total Costs		396,000	420,000	444,000
EBIT[1]		$ 36,000	$ 60,000	$ 84,000
Less Interest Expense		30,000	30,000	30,000
Taxable Income		$ 6,000	$ 30,000	$ 54,000
Less Taxes		2,400	12,000	21,600
Earnings after Taxes		$ 3,600	$ 18,000	$ 32,400
Number of Shares		3,000	3,000	3,000
Earnings Per Share (EPS)		1.20	$ 6	$ 10.80

[1]EBIT = Earnings Before Interest and Taxes

Percentage increase in EPS for 10% rise in sales:

$$\frac{10.80 - 6}{6} = \frac{4.80}{6} = 80\%$$

Percentage Decrease in EPS for 10% drop in sales:

$$\frac{6 - 1.2}{6} = \frac{4.80}{6} = 80\%$$

Profit Margin.   Profit margin can be calculated in many ways, to aid in studying operating efficiency of a firm. One can calculate and assess each of the following margin ratios:

1. Gross Profit Margin. This ratio is calculated by dividing gross profit by net sales. This ratio is a useful indicator of the productive efficiency on the plant floor of a firm. It should be analyzed in terms of its trend over time and in relationship to other companies operating in the same industry. As noted earlier, the method of inventory valuation used by the firm (e.g., L.I.F.O. vs. F.I.F.O.) is important, and the analyst must be sure that the figures used for comparison are comparable.

2. Net Operating Margin. This ratio is calculated by dividing net operating income by net sales. It is the complement of the net operating expense ratio, since the two when added must always equal 100 percent. This ratio indicates the percentage of sales dollars not used up in the generation of

sales. In other words, this is the percentage of sales dollars available to meet finance charges, pay taxes, and provide for dividends and financing corporate capital needs. Many analysts consider this ratio of equal importance with the number of times fixed charges are earned, when determining the quality of debt obligations and the risk of leverage.

3. Before-Tax and After-Tax Profit Margins. The before-tax ratio is calculated by dividing the earnings before taxes by the net sales. It is a more useful intermediate determinant of the return on assets than the after-tax profit margin, for purposes of assessing the efficiency with which assets are used. Industry statistics for profits per dollar of sales after taxes, are given in Table 11–2.

The percentage of sales brought down to before-tax profit may be low (as for a food chain), but if inventory turnover and capital investment turnover are high the rate of return on assets may still be big. Conversely, the before-tax margin may be relatively high (as for a public utility), but if inventory and/or capital asset turnover are low, the return on assets may be low. These ratios are components of the return on assets, and must be interpreted in relation to asset turnovers. It is the return on capital committed that is important to an investor, not how that return is generated. Breaking the return on investment into its basic components, however, helps gain a better understanding of the firms operating record and provides a better basis for forecasting.

The turnover of assets is calculated by dividing the net sales by the total assets. There are numerous combinations of asset turnover and margin that will yield a given return on assets. One should compare both the turnover ratios and the margins over time for a company to that of competitive companies, or companies in the same industry. Such an analysis, especially when buttressed by information gained in the analysis of the economy, can reveal weaknesses as well as the potential strength of a firm.

One must go beyond a mere calculation of these ratios and a comparison to competitors. A weak margin suggests problems in controlling expenses for a firm. Vertical and horizontal analysis can help explore these problems. Vertical analysis is accomplished by dividing each expense item in the income statement of a given year by net sales. One would expect expenses to rise as sales rise. When a particular expense item, however, rises at a faster rate than sales, it should be explored carefully. In horizontal analysis, each expense item of a given year is divided by that same expense item in the base year. This allows exploring changes in the relative importance of expense items over time and the behavior of expense items as sales change.

Changes in Asset Turnover and Expansion.   The turnover of assets may fall sharply when a firm undertakes a major expansion. The large asset investment involved causes this, since there has not yet been adequate time for these assets to generate the anticipated growth in sales that motivated undertaking the expansion. One must, therefore, be careful to review capital expenditures when assessing asset turnover ratios.

Leasing and the Asset Turnover Ratio.   Leased assets usually are not recorded on the balance sheet, and are not, therefore a part of the total assets shown on the balance sheet. Still, leased assets do result in sales. A rising or relatively high turnover ratio could, therefore, be generated by a firm that increases the use of leasing to acquire assets. This would not indicate more efficient use of asset investment.

Profitability Analysis and Physical Data Ratios

Analysts frequently calculate physical data ratios, and reduce them to a per share basis, to aid in studying profitability. These ratios are useful when calculated on the basis of specific characteristics of a given industry and used for comparing companies in that industry.

Physical Reserves.   Reserves are of utmost importance to companies dependent on wasting assets for their operations (such as oil or timber companies). Reported reserves by major companies normally provide a conservative representation of such assets. The analyst should note the quality or grade of reserves as well as the quantity, with special attention to changes in grade from year to year. Changes from year to year indicate current extractive policy and possibly "high grading" (mining primarily the highest grade ores in the deposit) in any given year.

Reserves of oil and gas, normally stated in terms of millions of barrels and billions of cubic feet respectively, frequently are reported on a per share basis. The estimated value of reserves can be computed by multiplying the number of units in reserve by the going market price per unit. The value of reserves per share often is compared to current market price per share when looking for undervalued companies. This is not necessarily a valid indicator of value since market prices for the physical resource can rise or fall sharply in the future (witness oil).

Capacity.   Producers and processors of various materials normally have specific productive or fabricating capacity that may be expressed in physical terms. These data can be reduced to a per share or a per employee basis for comparison between companies. Capacity also can be related to order backlogs, both in units and dollars. Persistent excess capacity often is a symptom of decline for a firm.

Production Data.   Production data in units can be related to capacity figures to assess whether or not excess capacity is present. This information should be compared to other firms in the industry. In companies concentrating principally on one type of product (e.g., crude oil, ingot steel, or copper), production data in units can be used to estimate selling prices, production costs and profits per unit. Such data also help the analyst determine the effects of changes in costs and selling prices not the profit margins of the company.

Freight Volume and Other Specialized Ratios.   Detailed information relative to volume, product composition, and geographical distribution of freight carried is valuable to the analyst in appraising the outlook for a transportation company such as a railroad, airline, trucking service, or barge line. Other examples of specialized physical ratios could be residential and commercial load for utilities, ton miles per dollar of debt for railroads or the load factor for airlines.

Short-Term Solvency Ratios

Short-term solvency ratios are used to judge the adequacy of liquid assets or meeting short-term obligations as they come due. Firms go bankrupt, or get into financial difficulty, because they cannot pay obligations as they come due, not merely because they are not profitable. An investor should, therefore, assure himself or herself that liquidity problems are not likely to appear before buying a stock.

A complete analysis of the adequacy of working capital for meeting current liabilities as they come due and assessing management's efficiency in the use of working capital would require a thorough analysis of cash flows, sources and applications of funds and forecasts of funds flows in future periods. Ratios can provide, however, a crude but useful assessment of working capital in many instances. We suggest using the five ratios listed below to assess the adequacy of working capital for a firm:

1. The current ratio.
2. The acid-test ratio.
3. The inventory turnover ratio.
4. The receivables turnover ratio.
5. The working capital turnover ratio.

Current Ratio.   The current ratio is calculated by dividing current assets by current liabilities. It indicates the company's coverage of current liabilities by current assets. For example, if the ratio were 2:1, the firm could realize only one-half of the values stated in the balance sheet in liquidating current assets and still have adequate funds to pay all current liabilities.

For many years it has been rather loosely stated that as a general rule this ratio should be 2:1 or better. For all U.S. Corporations, however, the ratio has only averaged about 1.85:1 in recent years and seemed adequate.

A general standard for this ratio is not useful. Such a standard fails to recognize that an appropriate current ratio is a function of the nature of a company's business and would vary with differing operating cycles of different businesses.

A current asset is defined as any asset that is expected to be converted into cash in the ordinary operating cycle of a business. Inventory, therefore, is a current asset. In a tobacco or liquor company, inventory may be as much as 80 to 90 percent of current assets. Yet for a liquor company that inventory may have to age four years or more before it can be converted into a salable asset. Such a company typically would require a much higher current ratio than average to have adequate liquidity to meet current liabilities maturing in one year. For a public utility company where there is no inventory or receivables collection problem, a current ratio of 1.1 or 1.2 to 1 has proved satisfactory. We suggest looking at industry averages, rather than considering an overall standard, as produced by organizations such as Dun & Bradstreet or Robert Morris Associates. Such averages have their.faults, but are preferable to general standards that do not recognize operating differences between companies.

The current ratio has a major weakness as an analytical tool. It ignores the composition of current assets, which may be as important as their relationship with current liabilities. Assume the current assets and current liabilities for a firm were as shown below.

Current Assets		Current Liabilities	
Cash	$ 1,000	Accounts Payable	$5,000
Receivables	1,000	Bank Loans	2,000
Inventory	12,000		
Total	$14,000		$7,000

While this firm has a 2:1 current ratio, which would more than meet the average in many industries, one could question its liquidity. The inventory has not been sold yet and appears high relative to the total of current assets. Therefore, current ratio analysis must be supplemented by other working capital ratios.

Acid Test (Quick) Ratio

Because the problem in meeting current liabilities may rest on slowness or even inability to convert inventories into cash to meet current obligations, the acid-test ratio is recommended. This is the ratio of current assets minus inventories, accruals, and prepaid items to current liabilities. This ratio does assume that receivables are of good quality and will be converted into cash over the next year. This ratio is only 2:7 in the above illustration, which would be low based on industry averages.

The key to whether or not the firm in the illustration above will have liquidity problems is the salability of the inventory. If all the inventory can be sold and the resulting receivables collected over the next year, the liquidity is adequate. We therefore need a test of the salability of that inventory.

Inventory Turnover

The inventory turnover is computed by dividing the cost of goods sold by the average inventory investment for a year. Dun and Bradstreet industry ratios, unfortunately, use net sales as the numerator for this ratio, and that numerator would have to be used in the calculation if one wants to compare to their averages. The analyst is interested in determining the physical turnover of the inventory, and needs a numerator (cost of goods sold) that is calculated on the same basis as the inventory. Price changes could distort this ratio, as an indicator of physical turnover, when net sales is used as a numerator.

A low ratio suggests the possibility that investment in inventory is too high for the sales capacity of the business. This will hurt future profitability, both because of the interest costs incurred by borrowing to support the inventory investment and the storage costs.

On the other hand, a high ratio relative to the industry tends to suggest that inventories are too low. This often is an indication of overtrading. This can result in a serious financial collapse and even bankruptcy if sales activity slows down temporarily. Debt is incurred increasingly as sales rise, and there is no reserve to draw on when cash flows shrink. Moreover, sales might be lost by a firm because of inadequate selection for its customers.

The number of days' sales outstanding in inventory can be calculated by dividing the number of days in a year (365) by the inventory turnover ratio, for example, if the inventory turnover ratio were 12, the number of days sales outstanding would be about 30. This would mean that if the firm continued to sell at the same rate it has in the past, it would sell the entire inventory shown on the balance sheet in 30 days.

Receivables Turnover

The time needed to translate receivables into cash could be important for purposes of judging the adequacy of working capital. The receivables turnover can be determined by dividing the net credit sales by the total of accounts and notes receivable. Net sales typically is used as the numerator because information is not available as to the portion of sales that were on credit terms. This does tend to overstate the liquidity of receivables when cash sales are significant, as for a retailer.

The turnover may be converted into the number of days sales outstanding in receivables by dividing the turnover figure into 365. One would expect the receivables turnover to be relatively in line with the firm's term of sale. The ratio also should be reviewed over time. A high receivables turnover could make a relatively low current ratio acceptable, from a liquidity standpoint, and lead to a higher return on assets. On the other hand, a high turnover cold suggest inadequate inventory for meeting customer's demands and/or an overly tight credit policy that is causing the firm to miss potentially profitable sales.

The average days sales outstanding in receivables and in inventory can be combined to obtain an "average age of conversion" of noncash current assets into cash. The age of conversion is a rough indicator of the length of the operating cycle of the firm. These figures are useful when attempting to project cash flows.

Capitalization Ratios

Analysts also calculate capitalization ratios to determine the extent to which the corporation is trading on its equity, the resulting financial leverage, and the degree of risk related to that leverage. These ratios can be interpreted only in the context of the stability of industry and company earnings and cash flow. The assumption is that the greater the stability of industry and company earnings and cash flow, the more the company is able to accept the risk associated with financial leverage, and the higher is the allowable ratio of debt to total capitalization (the total dollar amount of all long-term sources of funds in the balance sheet).

In the case of new companies or companies in highly cyclical industries, the use of any long-term debt may be unsound. If the fixed charges required to service the debt are covered by a large margin when studied in relation to likely cash flows in recession years, the debt can be acceptable. A highly leveraged capital structure can offer high returns on assets and equity in boom periods, but lead to serious financial consequences in recession years as illustrated by the railroads and airlines in 1960-61, 1970-71, and 1974-75. This can result in low prices for the securities of such companies in recession years. However, if an investor believes the worst has been experienced and that a decided improvement in earning power can be expected, a commitment in these securities while the prices are depressed and P/E ratios are relatively low can be rewarding.

Capitalization ratios can be calculated by dividing total capitalization by each major component of the capitalization structure; that is, dividing by total long-term debt, preferred stock, and common equity. It is useful to calculate common equity at market as well as at book value for purposes of determining these proportions. A market calculation for common equity may indicate considerably more or less financial leverage than a book calculation.

The proportion can serve as a screening device. When the common equity represents 70 percent or more of total capitalization, there normally is no need to be concerned with the risk of leverage. An analyst could then better spend his time studying more critical problems revealed by his or her analysis.

Leases and the Stock Equity Test

Many corporations rent buildings and equipment under long-term lease contracts. Required rental payments are contractual obligations similar to bond coupon and repayment obligations. However, assets acquired through leasing may not be capitalized and shown in the balance sheet. Two companies, therefore, might work with the same amount of fixed assets and produce the same profits before interest or rental payments, but the one leasing a high proportion of its productive equipment could show significantly lower debt relative to total capitalization.

Stock Equity Tests and Standards

Standards only can be established in a general sense. An electric utility, for example, with highly stable and recession resistant income can utilize more debt and preferred stock relative to equity than a company with more cyclical earnings, such as a steel or auto company. Debt could range from 50 to 65 percent of total capitalization, and up to 75 percent of total capitalization where preferred stock is included, for a public utility without suggesting excessive borrowing and leverage. A railroad or a highly cyclical company would raise serious questions long-term debt was as much as 50 percent of total capitalization. We would suggest questioning the capital structure for a cyclical company if the long-term debt represented more than 35 percent of total capitalization. For a company less subject to the business cycle, such as a food company, long-term debt safely could approach 50 percent of total capitalization. The key is the stability of the company's income over the cycle.

Earnings Coverage Tests

The earnings of a corporation are the basic source of cash flows. Coverage ratios are used to test the adequacy of cash flows generated through earnings for purposes of meeting debt and lease obligations.

Tests of the adequacy of earnings are applied to the past record of the company, although the future record is the one that will determine the soundness of the judgment exercised in buying a security. These ratios must, therefore, be interpreted in the light of the likelihood that the past financial record offers a reasonable indication of future performance.

Calculation of Earnings Available to Cover Fixed Charges

The calculation of an interest coverage or a fixed charges coverage ratio is simple: earnings available for paying the interest or the total fixed charges for a given year are divided by the annual interest expense or fixed charges. Interest expense and rental expenses are tax deductible and, therefore, all earnings before taxes are available for paying such charges. The proper calculation is shown in equation form below:

$$\frac{E_t + I_t + R_t}{I_t + R_t}$$

where
E_t = earnings before taxes during year t
I_t = interest charges paid during year t
R_t = rental payments made under long-term leases during year t.

Financial reporting services report coverage after taxes and also show average before taxes. Corporate annual reports often report the amount available for interest after taxes rather than before and many well not consider lease payments.

Minimum Standards for Coverage of Fixed Charges Coverage Ratios

Suggested standards are based on experience and empirical studies relating the incidence of defaults over a number of years to such ratios.[92]

Different standards are in order for a highly cyclical company than for a stable company. Data suggests that average coverage over a business cycle should be eight or better to be classed as higher grade for a cyclical company, while the coverage ratio should not fall below four in anyone year. For stable companies, an average coverage ratio of five or better and a minimum ratio of 2.5 in any year suggests relatively high quality.

Value Ratios

Ratios based on market price per share of the company's common stock offer investors important measures of growth and stability of earnings, and a crude indicator of relative value.

Price-Earnings Ratio

The P/E ratio was discussed in Chapter 10, and we refer the reader to that discussion. The range of the P/E ratio for a particular company's stock over a five- to ten-year period should be related to the range for the appropriate Dow-Jones and Standard & Poor's indexes for the same years, as well as the ratios of companies in the same industry. This will suggest whether a stock is high priced or low priced in relation to earnings. We suggest a low P/E out-of-favor stock selection policy, and this ratio is an initial screen.

An investor should aim at purchasing growth stocks whose future performance has not been over-discounted in their market price. A P/E ratio screen can help spot such companies.

An undervalued stock selection strategy tends to be oriented cyclically and long-term in approach. During economic recessions, the market tends to become

---

92 For example, see W. Braddock Hickman, Corporate Bond Quality and Investor Experience (New York: National Bureau of Economic Research, 1958).

undervalued in terms of any norm relative to the long-term secular trend of stock prices. At such times, the price of the stocks of some major companies may decline more than the averages, but in many years there are likely to be some undervaluations. Following this approach does require the emotional stamina to go against the crowd, and the patience to wait for the crowd to appreciate the facts. History suggests that investors tend to exaggerate both pessimism and optimism.

Not all low P/E stocks represent undervaluations. Undervaluation is found when a company's earning power can be expected to recover or has been underestimated by the market. Risk tends also to be minimized by concentrating stock selection on low P/E companies. The adverse expectations of the market already are reflected in the current stock price, lessening the downside risk of such selections. Moreover, low P/E stocks tend to offer high divided yields, giving further downside protection if expectations are not realized.

Dividends Per Share and Dividend Yield

The stability and growth of dividends on a compound annual basis should be calculated over the past five years, and explanations sought for significant changes in dividend payout policy. Dividend payout can be reviewed by dividing dividends per share by earnings per share. Also, it is useful to review dividends as a percentage of cash flow income over time.

PART III

Fundamental Analysis of Special Classes of Securities

CHAPTER 12

Regulated Industries: Utilities

The general legal and economic classifications of public utilities includes, among others: (1) electric light and power companies, (2) companies supplying natural or manufactured gas, either pipeline companies or direct operating companies, (3) telephone, telegraph, and other companies supplying communication services, (4) companies supplying water, and (5) railroads and other transportation companies.

In the financial community transportation companies are placed in a separate classification for separate analysis, and accordingly they will be discussed in the next chapter. Because electric utilities represent the major segment of investor interest in public utilities, they will be emphasized in this chapter. Space limitations permit only limited coverage of other types of utilities, such as gas and communication companies and water companies, that are nonetheless of significant importance in the investment field.

The Public Utility Industry

Public utility companies are required to meet the demands for service of all users, irrespective of fluctuation in demand. This requires maintenance of capacity to meet peak loads, with certain amounts of idle capacity at other times.

Characteristics of Public Utility Companies

Public utility companies can be identified by the following salient features:

1. They are affected with a public interest. Their service is a necessity for a large segment of the economy, and public utilities must meet public demand.

2. They operate under conditions where direct competition generally is not practical, although there may be competition between services, such as electric versus gas service for heating.
3. Because of the above factors, utilities are subject to broad regulation (especially rate regulation) by one or more governmental bodies or agencies.
4. Production of services is simultaneous with customer use and, unlike industrial companies, there is no inventory problem and a minimum of "receivables" problems.

Territory Served.   The territory served by a public utility is carefully defined by the franchises and certificates of necessity under which regulated companies operate. The analyst must carefully analyze the economics of the areas served as well as the geographic, physical, and atmospheric environment. Costs of operation, as for example, maintenance for railroads, are generally affected by physical and atmospheric environment.

Capitalization and Securities.   Regulators must approve the type of capitalization, the type of securities issued, and each sale of securities, including the method of sale and type of securities issued and their specific characteristics, as well as the use to which funds will be put.

Management.   Although management of regulated industries operates within a narrower decision scope than does management of industrial companies, management is still important, especially in its relations with the regulators and in the area of operations, such as efficiencies and ability and willingness to provide satisfactory service whenever and wherever needed. Labor relations are another important factor. Perhaps the most serious problem other than in the area of actual operations is public relations and related environmental problems.

Regulation of the Public Utility Industry

An analysis of a utility company should begin with an analysis of the regulatory climate, followed by an economic and financial analysis of the company. Unless the regulatory climate is satisfactory, the analyst should not proceed further. Earnings of utility companies actually are determined by regulatory authorities who must approve all rate changes.

Because utility companies often are natural monopolies that supply a necessary service to the public, they must be subject to government regulation. Electric utility companies are domiciled in the state in which they operate and are subject to regulation by state public utility commissions. States and local authorities with power delegated to them by their state regulate intrastate utilities.[93]

Regulation covers a broad area: rates, service rendered, purchase and sale of assets, issuance of securities, and a uniform accounting system. Utilities are required to conform to the uniform system of accounts to which most state utility commissions have subscribed. An excellent utility will make every effort to maintain good relations with its regulatory commission. However, it may have to apply to the courts for approval of rate increases, if the commission refuses to sanction equitable rates that would yield a fair return on the fair value of the property and that provide sufficient income to maintain the financial standing of the company's securities in the capital markets. The U.S. Supreme Court has the final decision in rate cases involving the question of fair return.

Franchises and Certificates of Necessity.   Contracts between the state (and local subdivisions) and public utilities authorize a particular utility to operate in a particular territory. Contracts may be perpetual, indeterminate, or limited in time. If a utility operates under a definitive term, questions may arise as the terminal date approaches concerning its renewal or at least the characteristics of the new contracts. A utility's bonds should not mature beyond the terminal date. In recent years the trend has been toward indeterminate life franchises continuing as long as service is satisfactory.

Federal Regulation.   Several agencies of the federal government are involved in the regulation of utilities as outlined below.

1. The Interstate Commerce Commission regulates the rates, service standards, financing and accounting of railroads, trucking companies and buses engaged in interstate business.
2. The Federal Energy Regulatory Commission regulates those electric utilities that use power from navigable streams as well as other users of these streams and rivers. It also governs utilities regularly transporting electricity and gas across state lines. Regulation includes approval of rates for electric power and gas crossing state lines, approval of mergers and securities

---

93 See Moody's *Public Utilities Manual* for information concerning regulating authorities and the National Association of Railroad & Public Utility Commissioners.

acquisitions by such companies and issuance of certificates for construction of interstate natural gas pipelines. Companies must file financial reports with the Energy Information Administration.

3. The Federal Communications Commission determines the rates and controls the accounts and basic practices of telephone and telegraph companies engaged in interstate commerce as they apply to the interstate activities of these companies.

4. The Securities and Exchange Commission, under the Public Utility Act of 1935, regulates public utility electric and gas holding companies that control operating companies in more than one state. Control is exercised over capital structures, financing and accounting of registered public utility holding companies in conjunction with State Regulation Commissions and their subsidiary operating companies.

5. The Civil Aeronautics Board regulates the air transport industry with authority over routes, schedules, rates, services, safety standards, accounting, mergers and acquisitions, and intercorporate relations.[94]

6. Proposals in connection with the new U.S. Department of Energy were the first attempt by the federal government to regulate overall rates the U.S. charges on both a retail and wholesale basis overriding state and local regulations. (Legislation recommended by House and Senate Conference, Nov.–Dec. 1977.)

The National Association of Railroad and Utility Commissions adopted a revised uniform system of accounts for electric and gas utilities in 1961. The Federal Energy Regulatory Commission requires essentially the same system for hydroelectric companies and utility companies that come under its jurisdiction. Other types of utility companies also are required to use a uniform system of accounting. Uniform accounting is a real aid to financial analysis of utility companies because the analyst can assume that accounts identified by similar names represent identical items as between utilities. However, although there is uniform accounting, there is a considerable divergence in actual accounting practices in published reports—for example, flow-through versus normalizing for depreciation methods, depending on state commissions.

---

94 Effective early January 1978, Congress legislated deregulation of rates and routes for air cargo carriers. The Civil Aeronautics Board still has the power to alter "predatory" or "discriminatory" pricing. Deregulation of passenger fares was being proposed as was also deregulation of rates applying to interstate truck and bus companies. In all cases, the industries concerned were fighting deregulation of rates claiming that cutthroat competition would result from deregulation.

Importance of Regulation to Investors. It has been noted that the regulatory climate in which a utility must operate is of vital importance to the investor, especially because of the effect of regulation on rates and service standards and on rate of return on investment. The rates charged must be approved by the regulatory commission, and the rates charged times the units sold determine the gross income of the utility. The utility has control over its costs but not its revenues. An electric utility company is permitted to earn a fair return on the fair value of its property used in the public service but is not guaranteed such a return.

The Hope Natural Gas decision by the U.S. Supreme Court in 1944 has been interpreted as releasing the regulatory commissions from the necessity of adhering to any specific method of determining the rate base. The method used by a commission in determining utility rate base valuation is no longer subject to judicial (U.S. Supreme Court) review. Rather, the overall effect of the rates charged on the company's credit standing in the capital markets has become the crucial issue. As most utilities are frequently in the capital markets to secure funds for expansion, the ability to secure their funds at a reasonable competitive cost is crucial and was so recognized by the Court (the cost-of-capital approach).

Methods of determining a fair rate of return vary widely. Some commissions use the accounting and statistical approach, while others have considered the rising cost of new money. There also is evidence in decisions of the recognition of "attrition" in earnings resulting from inflation (or the effect of inflation on the rate base).

Rate of Return on Rate Base. Utilities are permitted to charge rates that will produce the rate of return on their asset rate base approved by the regulatory commission. The allowed rate of return varies among states—the spread ranges from a low in some states of 5 percent, to a high in some states of 10 percent, with an average range of 5 to 7 percent.

The relatively few growth utilities have had two major factors that contributed to growth in earnings greater than that of the industry overall: (1) a favorable regulatory climate—average rate of return of 7.3 percent—on their rate base and (2) the advantage of operating in a rapidly growing area, such as Florida. Both factors need to be present. For example, in spite of the exceptionally rapid population and economic growth in California after World War II, the regulatory climate was not satisfactory, as the rate of return on the rate base tended to be held to an annual 5½ percent.

Therefore, California electric utility companies did not demonstrate nearly as high an earnings growth rate as did the Florida utilities in the post-World War II years, and this was reflected in stock prices.

Figure 12–1   Market Action

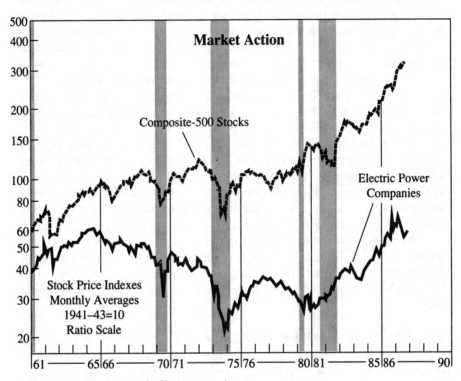

Shaded areas represent periods of business recessions

Source: Standard & Poor's Analyst Handbook (New York: Standard & Poor's Corporation, 1987).

The investor must know the rate of return permitted in the state where the utility under analysis operates, as well as whether there has been an up or down trend. The investor also should be familiar with the political climate in the state in regard to the utility commission or the probability of a change in the regulatory climate as a result of a changing political environment.

Of course, the rate base is as important as the allowed rate of return on the rate base. The investor should know the principle on which the commission calculates the rate base. For example, a rate base estimated on historical cost would be much lower than one based on reproduction cost or one that recognized the effect of inflation on property values.

Rate of Return on Investment. For electric utilities rates of return on total invested capital and stockholders' equity were satisfactory up to 1970. However, during 1970–1975 a serious lag developed between inflationary cost increases (particularly costs of fuel, costs of construction, and interest costs for new financing and refinancing), and rate increases. As a result, the rates of return on investment and the amount available to meet fixed charges and provide a return for stockholders fell to unsatisfactory levels from the standpoint of the investor, and this was reflected in the securities markets, as shown by the sharp drop in utility stock prices during the years 1971–75 (see Figure 12–1). The number of times fixed charges were earned for the industry overall fell well below two times, interest costs rose to nine to 10 per cent, and common stocks of many utilities fell below book values and sold at yields as high as 10 to 11 percent. After 1975 substantial rate relief was granted in a majority of cases, and the rates of return began to return to satisfactory levels, which in time was reflected in the securities market (see Table 12–1).

Table 12–1 contrasts key profitability and growth measures for the utility industry and all corporations covered in a *Forbes* study. Table 12–2 updates this information for the utility industry and provides additional data including forecasts. Figure 12–1 compares a price index for electric power company stocks to the Standard & Poor's 500 Stock Index.

It is not difficult to understand why utility stocks, on average, have such low P/E ratios, and that the prices of electric utility stocks are low relative to the S & P 500 Stock Index. They earn less on capital employed, and have shown insignificant earnings per share growth, especially since 1985. They are bought mainly on the basis of the high dividend yield these stocks offer, though substantial capital gains could have been made during the period 1980–85, when the operating expense ratio was dropping sharply.

Utility stock prices are highly sensitive to interest rate changes, and investors can purchase them for capital gain purposes when they believe interest rates will

Table 12–1   Profitability and Growth Measures, 1976–1980

	Profits After Taxes to:		Five Year Average Growth in:	
	Stockholders' Equity	Total Capital	Sales	Earnings Per Share
Utilities Serving:				
The Northeast	11.5	6.6	12.9	3.3
The Midwest	11.8	6.2	15.1	2.1
The Southeast	12.1	6.6	16.1	2.9
The Southwest	14.0	7.4	19.8	6.0
The West	11.8	6.6	15.8	2.7
All Industry Medians	15.5	10.9	14.0	12.5

Source: "34th Annual Report on American Industry," *Forbes*, January 4, 1982, pp. 104–108.

decline significantly. Investors become much more interested in purchasing tangible assets when real interest rates are negative (nominal rates trail the rate of inflation) and inflation is high. Stocks and bonds tend to fall out of favor during such a period, especially where their earnings growth trails behind the inflation rate. This did occur during the 1970s. Utilities also were hurt during this period because inflation rates exceeded the rate at which utility assets were being depreciated, thereby eroding asset values.

The inflation rate and interest rates were lowered sharply in the 1980s, leading to more favorable conditions for utilities. This was reflected in their stock prices (see Figure 12–1) through 1985.

Analysis of Gross Revenues

The annual report of a public utility generally will provide in the income statement or in a supplementary statement a breakdown of revenues and KWH's by class of customer, as illustrated in Table 12–3. Other useful data also is contained in the Table. A utility is to a large extent the prisoner of its geographic, economic and political environment—it may, at times, buy and/or sell electricity outside its territory. A reasonable balance between type of customer—residential, industrial, and commercial—is desirable.

Table 12–2 Key Financial Statistics and Ratios for Investor-owned Electric Utilities

	1980	1981	1982	1983	1984	1985	1986	E1987	E1988	E1989
Construction and Financing Requirements:										
Construction Expenditures										
(Million $)	28,335	30,690	35,350	35,565	35,285	33,294	31,023	26,928	24,748	22,689
AFUDC included above	4,365	5,358	6,612	7,816	7,923	6,941	5,659	3,893	2,647	2,498
New long-term financing (Million $)										
Debt	7,847	8,577	8,438	6,832	9,361	9,189	10,344	8,500	8,000	7,000
Preferred stock	2,003	1,174	2,097	1,902	888	655	985	500	400	300
Common stock	4,063	4,089	5,004	3,038	862	1,579	606	500	2,400	400
Total	13,913	13,840	15,539	11,817	11,111	11,423	11,935	9,500	10,800	7,700
Cash capital outlays finance externally (%)	61.7	62.0	65.2	54.6	50.3	61.2	60.0	55.0	54.0	52.0
Industry Financial Ratios										
Capitalization: (%)										
Long-term debt	50.4	50.2	49.3	48.4	48.2	48.2	48.0	47.0	46.0	45.0
Preferred stock	12.3	11.8	11.4	10.8	10.2	9.9	8.7	9.0	7.0	6.0
Common stock	37.3	38.0	39.3	40.8	41.6	41.9	43.3	44.0	47.0	49.0
S&P electric utility price–earnings ratio (High–Low)	7.25– 5.80	6.72– 5.63	7.11– 5.67	7.19– 6.38	6.88– 5.52	7.98– 6.70	10.29– 7.60	10.24– 7.85	9.00– 7.00	8.00– 6.00
Avg. interest rate on long-term debt (%)	8.4	9.3	9.6	9.7	9.9	10.0	9.8	8.5	8.2	8.4
Earned return on common equity (%)	11.4	12.6	13.4	14.4	14.5	13.8	13.7	13.0	12.8	12.5

Table 12–2 (continued)

	1980	1981	1982	1983	1984	1985	1986	E1987	E1988	E1989
Annual growth earnings per share—S&P Electric Utility Index (%)	3.1	8.9	10.1	11.4	7.5	1.6	1.3	1.0	0	0
Income Tax Rate	29.4	30.5	32.2	34.3	36.6	37.0	30.9	35.0	34.0	33.0
[1]AFUDC as a % of Common Earnings	54.5	52.8	53.8	53.7	48.8	50.7	36.1	30.0	28.0	27.0
Dividened Payout Ratio	75.8	72.9	70.9	69.3	65.7	74.6	65.6	66.0	67.0	68.0

[1]AFUDC—Allowance for funds used during construction (non cash item). E—Estimated by Standard & Poor's.

Sources: Edison Electric Institute; Standard & Poor's Industry Surveys, Vol. 2 (New York: Standard & Poor's Corporation, July, 1988), p. U33.

Table 12–3 Comparative Consolidated Information—Operations (American Electric Power Company, Inc. and Subsidiary Companies)

	1987	1986	1985	1984	1983	1982
Energy Supply						
System Capability (at December 31) (in thousands of kw)	22,930	23,486	23,384	23,351	22,453	22,387
Net System Peak Load (in thousands of kw)	20,936	22,056	20,357	21,021	19,477	19,301
Net Generation (in millions of kwh)	101,915	110,203	106,327	107,649	99,965	98,237
Net Purchased and Interchange Power (in millions of kwh)	4,133	4,603	5,585	15,266	11,917	6,618
Total System Load (in millions of kwh)	106,048	114,806	111,912	122,915	111,882	104,855
Efficiency						
Load Factor (%)	57.8	59.4	62.8	66.6	65.6	62.0
Heat Rate (Btu per kwh of net generation)	9,865	9,879	9,882	9,902	9,951	9,987
Coal Used (in thousands of tons)						
Purchased Coal (Estimated)	26,690	29,897	27,931	26,395	22,495	23,517
Coal from System Mines (estimated)	11,263	11,736	13,503	11,956	13,898	13,191
Total (actual)	37,953	41,633	41,434	38,351	36,393	36,708
Energy Delivery (in circuit miles of line)						
765,000-volt Transmission Lines	2,022	2,022	1,925	1,851	1,578	1,536
Other Transmission Lines[a]	19,703	19,687	19,674	19,635	19,648	19,679
Distribution Lines	97,484	97,024	96,559	96,152	95,734	95,268
Total Circut Miles	119,249	118,733	118,158	117,638	116,960	116,483
Customers—Electric (at Dec.31)						
Retail:						
Residential Without Electric Heating	1,742,724	1,736,469	1,733,509	1,731,297	1,733,245	1,735,546
Residential With Electric Heating	600,294	579,063	557,136	538,337	519,214	501,693
Total Residential	2,343,018	2,315,532	2,290,645	2,269,634	2,252,459	2,237,239

[a]Includes jointly owned lines   (P) Preliminary

Table 12-3 (continued)

	1987	1986	1985	1984	1983	1982
Customers-Electric (at Dec.31)						
Commercial	274,671	269,327	263,873	259,493	256,047	252,195
Industrial	21,427	20,960	20,599	19,852	19,039	18,247
Miscellaneous	11,005	10,918	10,961	10,633	10,498	10,406
Total Retail	2,650,121	2,616,737	2,586,078	2,559,612	2,538,043	2,518,087
Wholesale (Sales for Resale)	210	215	214	216	211	212
Total Electric Customers	2,650,331	2,616,952	2,586,292	2,559,828	2,538,254	2,518,299
Energy Use (in millions of kwh)						
Retail:						
Residential Without Electric Heating	14,297	13,547	13,458	13,171	13,618	13,073
Residential With Electric Heating	10,197	9,685	9,339	9,466	9,030	9,017
Total Residential	24,494	23,232	22,797	22,637	22,648	22,090
Commercial	16,846	16,073	15,571	14,849	14,398	14,078
Industrial	36,668	34,191	35,779	36,269	31,119	29,532
Miscellaneous	1,360	1,325	1,319	1,275	1,262	1,238
Total Retail	79,368	74,821	75,466	75,030	69,427	66,938
Wholesale (Sales for Resale)	18,840	31,679	28,964	40,186	34,792	31,027
Total Energy Used	98,208	106,500	104,430	115,216	104,219	97,965
Average Annual Use Per Customer (in kwh)						
Residential Without Electric Heating	8,227	7,817	7,779	7,610	7,857	7,521
Residential With Electric Heating	17,305	17,071	17,088	17,938	17,720	18,271
All Residential: AEP System	10,526	10,099	10,014	10,023	10,098	9,898
All Investor-Owned Utilities	8,861P	8,627P	8,487	8,500	8,379	8,261
Shareowners & Employees (at December 31)						
Shareowners	250,503	264,372	294,647	316,405	338,220	345,745
Employees	22,987	23,315	23,413	23,333	24,072	24,269

Note: Certain amounts for the years 1982–86 have been reclassified to reflect the presentation of 1987 amounts.

Table 12–3 (continued)   Financial and Operating Data, Principal Utility Subsidiaries

	Appalachian Power Company and Subsidiaries	Columbus Southern Power Company and Subsidiaries	Indiana Michigan Power Company and Subsidiaries	Ohio Power Company and Subsidiaries
Financial Data (in millions)				
Operating Revenues	$1,231.2	$ 744.4	$1,017.3	$1,343.7
Operating Income	233.1	130.9	223.0	295.6
Consolidated Net (income before preferred stock) Dividend Requirements	140.3	37.2	166.4	181.4
Utility Plant (less provisions)	2,299.3	1,516.3	3,035.0	2,753.6
Total Assets	2,794.5	1,930.3	3,956.6	3,460.6
Common Shareowner's Equity	901.0	536.4	973.6	1,073.3
Cumulative Preferred Stock:				
Not Subject to Mandatory Redemption	105.0	7.5	197.0	251.2
Subject to Mandatory Redemption (a)	81.8	103.5	32.0	—
Long-term Debt (a)	1,051.4	885.0	1,591.8	1,219.0
Operating Data				
Total Load (power generated and purchased in millions of kwh)	29,391	13,751	21,289	33,619
Transmission and Distribution Lines (circuit miles)	45,953	13,242(b)	19,104	27,404
Customers (at December 31)	778,441	518,755	463,982	630,668
Customers Energy Use (in millions of kwh)	26,856	12,786	19,833	31,276
Average Use Bill and Price:				
All Residential Customers:				
Kwh Used Per Customer	11,563	9,166	10,146	9,925
Annual Bill	$655.03	$642.88	$674.13	$665.37
Price Per Kwh (in cents)	5.66	7.01	6.64	6.70
All Customers:				
Price Per Kwh (in cents)	4.57	5.71	5.08	4.23

Table 12–3 (continued)

	Kentucky Power Company	Kingsport Power Company	Michigan Power Company	Wheeling Power Company
Financial Data (in millions)				
Operating Revenues	$250.1	$62.6	$46.8	$84.5
Operating Income	39.7	3.7	3.5	2.9
Net Income	16.8	1.8	10.8	0.4
Utility Plant (less provisions)	481.7	33.2	30.4	41.5
Total Assets	575.1	42.1	40.5	57.1
Common Shareowner's Equity	150.9	11.7	12.4	16.0
Long-term Debt[a]	259.8	17.0	10.0	22.0
Operating Data				
Total Load (power generated and purchased in millions of kwh)	6,121	1,483	811	1,916
Transmission and Distribution Lines (circuit miles)	9,376	1,177	1,360	1,634
Customers (at December 31)	149,958	37,122	30,904	40,520
Customers Energy Use (millions of kwh)	5,741	1,424	776	1,864
Average Use Bill and Price:				
All Residential Customers:				
Kwh Used Per Customer	13,123	16,375	7,994	9,217
Annual Bill	$665.46	$799.80	$570.90	$627.31
Price Per Kwh (in cents)	5.07	4.88	7.14	6.81
All Customers:				
Price Per Kwh (in cents)	4.28	4.38	5.97	4.45

[a] Including portion due within one year. (b) Includes jointly owned lines.

Residential Load.   The residential load for utilities has demonstrated, in general, great stability and sustained growth. Years ago lighting was the major load with the peak being in the evening and in December. Air conditioning now has become a major factor, causing loads to peak in the summer. Sales of electricity to residential customers increased about 5.3 percent from the comparable year-earlier period for the twelve months ended September 30, 1987, and residential demand is expected to continue to grow steadily.[95] Regional population shifts will affect demand for particular utilities. Our service-oriented economy has led to population growth in the metropolitan and coastal areas. The analyst should compare average residential loads and rates with other utilities, and be familiar with the economic and political characteristics of the area in which the utility operates.

Commercial Load.   This load has demonstrated nearly as much stability as the residential load. Customer classification includes stores, restaurants, gasoline stations, retail establishments in general, and the financial industry. This demand is expected to ease in the future, because of an expected slowdown in the services sector of our economy,[96] including: securities firms, money center banks and the insurance industry.

Industrial Load.   This load is less stable than the residential or commercial load in terms of the business cycle. The instability is greatest if sales to the durable consumer or capital goods areas represent a substantial portion of gross revenues. The investor should analyze the types of industrial service offered and the company's past record in this respect.

Street and Highway Lighting.   This load is as stable as the residential load, but political pressures on rates can be serious.

Sales to Other Companies for Resale.   Utilities have built up a large network of interconnections, and consistently sell or purchase power. Such sales may show considerable instability and should be analyzed carefully.

Regional Outlook.   Utilities serving the industrial Midwest and East Central Area are likely to realize good growth over the next few years because of the

---

95 Standard & Poor's Industry Surveys, Utilities, Electric (New York: Standard & Poor's Corporation, July, 1988) p. 18.

96 Standard & Poor's Industry Surveys, op. cit., p. 17.

resurgence of the industrial economy. This is likely to lead to increased off-system sales to utilities serving these areas to assure meeting demand.

Expenses

The major expense items in the income statement are maintenance, depreciation, federal income taxes, and other taxes. In the post-World War II years, the operating ratio for electric utilities (operating expenses divided by operating revenues) was generally at the 80 to 85 percent level until 1976, when it rose sharply reflecting higher costs not balanced by rate increases. Many utilities then received substantial rate relief and the ratio has again been in the 80 to 85 percent level since 1982.

The Nuclear Problem

There has been substantial efforts by community groups to stall the licensing process for nuclear plants. The Shoreham plant, owned by Long Island Lighting Company, and the Seabrook station owned by Public Service of New Hampshire and 11 other utilities are illustrative of the problems this can present. Congress recently expressed the sentiment that local officials should not be permitted to veto nuclear plant licenses. This should help bring resolution to the problem of bringing these plants into operation.

Investors should be cautious about acquiring the stock of an electric utility with nuclear plants facing political problems. They represent a costly investment, and the utility may not be allowed to include that investment in the rate base if they cannot operate the plants.

Allowance for Funds Used in Construction

This item is peculiar to utilities and often is a major expense item. The utility borrows funds and pays interest on these funds. The utility is permitted to capitalize a "reasonable" amount of interest and to show a noncash credit (income) item in its income statement for the same amount. If the amount is significant, the analyst must estimate what it will amount to over the next several years. The item ceases when the plant goes into operation, at which time it is hoped that additional income generated will offset the previous credit item in the income statement "Allowance for Funds Used in Construction."

Income Available for Fixed Charges

In the income statement of regulated companies the income available for fixed charges is "after taxes" because taxes were deducted in operating expenses. If the analyst wishes to calculate the coverage before taxes, income taxes must be added to the "income available for fixed charges." The income coverage should be at least two times. It fell below the level for the industry overall in years such as 1973–1975, but rate increases caused it to recover above two. The analyst recommending utility securities in the years 1973–1975 when they were selling at especially depressed prices and were distinctly out of favor had to feel reasonable assurance that rate relief was forthcoming, which indeed proved to be the case in most areas. The analyst also should calculate the coverage for fixed charges *plus* preferred dividends, allowing for the fact that preferred dividends are not tax deductible as is interest paid.

Comparative Financial Statistics

When considering purchasing a stock, including utilities, one should compare the companies earnings record and key balance sheet relationships with appropriate industry data. The *Standard & Poor's Industry Surveys* and the *Analyst Handbook* published by Standard & Poor's offer data for this purpose. Tables 12–4 and 12–5 contain per share data prepared by Standard & Poor's Corporation useful for comparative purposes. The industry surveys offer significant ratios for individual companies in the given industry.

Note the much higher average return earned on book value per share by the 400 industrials, than the electric utilities earned on net property per share (the equivalent). Also, the electricals payout a higher proportion of earnings as dividends than do the industrials, and offer significantly higher dividend yields. The growth characteristics, however, suggest greater capital gains potential for the industrials. The key question for the investor is whether or not the growth already is reflected in the price of the stock when purchase is considered.

Suggested minimum standards for electric utility companies are presented in Table 12–6.

Utility Industry Diversification

In recent years many utility companies have branched out from their traditional regulated businesses into new areas (primarily nonregulated areas). A multiple

Table 12—4   400 Industrials* (Per Share Data—Adjusted in Stock Price Index Level. Average of Stock Price Indexes. 1941–1943—10)

	Sales	Oper. Profit	Profit Margin %	Depr.	Income Taxes	Earnings Per Share	Earnings % of Sales	Dividends Per Share	Dividends % of Earn.
1956	54.73	8.36	15.27	2.04	2.96	3.50	6.40	1.84	52.57
1957	55.81	8.79	15.75	2.41	2.87	3.53	6.33	1.94	54.96
1958	53.48	7.70	14.40	2.38	2.40	2.95	5.52	1.86	63.05
1959	57.83	8.84	15.29	2.47	2.99	3.47	6.00	1.95	56.20
1960	59.47	8.73	14.68	2.56	2.87	3.40	5.72	2.00	58.82
1961	59.51	8.75	14.70	2.66	2.80	3.37	5.66	2.07	61.42
1962	64.63	9.81	15.18	2.89	3.16	3.83	5.93	2.20	57.44
1963	68.50	10.73	15.66	3.04	3.51	4.24	6.19	2.36	55.66
1964	73.19	11.67	15.94	3.24	3.70	4.85	6.63	2.58	53.20
1965	80.69	13.11	16.25	3.52	4.14	5.50	6.82	2.82	51.27
1966	88.46	14.48	16.37	3.87	4.35	5.87	6.64	2.95	50.26
1967	91.86	14.28	15.55	4.25	4.11	5.62	6.12	2.97	52.85
1968	101.49	16.08	15.84	4.56	5.14	6.16	6.07	3.16	51.30
1969	108.53	16.63	15.32	4.87	5.14	6.13	5.65	3.25	53.02
1970	109.85	15.54	14.15	5.17	4.23	5.41	4.92	3.20	59.15
1971	118.23	17.22	14.56	5.45	4.98	5.97	5.04	3.16	52.93
1972	128.79	19.39	15.06	5.76	5.90	6.83	5.30	3.22	47.14
1973	149.22	23.64	15.84	6.25	7.59	8.89	5.96	3.46	38.92
1974	182.10	27.97	15.36	6.86	10.22	9.61	5.28	3.71	38.61
1975	185.16	26.63	14.38	7.36	9.40	8.58	4.63	3.72	43.36
1976	202.66	29.23	14.42	7.58	10.21	10.69	5.27	4.22	39.48
1977	224.24	32.20	14.36	8.53	11.14	11.45	5.11	4.95	43.23

Table 12–4 (continued)

	Sales	Oper. Profit	Profit Margin %	Depr.	Income Taxes	Earnings Per Share	Earnings % of Sales	Dividends Per Share	Dividends % of Earn.
1978	251.32	36.19	14.40	9.64	12.14	13.04	5.19	5.37	41.18
1979	292.38	42.01	14.37	10.82	14.02	16.29	5.57	5.92	36.34
1980	327.36	43.08	13.16	12.37	13.67	16.12	4.92	6.49	40.26
1981	344.31	44.50	12.92	13.82	12.95	16.74	4.86	7.01	41.88
1982	333.86	42.67	12.78	15.30	10.95	13.20	3.95	7.13	54.02
1983	334.07	45.57	13.64	15.67	12.12	14.77	4.42	7.32	49.56
1984	379.70	51.50	13.56	16.31	14.15	18.11	4.77	7.51	41.47
R1985	398.42	53.23	13.36	18.19	13.68	15.28	4.77	7.87	51.51
P1986	388.44	52.36	13.48	19.44	10.95	14.57	3.75	8.15	55.94

	Price 1941–1943—10 High	Price 1941–1943—10 Low	Price/Earn. Ratio High	Price/Earn. Ratio Low	Div. Yields % High	Div. Yields % Low	Book Value Per Share	Book Value % Return	Working Capital	Capital Expenditures
1956	53.28	45.71	15.22	13.06	4.03	3.45	26.35	13.28	13.91	4.14
1957	53.25	41.98	15.08	11.89	4.62	3.64	29.44	11.99	13.50	4.84
1958	58.97	43.20	19.99	14.64	4.31	3.15	30.66	9.62	14.27	3.58
1959	65.32	57.02	18.82	16.43	3.42	2.99	32.26	10.76	14.93	3.65
1960	65.02	55.34	19.12	16.28	3.61	3.08	33.74	10.08	15.29	4.23
1961	76.69	60.87	22.76	18.06	3.40	2.70	34.85	9.67	15.84	3.97
1962	75.22	54.80	19.64	14.31	4.01	2.92	36.37	10.53	16.85	4.41
1963	79.25	65.48	18.69	15.44	3.60	2.98	38.17	11.11	17.64	4.41
1964	91.29	79.74	18.82	16.44	3.24	2.83	40.23	12.06	18.07	5.71
1965	98.55	86.43	17.92	15.71	3.26	2.86	43.50	12.64	18.80	6.87

Table 12–4 (continued)

	Price 1941–1943=10		Price/Earn. Ratio		Div. Yields %		Book Value		Working Capital	Capital Expenditures
	High	Low	High	Low	High	Low	Per Share	% Return		
1966	100.60	77.89	17.14	13.27	3.79	2.93	45.59	12.88	19.48	8.26
1967	106.15	85.31	18.89	15.81	3.48	2.80	47.78	11.76	20.74	8.35
1968	118.03	95.05	19.16	15.43	3.32	2.68	50.21	12.27	21.08	8.65
1969	116.24	97.75	18.96	15.95	3.32	2.80	51.70	11.86	21.05	9.70
1970	102.87	75.58	19.01	13.97	4.23	3.11	52.65	10.28	20.70	10.25
1971	115.84	99.36	19.40	16.64	3.18	2.73	55.28	10.80	22.61	9.96
1972	132.95	112.19	19.47	16.43	2.87	2.42	58.34	11.71	24.41	10.08
1973	134.54	103.37	15.13	11.63	3.35	2.57	62.84	14.15	26.49	11.65
1974	111.65	69.53	11.62	7.24	5.34	3.32	67.81	14.17	28.47	14.65
1975	107.40	77.71	12.52	9.06	4.79	3.46	70.84	12.11	30.47	14.43
1976	120.89	101.64	11.31	9.51	4.15	3.49	76.26	14.02	31.89	14.92
1977	118.92	99.88	10.39	8.72	4.96	4.16	82.21	13.93	33.28	17.02
1978	118.71	95.52	9.10	7.33	5.63	4.53	89.34	14.60	34.88	19.70
1979	124.49	107.08	7.64	6.57	5.53	4.76	98.71	16.50	36.32	26.44
1980	160.96	111.09	9.99	6.89	5.84	4.03	108.33	14.88	36.52	29.86
1981	157.02	125.93	9.38	7.52	5.57	4.46	116.06	14.42	35.98	33.03
1982	159.66	114.08	12.10	8.64	6.25	4.47	118.60	11.13	34.41	31.30
1983	194.84	154.95	13.19	10.49	4.72	3.76	122.32	12.07	36.55	25.24
1984	191.48	167.75	10.57	9.26	4.48	3.92	123.99	14.61	38.94	30.08
R1985	235.75	182.74	15.43	11.93	4.32	3.34	125.89	12.14	39.32	31.42
P1986	282.77	324.88	19.41	15.43	3.62	2.88	124.53	11.70	40.61	29.24

Note: 1983 data incls. results of "old" A.T.& T.; excls. $5.5 bil. charge; 1984 data reflect A.T.& T. divestiture.

*Based on 70 individual groups.

Stock Price Indexes for this group extend back to 1918.

Source: *Standard & Poor's Analyst's Handbook* (New York: Standard & Poor's Corporation 1987), p.1.

Table 12–5   Electric Power Companies (Per Share Data—Adjusted to Stock Price Index Level. Average of Stock Price Indexes, 1941–1943—10)

	Oper. Revs.	Maint.	Depr.	Income Taxes	Net Oper. Income	Oper. Ratio %	Earnings Per Share	Earnings % of Oper. Revs.	Dividends Per Share	Dividends % of Earn.
1956	13.07	0.88	1.21	1.69	2.44	81.33	1.62	12.39	1.13	69.75
1957	13.17	0.90	1.29	1.65	2.53	80.76	1.67	12.75	1.19	71.26
1958	13.54	0.91	1.37	1.68	2.68	80.21	1.78	13.15	1.24	69.66
1959	14.37	0.95	1.45	1.84	2.88	79.96	1.89	13.15	1.30	68.78
1960	15.10	0.99	1.55	1.89	3.05	79.80	2.01	13.31	1.37	68.16
1961	15.75	1.04	1.66	1.89	3.25	79.37	2.11	13.40	1.44	68.25
1962	16.72	1.11	1.79	1.92	3.56	78.71	2.34	14.00	1.52	64.96
1963	17.40	1.14	1.91	1.93	3.76	78.39	2.45	14.08	1.63	66.53
1964	18.12	1.21	1.98	1.97	3.92	78.37	2.65	14.62	1.74	65.66
1965	19.15	1.28	2.10	1.96	4.21	78.02	2.90	15.14	1.90	65.52
1966	20.60	1.36	2.23	2.05	4.51	78.11	3.09	15.00	2.04	66.02
1967	21.67	1.46	2.37	1.99	4.83	77.71	3.28	15.14	2.16	65.85
1968	23.03	1.51	2.50	2.15	4.98	78.38	3.25	14.11	2.27	69.85
1969	24.36	1.63	2.64	1.99	5.29	78.28	3.38	13.88	2.33	68.93
1970	25.55	1.79	2.75	1.44	5.50	78.47	3.40	13.31	2.40	70.59
1971	26.97	1.81	2.80	1.30	5.72	78.79	3.45	12.79	2.47	71.59
1972	28.84	2.01	2.92	1.33	6.10	78.85	3.69	12.79	2.53	68.56
1973	30.09	2.09	3.02	1.33	4.36	78.86	3.72	12.36	2.51	67.47
1974	35.73	2.18	3.09	1.24	6.56	81.64	3.47	9.71	2.49	71.76
1975	38.53	2.21	3.18	1.77	7.01	81.81	3.73	9.68	2.57	68.90
1976	38.88	2.25	3.16	2.22	6.91	82.23	3.85	9.90	2.58	67.01
1977	42.00	2.54	3.20	2.59	7.00	83.33	4.08	9.71	2.74	67.16
1978	43.05	2.74	3.31	2.60	7.00	83.74	4.12	9.57	2.94	71.36

Table 12–5 (continued)

	Oper. Revs.	Maint.	Depr.	Income Taxes	Net Oper. Income	Oper. Ratio %	Earnings Per Share	Earnings % of Oper. Revs.	Dividends Per Share	Dividends % of Earn.
1979	44.77	2.85	3.34	2.29	6.92	84.54	4.16	9.29	3.10	74.52
1980	49.07	3.01	3.27	2.38	7.27	85.18	4.29	8.74	3.20	74.59
1981	52.25	3.09	3.32	2.69	7.78	85.11	4.67	8.94	3.42	73.23
1982	51.34	3.16	3.28	3.40	8.01	84.40	5.14	10.01	3.62	70.43
1983	50.40	3.15	3.34	4.10	8.33	83.47	5.73	11.37	3.84	67.02
1984	52.02	3.38	3.50	4.40	8.80	83.08	6.16	11.84	4.06	65.91
1985	52.00	3.43	3.78	4.33	8.95	82.79	6.26	12.04	4.15	66.29
1986	50.45	3.40	4.19	4.86	9.59	80.99	6.34	12.57	4.21	66.40

	Price 1941–1943=10 High	Price 1941–1943=10 Low	Price/Earn. Ratio High	Price/Earn. Ratio Low	Div. Yields % High	Div. Yields % Low	Long Term Debt	Net Property Per Share	Net Property % Earned On	Capital Expenditures
1956	24.94	23.25	15.40	14.35	4.86	4.53	20.95	42.66	5.72	4.67
1957	25.41	22.29	15.22	13.35	5.34	4.68	23.15	45.19	5.60	5.49
1958	33.14	25.16	18.62	14.13	4.93	3.74	24.48	47.80	5.61	5.33
1959	34.43	31.94	18.22	16.90	4.07	3.78	25.72	50.02	5.76	4.96
1960	39.35	32.87	19.58	16.35	4.17	3.48	26.99	52.62	5.80	4.85
1961	52.91	39.47	25.08	18.71	3.65	2.72	27.92	54.99	5.78	4.72
1962	50.39	39.06	21.53	16.69	3.89	3.02	29.04	56.98	6.25	4.44
1963	53.51	48.66	21.84	19.86	3.35	3.05	29.64	58.97	6.38	4.51
1964	58.61	52.14	22.12	19.68	3.34	2.97	30.34	60.72	6.46	4.99
1965	60.90	57.26	21.00	19.74	3.32	3.12	31.80	64.16	6.56	5.82
1966	57.77	45.63	18.70	14.77	4.47	3.53	35.18	69.03	6.53	6.97
1967	55.03	46.16	16.78	14.07	4.68	3.93	38.06	74.37	6.50	8.23
1968	53.92	49.33	16.59	15.18	4.60	4.21	41.42	80.17	6.21	9.50

Table 12–5 (continued)

	Price 1941–1943—10		Price/Earn. Ratio		Div. Yields %		Long Term Debt	Net Property Per Share	Net Property % Earned On	Capital Expenditures
	High	Low	High	Low	High	Low				
1969	53.03	41.22	15.69	12.20	5.65	4.39	45.21	86.48	6.12	10.98
1970	45.62	35.53	13.42	10.45	6.75	5.26	48.90	92.14	5.97	12.56
1971	48.36	40.35	14.02	11.70	6.12	5.11	50.95	97.67	5.86	14.09
1972	45.39	38.53	12.30	10.44	6.57	5.57	53.22	103.77	5.88	14.54
1973	43.91	30.69	11.80	8.25	8.18	5.72	54.20	107.95	5.89	14.92
1974	34.17	20.41	9.85	5.88	12.20	7.29	57.19	110.09	5.96	14.58
1975	30.56	24.56	8.19	6.58	10.46	8.41	54.89	107.51	6.52	11.77
1976	35.17	29.44	9.14	7.65	8.76	7.34	53.06	106.68	6.48	12.48
1977	37.21	33.76	9.12	8.27	8.12	7.36	52.41	107.96	6.48	13.50
1978	35.52	31.38	8.62	7.62	9.37	8.28	52.45	111.33	6.29	14.53
1979	33.48	27.97	8.05	6.72	11.08	9.26	53.01	113.63	14.96	N.A.
1980	31.09	24.88	7.25	5.80	12.86	10.29	52.37	112.47	6.46	N.A.
1981	31.37	26.28	6.72	5.63	13.01	10.90	52.05	112.11	6.94	N.A.
1982	36.52	29.15	7.11	5.67	12.42	9.91	51.15	111.34	7.19	N.A.
1983	41.20	36.58	7.19	6.38	10.50	9.32	49.97	110.98	7.51	N.A.
1984	42.36	34.02	6.88	5.52	11.93	9.58	52.03	115.50	5.33	N.A.
1985	49.93	41.97	7.98	6.70	9.89	8.31	51.59	117.90	7.59	N.A.
1986	65.24	48.21	10.29	7.60	8.73	6.45	52.22	120.84	7.94	N.A.

Table 12-5 (continued)

Stock Price Indexes for this group extend back to 1918.

* American Elec. Pwr. (1-2-57)
* Baltimore Gas & Electric (1-9-35) (Formerly Cons. Gas El. Lt. & Pwr. of Baltimore) (Formerly Cons. Gas of Baltimore) (1-9-30 to 11-16-31)
* Central & South West Corp. (1-2-57)
* Commonwealth Edison (12-31-25)
* Consolidated Edison (1-2-18) (Formerly Cons. Gas)
* Detroit Edison (1-2-18)
* Dominion Resources (Formerly Virginia Electric Power) (4-30-52)
* Duke Power (6-30-76)
* FPL Group (Formerly Florida Power & Light) (6-30-76)
* Houston Industries (7-24-85)
* Middle South Utilities (1-2-57)
* Niagra Mohawk Power (1-4-50)
* Northern States Power Minnesota (7-13-49)
* Ohio Edison (7-17-57)
* Pacific Gas & Electric (1-2-18)
* Philadelphia Electric (5-31-44)
* Public Service Electric & Gas (7-7-48)

* Public Service of Indiana (6-30-76)
* Southern California Edison (12-31-25)
* Southern Co. (1-2-57)
* Texas Utilities (1-2-57)
Allegheny Power System (1-2-57 to 6-30-76) (Formerly West Penn)
Boston Edison (12-21-66 to 6-30-76)
Brooklyn Union Gas (1-2-18 to 12-5-56)
Cincinnati Gas & Elec. (2-26-47 to 6-30-76)
Cleveland Elec. Illum. Co. (7-16-47 to 6-30-76)
Consumers Power (2-26-47 to 6-30-76)
Dayton Power & Light (2-26-47 to 6-30-76)
Delmarva Power & Light (1-2-57 to 6-30-76)
Duquesne Light (1-2-57 to 6-30-76)
Florida Power Corp. (1-2-57 to 6-30-76)
General Public Utilities (1-2-57 to 6-30-76)
Gulf States Utilities (4-30-52 to 12-5-56)
Idaho Power (12-21-66 to 6-30-76)
Illinois Power (1-2-57 to 6-30-76)
Indianapolis Power & Light (9-26-45 to 6-30-76)
Laclede Gas Light (1-2-18 to 12-18-25)
Montana Power (1-2-18 to 12-28-25)

New England Electric System (1-2-57 to 11-30-83)
New York State Elec. & Gas (1-2-57 to 6-30-76)
Peoples Gas Ltd. & Coke (4-17-40 to 12-31-52)
Public Service of Colo. (12-21-66 to 6-30-76)
Union Electric (12-21-66 to 6-30-76)
Wisconsin Elec. Pwr. (2-28-58 to 11-30-83)

Source: *Standard & Poor's Analyst's Handbook* (New York: Standard & Poor's Corporation, 1987), p. 149.

Table 12–6   Financial Statement Tests—Electric Utility Companies

Balance Sheet

1. Current assets should be at least 10 percent of total assets.
2. Current ratio should be close to 1 to 1 and preferably over 1 to 1.
3. Cash and cash items should be close to 4 percent of total assets.
4. Net plant account should be between 82 percent and 90 percent of total assets.
5. Gross plant should not be over 4 times annual operating revenues for steam plants or 6 times for hydroelectric plants.
6. Net plant should not be over 3½ times annual operating revenues.
7. Plant capacity should provide reserves at peak load of at least 15 percent.
8. Long-term debt should not exceed 60 percent of capitalization.
9. Long-term debt plus preferred stock should not exceed 70 percent of capitalization.
10. Common stock equity should represent at least 30 percent of capitalization. This would mean that debt should not exceed 55 percent and preferred stock 15 percent of gross plant and 20 percent of net plant.
11. Allowance for accumulated depreciation should be at least 20 percent of gross plant and 25 percent of net plant for steam and for hydroelectric 15 percent of gross plant and 20 percent of net plant.

Income Statement

1. Operating revenues should be well balanced between the various classes of customers.
2. Operating ratio (with operating expenses including all taxes) should not exceed 82 percent for steam plants and 72 percent for hydroelectric plants.
3. Operating income should average at least 18 percent of operating revenues, and at least 7 percent of net plant.
4. Depreciation plus maintenance should not be less than 15% of revenues for steam plants and 12 percent for hydroelectric plants.
5. Ration of fixed charges on long-term debt to operating expenses should be at least 7 percent.
6. Fixed charge coverage for all debt, short term and long term, should be at least 2 times.
7. Coverage on the total of fixed charges plus preferred dividends should be at leat 1.90 times.
8. Earnings per share should be more than 10 percent of operating revenues per share.

regression study by Barry Abramson at Merrill Lynch[97] showed a positive impact on stock price for utilities that so diversified (electric, gas, and telephone). The findings showed that a company that earned more than 10 percent of net income from diversified activities would add four percentage points in market to book value ratio because of a higher return on owners' equity and an additional two percentage points because of the favor with which the market looked on a more diversified operating position.

The results of such diversification have proved to be mixed. Companies that diversified into energy-intensive industries such as oil and gas extraction, coal mining and uranium development aim at taking advantage of potential synergies with the utility. Falling energy prices has hurt the ability of such acquisitions to contribute profitably to the utility. If energy prices rise in the future, however, some of these acquisitions could still prove desirable. Some utilities acquired investment subsidiaries, which have not done well since the stock market crash in October 1987.

Analysis of the Gas Industry

There are three segments of the gas industry: (1) pipelines—intrastate and interstate; (2) distribution companies; and (3) integrated companies performing both functions of pipelines and distribution. Initially, most gas consumed, except in areas contiguous to oil-gas wells, was produced near the area of consumption, but such production today is uncommon. In recent years most gas consumed is brought by pipelines to the general area of distribution, such as a state, and then distributed by "distribution companies." Pipeline companies are classified as intrastate pipelines or interstate pipelines. The interstate pipelines may be subdivided into interstate transmission pipelines and interstate and integrated pipelines, the latter being both pipeline companies and distribution companies. Sales to consumers account for 35 to 40 percent of volume sales, but about 50 percent of revenues.

Demand for Gas

Many analysts feel that the traditional residential, commercial and industrial markets will post only modest growth in the future. New markets, however, are likely to be developed; such as the use of gas for environmental reasons.

---

97 Barry M. Abramson, "Utility Industry, Does Diversification Affect Utility Stock Prices?" (Pamphlet) (New York: Merrill Lynch, Securities Research Division, January 20, 1982).

The sharp drop in oil prices in the mid-1980s has led to deteriorating gas company earnings, as customers switched from gas to oil. The price of oil did rebound in 1987, and it seems reasonable to expect stable or rising prices for oil in the future. Moreover, interest rates were low in the mid-1980s, compared to the 1970s, which has benefitted the earnings of gas companies. If interest rates were to drop sharply in the future, however, the allowed rate of return for gas utilities might also drop, hindering earnings growth. Investors should monitor changing demand and interest rate conditions.

Supply of Gas

Proven reserves of natural gas have shown a downward trend since 1970 (see Figure 12–2). Additions to reserves were sharply higher in the early 1980s reaching a high ratio of discoveries to production of 0.92 percent in 1981 before falling to 0.57 percent by 1986.[98] The passage of the Natural Gas Policy Act in late 1978 stimulated exploration by removing the price disparity between interstate and intrastate natural gas and increasing the price for new gas.

The U.S. has been consuming more gas than it discovered since 1968, except for 1970 (when the reserves at Prudhoe Bay were discovered) and in 1981. Still, there has been a surplus of deliverable natural gas. The currently relatively low prices for gas and the oversupply situation were to a great extent caused by producers prior overproduction relative to demand.

Gas reserves do seem abundant relative to demand. The current oversupply situation is, however, expected to begin disappearing around 1990, and future years do look better for the gas industry.

Order 500

Order 500 was issued by the Federal Energy Regulatory Commission and implemented on January 1, 1988. It eliminates the right of firm—service customers to reduce the amount of gas for which they have contracted. Pipeline customers can fulfill contracted demand by either actually purchasing the gas outright or by having the pipeline transmit an equivalent amount of gas. This order benefits the pipelines.

---

98 Standard & Poor's Industry Surveys, op. cit., p. U88.

Figure 12–2   Gas Reserves—Lower 48 States

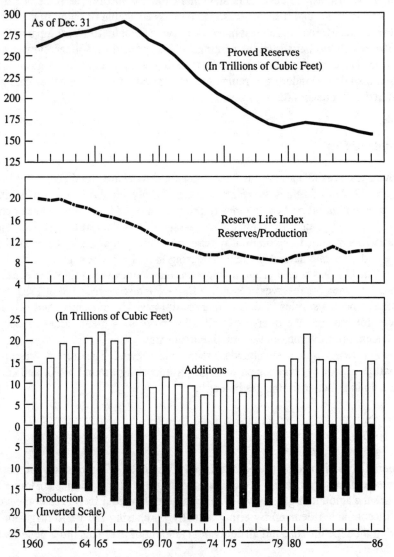

Source: Department of Energy. Reproduced from Standard & Poor's Industry Reports, December 3, 1987, p. 663.

Order 500 does allow pipelines to exact an inventory charge that reflects the cost of holding gas supplies. It is hoped this will allow pipelines to get their contract and service obligations in line with what customers will actually buy.

Distributors are likely to be the losers, as they will bear increased risks and gain nothing to offset those risks.

Regulation

Beginning with the federal Natural Gas Act of 1938, regulation of gas flowing in interstate commerce was placed under the jurisdiction of the Federal Power Commission (FPC). With the establishment of the new Department of Energy in the latter part of 1977, functions of many energy-related agencies were redistributed and new agencies established. The intent was to integrate responsibilities of like nature. The Department of Energy Organization Act of August 4, 1977, transferred to a newly formed Federal Energy Regulatory Commission many of the functions of the Federal Power Commission. Among the functions transferred were "the establishment, review, and enforcement of rates and charges for the transportation and sale of natural gas by a producer or gatherer or by a natural gas pipeline or natural gas company under sections 1, 4, 5, and 7 of the Natural Gas Act."[99]

Up until about 1970, the prices established by the Federal Power Commission were not sufficiently encouraging to attract new funds for new exploration. As a result, U.S. reserves of natural gas decreased because of the lack of opportunities for reasonable earnings growth in the interstate area of the business. In the early 1970s, the transportation of gas through interstate lines actually was declining. This tended to cause all gas pipeline securities to become relatively out of favor with investors. This was reflected in sharply decreasing price-earnings ratios through 1974, falling below price–earnings ratios for the general market averages.

In spite of a decline in earnings for interstate pipeline companies, in the 1970s there was a satisfactory earnings growth rate due to the higher rates of return and higher rate bases approved by the Federal Power Commission.

The energy legislation program that was enacted in 1978 has had a major impact on the pricing and other aspects of pipeline regulation, and has improved the outlook for gas companies.

---

99 *Department of Energy Organization Act*, 91 Stat. 565, Public Law 95–91, 95th Congress, August 4, 1977, Section 402.

Table 12–7 Composite Industry Data (Per Share Data Based on Standard & Poor's Group Stock Price Indexes)

Natural Gas—Distributors & Pipelines   The companies used for this series of per share data are: Costal Corp.; Columbia Gas System; Consolidated Natural Gas; Enron Corp.; ENSERCH Corp.; Houston Natural Gas (10-19-83 to 6-24-85); Oneok Inc.; Pacific Lighting; Panhandle Eastern Corp.; Peoples Energy; Sonat Inc.; Texas Eastern Corp.

	1979	1980	1981	1982	1983	1984	1985	1986
Operating Revenues	399.71	502.49	587.73	660.40	628.87	677.89	972.56	785.12
Maintenance	N.A.	N.A.	N.A.	N.A.	N.A.	N.A.	N.A.	N.A.
Depreciation	22.81	25.31	28.50	34.01	32.95	37.84	52.67	45.48
Income Taxes	20.08	22.99	24.71	15.16	23.45	26.16	17.17	d1.03
Net Operating Income	33.98	33.04	39.11	39.77	40.13	41.16	50.99	32.61
Operating Ratio %	91.50	93.42	93.35	93.98	93.62	93.93	94.75	95.85
Earnings	24.46	27.64	5.69	27.47	27.66	30.16	13.21	d5.41
Dividends	8.78	10.23	33.47	13.17	12.53	14.67	19.92	19.71
Earnings as a % of Oper. Revs.	6.12	5.50	11.56	4.16	4.40	4.45	1.32	def
Dividends as a % of Earns.	35.9	37.01	34.54	47.94	45.30	48.64	147.01	def
Price (1941–43 = 10) —High	202.25	287.90	249.07	207.72	243.91	261.34	334.18	342.81
—Low	121.50	178.58	195.82	140.65	164.82	219.83	240.25	def
Price–Earnings Ratios —High	8.27	10.42	7.44	7.56	8.82	8.67	25.30	def
—Low	4.97	6.46	5.85	5.12	5.96	7.29	18.19	def
Dividend Yield % —High	7.23	5.73	5.90	9.36	7.60	6.67	8.08	6.60
—Low	4.34	3.55	4.64	6.34	5.14	5.61	5.81	5.75

Table 12–7 (continued)

	1979	1980	1981	1982	1983	1984	1985	1986
Long-Term Debt	132.36	141.93	161.53	193.16	172.10	170.86	314.71	328.96
Net Property	298.65	304.00	362.83	413.81	409.47	420.25	681.14	592.07
% Earned on Net Property	11.38	12.48	12.12	9.61	9.80	9.79	7.49	5.51
Capital Expenditures	57.72	64.25	N.A.	N.A	67.73	53.93	N.A.	N.A.

Note: Per share data are expressed in terms of the S&P Stock Price Index, i.e., Stock Prices, 1941–43 = 10.Each of the items shown is first computed on a true per share basis for each company. Totals for each company are then reconstructed using the same number of shares outstanding as was used to compute our stock price index as of December 31st. This is done because the shares used on December 31st, although the latest known at the time, may differ from those reported in the annual reports, which are not available for six or eight weeks after the end of the year. The sum of these reconstructed totals is then related to the base period value used to compute the stock price index. As a double check we relate the various items to the dividends as these are the most stable series. So, for example, if total sales amount to 15 times the total dividend payments, then, with per share dividends at 3.50, the indicated per share sales will be (15 x 3.50) 52.50 in items of the S&P Stock Price Index. For comparability between the various groups, all data are on a calendar year basis, corporate data being posted in the year in which most months fall. Fiscal years ending June 30th are posted in the calendar year in which the fiscal year ends. RRevised. N.A.–Not Available.

Source: Standard & Poor's Industry surveys, Utilities—Gas (New York: Standard & Poor's Corporation, July, 1988), p. U 96.

Table 12–8 Selected Composite Analytical Ratios of Investor-owned Gas Utility Industry

Analytical Ratios	Total Industry					Transmission Companies		Integrated Companies		Distribution Companies	
	1970	1975	1980	1985	1986	1985	1986	1985	1986	1985	1986
Earnings											
Utility Operating Income as % of Total Plant	5.6	6.5	6.7	7.0	6.6	5.9	6.0	7.5	7.6	7.3	6.6
Utility Operating Income as % of Net Plant	7.8	9.9	10.9	12.0	11.2	12.9	12.6	12.6	11.8	10.7	9.8
Operating Revenues as % of Total Plant	²42.5	61.9	128.1	120.1	90.0	117.0	79.4	122.5	103.6	123.7	100.9
Common Dividend Payout Ratio (%)	67.6	57.2	58.2	108.2	116.7	124.5	167.4	154.6	83.3	81.3	100.4
Return on Common Equity (%)	²11.8	13.7	15.2	9.3	8.2	8.5	5.4	5.6	11.8	14.0	12.1
Expenses											
Operating Expenses as % of Operating Revenues	87.5	90.0	95.2	94.6	93.2	95.3	93.2	94.0	92.8	94.2	93.5
Maint. Exp. as % of Total Plant	1.1	1.4	1.8	1.9	1.9	1.3	1.4	2.2	2.2	2.4	2.4
Deprec. Exp. as % of Total Plant	2.9	3.6	3.6	3.7	3.7	3.8	3.9	4.0	3.1	3.3	3.4
Deprec. Exp. as % of Deprec. Plant	N.A.	3.6	4.1	3.7	3.9	3.8	4.1	4.0	3.1	3.4	3.9
Total Taxes as % of Total Plant	4.1	5.6	7.2	7.6	6.8	5.1	4.5	8.4	8.6	10.8	9.5
Total Taxes as % of Net Plant	5.6	8.5	11.8	13.1	11.5	11.0	9.5	14.1	13.4	16.0	14.0
Total Taxes as % of Net Inc. Plus Total Taxes	²52.4	53.9	53.6	63.5	64.4	53.0	59.3	71.7	64.5	69.4	70.1
¹Current Fed. Inc. Tax as % of Net Inc. Plus Current Fed. Inc. Tax	²29.8	30.4	27.4	40.0	45.0	39.6	49.4	51.4	43.6	33.4	43.0
Plant											
Total Plant Per $ of Total Operating Revenues	2.4	1.6	0.8	0.8	1.1	0.9	1.3	0.8	1.0	0.8	1.0
Net Plant Per $ of Total Operating Revenues	1.7	1.1	0.5	0.5	0.7	0.4	0.6	0.5	0.6	0.5	0.7
Deprec. Reserve as % of Total Plant	27.8	34.0	39.0	42.0	40.9	54.1	52.2	40.4	35.9	32.4	32.2
Deprec. Reserve as Total % of Deprec. Plant	N.A.	35.8	44.0	43.1	43.0	55.5	54.3	40.6	35.9	33.2	36.1
Total Plant Per Employee ($000)	182.1	251.6	328.1	423.2	445.3	844.0	909.0	328.0	291.5	281.3	299.5

Table 12–8 (continued)

Analytical Ratios	Total Industry					Transmission Companies		Integrated Companies		Distribution Companies	
	1970	1975	1980	1985	1986	1985	1986	1985	1986	1985	1986
Capitalization											
Long-term Debt as % of Net Plant	56.3	59.4	53.9	52.4	50.4	64.3	58.8	37.1	53.4	38.0	40.5
% Total Capitalization Represented by:											
Long-term Debt	54.7	50.1	42.9	40.0	40.2	36.4	34.9	40.6	45.6	42.4	44.8
Preferred Stock	6.8	6.5	7.1	5.2	4.6	4.3	3.4	3.7	4.6	4.2	3.4
Common Equity	38.5	43.4	50.0	54.8	55.2	59.3	61.7	55.7	49.8	53.4	51.8

[1]Includes "Provision for Deferred Federal Income Taxes" and "Portion of Current Federal Income Taxes Provided for in Prior Years."

[2]Not comparable with later data because of Federal Power Commission ruling requiring adoption of the equity method in reporting earnings of subsidiaries.
N.A.–Not Available

Sources: American Gas Association; Standard & Poor's Industry Surveys, Utilities—Gas (New York: Standard & Poor's Corporation, July, 1988), p. U. 94.

Key Financial Data

Per share data based on Standard & Poor's group stock price indexes for the natural gas industry are shown in Table 12–7, and selected analytical ratios in Table 12–8. Distributors and pipelines showed strong operating revenue growth (a 15.97 percent compound annual rate since 1979), but revenues and earnings fell sharply in 1986. Gas company earnings were adversely affected in 1986 by a falling price for oil which caused industrial customers to switch to the less expensive fuel. The price of oil rebounded, however, in 1987 and the gas companies recovered the sales lost in 1986, leading to some earnings growth. This earnings growth was not distributed evenly among gas companies. Pipelines with gas exploration and production operations suffered from falling gas prices in 1987. Order 500 also hurt many producers.

We do anticipate earnings improvement in the future, based on an expected increase in gas demand, benefits accruing from restructuring of operations, somewhat lower interest rates, and colder winters. Investors should monitor developments carefully in these areas.

Balance Sheet Analysis

Analysts often use the following rules of thumb, based on experience, when analyzing gas industry balance sheets:

1. Net plant should not exceed two times annual operating revenues and gross plant three times annual operating revenues.
2. Total debt should not exceeded 60 percent of total capitalization or about the same percentage of net plant.
3. Long-term debt plus preferred stock should not exceed 70 percent of total capitalization; and if it is 70 percent, long-term debt should not exceed 55 percent of total capitalization, leaving 15 percent for the preferred stock.
4. Common stock equity should represent at least 30 percent of total capitalization.

Income Statement Analysis

The following rules of thumb are suggested as standards when analyzing gas industry income statements.

1. Total operating expenses including taxes and depreciation should not exceed 88 percent of total operating revenues or 70 percent exclusive of depreciation and maintenance.
2. Depreciation plus maintenance should equal at least 10 percent of operating revenues.
3. The average rate of return on common equity should be at least 15 percent.
4. The rate of return on total capitalization should be at least 8 percent.
5. Coverage of fixed charges should be at least 2.75 times.
6. Coverage of fixed charges plus preferred dividends should be at least two times and should not exceed seven percent of operating revenues.
7. The balance available for the common should be at least seven percent of operating revenues.

The Telephone Industry

The telephone industry in the United States is dominated by AT&T and the seven Bell regional holding companies. There are nearly 1,400 other telephone companies, most of which are small, though some are large (such as United Telecommunications and G.T.E. Corporation).

Regulation

Regulatory developments have affected the long-term profit outlook of the telecommunications industry. There has been a philosophical shift toward fewer regulatory constraints, which has helped the non-Bell companies. The FCC contends rate-of-return regulation is a disincentive to cost-cutting and innovation. They wish to mandate lower price caps, but allow telephone companies to profit from cost cutting.

Rate cap legislation as proposed by the FCC is expected to hurt industry profitability in the short run, and the effect on longer-term profits is uncertain. Carriers will have to generate productivity gains three percent in excess of the overall economy to benefit from the legislation.[100]

---

100 Standard & Poor's Industry Survey's Telecommunications, op. cit., pp. T 1 & 2.

Specifics of Analysis of Telephone Company Securities

For the small, and sometimes even tiny, individual telephone company, the following requirements should be considerably stricter than for Bell companies because of the risks inherent in their very small size.

Balance Sheet Analysis

1. The current ratio should be above the one to one level.
2. Long-term debt should not exceed 45 percent of total percent capitalization, and debt plus preferred stock, 60 percent.
3. The turnover of net fixed assets (after depreciation) should be at least 2.8 times; i.e., annual revenue should be at least equal to 36 percent of the value of net plant.
4. The account "accumulated depreciation" should be equal to approximately 25 percent of gross plant account.

Income Statement Analysis

1. The operating ratio should not exceed 85 percent (operating expenses including income taxes). If income taxes are excluded from operating expenses, the operating ratio should not exceed 72 percent.
2. The ratio of maintenance plus depreciation to total gross revenue should not exceed 33 to 35 percent.
3. The rate of return on the capital structure (before deduction of fixed charges), i.e., amount available for fixed charges, should be at least seven to 7.5 percent.
4. The amount available for fixed charges before taxes should show a coverage of at least 3.8 times.

Water Companies

Most water companies are owned by the municipalities they serve. Some of these have issued revenue bonds that are held by private investors. There are still, however, many privately-owned water companies, but the ownership is often closely, even family, held. Some larger privately-owned municipal companies are located in Birmingham, Alabama; Indianapolis, Indiana; New Haven, Connecticut; New Rochelle, New York; and San Jose, California. One large privately-owned water company, American Water Works, controls about 75 companies operating in 15 states.

The gross revenues of water companies usually are stable, and in most areas exhibit consistent growth in revenues and earnings. In fast-growing areas the rate of growth reflects this environment. As with other utilities, fixed assets constitute the bulk of total assets, and the turnover of capital invested in these assets is relatively slow. The operations of water companies are relatively simple resulting in a relatively low operating ratio.

Financial Analysis

The following proportions should be present:

1. Gross fixed assets should not be greater than $5\frac{1}{2}$ to $6\frac{1}{2}$ times annual revenues.
2. The depreciation should be equal to at least 16 percent of gross plant.
3. Long-term debt should not be greater than two-thirds the value of net assets (gross assets less depreciation), and long-term debt plus preferred stock should not exceed three-quarters of total capitalization.
4. The common equity should represent at least one-quarter of the total capitalization.
5. The operating ratio should not exceed 70 percent.
6. The rate of return on the capital structure should at least be in the five to six percent range.
7. The fixed charge coverage should be at least two and one-half times earnings.
8. Total interest plus preferred dividends should be covered at least one and three-quarter times.
9. The amount of gross revenues carried down to the common equity should be at least 10 percent.

Summary

There are two broad categories of regulated industries: utilities and transportation companies. In general, regulated industries sell services that are affected with the public interest and in many instances, such as electric and gas utilities and telephone companies, enjoy a monopoly position and must be regulated to protect the public from excessive prices and poor service.

In analyzing regulated industries, the first and most important step is to determine the regulatory climate—essentially the attitude of the regulatory commission or agency as to rates and service requirements. The question is, "Is the utility permitted to earn a fair rate of return, fair in the judgement of investors, as expressed in the market yield of its securities compared to similar companies?" If it is determined that the regulatory climate is satisfactory from the investor's viewpoint, then the investor can proceed to analyze specific companies in that jurisdiction.

The financial analysis centers on the major financial statements as is the case with other companies. But each industry has its own special characteristics, and this fact must be given serious consideration in analyzing trends and ratios.

Closely correlated to the financial analysis is the analysis of related statistics that are available to the investor. Most of the larger utility companies furnish financial analysts with statistical booklets to supplement financial statements and other information appearing in annual reports.

CHAPTER 13

Regulated Industries: Transportation

Two major components of the transportation industry will be discussed in this chapter: the railroad industry and the trucking industry. In a broad legal context these regulated industries are public utilities. The most vital areas of control cover rates of return, mergers, consolidations, and abandonments, with rate of return being the most significant.

In the late 1970s the federal government was acting to decontrol the trucking and air transport industries, but the industries themselves and the unions were opposing decontrol, saying they feared cutthroat competition would develop. Air freight rates were decontrolled in 1978. Merger activity was accelerated in the early 1980s by changes in the regulatory environment.

The Railroads

Passenger traffic of the railroads has been shifted to agencies of the federal government—AMTRAK for long-haul traffic and CON-RAIL for commuter traffic. Passenger business has been a deficit operation for the railroads. Moreover, it has interfered seriously with freight traffic movements.

The share of railroads in total interstate freight fell from 75 percent in 1929 to a low of 36.7 percent in 1975, before rising to 37.2 percent in 1985 (see Table 13–1). Trucks and oil pipelines gained sharply at the expense of railroads until 1960. Railroads have managed to stabilize the situation since 1970 but have shown little growth in market share since then. Generally transportation experts assume that the railroads are most efficient for hauls of 400 miles or over while trucks have the advantage for hauls of 400 miles or less. This is the major reason why the eastern roads suffered most severely from truck competition on their relatively short hauls, and accounts for the poor record of the eastern roads relative to the southern and western roads.

Coal traffic has grown significantly over the past decade, and if this traffic is excluded, a serious weakening condition appears. Standard and Poor's, Inc. anticipates that future growth in coal consumption is likely to be well below levels of the past decade.[101]Moreover, grain traffic, which along with coal fueled much of the industry's growth during the 1970s also has proved disappointing recently. Piggyback shipments, however, are expected to post above average growth over the next decade and should help the railroads capture market share from the trucking industry.

Labor Costs

The railroad industry has made progress over the past decade in cutting labor costs and boosting productivity of its workers. Still, manpower levels do appear to be somewhat inflated, and the loss of traffic to trucks does reflect excessive labor costs and work rules that impair attaining efficient operations. Investors in railroads should watch labor costs and wage settlements.

Investment Favorites

The following railroads are considered to be representative of somewhat higher quality than the industry overall, based on compound growth rates recorded for operating revenues and net income (see Table 13–2). Notice that these railroads are concentrated in the south and the far west, where long-hauls are prevalent. Some regional rails are also looked upon favorably, such as the Chicago, Central & Pacific RR, which is reported to have slashed labor costs to 50 percent of operating costs from 75 percent.

Consolidations

Until legislation was passed in the 1950s, bringing about railroad mergers or consolidations was difficult, largely because of union opposition. However, after helpful 1958 legislation a series of consolidations began in 1959. Standard &

---

101 Standard & Poor's Industry Surveys, Vol. 2 (New York: Standard & Poor's Corporation, July, 1988), p. R17.

Table 13–1 Volume of U.S. Intercity Freight and Passenger Traffic—Millions of Revenue Freight Ton-Miles and Percentage of Total

Year	Railroads[a]	%	Trucks	%	Great Lakes	%	Rivers and Canals	%	Oil Pipelines	%	Air	%	Total
1929	454,800	74.9	19,689	3.3	97,322	16.0	8,661	1.4	26,900	4.4	3	—	607,375
1939	338,850	62.4	52,821	9.7	76,312	14.0	19,937	3.7	55,602	10.2	12	—	543,534
1944	746,912	68.6	58,264	5.4	118,769	10.9	31,386	2.9	132,864	12.2	71	—	1,088,266
1950	569,940	56.2	172,860	16.3	111,687	10.5	51,657	4.9	129,175	12.1	318	—	1,062,637
1960	579,130	44.1	285,483	21.7	99,468	7.6	120,785	9.2	228,626	17.4	778	—	1,314,270
1970	771,168	39.8	412,000	21.3	114,475	5.9	204,085	10.5	431,000	22.3	3,295	0.2	1,936,023
1980	932,000	37.5	555,000	22.3	96,000	3.9	311,000	12.5	588,000	23.6	4,840	0.2	2,486,840
1984	935,000	37.5	605,000	24.2	76,000	3.0	306,000	12.3	568,000	22.7	6,600	0.3	2,496,600
1985	895,000	36.4	610,000	24.8	76,000	3.1	306,000	12.5	564,000	22.9	6,710	0.3	2,457,710
1986[P]	896,000	35.8	627,700	25.1	72,000	2.9	321,000	12.8	579,000	23.1	7,340	0.3	2,502,340

Millions of Revenue Passenger-Miles and Percentage of Total (Except Private)

Year	Railroads[a]	%	Buses	%	Air Carriers	%	Inland Waterways	%	Total (except private)	Private Automobiles	Private Airplanes	Total (including private)
1929	33,965	77.1	6,800	15.4	—	—	3,300	7.5	44,065	175,000	—	219,065
1939	23,669	67.7	9,100	26.0	683	2.0	1,486	4.3	34,938	275,000	—	309,938
1944	97,705	75.7	26,920	20.9	2,177	1.7	2,187	1.7	128,989	181,000	1	309,990
1950	32,481	47.2	26,436	38.4	8,773	12.7	1,190	1.7	68,880	438,293	1,299	508,472
1960	21,574	28.6	19,327	25.7	31,730	42.1	2,688	3.6	75,319	706,079	2,228	783,626

Table 13–1 (continued)

Year	Rail-roads[a]	%	Buses	%	Air Carriers	%	Inland Water-ways	%	Total (except private)	Private Auto-mobiles	Private Air-planes	Total (including private)
1970	10,903	5.7	25,300	14.3	109,499	77.7	4,000	2.3	149,702	1,026,000	9,101	1,189,803
1980	11,000	4.5	27,400	11.3	204,400	84.2	N.A.	—	242,800	1,300,400	14,700	1,557,900
1984	11,500	4.0	27,100	9.4	250,700	86.6	N.A.	—	289,300	1,436,800	12,500	1,738,600
1985	11,400	3.6	23,800	7.6	277,800	88.8	N.A.	—	313,000	1,418,300	13,000	1,744,300
1986P	11,900	3.5	23,700	6.9	307,600	89.6	N.A.	—	343,200	1,459,700	12,100	1,815,000

[a] Railroads of all classes, including electric railways, Amtrack and Auto-train.

P These are preliminary estimates and are subject to frequent subsequent adjustments.

Note: Air carrier data from reports of CAB and TAA: Great Lakes and rivers and canals from Corps of Engineers and TAA: All 1980, 1984 through 1986 figures are from Transportation Policy Associations, except rail freight traffic is by the AAR.

Source: *Railroad Facts* (Washington, D.C.: Association of American Railroads, 1987), p. 32.

Table 13–2   Growth In Operating Revenues and Net Income for Better Quality Railroads

	Compound Growth Rate Operating Revenues			Compound Growth Rate Net Income		
	1 Yr.	5 Yrs.	10 Yrs.	1 Yr.	5 Yrs.	10 Yrs.
Burlington Northern (Substantial Coal Reserves)	–5.5	17.0	18.4	9.3	23.2	28.2
Santa Fe Southern Pacific (Substantial Natural Reserves)	–3.4	8.0	11.5	–4.3	24.7	20.1
Soo Line Corp. Holding Co.	90.3	14.5	14.4	NM*	NM	NM
Union Pacific (Substantial Natural Resources)	0.1	10.0	16.1	1.4	4.4	12.9
Norfolk Southern Corp.	8.5	19.4	13.8	3.7	16.6	19.0

* NM = Not Measurable.

Poor's reports that, "Since 1978 the number of Class I railroads (those with annual revenues exceeding $80 million) has been cut in half as a result of mergers, liquidations, and bankruptcies."[102] The top five rail systems generated 68% of industry freight revenues in 1985, and the top ten rail systems accounted for 86 percent of industry freight revenues. Rails have increased their specialization in long-haul freight with a growing dependence on bulk commodities and piggyback hauls.

Merger activity was stimulated in the early 1980s by changes in the regulatory environment. The Railroad Revitalization and Regulatory Reform Act of 1976 directed the ICC to facilitate mergers and streamline our railroad systems into healthier, more efficient carriers. The ICC, however, rejected a proposed combination of the Southern Pacific and Santa Fe railroads in July 1986, signalling an unfavorable shift in the regulatory climate for railroads. This creates doubt about the rapid approval of future merger proposals.

While a number of consolidations (or mergers) have worked out profitably, the massive Penn-Central bankruptcy shows that consolidation is not always the answer to problems, and does not always work out to the advantage of security holders. One must assess the likely impact on revenue generation, cost economies,

---

102 Standard & Poor's Industry Surveys, op. cit., p. R23.

and profitability, when considering whether a pending merger will or will not benefit investors.

The merger movement raises the threat that smaller independent railroads will be squeezed out of a number of markets, thereby threatening their survival.

Cyclical Traffic

Since a substantial portion of railroad traffic is in the area of heavy durable goods, the railroads are particularly subject to contractions in business cycles. High debt/capitalization ratios create high financial leverage. The combination of the cyclical nature of their business and the high financial leverage of most railroads causes their earnings records to be quite volatile over the business cycle.

Financial Analysis of Railroads

Table 13-3 shows the major items in the railroad income statement for selected years from 1929-1985. The distribution of operating revenues for 1986 is shown in Table 13-4. Operating revenues stayed in a relatively narrow range from 1950-1969 at $10 to $11 billion. During that period, however operating expenses rose sharply and profits tended to fall. Net income did not recover to the peak 1929 level until 1980. Net income then fell back sharply during the 1982 recession, again proving the railroads susceptibility to the business cycle. Operating income and net income reached new highs in 1984, but profits slid about 31 percent in 1985 and probably dropped further in 1986.

Standard & Poor's reports that 1985 and 1986 results were penalized by nonrecurring items, and that operating revenues are expected to inch forward in 1986.[103]

An examination of Table 13-3 shows the overall poor record of the eastern railroads, and the favorable results recorded by the Western district. The importance of labor costs (about 44 percent of total operating revenues), is clear when reviewing Table 13-4.

---

103 Standard & Poor's Industry Surveys, op. cit., p. R15.

Table 13–3   Condensed Income Statement—Class I Railroads

Operating Revenues

Railroad operating revenues amounted to $26.2 billion in 1986.
(Amounts shown in thousands)

	United States	Eastern District	Western District
1929	$6,279,521	$3,886,879	$2,392,642
1939	3,995,004	2,480,208	1,514,796
1944	9,436,790	5,416,089	4,020,701
1947	8,684,918	5,137,930	3,546,988
1951	10,390,611	6,083,725	4,306,885
1955	10,106,330	5,815,997	4,290,333
1972	13,409,815	7,084,616	6,325,199
1973	14,770,082	7,698,891	7,071,191
1974	16,922,841	8,862,595	8,060,246
1975	16,401,860	8,535,831	7,866,029
1976	18,536,482	9,557,098	8,979,384
1977	20,090,482	10,172,405	9,918,077
1978	21,721,332	10,620,862	11,100,470
1979	25,219,115	12,526,005	12,693,110
1980	28,102,946	13,434,101	14,668,845
1981	30,898,610	14,879,268	16,019,342
1982	27,503,503	13,357,745	14,145,758
1983	26,729,392	12,217,397	14,511,995
1984	29,453,446	13,566,348	15,887,098
1985	27,586,441	12,918,574	14,667,867
1986	**26,204,122**	**12,235,170**	**13,968,952**

Freight Revenue

Freight revenue of the Class I railroads totaled $25.3 billion in
1986, 5.0 percent below 1985. (Amounts shown in thousands)

	United States	Eastern District	Western District
1929	$4,825,622	$2,948,430	$1,877,192
1939	3,251,096	2,000,183	1,250,913
1944	6,998,615	3,991,866	3,006,748
1947	7,041,185	4,114,802	2,926,383
1951	8,634,101	4,983,440	3,650,661
1955	8,538,286	4,828,871	3,709,415

Table 13–3 (continued)
Freight Revenue

	United States	Eastern District	Western District
1972	12,570,326	6,511,514	6,058,812
1973	13,770,734	7,017,914	6,752,820
1974	15,766,710	8,065,016	7,701,694
1975	15,389,809	7,804,519	7,585,290
1976	17,400,241	8,730,863	8,669,378
1977	18,892,437	9,311,002	9,581,435
1978	20,236,065	9,531,536	10,704,529
1979	23,447,418	11,199,011	12,248,407
1980	26,200,348	12,036,953	14,163,395
1981	28,925,436	13,414,570	15,510,866
1982	25,627,354	11,943,959	13,683,395
1983	25,835,519	11,743,928	14,091,591
1984	28,471,789	13,032,248	15,439,541
1985	26,687,652	12,444,633	14,243,019
1986	**25,343,911**	**11,803,793**	**13,540,118**

Operating Expenses

Operating expenses totaled $24.9 billion in 1986, down 1.3 percent from 1985. Data for the past four years are not comparable to prior years because of the industry's conversion in 1983 to a standard Depreciation Accounting System which, on paper only, has the effect of decreasing annual costs. Operating expenses for 1985 were increased by $784 million and for 1986 by $1.8 billion due to the inclusion of special charges. (Amounts shown in thousands)

	United States	Eastern District	Western District
1929	$5,109,118	$3,178,515	$1,930,604
1939	3,511,310	2,146,729	1,364,519
1944	7,179,655	4,274,939	2,904,715
1947	7,725,423	4,690,309	3,035,115
1951	8,991,365	5,318,127	3,673,238
1955	8,621,255	4,989,033	3,632,224
1972	12,528,414	6,790,419	5,737,997
1973	13,844,765	7,368,054	6,476,711
1974	15,782,658	8,395,695	7,386,963
1975	15,935,542	8,517,851	7,417,691
1976	17,881,047	9,505,724	8,375,323

Table 13-3 (continued)
Operating Expenses

	United States	Eastern District	Western District
1977	19,533,970	10,277,500	9,256,469
1978	21,043,143	10,744,912	10,298,231
1979	23,994,154	12,136,793	11,857,361
1980	26,249,920	12,760,818	13,489,102
1981	28,586,890	13,740,751	14,846,139
1982	26,490,278	12,962,260	13,528,018
1983	24,106,254	11,017,643	13,088,611
1984	25,800,454	11,695,740	14,104,714
1985	25,225,295	11,947,595	13,277,700
1986	24,896,015	10,996,766	13,899,249

Principal Categories of Expenses

Expenditures to maintain way, structures and equipment and transportation expenses accounted for 87 percent of total operating outlays in 1986.

Data for the years 1978-1982 are not comparable to figures shown for the prior years due to extensive changes in expense accounts under the revised Uniform System of Accounts which became effective January 1, 1978, and data for 1983-1986 are not comparable with any of the prior years due to conversion to a Depreciation Accounting System. (Amounts shown in thousands)

	Maintenance of Way and Structures	Maintenance of Equipment	Transportation
1929	$855,355	$1,202,912	$2,079,954
1939	466,831	765,935	1,417,794
1944	1,263,292	1,587,485	2,973,910
1947	1,212,096	1,558,011	3,476,433
1951	1,478,766	1,945,022	3,974,458
1955	1,387,494	1,787,739	3,769,856
1972	1,920,395	2,397,596	5,207,652
1973	2,035,613	2,531,380	5,897,609
1974	2,351,973	2,809,237	6,766,355
1975	2,408,980	2,856,203	6,735,741
1976	3,047,236	3,213,892	7,337,593
1977	3,460,153	3,613,494	7,883,291
1978	4,055,105	5,421,182	9,617,066

Table 13–3 (continued)

Principal Categories of Expenses

	Maintenance of Way and Structures	Maintenance of Equipment	Trans- portation
1979	4,581,742	6,018,672	11,342,272
1980	4,923,403	6,387,976	12,646,893
1981	5,535,815	6,866,503	13,030,547
1982	5,208,584	6,413,196	12,366,145
1983	4,107,046	6,070,391	11,377,290
1984	4,250,275	6,572,696	12,281,567
1985	4,332,663	6,394,579	11,721,539
1986	4,779,691	6,573,065	10,196,636

Ordinary Income

Ordinary income (after income from outside sources and payment of fixed rentals, interest and other charges) amounted to $747 million in 1986, down 58.2 percent from 1985. Ordinary income for 1985 and 1986 were reduced due to the inclusion of special charges. (Amounts shown in thousands)

	United States	Eastern District	Western District
1929	$896,807	$560,037	$336,769
1939	93,182	122,073	(28,892)
1944	667,188	363,459	303,729
1947	478,875	216,370	262,505
1951	693,176	345,673	347,503
1955	927,122	503,093	424,029
1972	318,637	(18,555)	337,192
1973	359,343	3,965	355,378
1974	730,229	242,580	487,649
1975	144,362	(156,013)	300,375
1976	354,982	(98,552)	453,534
1977	325,582	(159,187)	484,769
1978	306,786	(228,417)	535,203
1979	938,254	286,442	651,812
1980	1,129,392	400,670	728,722
1981	2,041,265	978,245	1,063,020
1982	1,151,548	669,390	482,158
1983	1,777,916	897,755	880,161
1984	2,653,814	1,488,704	1,165,110
1985	1,788,151	779,626	1,008,525
1986	746,965	977,011	(230,046)

Table 13-3 (continued)
Net Railway Operating Income

Net railway operating income (NROI) for 1986 was $507 million, 71.0 percent lower than the previous year. Data for 1983-1986 are not comparable with prior years due to conversion to a Depreciation Accounting System.

Net railway operating income is the remainder of operating revenues after deducting operating expenses, current and deferred taxes, and rents for equipment and joint facilities, but before recording non-operating income and deducting fixed charges. "NROI" is the figure used to determine rate of return on investment. NROI for 1985 and 1986 were reduced due to the inclusion of special charges. (Amounts shown in thousands)

	United States	Eastern District	Western District
1929	$1,251,698	$767,277	$484,422
1939	588,829	410,714	178,116
1944	1,106,327	618,568	487,759
1947	780,694	407,125	373,570
1951	942,542	539,417	403,125
1955	1,127,997	678,557	449,440
1972	653,827	235,614	418,214
1973	649,828	235,237	414,591
1974	768,106	292,587	475,519
1975	350,682	(8,748)	359,429
1976	451,832	(48,421)	500,253
1977	343,093	(194,208)	537,301
1978	427,451	(200,893)	628,344
1979	837,232	159,553	677,679
1980	1,312,400	397,891	914,509
1981	1,360,611	622,966	737,645
1982	742,231	262,544	479,687
1983	1,837,854	870,047	967,807
1984	2,536,673	1,318,599	1,218,074
1985	1,746,386	760,143	986,243
1986	506,591	739,971	(233,380)

Source: *Railroad Facts* (Washington, D.C.: Association of American Railroads, 1987) pp. 12, 13, 14, 15, 17, and 20.

Table 13–4   Distribution of Operating Revenues (Dollar Amounts in Millions)

	1986
Total Operating Revenues	$26,204
Wages Charged to Expenses	8,675
Health and Welfare and Pensions	769
Payroll Taxes	2,183
Total Labor Costs	11,627
Income Taxes on Ordinary Income[1]	490
Provision for Deferred Taxes	(327)
Fuel and Power-Locomotives	1,486
Loss and Damage, Injuries, and Insurance	1,024
Depreciation	3,032
All Other Expenses[2]	8,365
Total Expenses and Taxes	25,697
Net Railway Operating Income	507

The Revenue Dollar—1986

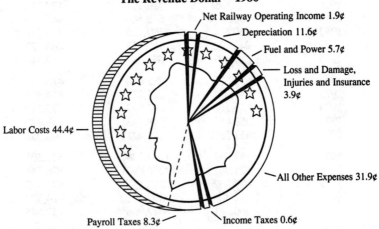

Net Railway Operating Income 1.9¢

Depreciation 11.6¢

Fuel and Power 5.7¢

Loss and Damage, Injuries and Insurance 3.9¢

All Other Expenses 31.9¢

Income Taxes 0.6¢

Payroll Taxes 8.3¢

Labor Costs 44.4¢

[1] Includes state income taxes
[2] Includes other materials and supplies, miscellaneous equipment, and joint facility rents, current taxes (other than payroll taxes and income taxes), and retirement charges and rent for income from leased roads and equipment.
Source: *Railroad Facts*, op. cit., p. 11.

Railroad Income Statement Analysis

"Revenues" in railroad accounting terminology means gross revenues (income) before deducting expenses. "Income" in railroad statements is synonymous with "net income" as used in industrial accounting. Also, while federal income taxes are deductible from net income on industrial company statements, they are included in the same categories as property and excise taxes in railroad accounting. Federal income taxes, therefore, reduce reported net railway operating income, whereas they would not affect net operating income of an industrial company.

Operating Revenues.   The major source of railroad revenues is freight income. The bases for analysis of revenues are therefore: (1) specific sources of revenues (commodity classifications) and trends of major components—the analyst has available in annual reports and ICC publications and statistical services complete breakdowns of freight revenues and tonnage by commodity classification and areas; (2) gross revenue carloadings and tonnage analysis and trends; (3) strategic position of traffic, i.e., traffic originated, terminated, and otherwise controlled; (4) trends of traffic between competing systems; (5) trends of traffic density-volume of ton-miles carried; (6) ton-miles carried per dollar of debt; (7) length of average haul; (8) stability of traffic through last two business cycles; and (9) review of trends of revenues over past cycles and estimates for the next five to six years of annual normal revenues by major commodity classification.

Analysis of Operating Revenues Expenses

The profitability of the railroad will depend on its freight traffic, the composition of the freight, the length of the haul, the traffic density, and the strategic position of the railroad in regard to its freight business. The analyst should study the territory served by the railroad to determine the source and the trends of actual and potential freight tonnage and revenues. Important factors are the natural resources in the area studied, the agricultural situation, the type and trend of industry and commerce in the area, the volume of traffic developed, population trends, and per capita income trends. A study of the major items carried by the railroad will give insight into its earning power, since those carrying higher freight rate commodities often will be in the most advantageous position. However, certain low-rate commodities such as coal—which can be handled with low labor costs, may also be profitable.

Trend of Revenues.   The trend of revenues over a period of years should be studied in relationship to the trend of the railroad industry as a whole, the trend of the region, competing roads within the region, competing modes of transportation such as motor carriers and barge lines, and GNP trends.

Tonnage Analysis.   Figures for a qualitative as well as quantitative analysis are provided in "Freight Commodity Loading Statistics," a report published by the ICC. Railway freight tonnage figures for each railroad are segregated in these reports into approximately 160 classes of commodities.

Strategic Position of Traffic.   In general, the greater the density of traffic, the greater the net profit. In this connection fairly diversified traffic is desirable, and it should be determined that the major source of traffic is stable and growing. Freight traffic density is measured by the net revenue ton-miles per mile of road.

Ton-Miles per Dollar of Debt.   The ton-miles per dollar of mortgage debt is an important ratio for the section of a railroad covered by a specific mortgage. The ratio generally should be at least 40.

Length of Average Haul.   Other things being equal, the longer the average haul for freight carried, the less expensive (on an average per-mile basis) it is to move and the more profitable it is to the railroad. Terminal expenses are major expenses because of high wage costs and the amount of labor costs involved; therefore, the longer the haul, the more these expenses can be allocated on a per-mile basis. The railroads are at a distinct cost disadvantage for hauls of less than 400 miles in competition with motor carriers.

Operating Expenses.   The major operating expenses of the railroads are maintenance, depreciation, transportation expenses, and traffic expenses. Labor costs are the largest individual expense item.

Maintenance.   Maintenance is a heavy factor in railroad expenses. In general, a railroad should spend at least 13 to 15 percent of gross revenue for maintenance of ways and structures, 17 to 19 percent for maintenance of equipment, and 38 to 40 percent for transportation expense.

Depreciation.   This item has in recent years averaged around five percent of gross revenues, or about the same as the amount available for the common stock. Because it is a tax-deductible expense, the effect on net income available for the common stock is apparent.

Labor Factors.   While railroad management has increased productivity of labor since World War II, reducing the number of workers by half since 1945 while carrying more freight volume, labor costs still represent 44 percent of total revenue. Average earnings of employees have approximately quadrupled. The benefits of capital expenditures and higher labor productivity have often been absorbed by employee wages with little or no benefit for security holders.

In 1929 the number of railroad employees was 1,660,850; in 1944, 1,413,672; and in 1947, 1,351,961. However, productivity so increased that the number of employees was reduced to 780,494 by 1960; to 566,282 in 1970, to 458,994 in 1980, and to 275,811 by the end of 1986. While total compensation was $4.35 billion in 1947 for 1,351,961 employees, it rose to $11.3 billion in 1980 for only 458,994 employees or from $3,218 annually per employee to $24,672 in 1980, and $35,894 by year-end 1986. Labor costs were 44 percent of total operating revenues in 1947, 47 percent of total operating revenues in 1980, and 44 percent in 1986. Therefore, labor costs relative to revenues were about the same in 1986 as in 1947 in spite of the great increase in labor productivity evidenced by the sharp decrease in the number of employees handling a large volume of freight.

Operating Ratio. The operating ratio is the ratio of operating expenses to operating revenue and consists largely of transportation expenses plus maintenance expenses. It is by far the most important ratio used in railroad analysis. But taken by itself as an indication of operating efficiency, the operating ratio may give a misleading picture, especially if maintenance is being skimped. Lease rentals, together with maintenance policy, may cause wide differences in operating ratios.

The average operating ratios for Class I railroads are shown in Table 13–5. The operating ratio for all Class I railroads rose to a high of 97.16% in 1975. The historically high ratios recorded in recent years (through 1987) are discouraging and suggest caution when selecting railroad stocks. In general, the better railroads will have lower operating ratios than the average.

Other Income. Most railroads have some income other than that from their normal railroad operations, and for some railroads this other income is significant. Many investors consider that substantial income from natural resource reserves is a favorable factor if normal railway operations consistently are profitable. Investors considering such railroads should not purchase securities on this basis unless railway operations have been and are expected to be profitable.

Available for Fixed Charges. Railroad fixed charges are regular annual fixed expenses such as interest on debt and rentals on leased properties. The amount available for fixed charges consists of (1) net railway operating income plus and (2) other income less other deductions. This is the amount available for all security

Table 13-5   Average Operating Expense Ratios* for U.S. Railroads—
Selected Years, 1929–1986

1929	81.36%
1939	87.89
1944	76.08
1955	85.30
1972	93.43
1975	97.16
1980	93.41
1981	92.52
1982	96.32
1983	90.19
1984	87.60
1985	91.44
1986	95.01

*Calculated by dividing operating expenses by operating revenues.

Source: Calculated on the basis of data provided in *Railroad Facts* (Washington, D.C.: Association of American Railroads, 1987) pp. 12 & 14.

holders, and it provides the numerator in calculating the number of times fixed charges are earned as published in ICC statistics.

For all Class I railroads the amount available for fixed charges in recent years has averaged about eight percent of gross operating revenues. The range was from actual deficits to highs of 21 percent, 24 percent, and 36 percent for certain roads.

Times Fixed Charges Earned.   The primary test for bonds is the number of times fixed charges are earned. This figure is calculated by dividing the amount available for fixed charges by the fixed charges. There is a wide range for various railroads for the number of times fixed charges are earned. The industry average in years of good business is around 3x. As with other bonds, the test is also the number of times fixed charges have been earned in recession years—the stability or lack of stability of the figures.

The amount of debt that a railroad can bear is determined by the traffic and the level of earnings and is measured in terms of the times fixed charges are earned and the adequacy of cash flow to meet debt amortization requirements.

Preferred Dividends.   Some railroads have preferred stock outstanding, and from the standpoint of the common stock, preferred dividends are a fixed charge. Therefore, the investor should calculate the coverage on an "overall basis," i.e., the number of times fixed charges plus preferred dividends are earned.

Earnings Available for the Common Stock.   This is the percentage of gross income after taxes and all prior charges including preferred dividends available for common stock. In good years it has averaged about eight percent of operating revenues for all Class I railroads. This is an important figure for the common stock because it indicates the margin of safety—how much all expenses and prior charges could increase before there would be nothing left for the common stock from the gross revenues.

Earnings Available Per Share of Common Stock.   As with all corporations, this figure is the most important item for common shareholders. The investor must analyze the record and trend over a period of years and make projections for five to six years in the future. The amount and ratio of "other income" to gross and net income frequently are significant.

Earnings available to common stock are divided by Shareholders' Equity to determine the rate of return earned on stockholders equity. The return on stockholder's equity reached a high of 10.54 percent for Class I railroads in 1981 but fell to a dismal 2.1 percent in 1986 (see Table 13–6). While returns earned in the 1980s compare favorably to the 1.4 percent earned during the years 1975–78, they still compare unfavorably to that earned in many other industries.

Railroad Balance Sheet Analysis

A review of the fluctuations and trends of revenues, costs, and profits (especially the number of times fixed charges are earned, the earnings per share, and the dividends received) as discussed in reference to railroad income statement analysis ordinarily provides a good indication of the prospective quality of a railroad security. However, balance sheet analysis also will provide necessary and useful information.

Working Capital.   Railroads have modest working capital requirements because receivables are short term and inventories are not a factor. Working capital for all Class I railroads in recent years has averaged six to seven percent of gross revenues, but the company-to-company range has been broad. Fixed charges must be paid out of working capital. In recent years working capital for Class I roads

Table 13–6   Rate of Return on Shareholders' Equity

The rate of return on shareholders' equity (ROE) for Class I railroads in 1986 was 2.1 percent. Due to conversion to a Depreciation Accounting System, the figures for 1983-1986 are not comparable with prior years.

ROE represents the relationship of net income (after income from outside sources, payment of fixed charges and adjustment for extraordinary items) to shareholders' equity (the sum of capital stock, capital surplus and retained income). (Dollar amounts in thousands)

Year	Net Income	Shareholders' Equity*	Rate of Return on Equity*
1967	$321,542	$18,083,434	1.78%
1968	564,505	17,978,627	3.14
1969	463,565	17,876,294	2.59
1970	76,179	17,546,055	0.43
1972	228,173	16,338,931	1.40
1973	409,223	16,224,367	2.52
1974	767,065	15,641,679	4.90
1975	278,819	14,943,468	1.87
1976	414,351	15,086,007	2.75
1977	338,580	15,478,492	2.19
1978	202,075	15,295,935	1.32
1979	913,450	16,718,846	5.46
1980	1,129,392	18,777,051	6.01
1981	2,140,905	20,320,268	10.54
1982	1,151,548	21,199,739	5.43
1983	1,797,483	24,775,112	7.26
1984	2,701,064	27,171,974	9.94
1985	1,881,522	27,528,127	6.83
1986	544,407	25,968,536	2.10

* Average beginning and end of year.

Note: Net income for 1985 and 1986 were reduced due to the inclusion of special charges.

Source: *Railroad Facts*, op. cit., p. 21.

has averaged 1.6× to 2× fixed charges for Class I railroads, but again a wide range is present among different roads (see Table 13–7). Net working capital (current assets—current liabilities—inventories) declined sharply until 1975, and again

Table 13–7   Net Working Capital for Class I Railroads—January 1, 1981
(Aggregates in Millions of Dollars)

	1958	1963	1969	1972	1975	1977	1980
United States	995	823	(184.8)	(60.7)	67.8	570.9	927.7
Eastern District	237	20	(313.9)	(159.7)	13.4	200.8	555.2
Southern District	166	125	64.3	12.9	17.7	105.4	282.8
Western District	593	678	64.7	86.1	36.7	264.8	89.7

*Parentheses indicate deficits.

Note: The association deducts current liabilities, including debt due within one year, from current assets, which include the material and supplies account. If material and supplies were excluded from current assets in 1977, the net working capital would become a $709.1 million deficit.

Source: *Yearbook of Railroad Facts* (Washington, D.C.: Association of American Railroads, 1981).

declined sharply in 1986. Current ratios fell below 1:1 for several railroad, and investors should be confident working capital is adequate before investing.

Property Accounts.   The major items on the asset side of a railroad balance sheet are investments in roadways and equipment. These items should be analyzed to determine the new equipment added annually, as well as the depreciation charged. There has been phenomenal modernization and improvement for the railroad industry as a whole since the end of World War II. The bulk of new capital funds in the railroad industry has gone into equipment, at times stimulated by the "investment credit."

Some analysts question whether railroads can maintain the present volume of capital expenditures, which is needed to exploit and accelerate traffic gains registered in recent years.

Capital Structure Proportions.   Railroad debt has been declining since the 1930s. Generally, debt for an individual railroad should not exceed 40 percent of total capitalization, and the remaining 60 percent should consist of preferred stock, common stock, and surplus. All additional debt issued to obtain funds since the 1930s has been in the form of equipment obligations.

The amount of debt that a railroad can bear is determined by the traffic and the level of earnings. The debt also is measured in terms of the times fixed charges are earned and the adequacy of cash flow to meet debt amortization requirements.

The Trucking Industry[104]

The trucking industry (motor freight carrier industry) has two major divisions: private and for hire. The private division comprises all those businesses that provide their own transportation through owned or leased lines. The for-hire division is subdivided into interstate, intrastate, and local. Interstate truckers subdivide further into contract and common carriers, with the former operating under continuing contracts with specific shippers. Both common and contract truckers are subject to ICC regulations.

For investment purposes we are concerned with publicly owned interstate ("intercity") common carriers. ICC regulations cover rates, routes, classes of commodities carried, accounting practices, finances, mergers, and acquisitions. ICC requires certificates of necessity that designate the specific routes for each carrier. In 1978, the Carter administration sought to decontrol the carriers but the carriers objected strenuously, fearing ruinous competition. The Teamsters Union also voiced strong opposition to deregulation. The Motor Carrier Act of 1980, however, deregulated the trucking industry, throwing it open to fresh competition, and this led to a host of new entrants. The industry did lose a measure of stability that regulation had provided, but gained the possibility of better control of labor costs. Many smaller carriers have gone out of business. Only the most efficient carriers will survive.

The cyclical nature of the trucking industry and its heavy financial leverage are demonstrated in the recovery year of 1976: gross freight revenues rose about 15 percent from 22.0 billion to $25.3 billion, but net income doubled from $400 million to $795 million. This data for 1975 and 1976 compares with gross freight revenues for railroads of $15.4 billion in 1975, $17.4 billion in 1976, net income of $144.4 million in 1975, and $272.5 million in 1976. In 1976 the motor carriers accounted for 54 percent of total revenues of all regulated carriers of freight versus 39 percent for the railroads. In 1960 the motor carriers accounted for 39 percent and the railroads 50 percent. The biggest carriers continue to grow larger through expansion of route systems and acquisitions. Bankruptcies have been on the rise, but excess capacity still remains to be wrung out (see Table 13–8).

Competition

In competition with the railroads, the truckers have taken the type of freight they desire (such as the less-than-carload business) from the railroads, leaving the latter

---

104 The basic source material for this section on trucking is *S & P Basic Analysis—Trucking.*

Table 13–8 Composite Industry Data (Per Share Data Based on Standard & Poor's Group and Stock Price Indexes)

Coal-Bituminous

The companies used for this series of per share data are: Eastern Gas & Fuel; North American Coal; Pittston Co.; and Westmoreland Coal.

	1978	1979	1980	1981	1982	1983	1984	1985
Sales	622.34	758.72	904.13	998.00	1,086.22	769.85	827.31	836.07
Operating Income	49.73	74.71	91.35	80.58	78.28	75.93	71.15	73.99
Profit Margins %	7.99	9.85	10.10	8.07	7.21	9.86	8.60	8.85
Depreciation	30.63	32.00	34.94	37.53	40.99	40.89	40.57	39.73
Taxes	cr 1.19	7.99	14.73	9.84	2.51	cr 6.10	cr 8.74	cr 4.97
Earnings	11.83	27.44	32.71	20.27	18.39	1.36	-7.54	6.60
Dividends	18.14	17.86	15.75	16.48	14.78	8.91	8.06	8.19
Earnings as a % of Sales	1.90	3.62	3.63	2.03	1.69	0.18	def.	0.79
Dividends as a % of Earnings	153.34	65.09	48.15	81.30	80.37	655.15	def.	124.09
Price (1941-43 = 10) —High	391.74	444.26	485.53	488.74	382.77	350.41	339.39	323.730
—Low	271.49	303.25	307.94	353.93	230.52	249.64	272.25	266.72
Price–Earnings Rations —High	33.11	16.19	14.85	24.11	20.81	257.65	def.	49.05
—Low	22.95	11.05	9.41	17.46	12.54	183.54	def.	40.41
Dividend Yield % —High	6.68	5.89	5.12	4.66	6.41	3.57	2.96	3.07
—Low	4.63	4.02	3.24	3.37	3.86	2.54	2.37	2.53
Book Value	294.01	294.07	313.11	316.78	280.20	272.14	258.19	253.25
Return on Book Value %	4.02	9.33	10.45	6.40	6.56	0.50	def.	2.61
†Working Capital	83.27	80.12	97.96	99.73	85.11	76.68	69.84	74.93
Capital Expenditures	67.87	64.52	101.82	66.48	81.87	42.98	N.A.	46.64

Table 13–8 (continued)

Truckers

The companies used for this series are: Consolidated Freightways; McLean Trucking (deleted 8-8-82); Overnight Transportation (added 6-2-82); Roadway Express; Yellow Freight Systems.

		1978	1979	1980	1981	1982	1983	1984	1985
Earnings		10.99	9.10	8.67	9.60	9.02	14.77	15.39	8.29
Dividends		2.47	2.93	3.28	3.80	4.01	4.62	5.30	5.70
Dividends as a % of Sales		22.47	32.20	27.83	39.58	44.46	31.28	34.44	68.76
Price (1943=10)	—High	†16.31	86.10	92.11	123.61	153.22	207.24	197.41	236.67
	—Low	88.75	68.96	62.37	84.02	84.89	142.04	130.01	158.73
Price–Earnings Ratios	—High	10.58	9.46	10.62	12.88	16.99	14.03	12.83	28.55
	—Low	6.26	7.58	7.19	8.75	9.41	9.62	8.45	19.15
Dividend Yield %	—High	3.59	4.25	5.26	4.52	4.72	3.25	4.08	3.59
	—Low	2.12	3.40	3.56	3.07	2.62	2.23	2.69	2.41

Railroads

The companies used for this series are: Burlington Northern; CSX (added 11-5-80); CNW Corp; Missouri-Pacific (deleted 12-29-82); Norfolk & Southern (added 6-2-82); Santa Fe Inds.; and Union-Pacific.

		1978	1979	1980	1981	1982	1983	1984	1985
Earnings		6.65	9.65	10.65	11.31	9.02	9.71	12.46	9.79
Dividends		2.64	2.85	3.23	3.58	3.87	3.98	4.20	4.49
Dividends as % of Sales		39.70	25.93	30.33	31.65	42.90	40.99	33.71	45.86
Price (1943 = 10)	—High	49.63	58.33	116.36	107.78	92.29	124.57	114.73	141.16
	—Low	42.04	43.67	55.28	76.17	60.22	86.67	87.59	103.94
Price–Earnings Ratios	—High	7.46	6.04	10.93	9.53	10.23	12.83	9.21	14.42
	—Low	6.32	4.53	5.19	6.73	6.68	8.93	7.03	10.62

Table 13–8 (continued)

Railroads

		1978	1979	1980	1981	1982	1983	1984	1985
Dividend Yield %	—High	6.28	6.53	5.84	4.70	6.43	4.59	4.80	4.32
	—Low	5.32	4.89	2.78	3.32	4.29	3.20	3.66	3.18

Note: Per share data are expressed in terms of the S&P Stock Price Index, i.e., stock prices, 1941–43 = 10. Each of the items shown is first computed on a true per share basis for each company. Totals for each company are then reconstructed using the same number of shares outstanding as was used to compute our stock price index as of December 31st. This is done because the shares used on December 31st, although the latest known at the time, may differ from those reported in the annual reports, which are not available for six or eight weeks after the end of the year. The sum of these reconstructed totals is then related to the base period value used to compute the stock price index. As a double check, we relate the various items to the dividends as these are the most stable series. So, for example, if total sales amount to 15 times the total dividend payments, then, with per share dividends at 3.50 the indicated per share sales will be (15 X 3.50) 52.50 in terms of the S&P Stock Price Index. For comparability between the various groups, all data are on a calendar year basis, corporate data being posted in the year in which most months fall. Fiscal years ending June 30 are posted in the calendar year in which the fiscal year ends. †Current assest less current liabilities, without allowance for long-term debt. R–Revised CR–Credit.

Source: *Standard & Poor's Industry Surveys*, Trucking (New ; York: Standard & Poor's Corporation, 1988), p. R63.

with the heavy freight that truckers cannot carry economically or the long-haul traffic. Therefore, the only real competition with the rails remaining is the piggyback freight handled by the railroads. The deregulation of the industry has led to fierce rate discounting, thereby limiting revenue growth.

Competition therefore is largely intra-industry, but as truck freight rates have risen steadily, competition is being felt in the form of freight forwarders using rail piggyback facilities.

While air freight competition is small, it is growing fast and takes the cream of the traffic—the high-value, high-rate traffic.

The Income Statement of Truck Carriers

As with the railroads, the largest expense items for the truckers are labor costs. The operating ratio for truck carriers generally ranges between 94 and 96 percent for the largest firms, the Class I truckers. Three items—transportation expenses, terminal costs, and maintenance of equipment—absorb about 73 to 75 percent of total revenue. The balance of revenue is absorbed as follows:

Operating taxes and licenses	6 – 6½%
Depreciation	3 – 3%
Traffic	3 – 3%
Insurance and safety	4 – 4½%
General and administration	6 – 6½%
	22 – 23½%

Key per share data for truckers is contained in Table 13–9.

The Balance Sheet of Truck Carriers

As with other regulated industries, the current ratio for the trucking industry is at 1.00 – 1.15 to 1 because there are no inventories (except tires and spare parts), and receivables are generally current, as most traffic is on a cash basis. The amount of working capital to cover cash operating expense is considered a more significant ratio than the current ratio.

As a measure of the quality of the funded debt, analysts calculate the ratio of all funded debt to total annual cash flow, i.e., how much of the funded debt could be paid off if all annual cash flow was used for that purpose.

Historically, carriers have attempted to purchase new equipment from annual cash flow, but in recent years they have used revolving credit agreements.

The general capital markets are not tapped too frequently for the sale of stocks or bonds; neither are private placements used normally.

Accounting Practices in the Industry

In reporting to stockholders, truckers may report either according to AICPA principles or in accordance with ICC procedures. Under AICPA principles, tax reductions resulting from accelerated tax depreciation and tax credits must be recorded as a deferred federal income tax liability charged to net income. But under ICC procedures this tax liability is not recognized, and tax reduction (savings) flows through to net income. Truckers may expense tires and tubes, as well as other prepaid expenses incurred, or may capitalize them and charge them off during their useful life. The method used will affect the current ratio, which normally is only between 1.0 to 1 and 1.2 to 1. Finally, the reported financial condition of the carrier will reflect the proportion of assets that are owned versus leased.

Rate of Return

The record of the rate of return on equity for selected trucking firms for the years 1981–85 is contained in Table 13–9. Note that the rate of return can vary sharply from year-to-year and between firms.

Summary of Analysis of a Trucking Company

The analyst should determine the economics of the area served, as well as the past and prospective growth trends of the carrier. The analyst also should determine the nature of routes used and the character of restrictions, types of highways, and tax levies. The past financial record then should be analyzed and compared to industry norms and trends in respect to items discussed above. Management's record in respect to the industry norms and management's policies toward mergers and acquisitions should be determined. Finally, the analyst should project revenues and earnings for the next five years, recognizing the cyclical nature of the industry and being especially alert to opportunities in periods of depressed stock markets, discounting general economic recessions.

Table 13–9 Return on Equity—Selected Trucking Companies, 1981–1985

General Commodity Motor Carriers	1981	1982	1983	1984	1985
American Carriers, Inc.	NA	NA	18.5%	11.7%	4.3%
Arkansas Best Corp.	16.2	NM	13.6	17.2	16.8
Carolina Freight Corp.	17.6	17.6	24.2	18.7	16.6
Consolidated Freightways	15.9	11.4	12.6	13.6	13.7
IU International Corp.	22.6	10.5	12.6	2.1	NM
Preston Corp.	8.6	7.2	8.0	9.0	4.3
Roadway Services, Inc.	19.6	17.8	20.2	18.1	12.7
Transcon Inc.–Calif.	NM	NM	9.6	22.5	6.0
Viking Freight, Inc.	NA	18.1	3.0	10.1	8.1
Yellow Freight System	8.1	5.0	21.3	16.7	18.5

Source: Standard & Poor's Industry Surveys, Railroads & Trucking, op. cit., p. R57.

CHAPTER 14

Financial Institutions

In this chapter we cover the two largest financial institutions—commercial banks and insurance companies. These institutions are different in their characteristics and regulations, and therefore they are treated separately. Commercial banks are covered in the first part of the chapter and insurance companies in the second part.

Commercial Banks

Commercial banks are engaged in a broad range of financial activities, including making both long-term and short-term loans to business firms, installment loans to consumers, mortgage loans to home buyers, offering trust services, and facilitating international transactions. They invest large amounts in U.S. Treasury and agency securities, securities of state and local governments, and money market instruments. Commercial banks are the primary, though not exclusive, provider of checking accounts and serve individuals through offering a large variety of savings accounts, money market instruments, and certificates of deposit. The nation's commercial banks hold the bulk of the cash assets of individuals, business firms, financial institutions, trust funds and pension funds, as well as the deposits of federal, state and local governments.

Banking: A Changing Environment

The banking industry has and continues to undergo tremendous change since the 1960s. First, there was the widespread adoption of the one-bank holding company form of organization during the late 1960s and early 1970s. Moreover, bankers realized early in the 1960s that interest bearing liabilities were likely to become the major source of funds for the support of future asset growth. Banks began to pursue more aggressive asset growth and operating strategies based on their seeming ability to expand liabilities almost at will.

309

The one-bank holding company form of organization facilitated the underwriting of a growing variety of assets and led banks into business areas not considered traditional areas of bank operations. Such changes offered large potential rewards, but increased risk also was present, as banks have learned to their sorrow. Relatively high dependence on borrowed funds to finance expansion, for example, weakened capital structures and made banks more sensitive to interest rate volatility.

Investors greeted the changes with great enthusiasm during the early 1970s, with bank stocks reaching all time highs in terms of price-earning ratios, and the relationship of these ratios to the average price-earnings ratio for the stocks included in the Standard and Poor's 500 Stock Price Index (See Table 14–1). Several bank stocks even sold for higher price-earnings ratios than recorded by the S&P 500 Stock Index during March 1974, rather than the usual discount.

The growing favor with which investors looked on bank stocks did not, however, last long. Severe problems became evident during 1974–75 and continue today. Moreover, there have been some spectacular failures or near failures among large bank institutions; First Pennsylvania, Continental Bank and the Texas banks are examples. This led to a reversal in investor attitudes, as exemplified by the sharp decline in price-earnings ratios for bank stocks by 1980–81. Price-earnings ratios recovered from the 1980–81 lows by 1986 but still remain below the March 1974 levels and generally sell at a discount to the S&P 500 Stock Index.

A paper presented at a Financial Management Association workshop noted six major developments that have altered the face of U.S. banking.[105] These factors should be carefully considered when assessing a bank stock. That list is summarized below with additions and alterations:

1. An increased dependence on purchased money leading to interest expense becoming a large and volatile number, approximating 50 percent or more of total expenses. The resulting leverage offered the potential for greater return, through expansion into new activities with borrowed money, but also increased risk. This becomes serious when the economy that absorbs the loans becomes depressed, as in Texas.

2. A "growth" philosophy, coupled with the need to cover rapidly rising expenses, led to the liberalization of lending policies and a sharp rise in loan losses. Critics feel that this liberalization went too far in several cases,

---

105 *Bank Analysis From External Sources*, (New York: Cates, Lyons & Co., Inc., 1979) pp. 3–14.

and one must consider the quality of bank assets when considering purchase of their stocks.

3. The erosion of bank capital. "In the early 1960s bank net worth generally exceeded ten percent of total assets, with few exceptions. The growth of assets since that Golden Age has so greatly exceeded the growth of capital that this key ratio now ranges between four percent and eight percent."[106] New risk-adjusted capital guidelines which central banks of ten nations have proposed in 1987 are out for public comment and will be accepted as suggested. These requirements are intended to create equitable competition internationally, and provide adequate capital for depositor and stockholder protection.

4. The growth of overhead resulting from the addition of new headquarters buildings, extensive branching networks, and the addition of computer hardware. Staff compensation also has risen sharply. Expense levels are too high at many banks, and they must concentrate on pruning away underperforming businesses and enhancing productivity.

5. Competition has intensified, both from other banks and other financial institutions.

6. While too early to make definitive judgments, many questions are being raised about mergers of the last several years. The expected efficiencies and synergies appear to be inadequate to support the high price paid in several instances.

7. The regulatory climate continues to change; but new powers granted the banks often are in thinner margined products that will not lead to immediate substantial gains.

8. Bank profitability has been trending down in the 1980s, and loan quality problems have continued to mount.

9. Security markets are providing the most significant competition to giant banks. Borrowers increasingly tap the money markets directly; for example, through the issue of commercial paper. Loans to large corporations actually are made at a loss at times to retain other profitable services sold to these corporations.

---

106 Ibid, p. 8.

Table 14–1 Comparative Market Valuation Statistics

Price/Earnings Multiples Relative to the S&P 500, By Quarter, 1974–86[a]

	1974				1975				1976				1977				1978				1979				1980			
	Mar	Jun	Sep	Dec	Mar	Jun	Sep	Dec	Mar	Jun	Sep	Dec	Mar	Jun	Sep	Dec	Mar	Jun	Sep	Dec	Mar	Jun	Sep	Dec	Mar	Jun	Sep	Dec
Bank of New York	58.9%	52.0%	62.9%	55.8%	52.5%	44.6%	42.6%	46.0%	49.6%	51.3%	52.7%	75.0%	71.4%	69.8%	70.0%	67.8%	70.7%	67.1%	66.3%	65.4%	61.8%	62.2%	58.7%	66.5%	58.2%	57.9%	46.5%	39.1%
Bankers Trust NY	74.1	65.3	62.9	59.7	48.5	44.6	39.8	44.2	59.7	70.8	71.8	73.2	75.5	85.4	84.4	79.3	80.5	70.6	62.9	65.4	62.3	70.3	72.0	58.9	52.2	46.1	40.7	46.7
Chase Manhattan	87.5	68.4	81.4	62.3	49.5	43.8	39.8	49.6	68.1	89.4	85.5	86.1	92.9	106.3	97.8	93.1	87.8	81.2	78.7	67.9	63.2	68.9	65.3	58.9	56.7	57.9	44.2	50.0
Chemical NY	78.6	64.3	67.1	58.4	50.5	44.6	36.1	38.9	49.6	60.2	58.2	62.0	61.2	68.8	66.7	69.0	65.9	63.5	62.9	61.5	61.8	63.5	60.0	56.2	56.7	53.9	44.2	41.3
Citicorp	174.1	142.7	132.9	144.2	125.3	114.1	84.3	92.9	102.5	107.1	94.6	93.5	89.8	87.5	84.4	86.2	79.3	80.0	79.8	78.2	73.7	86.5	78.7	74.0	66.7	65.8	51.2	64.1
Irving Bank Corp	68.8	55.1	60.0	53.3	47.5	41.3	37.0	37.2	44.5	48.7	49.1	53.7	58.2	60.4	62.2	62.2	63.4	64.7	61.8	59.0	60.5	64.9	62.7	58.9	53.7	53.9	46.5	53.3
Manufacturers Hanover	99.1	85.7	84.3	77.9	67.7	66.1	46.3	55.8	67.2	79.7	67.3	75.9	75.5	75.0	75.6	74.7	76.8	77.6	78.7	74.4	76.3	79.7	72.0	67.1	65.7	65.8	53.5	51.1
J.P. Morgan & Co	150.0	132.7	132.9	142.9	118.2	116.5	90.7	95.6	103.4	113.3	103.6	103.7	101.0	100.0	97.8	92.0	92.7	91.8	87.6	88.5	88.2	93.2	93.3	89.0	89.6	81.6	58.1	63.0
Manne Midland	64.3	56.1	75.7	62.3	59.6	51.2	50.9	76.1	187.4	—	—	125.0	115.3	93.3	105.6	106.9	122.0	108.2	103.4	98.7	88.2	91.9	89.3	75.3	52.2	51.3	54.7	52.2
Republic NY Corp	NA	NA	NA	NA	NA	NA	NA	NA	NA	NA	NA	NA	NA	NA	NA	NA	58.5	64.7	60.7	59.0	60.5	64.9	66.7	58.9	47.8	42.1	54.7	48.9
Bank of Boston Corp	89.3	71.4	72.9	70.1	61.6	58.7	54.6	57.5	73.1	75.2	69.1	76.9	77.6	81.3	82.2	74.7	76.8	72.9	69.7	69.2	63.2	66.2	66.7	57.5	55.5	52.6	45.3	46.7
First Chicago	146.4	118.4	95.7	84.4	63.6	71.1	58.3	60.2	70.6	79.7	72.7	88.9	86.7	82.3	84.4	75.9	73.2	80.0	83.1	74.4	71.1	75.7	72.0	72.6	76.1	85.5	94.2	101.1
Money Center Median	**87.5%**	**68.4%**	**75.7%**	**62.3%**	**59.6%**	**51.2%**	**46.3%**	**55.8%**	**68.1%**	**77.4%**	**70.5%**	**76.9%**	**77.8%**	**82.3%**	**84.4%**	**75.9%**	**76.8%**	**75.3%**	**74.2%**	**68.6%**	**63.2%**	**68.6%**	**60.3%**	**63.0%**	**58.7%**	**55.4%**	**48.8%**	**50.5%**
Fleet Financial	NA	NA	NA	NA	175.8%	192.6%	142.6%	56.6%	66.4%	80.5%	66.4%	67.6%	72.4%	72.9%	85.6%	70.1%	79.3%	68.2%	66.3%	64.1%	68.4%	66.2%	72.0%	60.3%	56.7%	56.6%	51.2%	46.7%
Norstar Bancorp	NA	NA	NA	NA	NA	NA	NA	NA	NA	NA	NA	NA	NA	NA	NA	NA	NA	NA	NA	NA	NA	NA	NA	NA	NA	NA	NA	NA
CoreStates Financial	62.5%	49.0%	60.0%	58.4%	54.5	47.1	44.4	44.2	56.3	60.2	58.2	68.5	68.4	69.8	66.7	77.0	78.1	75.3	66.3	57.7	63.2	62.2	64.0	58.9	61.2	55.3	52.3	51.1
Mellon Bank Corp	78.6	70.4	70.0	76.6	70.7	63.6	64.8	69.0	79.0	88.5	82.7	80.6	78.6	77.1	81.1	80.5	82.9	81.2	77.5	75.6	78.9	81.1	82.7	74.0	65.7	68.4	61.6	59.8
PNC Financial Corp	72.3	58.2	58.6	62.3	58.6	52.1	51.4	49.6	59.7	64.6	62.7	75.0	70.4	71.9	73.3	75.9	78.1	77.6	76.4	73.1	77.6	78.4	76.0	71.2	64.2	65.8	59.3	54.3
AmeriTrust Corp	67.9	61.2	61.4	63.6	53.5	51.2	49.1	46.0	52.1	57.5	60.9	71.3	69.4	78.1	71.1	74.7	76.8	77.6	70.8	66.7	76.3	74.3	74.7	71.2	56.7	60.5	61.6	53.3
Banc One Corp	96.4	102.0	127.1	77.9	73.7	58.7	62.0	60.2	61.3	73.5	70.9	70.4	78.6	85.4	92.2	89.7	87.8	81.2	77.5	80.8	82.9	82.4	81.3	78.1	68.7	78.9	73.3	72.8
National City Corp	67.9	59.2	64.3	72.7	62.6	53.7	58.3	56.6	61.3	69.9	70.0	83.3	82.7	83.3	88.9	85.1	91.5	89.4	82.0	83.0	86.8	87.8	92.0	86.3	67.2	76.3	61.6	55.4
NBD Bancorp	51.8	49.0	54.3	50.6	43.4	40.5	39.8	38.9	46.2	48.7	50.9	59.3	64.3	62.5	65.6	64.4	70.7	69.4	61.8	60.3	62.4	69.3	60.3	52.2	50.0	52.3	40.2	
First Bank System	142.9	100.0	111.4	113.0	93.9	95.9	86.1	86.7	89.9	99.1	88.2	96.3	85.7	84.4	83.3	83.9	87.8	87.6	78.7	78.2	75.0	78.4	80.1	78.1	67.1	67.1	59.3	58.7
Norwest Corp	137.5	93.9	85.7	100.0	84.9	81.0	72.2	77.9	81.5	92.9	88.2	100.9	99.0	90.6	90.0	89.7	86.6	87.1	84.3	88.5	81.6	86.5	89.3	82.2	68.7	73.7	62.8	69.6
NCNB Corp	183.9	126.5	82.9	92.2	121.2	119.0	91.7	78.8	99.2	94.7	90.0	93.5	94.9	87.5	90.0	92.0	90.2	89.4	89.9	75.6	72.4	79.7	78.7	75.3	67.2	69.7	58.1	56.5
Wachovia Corp	119.6	77.6	64.3	72.7	73.7	80.2	67.6	61.1	73.1	96.5	82.7	95.4	89.8	92.7	91.1	94.3	92.7	100.0	92.1	84.6	77.6	82.4	88.0	84.9	80.6	80.3	68.6	57.6
Barnett Banks	152.7	93.9	107.1	63.6	66.7	66.9	61.1	71.7	95.8	89.4	92.7	95.4	103.1	97.9	101.1	105.7	111.0	104.7	97.8	84.6	80.3	77.0	81.3	69.9	67.2	77.6	72.1	71.7
SunTrust Banks	139.3	102.0	77.1	67.5	75.8	86.0	137.0	136.3	141.2	132.7	104.5	138.9	155.1	155.2	148.9	139.1	150.0	141.2	125.8	107.7	101.3	95.9	101.3	89.0	74.6	81.6	73.3	73.9
InterFirst Corp	179.5	140.8	130.0	146.8	129.3	110.7	105.6	92.9	105.9	114.2	96.4	105.6	104.2	107.8	110.3	102.4	105.9	107.9	103.8	100.0	106.8	110.7	106.8	100.0	109.2	89.5	92.4	
RepublicBank Corp	106.3	86.7	61.4	61.0	65.7	66.1	54.6	62.8	65.6	80.5	83.6	89.8	96.9	96.9	87.8	92.0	87.8	94.1	94.3	87.2	77.6	85.1	92.0	98.7	110.5	104.1	110.7	105.5
Texas Commerce	159.8	132.7	137.1	133.8	118.2	109.1	100.0	97.3	100.0	114.2	103.6	104.6	105.1	103.1	105.6	109.2	108.5	105.9	108.9	98.7	110.5	104.1	110.7	105.5	104.5	107.9	102.3	100.0
BankAmerica Corp	124.1	100.0	97.1	111.7	97.0	90.9	82.4	85.8	95.0	108.0	93.6	116.7	105.1	100.0	105.6	96.6	96.3	87.1	93.3	93.6	89.5	91.9	92.0	91.8	83.6	67.2	71.1	60.5	66.3
First Interstate	72.3	50.0	57.1	58.4	61.6	61.2	52.8	49.6	61.3	69.0	66.4	74.1	69.4	71.9	72.2	73.9	72.2	69.4	71.9	67.9	68.4	82.4	78.7	75.3	67.2	71.1	60.5	66.3
Security Pacific	73.2	53.1	72.9	66.2	57.6	55.4	40.3	46.0	56.3	63.7	61.8	68.5	69.4	71.9	75.6	72.4	73.2	67.1	71.6	68.5	67.9	69.7	71.8	70.7	64.4	59.7	65.8	52.3
Wells Fargo & Co	104.5	70.4	62.9	68.8	59.6	60.3	50.0	54.0	64.3	73.5	66.4	73.8	81.8	83.7	80.2	78.9	77.0	73.2	67.1	68.5	67.9	71.8	64.4	59.7	65.8	52.3	58.7	
US Bancorp	92.0	74.5	71.4	68.8	72.7	62.0	64.8	54.0	60.5	76.1	71.8	81.5	83.7	81.3	78.9	93.1	89.0	87.1	88.8	84.6	90.8	93.2	96.0	86.3	89.6	84.2	74.4	72.8
Regional Median	**100.4%**	**78.0%**	**70.7%**	**68.8%**	**72.7%**	**66.1%**	**64.8%**	**61.1%**	**65.5%**	**80.5%**	**71.8%**	**81.5%**	**83.7%**	**84.4%**	**87.8%**	**89.7%**	**87.8%**	**85.9%**	**82.0%**	**78.2%**	**77.6%**	**81.1%**	**81.3%**	**75.3%**	**67.2%**	**71.1%**	**61.8%**	**58.7%**
35-Bank Median[c]	**94.0%**	**72.3%**	**73.2%**	**65.6%**	**66.2%**	**58.7%**	**55.8%**	**58.5%**	**66.8%**	**79.0%**	**71.2%**	**79.2%**	**80.7%**	**83.4%**	**86.1%**	**82.8%**	**82.3%**	**80.6%**	**78.1%**	**73.4%**	**70.4%**	**75.4%**	**75.3%**	**69.2%**	**62.0%**	**63.5%**	**55.2%**	**54.6%**

[a] Based on trailing 12-month earnings per share.
[b] Based on trailing 12-month operating earnings through the second quarter of 1986
[c] Average of subgroup medians
NA Not available

Source: "Comparative Market Valuation Statistics for 35 Banks by Quarter, 1974–86" (New York: Salomon Brothers, Inc., September 12, 1986).

Table 14-1 Comparative Market Valuation Statistics

	1990 Mar	Jun	Sep	Dec	1991 Mar	Jun	Sep	Dec	1992 Mar	Jun	Sep	Dec	1993 Mar	Jun	Sep	Dec	1994 Mar	Jun	Sep	Dec	1995 Mar	Jun	Sep	Dec	1996 Mar	Jun	Sep [b]
Bank of New York	58.2%	57.9%	46.5%	39.1%	43.0%	50.6%	52.6%	63.8%	56.6%	50.6%	47.2%	43.2%	40.7%	43.3%	43.2%	47.5%	47.1%	45.3%	52.0%	56.0%	55.6%	60.1%	55.6%	58.4%	67.8%	60.3%	63.2%
Bankers Trust NY	52.2	46.1	40.7	46.7	47.3	60.1	60.5	60.5	55.3	42.9	44.9	38.7	39.8	37.3	43.2	45.8	48.1	46.3	54.0	58.0	60.2	60.1	51.6	52.6	60.8	56.9	59.4
Chase Manhattan	56.7	57.9	44.2	50.0	49.5	64.4	64.5	53.8	52.6	53.2	47.2	52.3	54.5	35.1	36.0	36.4	45.2	42.1	49.0	54.0	52.8	56.4	42.0	46.5	56.7	50.6	46.1
Chemical NY	56.7	53.9	44.2	41.3	46.2	52.9	51.3	52.5	50.0	45.5	44.9	37.8	40.7	35.8	35.2	39.8	48.1	42.1	50.0	58.0	56.5	57.6	49.0	53.9	63.1	56.5	53.2
Citicorp	68.7	65.8	51.2	64.1	60.2	86.2	92.1	71.3	65.8	59.7	51.7	50.5	56.1	46.3	44.0	49.2	51.9	52.6	62.0	60.0	59.3	60.9	52.2	53.0	66.1	64.1	59.0
Irving Bank Corp	53.7	53.9	46.5	53.3	49.5	56.3	61.8	57.5	52.6	46.8	46.1	39.6	38.2	38.1	41.6	45.8	54.8	51.6	56.0	63.0	61.1	62.6	53.6	53.6	61.4	58.0	59.7
Manufacturers Hanover	65.7	65.8	53.5	51.1	49.5	64.4	61.8	58.8	55.3	45.5	43.8	47.7	43.1	39.6	37.6	41.5	45.2	36.8	52.0	59.0	55.6	57.0	45.8	47.2	64.4	42.4	38.3
J P Morgan & Co	89.6	81.6	58.1	63.0	59.1	75.9	89.5	73.8	73.7	70.1	61.8	56.8	55.3	47.0	51.2	54.2	58.7	61.1	66.0	66.0	67.6	67.7	54.7	62.8	69.1	68.5	72.9
Marine Midland	52.2	51.3	54.7	52.2	48.4	64.4	59.2	62.5	63.2	49.4	44.9	36.9	41.5	42.5	40.8	45.8	51.0	44.2	56.0	57.0	75.0	77.0	75.3	58.8	69.5	62.5	61.6
Republic NY Corp	47.8	42.1	54.7	48.9	53.8	79.3	76.3	77.5	67.1	61.0	50.7	60.4	65.9	50.0	62.4	56.8	59.6	56.8	65.0	66.0	70.4	70.5	76.8	65.6	84.7	73.8	81.5
Bank of Boston Corp	55.5	52.6	45.3	46.7	50.5	57.5	61.8	61.3	59.2	50.6	44.9	44.1	43.9	38.8	41.6	46.6	52.9	49.5	57.0	47.0	46.3	49.6	42.5	59.9	75.8	64.4	70.2
First Chicago	76.1	85.5	94.2	101.1	95.7	121.8	92.1	78.8	71.1	59.7	57.3	45.9	48.0	45.5	52.8	55.1	56.7	54.7	22.30	18.00	22.59	–	70.8	79.5	75.8	53.9	48.5
Money Center Median	56.7%	55.4%	48.8%	50.5%	49.5%	64.4%	61.8%	61.9%	57.9%	50.6%	46.8%	45.0%	43.5%	39.2%	42.4%	46.2%	52.9%	47.9%	56.0%	58.5%	50.7%	60.1%	52.9%	56.4%	67.0%	58.5%	60.0%
Fleet Financial	56.7%	56.6%	51.2%	46.7%	49.5%	58.6%	57.9%	61.3%	64.5%	51.9%	53.9%	48.6%	48.8%	51.5%	58.4%	58.5%	64.4%	80.0%	68.0%	73.0%	72.2%	83.3%	68.7%	66.4%	81.4%	88.2%	84.3%
Norstar Bancorp	NA	NA	NA	NA	NA	NA	NA	NA	NA	NA	NA	NA	NA	NA	NA	NA	NA	NA	NA	NA							
CoreStates Financial	61.2	55.3	52.3	51.1	52.7	60.9	56.6	57.5	51.3	48.1	47.2	45.0	41.5	39.6	32.8	45.8	52.9	62.1	63.0	64.0	78.7	84.3	85.3	85.3	85.4	75.5	69.9
Mellon Bank Corp	65.7	68.4	61.6	59.8	63.4	72.4	73.7	71.3	71.1	58.4	53.9	46.8	49.6	47.8	50.4	60.2	57.7	65.3	69.0	84.0	76.9	87.9	82.0	72.7	96.0	91.4	77.4
PNC Financial Corp	64.2	65.8	59.3	54.3	55.9	64.4	65.8	65.0	68.4	59.7	55.1	51.4	48.0	50.7	60.8	63.6	65.4	76.8	73.0	76.0	71.3	81.3	70.3	72.7	81.6	72.6	82.3
AmeriTrust Corp	56.7	60.5	61.6	53.3	51.6	62.1	57.9	58.8	59.2	62.3	59.6	53.2	47.2	54.5	68.8	73.7	74.0	69.5	76.0	77.0	74.1	85.5	79.7	71.4	85.2	80.8	77.7
Banc One Corp	68.7	78.9	73.3	72.8	73.1	85.1	90.8	88.8	93.4	100.0	82.0	89.2	77.2	66.4	83.2	77.1	79.8	83.2	86.0	89.0	81.5	97.6	95.4	96.1	107.4	93.2	82.9
National City Corp	67.2	76.3	61.6	55.4	57.0	67.8	71.1	67.5	67.1	55.8	58.4	47.7	44.7	43.3	54.4	51.7	52.9	55.8	56.0	70.0	63.9	67.1	62.6	55.1	65.8	68.6	63.9
NBD Bancorp	52.2	50.0	52.3	40.2	45.2	55.2	50.0	53.8	51.3	46.8	47.2	43.2	41.5	40.3	45.6	52.5	52.9	55.6	56.0	70.0	63.2	62.6	65.8	68.6	63.9	62.6	70.5
First Bank System	73.1	67.1	59.3	58.7	62.4	69.0	63.2	61.3	60.5	55.8	48.3	41.4	45.5	48.5	52.0	52.5	58.7	58.9	69.0	61.0	67.6	72.1	61.8	57.2	97.0	93.3	88.6
Norwest Corp	68.7	73.7	62.8	69.6	71.0	79.3	71.1	61.3	57.9	57.1	51.7	55.0	55.3	61.9	68.8	69.5	76.0	69.5	147.0	121.0	149.1	152.9	66.9	75.3	85.7	85.6	89.3
NCNB Corp	67.2	69.7	58.1	56.5	67.7	77.0	65.8	65.0	61.8	55.8	53.9	52.3	54.5	53.0	56.8	63.6	65.4	66.3	75.0	89.0	84.3	88.8	74.3	77.0	77.1	82.4	76.5
Wachovia Corp	80.6	80.3	68.6	65.6	65.1	78.9	78.8	72.4	68.8	76.4	59.5	61.0	57.5	64.8	68.6	75.0	82.1	84.0	87.0	91.7	84.7	81.1	78.1	93.3	97.0	89.7	
Barnett Banks	67.2	77.6	72.1	71.7	81.7	72.4	89.5	82.5	71.1	74.0	79.8	62.2	61.8	61.2	70.4	72.0	72.1	73.7	76.0	80.0	82.4	86.4	81.3	83.7	90.2	90.0	61.5
SunTrust Banks	74.6	81.6	73.3	73.9	79.6	89.7	80.3	78.8	84.2	85.7	79.8	71.2	65.0	62.7	71.2	69.5	68.3	74.7	83.0	103.0	99.1	104.3	85.8	80.4	84.9	96.4	85.2
InterFirst Corp	100.0	109.2	89.5	92.4	91.4	103.5	101.3	88.8	79.0	76.6	57.3	51.4	42.3	48.5	–	–	–	73.0	55.0	50.0	44.0	109.3	99.1	137.0			
RepublicBank Corp	77.6	84.2	73.3	76.1	81.7	89.7	89.5	88.8	71.1	66.2	59.6	48.6	47.2	47.8	52.0	57.6	72.1	68.4	77.0	59.0	60.2	54.1	56.1	53.9	52.5	74.6	68.7
Texas Commerce	104.5	107.9	102.3	100.0	103.2	110.3	113.2	105.0	94.7	79.2	70.8	63.1	52.8	58.2	60.8	63.6	76.0	77.9	83.0	69.0	60.2	62.4	78.3	185.5	203.2		
BankAmerica Corp	83.6	80.3	64.0	75.0	68.8	74.7	88.2	87.5	79.0	74.0	68.5	69.4	70.7	64.0	68.5	69.4	47.2	52.0	56.0				96.8	99.0	94.0	93.5	–
First Interstate	67.2	71.1	65.0	66.3	67.7	81.6	78.9	73.8	64.5	54.5	53.9	51.4	52.0	56.0	63.2	61.0	66.3	60.0	70.0	67.6	73.7	64.8	60.8	69.6	62.4	627.0	
Security Pacific	61.2	65.8	52.3	56.5	55.9	65.5	65.8	72.5	59.2	50.6	49.4	42.3														56.3	
Wells Fargo & Co	59.7	65.8	52.3	58.7	50.5	67.8	60.5	58.8	56.6	50.6	46.1	40.5	40.7	44.8	51.2	55.9	56.7	56.8	66.0	69.0	71.3	68.6	67.1	66.4	92.4	99.5	105.3
US Bancorp	89.6	84.2	74.4	72.8	76.3	86.2	85.5	77.5	89.7	82.3	62.9	55.0	54.9	66.4	74.7	66.1	73.1	65.3	86.0	82.0	89.8	83.0	73.6	69.1	84.6	90.4	71.3
Regional Median	67.2%	71.1%	61.6%	58.7%	65.6%	72.4%	71.1%	71.3%	67.1%	58.4%	55.1%	51.4%	46.8%	51.5%	60.8%	62.3%	57.3%	65.8%	72.2%	82.6%	82.7%	73.6%	72.7%	85.1%	81.6%	77.3%	
35-Bank Median [c]	62.0%	63.5%	55.2%	54.6%	57.6%	66.4%	66.5%	66.6%	62.5%	54.5%	50.9%	48.2%	46.2%	45.4%	45.1%	54.3%	60.1%	57.7%	64.5%	65.8%	71.2%	71.4%	63.3%	64.6%	71.1%	71.6%	68.7%

Financial Analysis of Commercial Bank Stocks

As with other industries, an investor is interested in the financial strength and the earning power of a bank. Ratio analysis of bank financial statements is the primary tool used by security analysts, paying attention to both the level and trend of the ratios studied. Any such analysis should be forward looking. The goal of any security analysis is to use past and present performance characteristics as a basis for assessing future prospects.

Earnings: The Key Variable. Banks must earn competitive rates on their capital if they are to be attractive to investors. The relative importance of various income and expense components for commercial banks is presented in Table 14–2. When analyzing bank operations, one should concentrate on bank earnings—that is, income before security transactions, not net income. One should not lose sight, however, of the fact that net income represents the base from which dividends to stockholders are paid and is the primary source of growth capital generated by bank operations. Salomon Brothers produces a useful publication entitled, "A Review of Bank Performance," that offers average ratios for selected banks that can be used for comparative purposes, as can the data in Table 14–2.

Rate Earned on Average Assets. This is the best indicator of the efficiency of bank operations and earnings performance. It is calculated by dividing net income by total average assets. Return on assets (ROA) for most banks falls within a range of 0.60% to 1.40%. Regional and community banks are likely to have an ROA in the upper range reflecting lower cost of funds and a higher yielding loan mix. Large regional and money center banks, on the other hand, may well have an ROA in the lower part of the range because of reliance on more expensive purchased funds. A stockholder, remember, is more interested in ROA as a component of return on common equity than in the number itself. One should not lose sight of this fact.

Float can distort the interpretation of this ratio since it is not an indicator of management performance.[107] Also, the portion of earnings derived from nonfunds using sources of income (such as trust services) can vary from bank to bank.

Rate Earned on Average Equity Capital. Prior tⱼ 1980, the rate of return earned on average equity capital was a bit below the average rate earned by manufacturing corporations. This could explain the lower price–earnings ratio

---

107 Checks in the process of collection can be a large or small fraction of total assets at any given time, thereby tending to raise or lower return on assets.

Table 14–2   Uniform Bank Performance Report National Data— All Insured Commercial Banks

	Summary Ratios				
	03/31/88	*03/31/87*	*12/31/87*	*12/31/865*	*12/31/85*
Number of Banks in Nation	13542	14073	13702	14198	14406
Earnings and Profitability					
Percent of Average Assets:					
Interest Income (TE)	8.91	8.90	9.01	9.80	10.82
– Interest Expense	4.80	4.67	4.72	5.29	6.07
Net Interest Income (TE)	4.14	4.26	4.32	4.55	4.79
+ Non-interest Income	0.73	0.74	0.74	0.74	0.74
– Overhead Expense	3.36	3.34	3.42	3.47	3.46
– Provision: Loan & Lease					
Losses	0.26	0.33	0.51	0.74	0.67
= Pretax Operating Income (TE)	1.29	1.30	1.15	1.03	1.36
+ Securities Gains (Losses)	0.00	0.02	0.02	0.09	0.04
= Pretax Net Operating Inc. (TE)	1.34	1.40	1.18	1.20	1.45
Net Operating Income	0.91	0.89	0.74	0.70	0.85
Adjusted Net Operating Income	1.00	1.00	0.80	0.79	0.98
Adjusted Net Income	1.00	0.97	0.80	0.75	0.92
Net Income	0.93	0.91	0.76	0.71	0.86
Margin Analysis					
Avg Earning Assets to Avg Assets	91.87	91.46	91.54	91.06	90.89
Avg Int-Bearing Funds to Avg					
Assets	77.53	77.65	77.26	76.22	75.14
Int Inc (TE) To Avg Earn Assets	9.73	9.74	9.86	10.77	11.93
Int Expense To Avg Earn Assets	5.24	5.11	5.15	5.81	6.68
Net Iht Inc-TE to avg Earn Asst	4.53	4.67	4.74	5.01	5.29
Loan & Lease Analysis					
Net Loss to Average Total LN&LS	0.76	0.94	1.04	1.38	1.12
Earnings Coverage of Net Loss(X)	9.49	7.84	6.44	4.83	6.16
Loss Reserve to Net Losses (X)	5.62	4.55	3.19	2.26	2.40
Loss Reserve to Total LN&LS	1.66	1.58	1.62	1.51	1.30
% Noncurrent Loans & Leases	2.42	2.95	2.37	2.79	2.66
Liquidity					
Volatile Liability Dependence	-10.51	-12.95	-9.92	-13.91	-10.93
Net Loans & Leases to Assets	51.47	50.64	51.47	50.43	50.43
Capitalization					
Member Primary Cap to Avg Assets	9.33	9.21	9.23	9.09	9.21
Nonmember Primary Cap to Avg Ast	9.30	9.18	9.20	9.07	9.20
Cash Dividends to Net Income	22.38	18.91	37.64	37.30	34.73
Retain Earns to Avg Total Equity	6.74	7.22	4.65	3.97	5.40

Table 14–2 (continued)

Summary Ratios				
	03/31/88	03/31/87	12/31/87	12/31/865	12/31/85

Growth Rates

	03/31/88	03/31/87	12/31/87	12/31/865	12/31/85
Assets	4.37	6.34	3.56	7.48	7.36
Member Primary Capital	5.29	5.40	5.61	5.81	7.86
November Primary Capital	5.35	5.43	5.65	5.86	7.66
Net Loans & Leases	7.25	4.33	6.43	4.85	6.72
Volatile Liabilities	19.06	1.48	13.31	4.37	12.02

	Overhead, Yield and Cost Ratios				
Percent of Average Assets	03/31/88	03/31/87	12/31/87	12/31/86	12/31/85
Personnel Expense	1.62	1.61	1.63	1.66	1.69
Occupancy Expense	0.50	0.50	0.51	0.52	0.53
Other Oper Exp (Incl Intangibles)	1.21	1.21	1.26	1.26	1.22
Total Overhead Expense	3.36	3.34	3.42	3.47	3.46
:Including Int on Mort & Leases	3.37	3.35	3.43	3.47	3.47
Overhead Less Non-Int Income	2.58	2.57	2.64	2.69	2.68

Other Income & Expense Ratios

	03/31/88	03/31/87	12/31/87	12/31/86	12/31/85
Avg Personnel Exp Per Empl ($000)	24.61	23.68	24.42	23.62	22.64
Avg Assets Per Empl ($Million)	1.65	1.59	1.65	1.61	1.50
Marginal Tax Rate	31.85	35.33	38.30	43.56	42.71

Yield on or Cost of

	03/31/88	03/31/87	12/31/87	12/31/86	12/31/85
Total Loans & Leases (TE)	10.88	10.85	10.98	11.73	12.76
Total Loans	10.84	10.80	10.92	11.64	12.66
Real Estate**	10.46	10.57	10.66	11.36	12.02
Commercial Time, Demand, Oth**	10.39	9.93	10.26	10.83	12.10
Installment**	11.72	12.02	11.97	12.76	13.55
Credit Card Plans**	14.53	14.74	14.59	15.23	16.96
Memo: Agricultural Lns in Above	10.33	10.04	10.15	10.76	11.93
Loans in Foreign Offices	8.16	7.19	7.25	8.82	10.62
Total Investment Securities (TE)	8.48	9.01	8.80	10.23	11.27
Tax-exempt (Book)	7.36	7.33	7.31	7.41	7.42
Tax-exempt (TE)	10.82	11.26	11.53	12.92	13.10
All Other Securities	7.93	8.18	8.02	9.18	10.53
Interest-Bearing Bank Balances	7.81	7.12	7.38	7.99	9.63
Federal Funds Sold & Resales	6.58	6.18	6.62	6.77	8.11
Total Int-Bearing Deposits	6.19	6.00	6.09	6.93	8.06
Transaction accounts	4.92	4.86	4.96	NA	NA
Money Market Deposit Accounts	5.40	5.24	5.38	NA	NA
Other Savings Deposits	5.16	5.13	5.19	NA	NA
Large Certificates of Deposit	6.74	6.27	6.47	7.30	8.67
All Other Time Deposits	6.96	6.88	6.87	NA	NA
Foreign Office Deposits	6.91	6.19	6.77	7.09	8.66

Table 14–2 (continued)

Percent of Average Assets	Overhead, Yield and Cost Ratios				
	03/31/88	03/31/87	12/31/87	12/31/86	12/31/85
Federal Funds Purch & Repos	5.42	4.89	5.70	5.79	7.01
Other Borrowed Money	4.98	6.55	5.10	4.50	5.01
Subordinated Notes & Debentures	8.96	8.23	8.22	8.46	9.17
All Interest-Bearing Funds	6.19	6.00	6.10	6.92	8.05

**Banks under $300 million in total assets report this loan detail (by type) using their own internal categorization systems.

Source: "Uniform Bank Performance Report" (Washington, D.C.: Federal Financial Institutions Examination Council, March, 1988).

typically accorded bank stocks during this period. However, the discount at which bank stocks sold relative to earnings performance seemed excessive.

Interestingly, the rate of return earned on stockholders' equity since 1982 by a selected sample of banks (see Table 14–3), has equaled or exceeded the average return for all manufacturing corporations (see Table 11–2). For example, the average for the composite bank sample in 1982 was 14.18 percent, while the average for all manufacturing corporations was only 9.2 percent in 1982. While bank price-earnings ratios are higher relative to the S&P 500 in the 1980s than they were through much of the 1970s, they still are at a discount. This could reflect a belief by the market that banks represent higher than average risk or that bank profits are overstated as we will suggest later.

Banks do employ leverage. Equity is a relatively small fraction of bank assets (4%–7%), and return on equity is accordingly much higher (10%–20%) than return on assets. The components determining return on equity and assets, as well as a detailed evaluation of the income statement, should be considered as a whole when evaluating a bank stock.

Leverage and Rates of Return. Changes in the level of bank earnings from year to year are determined by the rate earned on total bank assets, the rate of growth of those assets, and leverage factors as shown in Table 14–4. A rising return on assets and increased leverage (measured by dividing average total assets by average shareholders' equity) did result in a higher rate of return being earned on stockholders' equity after 1977 than before. Interestingly, bank price-earnings ratios, on average, still fell to a historic low 54.6 percent of the average P/E ratio for the S&P 500 stocks in the fourth quarter of 1980, before recovery. Bank

Table 14-3 Net Income, and as a Percentage of Average Total Equity, 1982–86 (Dollars in Millions)

	1982		1983		1984		1985		1986	
Bank of New York	$73	15.29%	$91	14.47%	$108	14.78%	$130	14.61%	$155	15.24%
Bankers Trust NY	223	16.13	257	15.49	307	15.66	371	16.11	428	15.93
Chase Manhattan	307	10.00	430	12.89	406	10.93	565	13.59	585	12.45
Chemical NY	241	13.61	306	14.37	341	14.16	390	14.59	402	13.63
Citicorp	723	15.83	860	15.99	890	14.39	998	14.15	1,058	12.56
Irving Bank Corp.	81	11.95	92	11.67	98	11.56	116	12.64	128	12.76
Manufacturers Hanover	295	13.45	337	13.06	353	11.33	407	11.94	411	11.22
JP. Morgan & Co.	394	15.50	460	14.78	538	15.29	705	17.40	873	18.25
Marine Midland	87	10.21	101	10.13	91	8.39	125	10.88	145	11.36
Republic NY Corp.	71	17.90	85	15.42	97	14.04	122	13.93	149	13.94
Bank of Boston Corp.	124	14.70	136	14.44	164	15.04	174	13.32	233	14.88
First Chicago	137	10.19	184	11.07	86	4.51	169	8.44	276	12.38
Money Center Total Composite	$2,756	13.71%	$3,337	14.05%	$3,477	12.76%	$4,273	13.87%	$4,843	13.70%
Fleet Financial	$55	16.94%	$71	16.44%	$87	16.80%	$106	17.36%	$137	19.08%
Norstar Bancorp	44	16.42	58	14.31	77	14.91	93	14.09	105	14.42
Midlantic Corp.	76	17.10	81	15.83	106	17.17	142	17.69	148	15.43
CoreStates Financial	61	13.91	91	15.62	116	16.56	115	13.86	148	15.54
Mellon Bank Corp.	134	13.20	184	14.25	159	10.35	202	12.26	183	9.79
PNC Financial Corp.	130	16.20	146	16.37	177	16.80	229	17.61	286	18.71

Table 14-3 (continued)

	1982		1983		1984		1985		1986	
AmeriTrust Corp.	64	10.54	55	8.57	76	11.16	86	11.80	89	11.10
Banc One Corp.	82	13.92	111	14.93	143	15.25	177	16.05	200	15.83
National City Corp.	44	11.33	48	11.84	66	13.87	108	15.51	135	16.76
NBD Bancorp	82	11.29	82	10.57	95	11.43	118	12.84	146	13.97
First Bank System	115	13.10	130	13.15	131	11.85	167	14.15	203	15.31
Norwest Corp.	89	9.36	125	11.53	70	6.03	108	9.04	122	9.59
NCNB Corp.	88	16.10	106	16.38	133	16.30	164	17.23	199	16.31
First Wachovia Corp.	91	14.52	133	18.73	156	19.05	188	19.57	194	17.68
Barnett Banks	49	12.36	81	16.16	106	16.72	134	16.51	162	16.77
SunTrust Banks	119	16.74	155	18.37	194	16.62	216	16.39	245	16.81
RepublicBank Corp.	144	17.08	130	13.82	137	12.81	140	11.91	54	4.40
Valley National	51	12.86	46	10.81	60	13.25	77	15.22	65	11.62
BankAmerican Corp.	395	9.29	390	7.82	346	6.68	-337	-6.83	-518	-12.16
First Interstate	221	13.12	247	13.01	276	12.68	313	13.11	338	12.92
Security Pacific	234	16.85	264	16.12	291	15.65	323	15.30	386	14.62
Wells Fargo & Co.	139	13.09	155	12.29	169	12.60	190	13.50	274	13.37
U.S. Bancorp	52	11.95	52	11.22	60	11.91	66	12.03	77	12.80
Regional Bank Total Composite	$2,560	12.94%	$2,942	12.74%	$3,232	12.35%	$3,125	10.85%	$3,376	10.56%
Total Composite	$5,316	13.33%	$6,279	13.40%	$6,708	12.56%	$7,398	12.41%	$8,218	12.21%

Source: T. Hanley, J. Rosenberg, C. D'Arista and E. Krahmer, A Review of Bank Performance: 1987 Edition (New York: Salomon Brothers, Inc, April, 1987), p. 29.

Table 14–4   The Interplay of Asset Leverage and Profit Margins on Return on Equity, 1982–86

	1982			1983		
	$Leverage^a$ ×	ROA^b =	ROE^c	$Leverage^a$ ×	ROA^b =	ROE^c
Bank of New York	25.6x	0.60%	15.3%	20.3x	0.71%	14.5%
Bankers Trust NY	28.7	0.60	16.1	23.5	0.67	15.5
Chase Manhattan	26.4	0.40	10.0	24.3	0.54	12.9
Chemical NY	25.9	0.54	13.6	22.6	0.64	14.4
Citicorp	26.7	0.60	15.8	23.9	0.67	16.0
Irving Bank Corp.	28.2	0.42	11.9	24.3	0.48	11.7
Manufacturers Hanover	27.0	0.50	13.4	23.8	0.55	13.1
J.P. Morgan & Co.	22.3	0.69	15.5	18.6	0.79	14.8
Marine Midland	22.8	0.45	10.2	20.9	0.49	10.1
Republic NY Corp.	24.9	0.76	17.9	17.9	0.90	15.4
Bank of Boston Corp.	20.7	0.71	14.7	20.0	0.72	14.4
First Chicago	25.9	0.39	10.2	20.8	0.53	11.1
Money Center Composite	25.7x	0.53%	13.7%	22.4x	0.63%	14.1%
Fleet Financial	16.3x	1.04%	16.9%	14.4x	1.15%	16.4%
Norstar Bancorp	12.8	1.29	16.4	11.3	1.27	14.3
Midlantic Corp.	15.4	1.11	17.1	15.9	0.99	15.8
CoreStates Financial	17.1	0.81	13.9	16.0	0.97	15.6
Mellon Bank Corp.	19.2	0.69	13.2	19.3	0.76	14.2
PNC Financial Corp.	15.7	1.03	16.2	15.5	1.06	16.4
AmeriTrust Corp.	10.0	1.06	10.5	9.6	0.89	8.6
Banc One Corp.	14.6	0.96	13.9	14.3	1.07	14.9
National City Corp.	14.9	0.76	11.3	15.4	0.77	11.8
NBD Bancorp	16.7	0.68	11.3	15.4	0.68	10.6
First Bank System	18.1	0.72	13.1	18.3	0.72	13.1
Norwest Corp.	16.5	0.57	9.4	17.1	0.67	11.5
NCNB Corp.	17.4	0.92	16.1	20.0	0.82	16.4
First Wachovia Corp.	16.5	0.89	14.5	16.8	1.12	18.7
Barnett Banks	18.3	0.68	12.4	19.1	0.85	16.2
SunTrust Banks	16.3	1.03	16.7	16.5	1.11	18.4
RepublicBank Corp.	19.0	0.90	17.1	18.5	0.75	13.8
Valley National	16.6	0.78	12.9	17.0	0.64	10.8
BankAmerica Corp.	28.2	0.33	9.3	24.6	0.32	7.8
First Interstate	22.6	0.58	13.1	21.4	0.61	13.0
Security Pacific	25.0	0.67	16.8	22.6	0.71	16.1
Wells Fargo & Co.	23.4	0.56	13.1	20.2	0.61	12.3
U.S. Bancorp	12.9	0.93	11.19	12.7	0.88	11.2
Regional Bank Composite	20.4x	0.63%	12.9%	19.2x	0.66%	12.7%
Composite	23.1x	0.58%	13.3%	20.8x	0.64%	13.4%

Table 14-4 (continued)

	1984 Leverage^a ×	ROA^b =	ROE^c	1985 Leverage^a ×	ROA^b =	ROE^c
Bank of New York	18.4x	0.80%	14.8%	17.3x	0.84%	14.6%
Bankers Trust NY	22.0	0.71	15.7	20.5	0.79	16.1
Chase Manhattan	23.3	0.48	10.9	20.9	0.65	13.6
Chemical NY	22.5	0.63	14.2	20.8	0.70	14.6
Citicorp	23.2	0.62	14.4	22.9	0.62	14.2
Irving Bank Corp.	24.1	0.48	11.6	23.1	0.55	12.6
Manufacturers Hanover	22.7	0.50	11.3	22.0	0.54	11.9
J.P. Morgan & Co.	17.5	0.87	15.3	16.4	1.06	17.4
Marine Midland	20.0	0.42	8.4	17.9	0.61	10.9
Republic NY Corp.	15.9	0.91	14.0	15.2	0.93	13.9
Bank of Boston Corp.	19.1	0.79	15.0	18.2	0.73	13.3
First Chicago	20.1	0.22	4.5	19.8	0.43	8.4
Money Center Composite	21.5x	0.60%	12.8%	20.3x	0.68%	13.9%
Fleet Financial	13.5x	1.25%	16.8%	13.1x	1.33%	17.4%
Norstar Bancorp	12.3	1.16	14.2	12.6	1.12	14.1
Midlantic Corp.	16.4	1.04	17.2	16.4	1.08	17.7
CoreStates Financial	14.8	1.12	16.6	13.9	1.00	13.9
Mellon Bank Corp.	19.2	0.57	10.4	19.4	0.67	12.3
PNC Financial Corp.	15.0	1.12	16.8	15.5	1.14	17.6
AmeriTrust Corp.	9.4	1.18	11.2	10.1	1.17	11.8
Banc One Corp.	14.0	1.13	15.3	13.5	1.23	16.0
National City Corp.	15.4	0.90	13.9	16.9	0.92	15.5
NBD Bancorp	16.0	0.71	11.4	16.5	0.78	12.8
First Bank System	19.0	0.63	11.9	20.2	0.70	14.1
Norwest Corp.	17.9	0.34	6.0	16.7	0.54	9.0
NCNB Corp.	19.4	0.84	16.3	18.7	0.92	17.2
First Wachovia Corp.	17.1	1.11	19.1	16.6	1.18	19.6
Barnett Banks	19.5	0.86	16.7	18.2	0.91	16.5
SunTrust Banks	16.0	1.04	16.6	16.0	1.03	16.4
RepublicBank Corp.	18.9	0.68	12.8	18.6	0.64	11.9
Valley National	17.7	0.75	13.3	17.6	0.86	15.2
BankAmerica Corp.	23.2	0.29	6.7	24.1	−0.28	−6.8
First Interstate	19.8	0.64	12.7	19.5	0.67	13.1
Security Pacific	22.0	0.71	15.6	22.2	0.69	15.3
Wells Fargo & Co.	20.3	0.62	12.6	20.3	0.67	13.5
U.S. Bancorp	13.5	0.88	11.9	14.2	0.85	12.0
Regional Bank Composite	18.7x	0.66%	12.4%	18.6x	0.58%	10.8%
Composite	20.1x	0.63%	12.6%	19.5x	0.64%	12.4%

^{a}Average total assets divided by average shareholders equity.

^{b}Net income divided by average total assets.

^{c}Net income retained after dividends on redeemable preferred stock divided by average shareholders equity.

Table 14–4 (continued)

	1986		
	$Leverage^a$	$\times ROA^b$	$= ROE^c$
Bank of New York	17.9x	0.85%	15.2%
Bankers Trust NY	20.2	0.79	15.9
Chase Manhattan	19.3	0.65	12.5
Chemical NY	19.6	0.70	13.6
Citicorp	21.9	0.58	12.6
Irving Bank Corp.	21.3	0.60	12.8
Manufacturers Hanover	20.8	0.54	11.2
J.P. Morgan & Co.	15.3	1.19	18.3
Marine Midland	17.4	0.65	11.4
Republic NY Corp.	16.6	0.85	13.9
Bank of Boston Corp.	19.0	0.78	14.9
First Chicago	17.4	0.71	12.4
Money Center Composite	19.4x	0.71%	13.7%
Fleet Financial	14.0x	1.37%	19.1%
Norstar Bancorp	13.5	1.07	14.4
Midlantic Corp.	16.3	0.95	15.4
CoreStates Financial	14.4	1.08	15.5
Mellon Bank Corp.	19.1	0.54	9.8
PNC Financial Corp.	15.4	1.22	18.7
AmeriTrust Corp.	10.8	1.03	11.1
Banc One Corp.	13.3	1.23	15.8
National City Corp.	15.4	1.09	16.8
NBD Bancorp	16.8	0.83	14.0
First Bank System	20.0	0.76	15.3
Norwest Corp.	15.4	0.62	9.6
NCNB Corp.	19.5	0.84	16.3
First Wachovia Corp.	15.4	1.15	17.7
Barnett Banks	18.2	0.92	16.8
SunTrust Banks	16.4	1.03	16.8
RepublicBank Corp.	17.8	0.25	4.4
Valley National	17.4	0.67	11.6
BankAmerica Corp.	26.7	–0.45	–12.2
First Interstate	19.1	0.68	12.9
Security Pacific	20.6	0.71	14.6
Wells Fargo & Co.	18.3	0.73	13.4
U.S. Bancorp	14.2	0.90	12.8
Regional Bank Composite	18.4x	0.58%	10.6%
Composite	18.9x	0.65%	12.2%

Source: T. Hanley et. al, op. cit., pp. 56 and 57.

performance just doesn't seem to explain the disfavor into which their common stocks had fallen by the end of 1980. Selective purchases of bank stocks in 1980 would have led to good results.

Noninterest Income and Expense.   Noninterest income is generated by a variety of sources, including service charges, trust department income, and profits on currency and bond trading. Noninterest income has been rising in relative importance and constitutes about 30 percent of net revenues at most banks. Larger banks tend to have a greater proportion of noninterest income than smaller banks.

Noninterest expenses also have been rising relative to total income for many banks, often reflecting higher personnel and computer costs. When the level is rising at a particular bank it can be an indication of inefficient operations. Rises in noninterest expenses should be carefully investigated to determine if they are justified.

Other Key Performance Ratios.   Other ratios useful in analyzing bank performance and financial strength are reviewed as follows:

1. The following four ratios should be reviewed to give an indication of possible asset quality problems resulting from the loan decisions of the bank:
    (a) Period-end reserve for loan losses to period-end loans.
    (b) Net loan charge-offs to average total loans.
    (c) Provision for loan losses to net charge-offs of that period.
    (d) Nonperforming assets to loans. This ratio indicates the proportion of total loans that are in default.
2. Financial strength is measured by balance sheet as well as income statement ratios. The following are important ratios to study over time.
    (a) Subordinated debt to total capital accounts. Although this ratio is low for "all insured commercial banks," it tends to be large for large money center banks. While the subordination reduces risk somewhat for the purchaser of such instruments, it really does not reduce bank risk.
    (b) Ratio of capital accounts to assets, deposits, and loans. In the early 1960s bank capital accounts generally exceeded 10 percent of total assets. Asset growth, financed mainly by adding bank liabilities, has reduced this ratio to four to eight percent today, depending on bank size, location, and management policy. There has been an erosion of bank capital, and the low P/E ratios, already reviewed for bank stocks, make raising new equity capital painful. Bank analysts should and do

watch the capital formation rate from internal sources in relation to the rate of asset growth. They also monitor the maturity of debt, as well as the total outstanding.

(c) Ratio of time and savings deposits to total deposits. The higher the proportion of time and savings deposits to total deposits for a bank, the greater the interest cost. Time and savings deposits represented only about 22 percent of total deposits for the average bank in 1945. By December 1980 this ratio was about 64 percent. The increased interest expense resulting from this change in deposit makeup has led banks to reach for higher-yielding loans and asset mixes, no doubt, thereby, increasing investor risk.

(d) Ratio of cash and U.S. government securities to total assets and deposits. This ratio indicates the immediate liquidity of the bank. Analysts expect the ratio to be at least 12 percent of total assets and 15 percent of deposits.

(e) Dividends per share divided by earnings per share (the payout ratio).

The Net Interest Margin.   Banks have depended increasingly on purchased money (the incurrence of liabilities) to finance asset growth since 1961. Steadily rising interest rates throughout the 1970s, coupled with the rapidly increasing debt taken on by banks, has resulted in interest expense becoming a large and volatile number. This has led analysts to stress the concept of "net interest margin." Net interest margin is measured by dividing net interest income by average earning assets. This ratio should be considered in terms of the history of the bank being reviewed and the average ratio for similar-sized banks. A net interest margin below the average suggests inefficient use of assets. On the other hand, a ratio that much exceeds the average for similar banks could suggest a bank that has courted high risk loans and investments.

A break-even yield also can be computed for a bank by dividing total interest expense by average gross earning assets. The break-even yield indicates the yield required on earning assets merely to cover interest expense. "For a retail-oriented bank, heavy in demand and savings type deposits, the norm for break-even yield tends to range between two and three percent, changing little from year to year. For many wholesale banks, which 'buy' most of their investible funds, the break-even yield is not only much higher (five to seven percent), but fluctuates according to interest rate movements."[108]

---

108 *Bank Analysis from External Sources*, p. 31.

Financial Reports Tend to Confuse.[109]

In a recent paper, David Cates identifies five frontiers of confusion that hamper effective analysis of bank financial statements. Each of these is discussed below.

1. Recurring profitability often is masked by the handling of nonrecurring and discretionary accounting events. For example, security gains taken in a rising market "may reflect transient trading opportunities captured by an active manager" that may not be repeated in the future. Another example is the highly discretionary approach taken by various banks toward their loan loss provisions. Also, banks have abused the concept of operating earnings by throwing in office building sales, debt buy-back gains, pension re-accounting, and discretionary recognition of gains on all manner of investments. "To illustrate, of the 50 largest bank holding companies reporting in 1986, 24 showed nonrecurring gains and/or net securities gains (all after tax) equal to 15% or more of net income, and 14 (excluding Texas banks) reported such items equal to 25% or more of net income."[110] This will overstate return on assets in a comparative sense. Investors should attempt to assess recurring earnings when studying bank statements, and reflect this number in return on asset comparisons.

2. Banks are currently permitted to include "equity contract notes" in primary capital. These obligate the bank to sell common stock sufficient to retire the note at or before maturity. This poses possible large dilution to earnings per share, but the amount of dilution is just about impossible to calculate. For a high quality bank the danger is probably not great, but the damage could be serious for a low quality bank that has a poor standing in the stock market. Pooling of interest accounting also can distort earnings per share comparisons, as we have previously discussed in the book.

3. While assets classified as investment can be restated to market, it is difficult to make similar adjustments for loans. Analysts evaluate loans from signals given by: (a) loan yield; (b) loan mix; (c) demand deposit level; (d) non-performing loan statistics; (e) net lost interest income; (f) secondary-market bids for LDC debt; and (g) junk bond yields.

4. Large banks have accumulated huge commitments and contingencies represented by off-balance-sheet items. Off-balance-sheet assets may dwarf

---

109 This section is based on an unpublished paper by David C. Cates, "The Intelligibility of Banks Has Faded Again" (New York: Cates Consulting Analysts, Inc., Summer, 1987).

110 Ibid, p. 11.

recorded assets. Income does often include the earnings of these assets, and return on assets is distorted. Analysts need to know much more than is presented in annual reports to properly evaluate the contribution of these activities to the bank and the risk involved.

5. Accounting statements "create fictional capital whose reality must be tested by the market value of assets and by the market value of capital itself."[111] The adequacy of capital must be judged in relation to the risk profile of the bank. Regulators focus on depositor safety, and their measures are not likely to represent stockholders' best interests, which should be the focal point of a stock analysis.

Insurance Company Stocks

Insurance companies can be divided into two major groups: (1) fire and casualty companies, and (2) life insurance companies. The characteristics of these two groups are different so they will be dealt with separately. One difference is that contracts for property and liability companies are relatively short, usually one, two, or three years, while contracts issued by life insurance companies usually run for many years. Some companies are writing multiline life insurance, health and accident policies, and fire and casualty policies. Insurance companies are also classified as either (1) mutual companies, or (2) stock companies, sStock companythe latter being the only ones in which investors can invest.

Insurance Accounting-Regulatory vs. GAAP Accounting

Historically, until the late 1960s and early 1970s, fire, casualty, and life companies reported to stockholders in the manner required by state insurance commissioners. Because statutory accounting differs in significant ways from GAAP (generally accepted accounting principles) accounting, the analyst had to adjust reported

---

111 Ibid, p. 19.

statements to conform with GAAP accounting.[112] However, as a result of reports and requirements issued by the AICPA, and also SEC requirements and pressures from the Financial Analysts Federation, most companies whose securities are traded publicly now submit supplementary schedules in addition to statutory reporting. These are necessary for statutory accounting to be reconciled to conform with GAAP accounting. Therefore, analysts operating outside the company are given the reconciliations or can make them with data supplied.[113]

The Property and Casualty Industry

Approximately 3,600 companies operated in the highly competitive environment called the property–casualty industry. About 900 of those firms account for most of the business, but no one company controls more than 10% of the market.

Property insurance is designed to protect individuals and businesses from the impact of financial risks associated with the ownership and operation of property. Casualty insurance is designed to insure against potential liabilities arising from harm caused others.

Analysis of Property and Casualty Insurance Companies

The income of insurance companies consists of underwriting premiums collected plus investment income. The expenses consist of underwriting expenses, losses and expenses associated with covered policy losses, and proportionate general and administrative overhead.

While the demand for property and casualty insurance is fairly stable (reflecting basically real growth of the economy and inflation), the supply curve

---

112 Statutory reporting prorates the income over the life of the policy as under GAAP but, unlike GAAP, does not prorate the expenses of placing policies on the books, but instead burdens the initial fiscal period with all the initial expenses.

113 See (a) Audits of Fire and Casualty Insurance Companies, an AICPA Industry Audit Guide, prepared by the Committee on Insurance Accounting and Auditing of the American Institute of CPA's, New York, 1966. See also, annual editions of Financial Reporting Trends-Fire and Casualty Insurance, Ernst and Ernst, New York.

(b) Audits of Stock Life Insurance Companies. An Industry Audit Guide prepared by the Committee of Insurance Accounting and Auditing of the American Institute of CPA's, New York, 1972.

(c) See also, annual editions of Financial Reporting Trends-Life Insurance, Ernst and Ernst, New York.

is volatile. As interest rates rise the willingness of companies to offer such insurance increases, because each premium dollar generates more investment income. Property and casualty companies often have shown little or no underwriting profits, depending on successful investment results to earn adequate returns for the owners (see Table 14–5).

Underwriting Tests of Profitability.   There are three major tests of underwriting profitability: the loss ratio, the expense ratio, and the combined loss and expense ratio. The historic ratios for the insurance industry are shown in Table 14–6.

Loss Ratio.   This ratio is generally taken as the ratio of losses incurred, plus directly related expenses, to premiums earned, although sometimes the ratio is calculated to premiums written. This is a test of the quality of the risks that are underwritten.

Table 14–5   Property/Casualty Operating Results, 1983–86 (Dollar Figures in Millions)

	1983	1984	1985	1986
Net Premiums Written	107,803	117,744	143,882	176,993
Percent Change from Previous Year	4.6	9.2	22.2	23.0
Net Premiums Earned	105,787	114,257	132,651	166,381
Percent Change from Previous Year	4.6	8.0	16.1	25.4
Pure Losses	74,623	87,917	102,243	116,852
Loss Adjustment Expense	11,459	12,731	15,631	18,914
Underwriting Expenses	30,796	32,981	37,365	44,587
Total Expenses	116,878	133,628	155,239	180,353
Underwriting Gain/(Loss)	(11,091)	(19,371)	(22,587)	(13,972)
Policy Holder Dividends	2,194	2,084	2,199	2,165
Underwriting Gain/(Loss) After Dividends	(13,285)	(21,455)	(24,788)	(16,137)
Net Investment Income	15,784	17,448	19,375	21,924
Other Income	(308)	46	(113)	476
Pre-tax Operating Income	2,191	(3,961)	(5,525)	5,312

Source: A.M. Best. As reproduced in Standard & Poor's Industry Surveys, Insurance & Investment (New York: Standard & Poor's, Inc., 12/31/87), p. I 28.

Table 14-6   Combined Ratio and Its Components—Property/Casualty Insurance, 1980–86 (All figures in percent)

Year	Loss Ratio	Expense Ratio	Dividend Ratio	Combined Ratio
1987	77.9	25.3	1.3	104.6
1986	81.6	25.2	1.3	108.1
1985	88.9	25.9	1.6	116.5
1984	88.2	28.0	1.8	118.1
1983	81.5	28.4	2.1	112.0
1982	79.7	28.0	2.0	109.7
1981	76.8	27.3	1.9	106.0
1980	74.9	26.5	1.7	103.1
1975	79.3	27.3	1.3	107.9
1970	70.8	27.6	1.7	100.1

Source: Best's Aggregates & Averages: Property/Casualty (Oldwick, New Jersey: A.M. Best & Co., 1988), p. 83.

Expense Ratio. This ratio is generally taken as the ratio of operating expenses to premiums written but may be taken as a ratio to premiums earned. It is a test of managements' efficiency in operations.

Combined Loss and Expense Ratio. This ratio is the sum total of the loss ratio and the expense ratio and, if under 100, indicates the degree of profitability of underwriting and, if over 100, the degree of unprofitability.

Recent Profit Experience. Insurance Services Office reported that losses and loss adjustment expense accounted for 75 percent of total industry expenses in 1986. Losses and expenses exceeded earned premiums in 1986, resulting in an underwriting loss of $15.9 billion after policy holder dividends of $2.0 billion. While this is a large loss, it represents a 35 percent improvement over the $24.8 billion loss incurred in 1985. Operating results were aided in 1986 by a low level of insured catastrophic losses in 1986, and the improved 1986 results may, therefore, not be an accurate gauge of the future.

The relatively favorable performance recorded by the industry in 1986 reflects rising premium revenues, lower underwriting losses, and increased investment income. The industry earned over $5 billion in 1986 as pretax net operating income, compared to losses of close to $4 billion in 1984 and over $5 billion in

1985. On the other hand, the pace of increase in premium revenues began to slow in 1986, and losses are difficult to predict.

Recurring Cycles in Fire and Casualty Business.   An examination of past history indicates the cyclical nature of underwriting. The business will experience profitability for a period of years and then, especially in years of inflation, the business will become unprofitable. When it is unprofitable, the companies will seek rate increases. Increases in rates for the industry as a whole have always been granted by state insurance commissioners, and the industry then has returned to a period of profitability, which again is followed by a period of unprofitability. Purchasers of fire and casualty insurance stocks during the unprofitable and out-of-favor phase of the cycle must assume a return to profitability, which to date has always followed, as it did in 1986.

In the period 1956–1980, for the stock companies, the lowest combined ratios were 95.4 in 1972 and 95.8 in 1971, and the highest ratio was 107.9 in 1975. The combined ratio (ignoring dividends) reached an all time high of 118.1 in 1984 before declining to 104.6 in 1987. Investors can expect only slight total profitability when underwriting is unprofitable because the net loss must be absorbed by investment income, which is the source of dividends and the basis for capital gains secured by investors. These ratios represent industry averages. But, of course, certain companies have a better record than the averages and other companies a poorer one.

In general, investors in property and liability insurance companies do not expect much in the way of underwriting profits, only wanting the combined loss and expense ratio to be equal to or somewhat below 100 percent. Their major expectation for income and capital gains centers on investment performance and investment income. Therefore, the investor making an analysis of an insurance company must give major attention to the company's investment portfolio and investment results over a period of years. The comparative investment and underwriting record for selected years over the period 1970–87 is shown in Table 14–7.

Troublesome Underwriting Losses.   The stock property-casualty companies have recorded underwriting losses during the 1980s. Moreover, rising interest rates could erode the value of insurers bond portfolios.

Analysts feel the industry is suffering from excess capacity brought on by the attraction of relatively high rates of return on equity capital in recent years. High interest rates in the late 1970s encouraged rate cutting to attract funds to invest. Rising inflation rates further exacerbated the problem by causing claim settlements and operating expenses to rise sharply. Price competition again

**Table 14-7   Property and Casualty Stock Insurance Companies—
Comparative Investment and Underwriting Record
(Dollar Figures in Millions)**

Year	Investment Income		Underwriting Profit or Loss	
	Dollars	Percent of Mean Assets	Dollars	Percent of Earned Premiums
1987	18,824	6.03	(5,450)	(4.14)
1986	16,872	6.35	(10,446)	(8.95)
1985	14,957	6.73	(17,879)	(19.40)
1984	13,695	6.91	(15,670)	(19.84)
1983	12,381	6.58	(9,090)	(12.41)
1982	11,846	6.79	(6,475)	(9.17)
1981	10,291	6.37	(3,681)	(5.41)
1980	8,836	6.02	(1,956)	(2.98)
1975	3,143	4.83	(2,880)	(8.34)
1970	1,439	3.57	(154)	(0.72)

Source: Best's Aggregates & Averages: Property/Casualty (Oldwick, New Jersey: A.M. Best & Co., 1988) p. 87.

emerged in 1988, and the growth in industry wide premiums slowed in 1987. Still operating earnings are expected to advance in 1988, though declines are likely in the 1989–90 period. These trends will have to be watched closely by investment analysts.

Investment Policy Requirements.   Investment policy is based partly on regulations and partly on management decisions. Regulations governing fire and casualty investments are considerably less restrictive than regulations controlling investments of life insurance companies. For fire and casualty companies there is no specific limitation on stock investments.

The minimum capital required must be invested in cash and U.S. government securities, which in recent years has averaged about eight percent of assets. Unearned premium reserves and required reserves must be invested in cash, government securities, and approved corporate bonds. The balance of funds may be invested in either stocks or bonds as long as the issuers have maintained satisfactory records of interest and dividend payments and are solvent.

Investment Policy.   Investment income is the principal component of the earnings of property and casualty insurers, and have kept the industry profitable during every year since 1975, except for 1984.

The bulk of investment funds of property and casualty insurers are kept in investments that can be sold readily, including stocks and bonds. The portion invested in bonds increased to 73.38 percent in 1984 from 59.6 percent in 1973.[114] Holdings of common stocks declined to 19.67 percent from 26.32 percent over the same time period.

The dollar growth in municipal securities from 1975 to 1981 was impressive. Special revenue bonds of colleges, universities and public works programs dominated the fixed income portfolio at the end of 1984, representing 30 percent of the total fixed income portfolio. Property and casualty companies find such securities particularly interesting if the combined ratio is below 100 percent, since they are certain to face a federal income tax on investment earnings.

The higher the ratio of capital and surplus to unearned premium reserves for a company, the more justifiable is a large investment in common stocks. Analysts should relate the common stock investment to capital funds and estimate the effect of a given decline in market value of common stocks on capital and surplus of the company.

Investment Results.   An insurance company's total earnings consist of the adjusted underwriting gain (or loss) plus net investment income. The underwriting earnings tend to be quite variable, fluctuating considerably over the years, and in numerous years companies experience underwriting losses. The pattern is suggested in Table 14–7. But fortunately investment income, largely from debt instruments, tends to be stable and rising. This means that dividends are paid generally or entirely from investment income. Earnings per share should be calculated after income taxes and their trend and cyclical nature determined.

While companies experience both capital gains and losses in their investment portfolios, security analysts generally do not include portfolio gains or losses in calculating annual earnings. This is in line with the usual accounting practices of excluding nonrecurring gains from income on an annual basis.

Summary of Major Factors to Consider in Analysis of Fire and Casualty Companies.   After analyzing the underwriting record and the investment record of a company, the analyst should determine growth in each of several categories. Growth factors for which the compound annual growth should be determined are:

---

114 As reported by the Insurance Information Institute.

1. Assets.
2. Capital funds.
3. Total income.
4. Premium income.
5. Other income.
6. Net income from operations after income tax.
7. Earnings per share.
8. Dividends per share.
9. Liquidating value per share (adjusted book value).

Stability of items 3 through 9 also is of interest. The following analytical tests for fire and casualty insurance companies are suggested:

1. Cash and investment grade bonds (rated in the top four grades) should be at least equal to 90 percent of liabilities with cash and U.S. government securities at least equal to 20 percent of total assets and 30 percent of liabilities. The higher the ratio the less concern for market fluctuations in securities, especially common stocks.
2. The ratio of common equity (exclusive of equity in unearned premium reserve) to total assets should be at least 35 percent.
3. The analyst should calculate the effect on capital and surplus if stock prices should decline 50 percent.
4. The loss ratios over both the last five and 10 years should not average over 72 percent.
5. The expense ratio over the last five and 10 years should not average over 23 percent.
6. The combined loss and expense ratios should not average over 95 percent for the last five and 10 years.
7. The rate of return on average assets should have been at least five percent over the most recent five years.
8. Investment income should rise on the average at least as fast as the growth in assets plus the rate of growth in interest rate on "A" rated bonds.
9. There should be a satisfactory record of at least 10 years of growth in assets, net income, earnings per share, and dividends per share.

Life Insurance Companies

The life insurance industry is a major and growing component of the American financial scene. Total assets of U.S. life insurance companies grew from $351.7 billion in 1977 to $931.6 billion at year-end 1986, recording a compound annual growth rate of 11.43 percent (see Table 14–8).

The life insurance industry traditionally has been dominated by mutual companies, which are both older and larger than the stockholder owned companies. We, of course, are interested in the stockholder-owned companies.

Growth of Life Insurance Industry.   The life insurance industry is well known for its continuous and considerable growth over long periods, including the growth of investment income. This is in sharp contrast to the erratic underwriting record of fire and casualty insurance companies.

In the post-World War II years the life insurance industry has shown a fairly steady growth rate although the rate of growth slowed in the 1955–1970 period only to regain the 1945–1955 growth rate after 1969. Growth rates for major categories are shown for the period 1976–86 in Table 14–9.

The evolution into financial services continues in this industry. Life insurance companies, therefore, compete not only among themselves for the consumers' savings dollar, but also against other financial institutions, such as banks and brokerage houses.

Relatively high interest rates and inflation in late 1970 and the early 1980s, and a low rate of return, on the savings feature, for consumers whole life policies (approximately five percent), caused many buyers to shift to lower margined term insurance and invest the difference at higher rates of return. This led to an increase in policy terminations and policy loans, heightening liquidity and profitability problems for the industry. The sharp increase in lapses and surrenders in the 1980s is highlighted in Table 14–10. While the factors that spurred these changes have abated recently, investors should watch to see if the rate of lapses and surrenders slows down.

Earnings prospects for the industry were unexciting at the time of writing this material. The following factors cloud the near-term earnings horizon:

1. Fear of rising interest rates, which could accelerate the trend away from whole life and would have an adverse effect on the value of large bond holdings by the industry.
2. Higher tax rates beginning in 1987.

Table 14-8 Assets of U.S. Life Insurance Companies (In Millions of Dollars)

Year	Total Assets	Government Securities	Corporate Securities Total	Bonds	Stocks	Mortgages	Real Estate	Policy Loans	Other Assets
1986	937,551	144,616	432,831	341,967	90,864	193,842	31,615	54,055	80,592
1985	825,901	124,598	374,344	296,848	77,496	171,797	28,822	54,369	71,971
1984	722,979	99,769	322,463	259,128	63,335	156,699	25,767	54,505	63,776
1983	654,948	76,615	296,991	232,123	64,868	150,999	22,234	54,063	54,046
1982	588,163	55,516	268,502	212,772	55,730	141,989	20,624	52,961	48,571
1981	525,803	39,502	241,760	193,806	47,670	137,747	18,278	48,706	40,094
1980	479,210	33,015	226,969	179,603	47,366	131,080	15,033	41,411	31,702
1979	432,282	29,719	208,747	168,990	39,757	118,421	13,007	34,825	27,563
1978	389,924	26,552	191,562	156,044	35,518	106,167	11,764	30,146	23,733
1977	351,722	23,555	171,652	137,889	33,763	96,848	11,060	27,556	21,051

Source: Standard & Poor's Industry Surveys, Insurance and Investment (New York: Standard & Poor's Corporation, July, 1988), p. I-15.

Table 14-9   Key Life Insurance Statistics

	1976	1985	1986	% Change 1985-84	% Change 1986-85
Life Insurance in Force in the United States (000,000 omitted)					
Ordinary	$1,177,672	$3,247,289	$3,658,203	12.5	12.7
Group	1,002,647	2,561,595	2,801,049	7.1	9.3
Industrial	39,175	28,250	27,168	-6.2	-3.8
Credit	123,569	215,973	233,859	13.7	8.3
Total	$2,343,063	$6,053,107	$6,720,279	10.1	11.0
Average Amounts of Life Insurance in Force in the United States					
Per Family	$30,100	$63,400	$69,100	8.0	9.0
Per Insured Family	$35,000	$74,600	$81,200	9.2	8.8
Life Insurance Purchases in the United States (000,000 omitted)					
Ordinary	$213,784	$ 910,944	$ 933,592	11.0	2.5
Group	104,683	391,503	374,741*	8.9	17.3
Industrial	6,382	722	418	-23.4	-42.1
Total	$324,849	$1,231,169	$1,308,751*	10.4	6.3
Benefit Payments in the United States (000,000 omitted)					
Payments to Beneficiaries	$9,593	$18,226	$19,479	8.8	6.9
Payments to Policy Holder	10,599	27,025	26,169	4.9	3.2
Payments to Annuitants	4,419	21,259	22,657	18.7	6.6
Total	$24,611	$66,510	$68,305	10.1	2.7
Premium Receipts of U.S. Life Insurance Companies (000,000 omitted)					
Life Insurance	$31,358	$ 60,127	$ 66,213	17.3	10.1
Annuity Considerations	13,962	53,899	83,712	25.8	55.3
Health Insurance	21,059	41,837	44,153	2.9	5.5
Total	$66,379	$155,863	$194,078	15.6	24.5
Assets of U.S. Life Insurance Companies (000,000 omitted)					
Government Securities	$ 20,260	$124,598	$144,616	24.9	16.1
Corporate Bonds	120,666	296,848	341,967	14.6	15.2
Stocks	34,262	77,496	90,864	22.4	17.2
Mortgages	91,552	171,797	193,842	9.6	12.8
Real Estate	10,476	28,822	31,615	11.9	9.7
Policy Loans	25,834	54,369	54,055	-0.2	-0.6
Other Assets	18,502	71,971	80,592	12.8	12.0
Total	$321,552	$825,901	$937,551	14.2	13.5
Net Rate of Investment Income of U.S. Life Insurance Companies (Before Federal Income Taxes)					
Including Separate Accounts	6.55%	9.63%	9.35%		
Excluding Separate Accounts	6.68%	9.87%	9.64%		

* Includes Servicemen's Group Life Insurance of $51.0 Billion and Federal Employees' Group Life Insurance of $10.8 Billion

Source: *Life Insurance Fact Book Update* (Washington, D.C.: American Council of Life Insurance, 1987), p. 4.

3. A cyclical decline in group health results and the danger represented by AIDS. Insurers have instituted price hikes in the health area which should help alleviate this problem.

New and Discontinuing Companies. Each year many new companies are established, and many companies go out of business. Sometimes promoters start companies and accept low quality risks at low premiums to show a rapid increase in "insurance in force," expecting that the price of their stock will rise rapidly permitting them to sell out at a large profit before the low quality of risks produces poor results. Furthermore, the "insurance in force" figure may rise rapidly without a significant increase in assets if most new policies are term policies. New companies, therefore, usually are of such high risk as not to fit the objectives of most long-term investors.

Financial Statements of Life Insurance Companies. Tables 14–11 and 14–12 offer historical balance sheet information for life insurance companies, which

Table 14–10   Lapses and Surrenders—Voluntary Termination Rate (Ordinary Policies in force in the United States)

Year	Policies In Force Less Than 2 Years	Policies In Force 2 Years or More	All Policies In Force	Year	Policies In Force Less Than 2 Years	Policies In Force 2 Years or More	All Policies in Force
1951	9.4%	2.2%	3.2%	1975	20.9%	4.5%	6.7%
1955	11.4	2.5	3.8	1976	19.7	4.6	6.6
1960	14.5	3.7	5.2	1977	19.5	4.7	6.6
1965	15.4	3.5	5.1	1978	19.6	4.6	6.6
1966	16.2	3.5	5.2	1979	21.0	5.1	7.2
1967	16.5	3.6	5.2	1980	22.4	5.8	8.1
1968	18.0	3.7	5.5	1981	23.5	6.6	8.9
1969	18.3	3.7	5.6	1982	24.4	7.6	10.0
1970	19.3	3.9	5.9	1983	25.1	8.6	11.0
1971	19.0	3.9	5.8	1984	23.0	9.6	11.9
1972	19.3	3.9	6.0	1985	20.9	10.3	12.3
1973	18.8	4.3	6.3	1986	21.7	9.0	11.1
1974	19.5	4.5	6.5				

Note: The rate is the ratio of the number of policies lapsed or surrendered to the mean number of policies in force.

Source: *Life Insurance Fact Book Update* (Washington, D.C.: American Council of Life Insurance, 1987,) p. 26.

should be understood and used for comparative purposes in analyzing particular companies. Table 14–11 presents the major assets and Table 14–12 the major liabilities, reserves, capital, and surplus items.

Analysis of Assets of Life Insurance Companies.   Utilizing the data in Table 14–11, we find that debt instruments (government securities, bonds, mortgages, and policy loans), represented 78.3 percent of total assets in 1986, and 80.4 percent in 1980. This breakdown is typical for life insurance companies. State regulations governing the investments of insurance companies generally limit investment in equities to 10 percent of total assets, except for pension fund assets, which are set aside in separate accounts.

Pension fund assets are segregated since such assets may be invested entirely in common stock if the insurance company wishes to do so. Insurance companies had invested only 49.4 percent of total separate account (pension fund) assets in common stocks at the end of 1980. The rate of return earned is a bit lower when separate accounts are included than when they are excluded, as shown in Table 14–13. This occurs because of the higher proportion of common stocks held in these accounts.

The largest class of securities is corporate securities, representing 47.4 percent of all assets in 1980 (37.5 percent bonds and 9.9 percent equity), and 46.2 percent in 1986. The next largest class is mortgages, representing 27.4 percent of assets in 1980 and 20.6 percent in 1986, which is among the lowest levels for this category since 1954. Policy loans represent 5.8 percent, real estate 3.4 percent, and miscellaneous assets 8.6 percent in 1986.

The Income Statement.   A typical income statement of a stock life insurance company is presented in Table 14–14. Premium income represents about 68 percent of total income and net investment income about 27 percent. Benefits, related payments and additions to policy and special reserves absorbs about 80 percent of income. Operating expenses absorb another 15 percent, and income taxes about 1.5 percent, leaving 3.5 percent for dividends and additions to surplus.

The actual proportions in the income statement can vary by size of stock company. Smaller companies (those with assets of less than $500 million), could show as much as 78 percent of income derived from premium receipts. Expense proportions also may vary, depending on such factors as types of coverage offered by a given company and its ratio of recently issued insurance to total insurance in force. The figures given are general averages for all stock insurance companies.

Sources of Earnings—Underwriting.   Normally the investor can take a non-insurance company's sales for a given period and subtract the costs to arrive at the

Table 14–11 Life Insurance Assets—Distribution of Assets of U.S. Life Insurance Companies

Amount (000,000 omitted)

Year	Government Securities	Corporate Securities Bonds	Stocks	Mortgages	Real Estate	Policy Loans	Misc. Assets	Total
1917	$562	$1,975	$83	$2,021	$179	$810	$311	$5,941
1920	1,349	1,949	75	2,442	172	859	474	7,320
1925	1,311	3,022	81	4,808	266	1,446	604	11,538
1930	1,502	4,929	519	7,598	548	2,807	977	18,880
1935	4,727	5,314	583	5,357	1,990	3,540	1,705	23,216
1940	8,447	8,645	605	5,972	2,065	3,091	1,977	30,802
1945	22,545	10,060	999	6,636	857	1,962	1,738	44,797
1950	16,118	23,248	2,103	16,102	1,445	2,413	2,591	64,020
1955	11,829	35,912	3,633	29,445	2,581	3,290	3,742	90,432
1960	11,815	46,740	4,981	41,771	3,765	5,231	5,273	119,576
1965	11,908	58,244	9,126	60,013	4,681	7,678	7,234	158,884
1970	11,068	73,098	15,420	74,375	6,320	16,064	10,909	207,254
1975	15,177	105,837	28,061	89,167	9,621	24,467	16,974	289,304
1976	20,260	120,666	34,262	91,552	10,476	25,834	18,502	321,552
1977	23,555	137,889	33,763	96,848	11,060	27,556	21,051	351,722
1978	26,552	156,044	35,518	106,167	11,764	30,146	23,733	389,924
1979	29,719	168,990	39,757	118,421	13,007	34,825	27,563	432,282
1980	33,015	179,603	47,366	131,080	15,033	41,411	31,702	479,210
1981	39,502	193,806	47,670	137,747	18,278	48,706	40,094	525,803
1982	55,516	212,772	55,730	141,989	20,624	52,961	48,571	588,163
1983	76,615	232,123	64,868	150,999	22,234	54,063	54,046	654,948
1984	99,769	259,128	63,335	156,699	25,767	54,505	63,776	722,979
1985	124,598	296,848	77,496	171,797	28,822	54,369	71,971	825,901
1986	144,616	341,967	90,864	193,842	31,615	54,055	80,592	937,551

Table 14–11 (continued)

Percent

Year	Government Securities	Corporate Securities		Mortgages	Real Estate	Policy Loans	Misc. Assets	Total
		Bonds	Stocks					
1917	9.6%	33.2%	1.4%	34.0%	3.0%	13.6%	5.2%	100.0%
1920	18.4	26.7	1.0	33.4	2.3	11.7	6.5	100.0
1925	11.3	26.2	.7	41.7	2.3	12.5	5.3	100.0
1930	8.0	26.0	2.8	40.2	2.9	14.9	5.2	100.0
1935	20.4	22.9	2.5	23.1	8.6	15.2	7.3	100.0
1940	27.5	28.1	2.0	19.4	6.7	10.0	6.3	100.0
1945	50.3	22.5	2.2	14.8	1.9	4.4	3.9	100.0
1950	25.2	36.3	3.3	25.1	2.2	3.8	4.1	100.0
1955	13.1	39.7	4.0	32.6	2.9	3.6	4.1	100.0
1960	9.9	39.1	4.2	34.9	3.1	4.4	4.4	100.0
1965	7.5	36.7	5.7	37.8	3.0	4.8	4.5	100.0
1970	5.3	35.3	7.4	35.9	3.0	7.8	5.3	100.0
1975	5.2	36.6	9.7	30.8	3.3	8.5	5.9	100.0
1976	6.3	37.5	10.7	28.5	3.3	8.0	5.7	100.0
1977	6.7	39.2	9.6	27.5	3.2	7.8	6.0	100.0
1978	6.8	40.0	9.1	27.2	3.0	7.8	6.1	100.0
1979	6.9	39.1	9.2	27.4	3.0	8.1	6.3	100.0
1980	6.9	37.5	9.9	27.4	3.1	8.6	6.6	100.0
1981	7.5	36.8	9.1	26.2	3.5	9.3	7.6	100.0
1982	9.4	36.2	9.5	24.1	3.5	9.0	8.3	100.0
1983	11.7	35.4	9.9	23.1	3.4	8.3	8.2	100.0
1984	13.8	35.8	8.8	21.7	3.6	7.5	8.8	100.0
1985	15.0	36.0	9.4	20.8	3.5	6.6	8.7	100.0
1986	15.4	36.5	9.7	20.6	3.4	5.8	8.6	100.0

Note: Beginning with 1962, these dates include the assets of separate accounts

Source: *Life Insurance Fact Book Update* (Washington, D.C.: American Council of life Insurance, 1987), p. 36.

Table 14–12 Obligations and Surplus Funds—U.S. Life Insurance Companies (000,000 omitted)

Year	Policy Reserves	Policy Dividend Accumulation	Funds Set Aside For Policy Dividends	Other Obligations	Surplus Funds	Capital (Stock Companies)	Total
1952	$62,579	$1,675	$ 841	$3,024	$4,884	$ 372	$73,375
1955	75,359	2,239	1,201	4,625	6,475	533	90,432
1960	98,473	3,381	1,780	6,268	8,827	847	119,576
1965	127,620	4,326	2,647	10,455	12,468	1,368	158,884
1970	167,779	6,068	3,540	12,544	15,651	1,672	207,254
1975	237,116	8,814	4,875	17,936	18,635	1,928	289,304
1976	262,775	9,633	5,252	21,881	20,077	1,934	321,552
1977	287,932	10,427	5,839	23,907	21,669	1,948	351,722
1978	318,483	11,319	6,380	27,495	24,285	1,962	389,924
1979	351,637	12,112	7,158	31,372	28,023	1,980	432,282
1980	390,339	12,727	7,659	34,127	32,274	2,084	479,210
1981	428,031	13,261	8,355	38,734	35,211	2,211	525,803
1982	479,360	13,706	8,914	44,732	39,105	2,346	588,163
1983	532,441	13,939	10,078	52,106	43,978	2,406	654,948
1984	584,193	14,395	10,745	63,299	47,800	2,547	722,979
1985	665,302	14,638	11,710	77,471	54,039	2,741	825,901
1986	761,924	15,174	11,704	84,600	61,314	2,835	937,551

Source: *Life Insurance Fact Book Update* (Washington, D.C.: American Council of Life Insurance, 1987), p.35.

Table 14–13   Net Rate of Investment Income—U.S Life Insurance Companies

Year	Rate	Year	Rate
1915	4.77%	1940	3.45%
1920	4.83	1945	3.11
1925	5.11	1950	3.13
1930	5.05	1955	3.51
1935	3.70	1960	4.11

	Rate			Rate	
Year	Including Separate Accounts	Excluding Separate Accounts	Year	Including Separate Accounts	Excluding Separate Accounts
1965	4.61%	4.61%	1976	6.55%	6.68%
1966	4.73	4.73	1977	6.89	7.00
1967	4.82	4.83	1978	7.31	7.39
1968	4.95	4.97	1979	7.73	7.78
1969	5.12	5.15	1980	8.02	8.06
1970	5.30	5.34	1981	8.57	8.53
1971	5.44	5.52	1982	8.91	8.87
1972	5.56	5.69	1983	8.96	9.06
1973	5.88	6.00	1984	9.45	9.65
1974	6.25	6.31	1985	9.63	9.87
1975	6.36	6.44	1986	9.35	9.64

Note: The net rate of investment income is calculated using industry aggregates, and represent the ration of (1) net investment income to (2) mean invested assets (including cash) less half the net investment income. Before 1940, some federal income taxes were deducted from net investment income: beginning with 1940, the rates are calculated before deducting any federal inceome taxes.

Source: Life Insurance Fact Book Update, op. cit., p. 32.

company's profit. In life insurance the sales unit referred to is a promise by the company to pay $1,000 at a future time. The amount received by the company is usually no more than a year's premium, which is a small fraction of this $1,000. It is the premium payment received each year and not the contract sale that provides income for the insurance company.

Fixing Premiums.   In fixing premiums the insurance company will calculate the amount that must be received each year so that, with interest earned, the amounts received will equal the benefits expected to be paid out over the duration of the contracts. This amount per year is called the net level premium and

Table 14–14   A Typical Condensed Income Statement of a Life Insurance Company

Sources of Funds—Income		
Premiums Receipts	69.8%	
Net Investment Income	26.7	
Other Income	4.5	
		100.0%
Use of Funds or Distribution of Income		
Benefits including surrender benefits	42.5	
Annuities and mutual endowment	7.5	
Miscellaneous deductions	5.5	
Increase in policy and special revenues	24.5	
		80.0
Expenses of Operation		
Agents' commissions	6.0	
General expenses	6.3	
Taxes other than income taxes	2.7	
		15.0
Total of Above		95.0
Income Taxes		1.5
Total		96.5
Net Gain After Income Tax, Before Dividends		3.5
Dividends to Policyholders		2.3
Net Gain After Dividends to Policyholders		1.2
Charges to Surplus		
Surplus beginning of fiscal period		xxxx
Add: Net gains after income tax	3.5	
Net gain from sale of investments	.5	
Increase in market value of investments	1.0	
Total increase in surplus		xxxx
Less: Dividends to policyholders	2.3	
Increase in security valuation reserves	1.0	
Surplus at end of fiscal period		xxxx

corresponds to the cost of goods sold for an ordinary business. To this net level premium the company then adds an amount that it estimates will cover its costs, including commissions, and give it a small margin of profit. This amount is called the load and is the same as the markup for a seller of goods.

Conservative Nature of Reported Earnings.   In calculating the profit that a life insurance company will make, it must be emphasized that most of the cost factors are estimates and assumptions for long periods of time in the future. The differences between these estimates and the actual costs that occur are the sources of additional possible profit or loss to the company. Since the estimates and assumptions used have been conservative (that is, have tended to overstate the costs), these differences have more often been profits than losses.

Determining Companies to Consider.   The quantitative measures discussed in the following paragraphs are useful in assessing the quality and potential return for life insurance stocks.

Measures of Efficiency.   The tests of management in this area, as in other companies, are such measures as the return on stockholders' equity and the growth of earnings. Also it will be helpful to look at specific indicators, especially in the area of expenses. Renewal expense and investment yield are useful.

1. To calculate renewal expense per $1,000 of old business in force, renewal expense first must be estimated. This is done by subtracting from general insurance expense the identifiable first-year expenses that are contained in this item. The renewal expense per $1,000, particularly when calculated separately for ordinary business, provides a measure that is suitable for comparison between companies or with a general standard.
2. Investment yield is the ratio of net investment income to mean assets. The trend of a company's investment yield should be rising in line with the general trend for the industry.

Growth in Earnings.   Growth in earnings per share is by far the most important factor to be considered in measuring the growth of a company. The rates of growth of both reported and adjusted earnings should be at a satisfactory level. Any divergence of the two over a period of several years should be investigated.

Quality of Business.   The investor must attempt to measure the quality of the business. This also indicates the quality of the earnings. The following factors will be of assistance in this effort.

1. **Lapse Ratio.** This is the ratio of voluntary terminations (including both lapses and surrenders) to business in force (average of beginning and ending). The lower the lapse ratio, the longer a company's business is remaining in force on the average and the greater is the profit that can be expected.

2. **Composition of Business in Force.** The proportion of most profitable lines, particularly ordinary life (whole life and endowment), and the trends are important. Investors should prefer life insurance companies that have concentrated on ordinary life rather than group business.

3. **Composition of Premium Income.** As with the composition of business in force, the composition of premium income measure should show a substantial proportion of premium income from ordinary life insurance.

Return on Stockholders' Equity. This is the most important single measure of benefit to stockholders in any line of business. It shows how well management is using the funds provided by stockholders and is used for comparison with other companies. It should be calculated using both reported and adjusted earnings and stockholders' equity. The adjusted figures may be more accurate, but a satisfactory return should be indicated by both calculations.

Standards for Quantitative Measures. Table 14–15 presents standards that should be applied in the analysis of a life insurance company stock.

Performance of Life Insurance Stocks. Life insurance stocks enjoyed a period of extreme popularity during the period 1946–56; the S&P Monthly Index of Life Insurance Stocks rose nearly ten times from 18.6 to 177.7 while the S&P 500 rose only 2.4 times. Life insurance stocks then moved pretty much horizontally from 1961–1981.

Life insurance stocks were one of the popular groups in 1961 and rose strongly from about 180 to about 280 in terms of the S&P Index of Life Insurance. Life insurance stocks then fell before reaching a high of about 365 in 1964. That peak was not surpassed until the 1980s. The index had bear market lows of 190 in 1966, 147 in 1970, and 115 in 1974.

In 1981 the index began rising sharply, reaching a peak of about 823 in 1986 before beginning to fall again. Life insurance stocks have been passed over by investors in recent years, who seek stocks with more exciting growth prospects. The primary problem area for life insurance company prospects has been the troubled group health area and the related specter of AIDS.

Table 14–15   Suggested Standards for Ratios for Life Insurance Companies

	Minimum	Maximum
Stockholders' equity ratio	8%	
Maximum decline in earnings in a given year:		
Reported		20%
Adjusted		15%
Years of earnings decline in past 10 years		3
Renewal expense per $1,000		$2.50
Yield on investments	4.5%	
Growth rate of earnings per share	6%	
Lapse ratio		8%
Composition of business in force:		
Ordinary and industrial	50%	
Term		30%
Group		30%
Composition of premium income:		
Ordinary and industrial	50%	
Health insurance		20%
First-year compensation		90%
First-year expense ratio		125%
Return on stockholders' equity	10%	

Summary

The main functions of commercial banks are to receive deposits from other segments of the economy and to make loans and discounts to industry, commerce, agriculture, and individuals; and to federal, state, and local governments through purchase of their securities. The nation's commercial banks hold the bulk of the cash assets of individuals, business firms, and financial institutions. This means that in total the assets and deposits must grow with the growth of GNP. In fact the growth rates are interrelated.

While management is important with all corporations, it is of special importance in the case of banks because the quality of assets, especially loans, is the most important factor in the determination of the investment status of a bank.

About 90 percent of a bank's assets consist of cash, security investments (currently about evenly divided between U.S. government and agency securities on the one hand and municipals on the other), and loans and discounts, with the latter representing 50 to 60 percent of total assets. Again, the quality of these loans is the crucial factor, and, as recent experience has proved, it is difficult for the analyst or investor outside the bank to determine accurately the quality of loans.

In addition to aggressively seeking time deposits and certificates of deposits, the large banks have actively entered the capital market for funds by selling debentures, which they are permitted to include in the category "capital accounts." Banks have had strong pressure to increase their equity capital because of the substantial increase in deposits, and substantial increases in debentures and other debt outstanding. However, in many cases the fact that market prices of several bank stocks have been below book values has created difficulty in selling more stock in addition to the relatively high cost of equity under such conditions.

As with other industries, the investor is interested in the financial strength and liquidity of the corporation (bank) and then in the growth rate of earnings past and expected. It must be noted that while earnings may grow satisfactorily for a time based on lower-quality loans, this will result in loan losses that will penalize current and retained earnings.

Insurance companies can be divided into two major groups: (1) fire and casualty, and (2) life insurance companies. Historically, insurance companies reported to stockholders in the same form as to regulatory authorities—that is, statutory reporting—and the analyst was forced to attempt to adjust reported earnings to conform with GAAP. However, as a result of pressure from financial analysts, the SEC, stock exchanges, and the accounting profession, insurance companies recently have followed the practice of not only reporting on a statutory basis but also on a GAAP basis. This has reduced the problem of analysis.

For fire and casualty insurance companies the three most important ratios are: (1) the expense ratio, which measures the operating efficiency of the company; (2) the loss ratio, which measures the quality of the business; and (3) the combined expense and loss ratio, which indicates the operating profit or loss of the business.

Investment policy is based on regulations and on management decisions. The higher the ratio of capital and surplus to unearned premium reserves (liabilities), the more justification for a relatively large investment in common stock.

Debt instruments represent about 90 percent of the assets of life insurance companies and equity investments only about ten percent. Therefore, the almost continuous upward trend of interest rates 1946–1981 was a favorable factor for the life insurance companies. This was particularly noteworthy in the period after 1966–1968 when the level of common stock prices remained in a wider but fairly horizontal channel. Interest rates fell after 1981 and are not expected to rise much in the near future. Problems in the group health area have plagued life insurance companies in recent years, and they remain a drag on earnings. AIDS could be a serious threat to growth in this industry.

A number of quantitative measures for assessing the quality and potential return for life insurance stocks have been presented. As with other corporations the most significant factors are those that contribute to past and expected growth and stability of earnings. In recent years P/E ratios, having come down from their peaks of earlier years have contributed to a return of some investment interest in such stocks.

Appendix

Types of Questions Analysts Ask When Visiting Companies[115]

Sales

1. Percentage gain or loss, year to date vs. year before.
2. Estimates for full year:
   (a) Units and dollars.
   (b) Identical store sales (retailing).
3. Explanation of sales changes, either way.
4. Sales breakdowns (year to date):
   (a) By divisions.
   (b) By major product groups.
   (c) By major consuming markets.
5. Explanation of sales trends above or below the industry average.
6. Demand prospects: near, intermediate, and longer term.
7. Inventory status of company, its distributors, ultimate users.
8. Price levels vs. year ago—impact on unit and dollar sales.
9. Outlook for selling price: firm, up or down. Why?
10. Company's percent of industry sales (i.e. "trade position"?).

---

115 Joseph M. Galanis, "A Primer for Field Contact Work," *Financial Analysts Journal* (August 1956).

11. Foreign sales aspects:
    (a) Percent of export sales.
    (b) Percent contributed by foreign branches.
    (c) Outlook abroad by countries.
12. Percent of sales derived from government business—type of work.

Selling and Distribution

1. Methods used: direct to users, via wholesalers, retailers, branch warehouses, or combination of these.
2. Percent of selling costs to total sales.
3. Methods of compensation to selling forces: number of salespeople employed.
4. Advertising and promotional efforts, use of TV and other publicity media, with actual costs of this type of expense.
5. Extent of geographic coverage of the nation: plans, if any, to extend marketing areas, add new distributors, etc.
6. Economic radius of distribution from individual points; importance of freight rates.

Competition

1. What concerns are viewed as chief competitors?
2. Few or many competitors?
3. Is competition cutthroat or live-and-let-live type?
4. Are competitors strongly or weakly financed units?
5. In what way do company's products and services have an advantage, if any, over competition?
6. Is new competition entering field?
7. Where does company rank in its field or fields?
8. Importance of brand names, trademarks, patents, or servicing methods.

Patent Aspects

1. Importance re sales and prices.
2. Expiration dates of basic or supplementary patents; expected impact on sales, price structure, profit margins, etc., upon expirations.

Production

1. Rate of operations to date vs. year ago; prospective rates of operation over foreseeable future.
2. Basis of operations: 1-2-3 shift, 7-8 hour day, or continuous operations?
3. Overtime premium pay?
4. Number of plants and character of their construction; multistory or single-story (modern)
5. Status of equipment: new, modernized, or obsolete?
6. Does company rate as a low-cost, high-cost, or average-cost producer?
7. Steps, if any, being taken to improve production methods and to increase productive efficiency.

Raw Materials

1. Major raw materials used; sources, domestic and foreign. Ample supplies of storage?
2. Price history of raw materials used. Volatility?
3. Extent of integration.
4. is LIFO method of inventory valuation used?

Financial

1. Most recent capitalization and changes.
2. Any current bank loans outstanding? Explanation.
3. Adequacy of working capital in relation to current and anticipated sales, compared with earlier years.
4. Near term maturities? Refundings? Retirements? Comment on ability to meet these obligations.

5. Any new financing in offing? Kind.
6. Insured, replacement, or appraisal value of fixed assets (especially natural resources) vs. book value.

Dividend Policies and Prospects

1. Payout policy, percent of earnings, percent of cash flow.
2. Prospect for extras.
3. Prospect for stock dividends.
4. Chances for increase (or decrease) in regular annual rate.

Earnings

1. Trend of labor and materials costs, percent of each to sales.
2. Ability to adjust selling prices to higher costs.
3. Cost savings programs, and comments.
4. Profit margins vs. year ago.
5. Trend of earnings to date vs. year ago.
6. Per share earnings for full year.
7. Nonrecurring items. Explanation.
8. Nonoperating sources of income vs. year ago.

Miscellaneous Topics

During the average interview, the analyst will think of spur-of-the-moment questions induced by information or comments of the contact. In addition, it may prove advisable to request comment on such individual topics as

1. Status of current litigation.
2. Impact of Government Consent Decree.
3. Status of particular long-term sales contracts.
4. Problems arising as result of a current strike or aftermath of one settled.
5. Extent of insurance coverage in connection with floods or other disasters.

Expansion

1. Details of program: plant locations, additional, product lines to be added.
2. Capital outlays involved; methods of financing, if any, contemplated.
3. Percent to be added to plant capacity on a square foot basis, or in physical units, or in dollar sales volume.
4. Any certificates of necessity or fast amortization of new facilities involved?
5. Any new acquisitions in mind?
6. Costs of new construction and equipment per unit added production vs. one to five years ago.
7. Expected sales per $1 of new plant account investment vs. other years.

Research

1. Amounts, or percent, of sales spent annually on research.
2. Number employed and number possessing advanced degrees.
3. Record of recent patents granted as result of research.
4. New products on the fire and their prospects.
5. Percent of current sales from new products traceable to research over the past five to fifteen years. (This is the most important factor in evaluating research.)

Management

1. Does management show continuity or frequent changes?
2. Average age of top management officials.
3. Is the company a one-person outfit?
4. Methods of recruiting and training executives.
5. Is management centralized or decentralized?

Employee Relations

1. Long-term strike record.
2. Percent of employees unionized—which plants?
3. Management policies on labor relations.
4. Chief employee benefits.
5. Labor turnover rates.

Index

354

About the Author

John C. Ritchie, Jr. is Professor of Finance and Associate Dean for the School of Business and Management at Temple University in Philadelphia. He also serves as a consultant to the Provident Capital Management Corporation. Dr. Ritchie received his Ph.D. in finance from Temple in 1963 and in addition to teaching finance has been a consultant to a number of corporations, industry trade associations and pension funds. He has authored numerous articles which have appeared in business and financial journals and as chapters in books on financial and investment topics.